For My Foot Being Off:
A Narrative in Documents and Letters Relating to the WWI Experiences of Infantry Lieutenant Alfred Barlow

(Second Edition)

Edited by
Aaron Barlow

Shakespeare's Sister, Inc.
Brooklyn, NY
&
lulu.com
2005

Dedicated to
Alfred Barlow's Mother,
Eva Browne Barlow,
and to his Children,
John Alfred Barlow, Anne Barlow Nygren, and Patricia Barlow Paterson,
his Other Grandchildren,
Bu Nygrens, Leopoldo Alfredo Farias, Patricia Anne Farias,
Jamie Barlow Nygren, Joel John Barlow, Mariana Farias, and
Michael John Barlow,
his Great-Grandchildren
Miranda Maureen Liles, Carla Anne Liles, Leopoldo Jesus Farias,
Eric Estephan Farias, Daniel Farias, Eli Wood Nygren,
Dashiell Michael Barlow, Lilith Ana Barlow, Carmen Patricia Sanchez,
and Samuel Michael Barlow,
and his Great-Great-Grandchildren,
Isaac Jacob Trent and Christian McIver Hill

Foreword

His report, as it was caught on the typewriter in some message center far behind, will some day gather dust in the archives of the War Department at Washington.

From a story on the Argonne offensive in
The Stars and Stripes, France, October 4, 1918

The *written* First World War began in its first shots' echoes. Battlefield poetry, journalists' reports, letters, and works of fiction: all sprang forth as the soldiers fought—and died. Words integral to the fighting itself, words from within the military, had impact, too, often even propelling the war. This war often traveled on logistics and bureaucracy writing from afar—did so to a degree never before imagined, a degree made possible by new technological advances such as the typewriter and the linotype machine, a degree made necessary by the immense numbers and distances now associated with wars and armies.

Over the course of time, through the more-than three-quarters of a century since that war, the words of that time—except in literature—have been mostly forgotten. Yet words documented this war in ways never before possible or even imagined, words put on paper by clerks and aides de camp, by brevet majors and even major generals. Almost all of them now lie forgotten and unread, on crumbling paper in dusty folders in government archives.

Today, perceptions of the First World War usually come through words written long after the conflict ended. We see the war through analyses made by those to whom time has presented broader pictures. Rarely do we see the war as it was presented, through writings of the time, to those involved. Though the newer, broad pictures help place the war within historical perspectives, they do little to aid the seeker of an approximation of the direct experience of that war. Fiction can provide that aid, but only subjectively and at its own deliberate removes. Sometimes neither histories nor these fictions provide satisfactory understanding to those seeking to comprehend even a small part of such monumental disasters as the First World War.

My intent here is to bring back a bit of contemporary understanding of the First World War to readers now so far removed from it that they may not have even met participants in it. The military documents I have selected pertain to the actions of one particular American division—not to build any broader picture or vision of the war, but to help us see something of the unit's day-to-day activities. To give these life, they are spliced with stories from the France edition of *Stars and Stripes*, the letters sent home by one of the officers of that battalion (my grandfather and the spark that ignited this project), and articles from his hometown newspaper.

Little in this volume provides explanation for the great events of the war, or even details them. Instead, primarily in words that Lieutenant Alfred Barlow wrote or read, or could have read at the time or soon after, I have tried to gather an impression of what his life as an infantry officer must have been. For this second edition, I have also tried to present the documents in an approximation of the form they came to me, using a variety of typefaces but trying to keep a sense of the original--and have added in new items, such as the awards citations, that have come my way since publication of the first edition.

Except for the news stories from *The Stars and Stripes*, this volume lacks description of the details of life on the front, either in its colossal dreariness or excitement. Barlow's letters deal with the mundane side of army life, not with the stuff of good fiction or drama. And the Special Orders and army messages included show little of the events that generated them—or that they, themselves, generated. But not much of army life was anything more than worrying that the local paper and letters from home were not arriving, than making sure that the details of a specific Field Order were followed. These and similar small matters, not battles, made the bulk of the American Expeditionary Force experience; their accompanying words make the bulk of this book.

Taken together, I hope these documents provide a feeling for the First World War as it saw itself, in its own words, words of immediate participants or observers. Thanks to the typewriter and the explosion of writing stemming from it, they show war in a way no war ever before it could have been seen.

Introduction

This "story in documents" grew out of a box of letters and clippings saved by Alfred Barlow's mother Eva from 1918 until her death in 1952. The box kicked around amongst Barlow's children's families for the next thirty-five years, ending up in my hands in 1987.

Because the paper was aging poorly and the letters were becoming difficult to read, I deciphered them and typed them into my computer and prepared a printout, making the letters once more easily accessible to family members.

While I was doing so, stories the letters only hinted at began to intrigue me. My curiosity about this war that had so changed my grandfather's life—he lost a leg and, partly as a result, became a lawyer rather than a farmer—was piqued; I started to wonder about the many obscure allusions and unilluminated incidents mentioned in the letters. I understood that my grandfather had been unable to write about much of what he was doing—the standards of censorship were strict and he was one to keep to them—but was frustrated by the unseen pictures hinted at through his poor, stilted prose.

The history books I picked up, hoping to use them to somehow see my grandfather's war, proved little more able to satisfy my curiosity. Soon, I began looking for other means of access, finally looking for documents from the time of the war itself, documents that could bring to life my grandfather's frustrating (to me) letters.

My search quickly led to the National Archives in Washington, where I paged through forgotten, long-ago declassified Army documents, sorting through the remnants of military actions three-quarters of a century past, at last painting for myself a better picture of what that war had been to my grandfather, to one involved in its actions.

Barlow's experience was not unique to him, but fit the pattern of his time. He, and what he did, were typical of the American soldier in the First World War. Even the particular division he served with had few peculiarities. A simple infantry division, rather generic and undistinguished, its story is common to many of the divisions sent to France. It saw action, sustained losses, and gained ground against an exhausted German opposition.

In the box Eva Barlow saved, I found the following description of the service of the 37th Division. As I used it as the starting point of my search and my guide as I studied at the National Archives, it should also start this book, for it provides the frame for the entire project:

A BRIEF HISTORY OF THE

THIRTY-SEVENTH DIVISION

In compliance with General Orders, No. 101, War Department, 1917, the 37th Division--known as the Buckeye Division--was organized at Camp Sheridan, Montgomery, Alabama, beginning in August, 1917, when the first units of the Ohio National Guard arrived and completed in October when the last had reached camp.

The Division was built around the 1st, 2d, 3d, 4th, 5th, 6th, 7th, 8th and 10th Ohio Regiments, 1st Ohio Field Artillery, 1st Ohio Cavalry, 1st Ohio Engineers, and the Ohio Signal Field Battalion.

On May 20th the Division, less its artillery, was sent to Camp Lee, Virginia, where it was filled to war strength and on June 11th, Headquarters and Headquarters Troop, 134th Machine Gun Battalion and 73rd Infantry Brigade began the movement to Hoboken, sailing on June 15th and arriving in France June 22, 1918. The 74th Infantry Brigade and Engineers left Camp Lee June 21st and sailing via Newport News arrived in France July 5th.

Field Artillery Brigade, Trench Mortar Battery, Sanitary Train, Military Police and 114th Veterinary Second, left Camp Sheridan, Alabama, June 14th, for Camp Upton, sailing from there June 27th via England.

With the exception of the Field Artillery Brigade and Ammunition Train (less small arms section) the Division was sent to the Bourmont Area for training, and on August 4th went into the front lines in the Baccarat Sector in the Vosges mountains where it trained under the 6th French Corps.

On September 16th it was relieved from this sector and proceeded by rail to the vicinity of Robert-Espagne. After four days it was moved by bus to Recicourt and as part of the 5th Corps entered the Argonne drive at Avocourt. Relieved on October 1st after having advanced to Cierges, the Division was sent to Pagny-sur-Meuse from which point it was sent to hold a portion of the line in the St. Mihiel sector with headquarters at Euvezin.

After nine days in this sector the Division was withdrawn to Pagny-sur-Meuse and on October 18th began its move by rail to Belgium where with Division Headquarters at Hooglede in the Lys Sector it was attached to the French Army 30th Corps on October 22nd. Advancing to and crossing the Escaut river in a sector with Sygem as its headquarters. Forcing a crossing of the Scheldt (Escaut) river on the night of November 10-11, the advance was begun early on the 11th and pushed forward some 5 kilometers to the towns of Dickele and Hindelgem where the armistice at 11 A. M. brought the fighting to an end.

The Artillery was sent to Camp de Souge for training and assigned to the 1st Army in the Argonne offensive, never serving with its own division. It served successively with the 4th American Corps, 2d American Army, Second French Colonial Army, and 17th French Corp. At one time the three regiments of the Brigade served with three different divisions, the 28th, 33d, and 92d, and only joined the division just prior to its return to the United States.

Major General Charles G. Treat was the first commander of the Division, being relieved April 24th. On May 8th, Major General Chas. S. Farnsworth was assigned to and commanded until its return to the States.

The Division made the following captures from the enemy: Officers, 26; enlisted men, 1,747; Artillery, 19-77's; 4-195's; 10-155's; 7 Trench Mortars; Machine Guns, 261; besides many rifles and a great deal of ammunition of all calibers.

This Division made a total advance against resistance of 30 and 3/4 kilometers.

During active operations the Division suffered the following losses (as reported to War Department 10 May, 1919):-

Battle deaths, 992; wounded 4,931; prisoners of war, 23. One thousand two hundred and fifty replacements were furnished the 37th Division.

The following units composed this Division:- 73rd and 74th Infantry Brigades; 145th, 146th, 147th and 148th Infantry Regiments; 135th and 136th Machine Gun Battalions; 62nd Artillery Brigade; 134th, 135th and 136th Artillery Regiments and Train; 112th Trench Mortar Battery; 134th Machine Gun Battalion; 112th Engineers Regiment and train; 112th Field Signal Battalion; 112th Train Headquarters and Military Police; 112th Supply Train; 112th Ammunition Train; 112th Sanitary Train; 145th, 146th 147th and 148th Ambulance Companies. and Field Hospitals.

As it claims, this is but a brief history, an outline. It tells little of what happened, only that things did. It tells nothing of the changes wrought by the war, yet the soldiers of the 37th Division, like all who experience war or are touched by it, were changed by it. An important point: when they and the other veterans returned home, the soldiers also changed the United States.

The story of this book, of change through war, not of glorification of war, is told through Barlow's letters, official war diary entries, field messages, field orders, newspaper articles, and other documents from the time. Some additional bits come from an history of the division published in 1926, just eight years after the end of the war. I provide some connecting material throughout, but as little as I thought possible.

Chapter One

Each room in the little house at 1066 First Avenue, Gallipolis, Ohio led into a bathroom. Marion Barlow had built it so. He had to. He had gorged himself on salt pork and unripe crab apples after three famine days during service with the 192nd Ohio Volunteer Infantry in the Shenandoah Valley during the Civil War. His bowels long ruined, in 1880 he moved back home to Gallipolis and built the house facing the Ohio River, having sold his Pekin, Illinois shoe store, to "retire" to less taxing work at the ancient age of forty-two.

His younger son, Alfred, or "Skip," as he preferred to be called, grew up in that house facing the Ohio River. He must have been reminded daily of the, well, less romantic side of war. Like his father, he, too, would later suffer it, eventually living most of his life crippled by combat wounds. He handled his disability with equanimity, though, perhaps because of what he saw during those early years, at home and among his father's aging friends, also veterans of the Civil War.

Barlow suffered from his injuries as much as any from that earlier, less medically advanced, war: years later, after Barlow's funeral at Arlington, an elderly man approached his son John (my father). "I saw the obituary and had to come," he told him. "I remember helping hold him down during an amputation on the boat back home. No anesthetic. I never forgot that poor, pale, brave officer." Barlow probably would have been prouder of that acknowledgement than of almost any other. The sad part is that the amputation on the boat was but one of at least nine (some say as many as fifteen), as gangrene inched up from each new cut.

Barlow's hometown had but one claim to fame: General Lafayette had stayed overnight there, on his triumphal return tour of the United States years after the Revolution. Its population of a couple of thousand made the town really little more than a farming village by the river, though it did serve as the seat of Gallia County. Its youth dreamed of leaving, of finding the fame and excitement of the cities, the sea, and foreign lands. According to one story, Barlow, hating his given name, admitting to his personal dreams, chose his own nickname as a boy, swearing to his friends that he would one day be skipper of an ocean ship. Like its fictional counterpart, Sherwood Anderson's Winesburg, Ohio, Gallipolis was a place for youth to come from—not a place to stay.

At 6'1", Barlow was more than a little bit tall for his time. He was skinny as well, and wore glasses that made him appear serious, almost glum. He left Gallipolis for the first time for education, studying at Ohio State University up in Columbus whenever he could afford to. By the end of 1916, when he was 25, he had finished only a couple of years of study–a normal course of events for students at the land grant institutions of the time. Young people had to scrimp and save to attend even state schools, and would return home to help with the business or the farm whenever needed. By 1916, Barlow's finances had become particularly precarious: he'd never managed money well, and now his father's health was deteriorating, eating up both family savings and income possibilities.

Leaving school probably didn't bother Barlow, just then. He certainly had been following world events and Washington reactions to them; he knew war was coming and fully expected to find himself a part of the conflict. Graduation, no matter what else might happen, would not occur in his immediate future. So Barlow returned home to look after his father, mother, and grandmother.

By March, his father recovering slightly, Barlow had enrolled in classes at nearby Rio Grande College and was looking for ways to earn a bit of money. He continued reading the local newspaper, The *Gallipolis Daily Tribune*, watching and waiting as events edged the reluctant United States towards war.

By late February, when President Wilson saw the Zimmerman telegram (which offered Mexico German assistance in regaining Texas if Mexico joined with Germany), U.S./German diplomatic relations had already been broken for a month. Soon before that, Berlin had informed Washington that unrestricted submarine warfare would be resumed, and that American shipping could not expect to be spared. U.S. entrance into the European conflict, though still resisted by many, was becoming more assured, and plans were being made for mobilization. Barlow was already angling to insure he participated in the conflict–even as he saw his father through the last days of life.

On March 12, the following appeared in the local paper:

Gallipolis Daily Tribune, March 12, 1917

M. S. BARLOW PASSES

Was a Well Known and Respected Citizen

Marion Stephen Barlow departed this life Saturday, March 10, at 6:30 p.m. Though he had been in failing health for some time he had been sick in bed only a little over a week. Despite the seriousness of his condition the end came as a surprise, as up to a short time before his death his condition was thought to be improved.

Mr. Barlow was born in Gallipolis December 24, 1838, and was in his 79th year.

As a young man he attended the Gallia Academy under Prof. and Mrs. A. G. Sears and left school to join Company B of the 91st Regiment Ohio Valley Infantry in which he served three years.

After the war he went to Illinois where he was in the shoe business. Then he married Miss Eva Browne in 1875.

In 1880 he came back to Gallipolis and for several years engaged in the coal business, which however because of ill health he was compelled to give up.

On March 2 last Mr. Barlow remarked that sixty years ago that day he joined the Methodist Episcopal Church. In this church he was up to the last few years of his life always an active member. He had been a Sunday School teacher and superintendent, a member of the choir, and was for many years a member of the official board of Grace M. E. Church.

He leaves to glory in his gain his widow and two sons, Edwin Morley of Chicago, and Alfred M, at home. He is also survived by three brothers, Tell and Bryson of Streator, Illinois, and John of Los Angeles, and one sister, Mrs. William Lanning of Wilwankee.

He was preceded to the Great Beyond by one brother and one sister-- Mr. B. Frank Barlow and Mrs. Fannie A. Cating, the mother of J. Earnest Cating of this city.

Mr. Barlow's family were early settlers both of America and of Gallia County, coming to Connecticut in 1630 and here in 1803. He was a descendant of Nathaniel Hull and a great grandson of Col. Aaron Barlow of the

Revolution. His great uncle was Joel Barlow, secretary of the Scioto Land Company that settled Gallipolis.

Morley Barlow accompanied by Mrs. Barlow's mother, Mrs. M. M. Browne, and sister Mrs. T. D. McGuire, arrived from Chicago this morning.

The funeral will be from the home tomorrow, Tuesday, at 2 P.M., by the Rev. Dr. Cherington with interment by Wetherholt at Pine Street cemetery.

The pall-bearers are Capt. J. C. Hutsinpiller, J. G. Damron, A. W. Kerns, John Stone, A. R. Weaver and H. C. Zimmerman.

It was Barlow's mother, Eva, who saved this clipping, and many of the others, along with Barlow's letters, until the time of her death in 1952. Marion's grandfather Samuel had moved his family out to Ohio after many of the initial settlers of Gallipolis had either given up or died. Many of them had been French, fleeing the revolution in their homeland. Joel Barlow, while an American diplomat in Paris, had helped encourage them to emigrate. Joel was also well-known as a poet, as one of the 'Connecticut Wits' and, later, as author of *The Columbiad*, one of the first American best-sellers, an epic poem of the vision of Columbus and America. He died in Poland, in 1812, again in diplomatic service, trying to deliver a treaty to Napoleon during his retreat from Moscow.

Barlow, now that his father was gone, felt responsible for the finances and care of his mother and grandmother. His brother Morley, after all, had long before left home (he was much older), establishing his own life in far-away Chicago. Barlow's letters throughout the war would show concern for their finances, even as he struggled unsuccessfully to manage his own.

Marion Barlow had left his family little more than a bit of farmland and that small house he had built that still stands along the road by the Ohio River. After Marion's death, it was shared by Barlow and his mother and grandmother. No longer could any family money be forthcoming for education, so Barlow again gave up the idea of returning to Columbus. He therefore decided to switch to the local company of the Ohio National Guard (he had previously been a sergeant with the company at OSU). Within weeks of his father's death he had also taken the officer's exam.

Unlike many of the people of Ohio, Barlow's ancestry was strongly English. His mother's father, Morely Browne, had emigrated in the 19th century, at a time when much larger bodies of immigrants were coming from Germany and Ireland, just two name two of the main sources of the state's exploding population. In fact, Barlow would eventually marry Marian Sullivan, an Ohio native whose ancestry was a mix of German and Irish—nothing unusual in the state at that time.

Found in *The 37ᵗʰ Division in the Great War, Vol 1*
by Ralph D. Cole and W.C. Howells
(Columbus, OH: The Thirty-Seventh Division Veterans
Association, 1926)

Of the foreign born whites resident in Ohio in 1910, one hundred and seventy-five thousand were born in Germany, while there were three hundred twenty-eight thousand whose parents were born in Germany but who were classed as native born. There were seventy-three thousand who had been born in Austria and forty-six thousand whose parents were born there; there were eighty-six thousand who were born in Hungary, and twenty-eight thousand whose parents were native Hungarians. (36)

Not surprisingly, given the high numbers of people with Germanic backgrounds in the state, sentiments in Ohio, as in much of the United States, were not completely in favor of England, Russia, and France in the European war, though the weight of public opinion had long been moving in that direction. In late March, however, the renewed German submarine attacks on merchant shipping claimed four American ships. Views shifted fast away from Germany and Barlow moved closer to his own participation in the war.

Gallipolis Daily Tribune, April 5, 1917

Lieutenant
Alfred Barlow

Alfred Barlow on the recommendation of Col. Crosson has been appointed Second Lieutenant of Company F, Ohio National Guard by the Adjutant General. Lieut. Barlow successfully passed the examination at Columbus Wednesday we are pleased to state.

That "Wednesday" would have been April 4, 1917. Changes were coming fast and furious in Barlow's life. First, his father had died. Now, just a month later, he was no longer a simple National-Guard sergeant, a non-commissioned officer, but would have to start taking on the responsibilities of an officer beholden to a commission. Just two days later, perhaps even sooner than an anxious and expectant Barlow could have hoped, The *Gallipolis Daily Tribune* headlined war's arrival:

Gallipolis Daily Tribune, April 6, 1917

UNITED STATES ENTERS WORLD WAR.

Passage of "State of War" Resolution by the House Settles the Long Uncertainty.

Legislation for Men, Money, Equipment and Military Training to be Passed

------

Washington, April 6.--The resolution declaring that a state of war exists between the United States and Germany, already passed by the senate, passed the house shortly after three o'clock this morning by a vote of 373 to 50.

President Wilson will sign the resolution as soon as Vice President Marshall has attached his signature in the senate. It formally accepts the state of belligerency forced by German aggression and authorizes and directs the President to employ the military and naval forces and all the resources of the nation to bring war against Germany to a successful termination.

Without roll calls the house rejected all amendments including proposals to prohibit the sending of American troops overseas without congressional authority.

Passage of the resolution followed seventeen hours of debate. There was no attempted filibuster, but the pacifist group, under the leadership of Democratic Leader Kitchen, prolonged the discussion with impassioned speeches declaring conscience would not permit them to support the president's recommendation that a state of war be declared.

Miss Rankin of Montana, the only woman member of congress, sat through the first roll call with bowed head, failing to answer to her name, twice called by the clerk.

On the second role call she rose and said in a sobbing voice, "I want to stand by my country, but I cannot vote for war."

For a moment then she remained standing supporting herself against a desk, and as cries of "vote," "vote," came from several parts of the house, she sank back into her seat without voting audibly. She was recorded in the negative.

Washington, April 6.--How the government plans to raise a war army of a million men within a year and two million within two years was disclosed upon passage of the war resolution by the house.

A bill prepared by the general staff and approved by the President for submission to congress provides for the immediate filling up of the regular army and national guard to war strength of more than 600,000 by draft unless enough volunteers enlist quickly, and for bringing into the service by late summer of the first 500,000 of the new force of young men between the ages of 19 and 25 years to be called to the colors by selective conscription.

Train 10,000 Officers

In drafting its program, the staff recognized the fact that the United States must start at the beginning and train first an army of 100,000 officers and non-commissioned officers to undertake the training of the thousands of youths who will enter the service with no notion of military duty or life.

Expansion of the present regular army to its full war strength of 287,000 enlisted men and 11,700 officers, means many new regiments of all arms to be created by dividing existing regiments and filling each half to war strength with volunteers or conscripts. The national guard regiments, all of which can be called in the federal service under existing law, will have approximately 327,000 men and 10,300 officers at war strength.

For five months these expanded forces will be subjected to training of a character hitherto unknown in this country. Simultaneously the registration of all men between the ages of 19 and 25 will be carried out with federal, state and municipal authorities cooperating.

In August or in September, the first 500,000 of this new army composed exclusively of young men summoned to the colors under the principle of universal military service with those supporting dependents or needed by the nation in civil life exempted, would be assembled for training.

MEN WANTED FOR COMPANY F

F Company of the Seventh Regiment, O.N.G. is still in need of men to fill it to its proper strength.

Now that a state of war has been declared between Germany and the United States, the appeal for men to serve their country is made more earnestly than before. Men will be received up to 45 years of age

It may have seemed to Barlow that, just now, when he was already 25 years old, his life was finally coming to some purpose. He had not been drifting, exactly, before this time, but he certainly must have been waiting. The war, after all, was nearly three years old when the United States finally got directly involved. But Barlow must have known, for most of that time, that it would, and that he would be one of the participants.

Still, little changed right away.

Found in *The 37th Division in the World War*

Office men huddled deeper into their overcoat collars and spread open the morning paper that was to tell them they were now citizens of a nation at war. It was to tell them—too—of the ordinary routine of peace time civilian activities; that a congressman in a distant state had resigned because a jury had convicted him of a crime; that two storage plants in Cleveland had been dynamited in some labor troubles; that an automobile had killed a woman hurrying home from shopping the night before; that a heavyweight had been discredited in the sporting world; that engagements to wed had been announced and women's clubs had met; that Easter had livened local markets. A young actress named Mary Pickford was playing in "A Poor Little Rich Girl;" Raymond Hitchcock, the popular comedian, was in "Betty;"John Mason in "Common Clay," and Marie Cahill in "The Masque of Life." At motion picture houses, audiences watched the diminutive Marguerite Clark in "The Fortunes of Fifi," and Blanche Sweet in "Those Without Sin." Charlie Chaplin, already well on his way to stardom, was in "The Cure," and "The Birth of a Nation" was incitement enough for a lively and diverting controversy in which its propriety was the central theme. Robert Warwick, Anita Steward, Richard Walton Tully, and Clara Kimball Young were the favorites of the day; audiences at the revues still thrilled at the novelty of the innovation when the chorus galloped down the runway and out into the orchestra rows and danced and sang over their heads; the open saloon and the free lunch were accepted American institutions. (Vol. 1, 27)

Going back to school, or even setting up as a farmer, was now out of the question, though Barlow had never really been destined for that. All of the other possibilities, all of the suggestions from family and friends, could now safely be ignored. Barlow would not have to worry about his future, at least, not for a while. His war would now have him. And many, many more like him, though the getting was not often easy.

Found in *The 37th Division in the Great War*

The first problem the Thirty-Seventh Division faced in its formative stages was that of recruiting its commissioned and enlisted strength. In its effort to solve this problem the division was to deal with all of these varying and variable factors through days of discouragement and disappointment, but likewise through days when all communities rallied in well intentioned and effective support. But the million men the noisy and unthinking patriot had predicted would sprint to arms over night did not spring. (Vol. 1, 36)

Not everyone was completely enthusiastic about the war from the first, despite the new enthusiasm for war in Washington. In Ohio, many still wondered if involvement were really such a good idea, and this hurt recruitment. The papers, by now all in favor of the war, tried to make recruitment look better than it was, or at least the best they could:

Gallipolis Daily Tribune, April 7, 1917

High School Boys Enlist.

About fifteen of the High School boys have offered to join Co. F by signing their names to a paper, providing other members of their class will.

New Recruits for Co. F.

Capt. H. E. Houck of Co. F. O.N.G. said today that a few new recruits were enlisting but many more were needed to fill out the company. Capt. Houck believes that many young unmarried men will have to be drafted to raise the number of soldiers needed in the army. Capt. Houck hopes soon to have a crack company enlisted to full strength.

He said all can not be officers and that fact should not influence young men from coming quickly to the front and enlisting.

"Dot" Kennett who is a well known chef and former steamboat cook has agreed to go with Co. F as their cook.

Gallipolis Daily Tribune, April 18, 1917

New Recruits for Company F.

Captain Houck gives us a list of the new recruits who have enlisted in Co. F during the past week:

Wm. Rose, Selby Rupe, Fred McGoun, Stanley Sims, Lewis Kennett, Verne Niday, Clarence Gilmore, Floyd Brown, Charles M. Smeltzer, Bing White, James Scott, Ross Thompson, James Saunders, Gilbert Bush, Harry and Alfred Mayes, Fred Rader, Raymond Rupe, Reuben Benson, John Moss, Pearl and John Rusk, James Evans, Everett Benson.

Alfred Mayes would eventually become a sergeant, serving without a scratch, and would almost make it home, in company with Barlow. His story, however, belongs to the end of the war and one of this book's final chapters, not its start.

For obvious reasons, many young men considering enlisting were concerned about the duration of their service. The army needed to make clear that commitment would end with the war.

Gallipolis Daily Tribune, April 23, 1917

Capt. Houck Receives an Order.

The following telegram received by Capt. Houck of Co. F from the Chief Militia Bureau, is officially published for the guidance of all recruiting officers in the State's service:

"Secretary of War directs that you be informed that it is the policy of War Department to discharge all men who have enlisted since declaration of war upon termination of emergency period. This to apply to Regular Army and National Guard."

MANN, Chief Militia Bureau.

By Command of Governor Cox:

GEORGE H. WOOD,

The Adjutant General.

Five new recruits joined the ranks of Co. F Saturday. Charles Houck, son of the Mayor, and four other boys by the names of Pinkerman, Burnett, Plantz and Woodyard.

Though the papers had been trying to show that there was a real enthusiasm for enlistment, the following article lets slip that there really was not. Not yet, at least.

Gallipolis Daily Tribune, May 15, 1917

FIFTY MORE FROM GALLIA

County Must Send 130 to New Army and 50 to Regulars.

The Cincinnati Recruiting District, of which Gallia County forms a part, must furnish to the Regular Army a quota of 1600 men within thirty days after the passage of bill now before Congress. The quota of Gallia County is 50, of which practically none have enlisted.

The overshadowing war fact must be realized in Gallia County. Of the male voters between 21 and 31 years of age, 180 must go to the war soon. With the exemption of farmers, married men, and the otherwise disqualified this will be a heavy draft on our resources of young men, particularly in the villages and in Gallipolis.

Present indications are that another 500,000 will be called for just as soon as the first half million get a good start in training. The condition of affairs in Russia is far from what the Allies desire, and if her internal troubles keep her from active war service, as now seems almost certain, the

United States is likely to send soldiers by the million to the Western front in Europe.

Not only were "affairs in Russia far from what the Allies desire," but they would soon devolve into revolution and a civil war that would last into the next decade. The collapse of Russia also meant that Germany could soon start to move hundreds of thousands of men from the eastern front to the western. The urgent need for quick American participation became more obvious daily.

Gallipolis Daily Tribune, May 21, 1917

CO. F. O.N.G.

Will Probably Be Called Within 30 Days.

That Co. F of Gallipolis will be called to a mobilization field within thirty days is the opinion of Capt. Houck who has been in touch with Col. T. S. Crosson of the Seventh Regiment.

It was Capt. Houck's intention to attend the national meeting as a delegate from the local lodge of the Junior Order of American Mechanics which meets in Ashville, N.C., June 19.

Col. Crosson advised Capt. Houck not to leave and be ready for a call at any moment to a mobilization point. 150 men will be recruited.

Co. F now has 107 men all in the condition and ready to leave for the front on an hour's notice. One of the latest recruits to Co. F is Attorney Edwin Barger of the Gallia County bar who enlisted today.

A regular medical examiner arrived today to examine all new recruits who have enlisted since war was declared by the United States with Germany.

In late May, despite his now daily involvement with Company F, Barlow's life still covered more than the military. He even prepared at least one simple lesson plan for a stint as a substitute teacher. Though not an impressive plan and obviously that of an amateur, Alfred's mother, Eva, saved it and later placed it with the letters she received while her son was off at war.

LESSON PLANS FOR MAY 24, 1917

[Marked "O.K." in another hand]

A M Barlow

Teacher's aim: to acquaint the pupils of both the history and geography classes with a little of the history of the Spanish conquests of Peru and of the adventure of the English Buccaneers and also some of the principle characteristics of Spanish life including bull fights.

Conquest of the Moors

    Influence on Spanish character

The Incas

      Civilization and wealth

Customs and Temperament

    Bull Fights

    Temperament

Not surprisingly, given his situation, Barlow shows as much interest in the excitements of conquistadors, buccaneers, and bullfighters as in Spanish life, customs, and temperament. His naïve view—even if of history as it was to be taught to very young students—reflects, perhaps, the innocence of his Ohio River milieu, not simply his own. For, though already better educated than most people of his time and community, Barlow was a fairly typical son of his small-town environment. And, even though he knew from his father's generation how war could destroy or maim a person, he still believed in its glory and adventure.

Enthusiasm for the war began to grow, as did enlistment. Finally, the Ohio National Guard was building up its strength, and its top officers had begun to lobby Washington for creation of an Ohio division, one to be built out of the National Guard units that were now coming together.

Found in *The 37ᵗʰ Division in the Great War*

During May and June, fifteen thousand men had enlisted in the Ohio National Guard; in the first half of the latter month, the state had led all others in the number of recruits enrolled. Ohio now had three infantry brigades, a complete artillery brigade, a regiment of engineers, a filed signal battalion, and a sanitary train. (Vol. 1, 77)

Though most of the Ohio National Guard would eventually become the major part of the 37ᵗʰ "Buckeye" Division, a part of it would be called overseas more quickly, as part of the "Rainbow" Division that represented America's first substantial contribution to the war effort in France.

Gallipolis Daily Tribune, June 4, 1917

TO FRANCE BY FALL

O.N.G. to Go With 100,000 Other State Troops.

Washington, June 3.--National Guard troops will be on the battlefield of France before snow files. That became a virtual certainty today, when it was learned officially that the General Staff of the army is giving final consideration to a plan to send between 100,000 and 125,000 national guardsmen to Europe within the next three months, and Secretary Baker said that the first to go into training would be the first to go.

Pennsylvania is in the first of the three increments of the National Guard to be called out for Federal service under the orders of the War Department, and in view of the fact that a large part of the men now in the State organization recently had intensive training on the Mexican border it is considered certain they will be counted in the first National Guard troops to go abroad.

The first of the National Guard troops, which includes all of the Ohio guard organizations are to become a part of the Federal fighting force on July 15. The next increment will begin training July 25 and the third August 5, unless there is a postponement. In any event the Ohio troops will be among the first in the field and therefore in the first contingent sent to France.

Orders to National Guards that they were to be taken into the Federal service on July 15, General Mann said, ought to be enough information for them to know that they would be expected to do the imperative duty within a short time. As the National Guards of half a dozen States--New York, Pennsylvania, Illinois, Massachusetts and Ohio--are in fine military condition, resulting from their border campaign, the war officials hold that the 100,000 would be picked from these guards.

As an evidence that the Secretary of War has decided that the National Guards shall follow the Pershing expedition to France, there is the recent letter written to Senator Jones, of Washington. In this he said: "The National Guards of your State will have an opportunity to show their training in France before the snow flies."

It would not be so soon, not for all anticipation and optimism of the early days of the war, at least, not for Barlow and Company F. Barlow must have felt a great deal of frustration as he taught, took care of the family, and waited.

Gallipolis Daily Tribune, July 11, 1917

NATIONAL GUARDSMEN

Will Be Drafted Into U. S. Army August 5.

Washington, July 10.--The last step necessary to make the entire national guard available for duty in France was taken yesterday by President Wilson with the issuance of a proclamation drafting the state troops into the army of the United States August 5.

Gallipolis Daily Tribune, July 13, 1917.

CAPT. HOUCK

Will Mobilize Co. F on Park Front Sunday

Capt. Houck has returned from New Lexington, O, where he met with all the officers of the Seventh Regiment to take instructions from Col. Crosson.

The members of Co. F will mobilize in front of the Park Sunday and go to the armory for two weeks camp at least before being mustered into the Federal army.

Company F is badly in need of two gas ranges to use in the armory during their camping in the city and will appreciate the use of them and if not donated will pay for them.

Capt. Houck states that Capt. Tom Jones of Middleport will not mobilize his Company C in Pomeroy and that all equipment will be removed from the Pomeroy Armory. The citizens of Middleport donated a free building, gas and other necessities. Each National Guardsman is allowed but forty cents per day to exist on.

Those "two weeks" of camp in the center of town dragged out for three months, with daily expectation of orders to move to training camp. It must have been frustrating: the tedium, the dashed hopes for early deployment. Dates for departure were given and passed and given again:

Found in *The 37th Division in the Great War*

On 13th July, the war department announced that the Ohio troopers were to encamp and train at Camp Sheridan, Montgomery, and that General Charles G. Treat had been given command of the division.

When the division was to move to Alabama, it would pass through Cincinnati, the old gateway to the south, the city where General William T. Sherman (that Ohio soldier for who the camp at Chillicothe was named) had set in a hotel room pouring over maps as he planned his march to the sea. When it should detrain, it was to be at Montgomery, capital of Alabama and cradle of the Southern Confederacy, the first capital of the seceding states. (Vol. 1, 181)

Unfortunately, Company F would end up being one of the last units of the ONG to move to Alabama. In the meantime, rumors of departure dates and destinations came and went:

Gallipolis Daily Tribune, July 14, 1917

NATIONAL GUARDSMEN

To Train For Action in South.

Draft May Come Soon.

A dispatch from Washington says that the Ohio National Guardsmen will train this winter at Augusta, Ga. The Guardsmen will train two weeks at home before starting south on August 1st. Capt. Houck says the Guardsmen, it is expected, will first go to Camp Perry near Lake Erie, before going south.

Co. F will be vaccinated here and inoculated against typhoid germs. The inoculation will take two weeks. Further orders have not been received by Capt. Houck.

The draft may take place the first of next week but officials at Washington refuse to give out exact details of draft plan. Newspapers are appealing to government officials to be permitted to publish names of men exempted and the cause for same.

Company F will go into camp in their tents on the park front Sunday.

Gallipolis Daily Tribune, July 18, 1917

DRILLING HARD

In Company F Preparatory to Going South.

Co. F, Capt. Houck, is drilling daily. The new recruits are being drilled by Lieut. Mackenzie and Lieut. Barlow and they make a fine looking bunch of soldiers.

Good order is being maintained in the Park Camp and guards are on duty day and night.

Capt. Houck will take Company F on a 20 mile hike up to Pomeroy next Tuesday and back again the same day, we are informed. Co. F will leave for the southern mobilization camp in Alabama about August 5th it is expected.

Harold Mackenzie, the other company F lieutenant, had become one of Barlow's best friends. The two would be together almost until the moment of embarkation for France. While they waited, camped in the park, others started the long voyage across the Atlantic:

Found in *The 37th Division in the Great War*

During June, July and August, while Ohio troops continued under the routine of drill, alternating now and then with recruiting, with physical examinations, and with the formality of being mustered into the United States Army, the stream of soldiers continued to flow across the Atlantic. In June, 11,750 embarked; in July, 3,500, and in August, 5,000. (Vol. 1, 81)

Gallipolis Daily Tribune, July 19, 1917

PLANS ALL LAID NOW

To Equip Seventh Regiment with Suitable Social Facilities

At a meeting held yesterday in regard to establishing a social center for the Seventh Regiment, O.N.G., Dr. Kineon, H. C. Johnston and Mrs. Joe Moeh were appointed as a finance committee and Judge Mauck, S. H. Eagle and Dr. Ella Lupton as a permanent committee representing the citizens of Gallipolis in all affairs relating to the local company.

The social center of the regiment will have to do with the sports, music and amusements generally of the boys, all under control of the chaplain of the regiment, Lieut. S. L. Martin.

Each soldier will be supplied with stationary for two letters a week, and a regimental editor will send a letter a week to each of the Gallipolis newspapers. The regiment will have a library of 500 books and 158 magazines.

Portsmouth has raised $1,000 for this work and Ironton $500. Gallia county is pledged to not less than $300.

When considering your subscription remember that these volunteers have saved Gallia from a draft.

Co. F. Praised by Col. Wolser.

Co. F was highly praised by Col. Wolser while here, saying it was one of the best companies he had inspected and was well drilled considering the length of time they had been guardsmen, so many of them being raw recruits.

They went on a hike to Mills Station this morning.

Gallipolis Daily Tribune, July 24, 1917

COMPANY F

Is Being Mustered Into the Federal Service

Capt. Cooley, of the Sixth Regiment, a mustering officer of the O.N.G., is here mustering into the Federal service members of Company F.

The Company will also be inoculated and vaccinated, which will no doubt cause some illness to some of the members for a short time.

Capt. Houck does not expect Co. F to leave Gallipolis for several weeks, probably not before some time in September, although no one can tell how soon they may be called and started on the way to France or Belgium.

Capt. Houck said Monday evening that he needed twenty men yet to fill Company F.

The hike to Pomeroy has been given up for the present. It would be a long, hot and dusty tramp for the soldier boys to take until they are more thoroughly seasoned.

Found in *The 37ᵗʰ Division in the Great War*

A total of 25,187 men and officers was mustered into federal service with the Ohio division, including 24,360 men and 827 officers, exclusive of the 951 National Naval Volunteers with the U.S.S. Essex Ship Company in Toledo and the U.S.S. Dorothea Ship Company at Cleveland. This included 1,832 men of the First Infantry, 1,583 in the Second, 1,636 in the Third, 1,895 in the Fourth, 1,806 in the Fifth, 1,613 in the Sixth, 1,867 in the Seventh, 1,846 in the Eighth, 1,730 in the Tenth and 600 in the Ninth Separate Battalion. It included 1,275 men in the First Field Artillery, 1,265 in the Second and 1,242 in the Third; 1,065 in the First Engineers, 235 in the Signal Corps; 294 in the Military Police; 643 in the Ammunition Train; 306 in the Supply Train; and 166 in the Engineer Train. The four ambulance companies had from 140 to 153 men, and the four field hospitals, from 77 to 80. (Vol. 1, 176-177)

Gallipolis Daily Tribune, July 26, 1917

Co. F Mustered Into Federal Service.

Company F was mustered into Federal service (this) Thursday afternoon, July 26, 1917, by Capt. John M. Cooley of the Sixth Ohio.

Lieut. Copeland of the United States Reserves gave the members of Co. F a physical examination and he will vaccinate and inoculate the men.

A few members of Company F were rejected after physical examination.

Found in *The 37ᵗʰ Division in the Great War*

For the Seventh Infantry the problem of recruitment was not vastly different [from the other Infantry outfits]... excepting that its units were scattered over considerable territory, being located in a number of small cities instead of concentrated in one large center of population. When mustered into federal service for the World War, its officers, their organizations and locations were as follows:

Regimental Officers and Chaplin

Colonel	Tom O. Crosson
	New Lexington
Lieut. Colonel	Elmer P. Walser
	Somerset
Chaplin	Summer L. Martin
	Pleasantville
Battalion Commanders Major	E.P. Lawler
	McConnelsville
Major	Van A. Snider
	Lancaster

Major	Samuel M. Johnson
	Athens

...

Company F, Gallipolis

Captain	Hiram E. Houck
First Lieutenant	Albert H. Mackenzie
Second Lieutenant	Alfred M. Barlow...

Colonel Crosson had been commissioned captain of Company H of the Seventh on 26th June, 1902, major on 21st July, 1905, lieutenant colonel on 27th June, 1913, and colonel on 29th December, 1916. Lieutenant Colonel Walser was commissioned captain of Company D of the Seventh on 27th September, 1905, major on 15th November, 1909 and lieutenant colonel on 29th December, 1916. (vol. 1, 142-144)

Gallipolis Daily Tribune, July 27, 1917

FLAG FOR F COMPANY

Presented in Impressive Speech by Capt. Verne Bovie.

At 6:30 Thursday evening, after a lively shower, the flag purchased by a few citizens was formally presented to F Company by Capt. Bovie. The boys were drawn up in a long double line on the walk in the Public Square, extending from the band stand to the fence fronting the river.

Capt. Bovie delivered a speech addressed to the Company and the large crowd of spectators, that was beautifully phrased, profoundly touching and inspiring, and admirably conceived from start to finish. He was frequently applauded, and rose to the full height of what was a really historic occasion for Gallipolis.

Edwin S. Barger, a private in the Company, made a well thought out and happy response in behalf of his soldier comrades, in which he pledged them to devoted service to their Flag and Country in whatever situation fate might place them. He and his comrades appreciate fully the fact that the honor and reputation of Gallia County has been entrusted to them in this

war, and nobody who looked down the imposing line doubts for a moment
that they will acquit themselves bravely and nobly in the months to come.

Capt. Houck received the flag for the Company. It is a serviceable bunting.

Not all of Captain Houck's duties during this time were so pleasurable,
and the soldiers, certainly, did not always look so imposing:

Gallipolis Daily Tribune, July 28, 1917

BOOZER'S RENDEZVOUS

Invaded by Capt. Houck Friday Night.

Capt. Houck received a tip Friday that members of Co. F had been
gathering in the cellar of a residence in the city where booze was being furnished them.

He walked in on them alone last night and discovered the truth finding five men in uniform and three women and one man in civilian dress all
drinking.

The soldiers were placed in the guardhouse, three later making their escape are now carrying bricks from one end of the park to the other as punishment imposed for breaking out.

Gallipolis Daily Tribune, August 4, 1917

COMPANY F

Makes Hike to Cheshire and Returns in Good Shape.

Company F, in charge of Capt. Houck, made the hike to Cheshire
Friday morning in three hours and returned in the evening. They hiked
back in three hours and a half and were in fine condition after walking all

told 25 miles, and in spite of the fact that the heat was intense, only two or three "fell down" on the trip.

Three ran away from the Company at Cheshire and returned on the Hocking Valley train. Capt. Houck will see that they are punished for leaving the Company without permission.

The ladies of Cheshire treated Co. F most royally. An elegant dinner was served the soldier boys both at noon and again late in the afternoon before they started on the return trip.

Company F arrived home at Camp Crosson shortly after 9 o'clock.

Captain Houck who led the Company had a blistered foot as a result of his long walk but he was going about as usual today.

Lieut. Barlow, a very popular officer in Co. F, was compelled to back down stairs this morning on account of stiff knees after his long walk.

Now in Federal service, having been an officer in the ONG, Barlow did what he could, including asking for letters of recommendation, to insure he would continue at commissioned rank. This is one he was given:

ROBERT M. SWITZER
Ohio, Tenth District

HOUSE OF REPRESENTATIVES
WASHINGTON

Gallipolis, Ohio, August 20, 1917.

Adjutant General, U.S. Army,
                Washington, D.C.,

Sir;-
    Alfred M. Barlow a constituent of mine and a
Second Lieut. in Company F., 7th Ohio infantry
and whose post office address is Gallipolis, Ohio,
is making application for a commission in the
Regular Army and I desire to endorse him as a very

worthy young man and one who will make an efficient
officer.

He is from an old and highly respected family
of this vicinity and has had the benefit of a
public school education and several years at
college, attending the Ohio State University two
and one half years where he received military
training under Major Converse, U.S.A. I have
personally known Lieut. Barlow practically all his
life and recommend him as exceedingly energetic,
quick to grasp the details of any work that may
be assigned him and possessing good executive
ability, and I feel sure he possesses the mental
and physical requirements needed for military
work. Trusting that his application may meet with
your favorable consideration. I am.

                    Very respectfully,

                    R M Switzer

The waiting for orders, however, and the camping in the park, continued.

Gallipolis Daily Tribune, September 10, 1917.

Soldiers Suffer.

The soldiers in the Park suffered from the cold Sunday night. Additional
blankets were issued today from the supply department.

It is not known when the men of Co. F will leave here, but it is thought
they will get away before very long.

At least they were camped at home, and, every once in a while, could have
a little fun with families and friend:

Gallipolis Daily Tribune, September 18, 1917

CO. F DANCE

A Benefit Dance at Elks Hall Wednesday Night.

Company F will give a benefit dance at the Elks Hall tomorrow night from 8 to 12. The price of tickets will be $1.00.

Good music will be furnished by the Kuhn orchestra.

This dance is given by Company F to help their mess fund and every body should buy a ticket and help this good cause.

Tickets can be secured from the soldiers and at Albert Merriman's jewelry store and the Ganey Co.

Clerk Fred Johnston and Corporal Charlie Rathburn of the Company were out today booming the dance which will no doubt be a great success and we hope net the boys a nice sum.

Gallipolis Daily Tribune, September 24, 1917

COMPANY F

Makes a Hit With the People of Pt. Pleasant.

We take off our hats and extend our hands in congratulations to Captain Houck and his company of soldiers of Gallipolis, Ohio, upon their splendid appearance while in our city yesterday. Our one great regret is that they did not have more time to spend with us. The miracle which has been wrought in these men is hardly conceivable from the raw recruits who came here on guard duty upon our entrance in the war to the rugged, well disciplined, fine looking bunch of soldiers they are today.

It is our opinion that they will compare most favorably with many of our soldiers who have been in the service for a longer period of time. And, again, we think that by far the greater part of this success is due to the untiring efforts and farsightedness of their splendid officer Capt. Houck.

And the courtesy shown by these soldiers from Gallipolis to our boys who were leaving for Camp Lee, yesterday, has cemented and made stronger the great sisterhood between Gallia county, Ohio and Mason county, this state.

Capt. Houck and your gallant soldiers, we join with your home county of Gallia, in pledging to you our love and devotion as you go forth in the name of humanity.--Saturday's *Pt. Pleasant Register*.

Point Pleasant, West Virginia lies across the Ohio River from Gallipolis.

Gallipolis Daily Tribune, October 3, 1917

Co. F Ready For Call

The local company's latest orders were to have everything in readiness to leave in a few hours.

Two tents were taken down and packed this afternoon.

Gallipolis Daily Tribune, October 6, 1917

TWO SOLDIERS

Desert F Company--One Caught at Pt. Pleasant.

Two soldiers have deserted F company recently. One, a young man named Shamblin, has been gone about three weeks. The other, Fred Rader, left a few days ago, but was captured at Pt. Pleasant Friday and locked up. The whereabouts of Shamblin is unknown.

It is not known just when the company will leave the Gallipolis camp for the south, but they are in good shape and ready to go on a few hours notice. The boys are tired out waiting and most of them are anxious to get to the front.

The penalty for desertion is very severe.

Gallipolis Daily Tribune, October 11, 1917

COMPANY F

To Leave Sunday Morning For Alabama Camp.

Capt. H. E. Houck, in command of F Company, received the official word today that our company would entrain at 7:30 Sunday morning for Camp Sheridan, Montgomery, Ala.

The boys are in excellent condition for the trip and no doubt will feel relieved, knowing the definite time for their departure as they have been kept in a state of anxiety for three months awaiting orders to move.

It is expected that quite a farewell demonstration will be given the soldiers at the depot.

More than six months after the United States entered the war, most of it spent waiting in the part, drilling and waiting, marching and waiting, Company F was finally off to begin its real training.

Gallipolis Daily Tribune, October 12, 1917

SOLDIERS LEAVE SUNDAY

Big Goodbye Demonstration Planned by Loyal Citizens

Sunday morning at 9:00 Company F will leave for their Southern training quarters. Not later than 8:30 o'clock the Company will march up Second Avenue to the Hocking station, accompanied by an escort of citizens and a band of music. The whole city is invited to join in this farewell to the boys, and residents along the line of march are urged to have their flags flying.

Street car service from Kanauga will begin at 7 o'clock, and early cars will carry people to the station who do not care to march.

Capt. Houck announces that all boxes and packages for the boys must be delivered at the Armory by 3 p. m. Saturday, plainly marked. Each package will be delivered to the soldier whose name is on it after the Company entrains.

Gallipolis Daily Tribune, October 15, 1917

SEEING THE BOYS OFF

Citizens Escort Co. F to Station, Where 3,000 Assemble.

Sunday morning was a time to be remembered in Gallipolis. At 8:30 the Elks, Civil War veterans, the Jr. O.U.A.M. and the Woodman, all led by the Woodman Band, with Clark's Band in front of Co. F, escorted the soldiers to the Hocking Station with flags flying.

It was a quiet crowd, very closely packed, at the station, estimated at from 2,000 to 3,000 people.

As soon as the halt was made relatives, friends and citizens generally pressed down the line of soldiers saying their farewells. There were tears and kisses and mobs and choking utterances all along the line, and tears rolled down the cheeks of many of the boys in khaki.

Learning that it would be an hour before the train arrived, an impromptu religious service was given. America was sung, led by Clark's band, after which a fervent and patriotic prayer was made by the Rev. Mr. Yoakley of the First Baptist Church. The Rev. Mr. McClure of Grace M. E. Church followed in a stirring address ten minutes long on the war, its causes, and its justification on religious principles. The Rev. Mr. Beery then spoke on the maintenance and improvement in Christian character possible for our soldiers. "Onward, Christian Soldier," was sung, led by the band, and Mr. Beery pronounced the benediction. It was all a happy, appropriate, and eminently fitting incident in the "Godspeed you" spirit, and bubbling with deep, true patriotism. It must have impressed the Company, as it did their friends. There were many regrets that the Rev. Mr. Wilder of the Episcopal Church had to be with his people in Pomeroy.

At 10:30 the train pulled in and the boys entered the cars after final hugs, kisses and blessings from wet-eyed wives, sweethearts, mothers and sisters. There were few dry eyes when the train pulled out. Cheers arose, but there was so much pent up emotion behind them that they were not, could not, be loud.

The boys are off! God bless and keep them every one!

Chapter Two

Gallipolis Daily Tribune, October 17, 1917

SOLDIER SHOT

Member of Company F First to Be Injured.

Merl Vance, Company F, Seventh Ohio Infantry, of Gallipolis, was shot accidentally in the left leg by a revolver he was handling Tuesday at Camp Sheridan. He lost much blood and was carried to the base hospital for treatment. Vance is the first member of the division to suffer a bullet wound since the Ohio soldiers arrived.

Vance is the son of Mrs. William Scarberry of this city and about 20 years old. He joined the company when their first call for volunteers came.

This distressing story was the first bit of news Gallipolis received about its departed National Guard company, now in training in Alabama at one of the camps established soon after the United States had entered into the war. The camp is the one where, some months later, another young lieutenant and nascent writer named F. Scott Fitzgerald would train, visit Montgomery, and court his future wife, Zelda Sayre.

Found in *The 37th Division in the Great War*

Major General Leonard Wood was... commanding the Department of the Southeast, in which Montgomery was located. As early as May [1917], that city had sought consideration as a possible location for a camp and on 7th May, Major General Wood visited Montgomery to investigate and report on the question of the advisability of establishing a camp [Camp Sheridan] there.[...]

The task that confronted the officers with construction of the camp was a gigantic one. A city that would house 40,000 men must spring up out of the cotton and corn fields, and out of the meadows and waste land spotted with underbrush and weeds. Before the camp should be completed, five miles of railroad tracking had been laid over which supplies and troop trains would be handled. Ten miles of dirt road was to be built, within the camp, in addition to the main thoroughfare that were to serve division and regimental warehouses. A water plant was to be installed that would furnish about 350,000 gallons daily to the camp; and 250 miles of wire was strung to and through the site to convey electric current. Three thousand shower baths and 4,000 sinks were installed. In addition to the main camp, a base hospital, remount station and target range were to be provided. The whole was planned to accommodate 41,593 troops, and when it was completed, 1,277 buildings had sprung up.[...]

The camp was located three and one-half miles north of the center of Montgomery. A street railroad, later double tracked, ran between the camp and the city and there were two gravel roads leading into town. The camp, and the city of Montgomery as well, were amply supplied with steam roads. The Seaboard Air Line ran along the southern boundary of the camp, and the Western Railway of Alabama cut through the northwestern corner and ran along the northern border.[...]

The site selected for the main camp was a rolling plateau about fifty feet above the level of the business center of the city, and from 250 to 235 feet above sea level. The soil throughout was well suited for camp purposes. The surface was usually a sandy loam with an occasional outcropping of sand and of sand mixed with gravel.... The reservation contains a total of about 30,000 acres and was of irregular shape with a maximum length of two and one-half miles and a maximum width of two miles. [...]

The rifle range was situated east of the city and of the main camp, in Elmore county. Twelve miles from the camp, it was partially connected by a good gravel road that reached a point four miles from the range. From that point, a dirt road (that was improved by grading and draining) led to the range. This reservation contained about 1,600 acres. (vol. 1, 187-189)

Advanced detachments from the 5th and 8th Ohio Infantry, First Ohio Artillery, and the entire supply train and Second Ambulance Company, comprising approximately two thousand men arrived on August 25th, and approximately two thousand men, the advance detachments of practically all the remaining Ohio units arrived the following day with other advance detachments on the 27th and 28th. Troops were arriving almost daily from that time until October 16th, when the Seventh Ohio Infantry reached camp. (vol. 1, 196-197)

Gallipolis Daily Tribune, October 18, 1917

SEVENTH REGIMENT

Col. Crosson Desired To Go Into Battle As Unit.

Camp Sheridan, Ala, October 17.--Camp Sheridan's Ohio population took another jump and went above the 20,000 mark Tuesday with the arrival of the old Seventh Ohio Regiment of Infantry, which has been reorganized into the Seventh, Eighth and Ninth Training Battalions of the Sixty-second Depot Brigade.

Led by Colonel Tom O. Crosson of New Lexington, who lives in the neighborhood of General Phil Sheridan, whose exploits in the Civil War brought him recognition in the naming of Camp Sheridan, the regiment detrained here during the day, and at the sound of retreat was encamped in walled tents which had been arranged by other detachments.

With the exception of two small units, the movement of the old Ohio National Guard has been completed. Attention now will be given to the transportation of selectmen [draftees] from Ohio and other states to fill the gaps in the division caused by changes in plans of the War Department. This movement is expected to begin within 10 days.

Colonel Crosson is determined to do all in his power to prevent the breaking up of his regiment into training battalions. He and his men desire active service at the front. They fear they will be kept in camp in the United States if they become a part of the depot brigade.

The regiment recruited in Southeastern Ohio desires to maintain its identity and to go into battle as a unit. Colonel Crosson fears this cannot be realized if the regiment is broken up into training battalions.

With the 5,000 selectmen already provided, the Ohio division will be increased to more than 27,000. More men probably will be needed, and it is believed intensive training will be started when the units have been recruited to war strength, with no less than 30,000 men in camp.

Dissatisfied over the prospect of lounging about Camp Sheridan while their comrades of Ohio are fighting in France, more than 1,000 member of the Sixty-second Depot Brigade, who have been assigned to the three training battalions, have requested transfers to the fighting units, and their requests will be granted.

Ohio election officials who will receive the votes of Ohio soldiers in the municipal elections next months began to arrive today, and during the next few days several score will be here to receive the ballots, which will be counted at the close of the election. Ten officials of Cincinnati and Hamilton County arrived today.

Chief interest at Camp Sheridan hinges about the question of prohibition, while woman suffrage is second in importance.

Capt. Jones at Camp Sheridan.

Capt. Tom Jones of Co. C, from Meigs county, is making a hit in Camp Sheridan. Capt. Jones recently celebrated his 44th birthday in the Camp and he has been appointed judge advocate of the general court martial. Each tent at Camp Sheridan is walled up, has a floor and a stove therein. Every soldier can live in comfort down there.

The integrity of the units that Colonel Crosson desired, however, would not be maintained. Despite his vows, Colonel Crosson found himself soon gone, taking over command of Military Police, instead. He was replaced by Colonel Robert L. Hubner, a native of Dayton but still a stranger to the old Seventh. Other officers and, indeed, whole units, were also moved of split up. Among those transferred was Skip Barlow who, after bouncing around a bit, came to rest with Company L of the 3rd Battalion of the 148th Infantry Regiment, where he would stay for the rest of the war.

Found in *The 37th Division in the World War*

Throughout the months of October and November, training was carried on steadily if somewhat uncertainly, and the reorganization of the division was completed.[...]

The Seventh Infantry, whose headquarters had been at New Lexington, was split up as follows: parts of Companies F (Gallipolis), G (Logan), H (New Lexington), I (Ironton) and M (McConnellsville) to the 148th Infantry. (vol. 1, 227-228)

The experience [of personnel changes], heartbreaking as it was, was not peculiar to Ohio, nor to the United States. Privates, lieutenants, captains, field officers and general officers all suffered through it. When companies were broken up, men who had enlisted together were separated. Others who enlisted under some one unit commander found themselves torn from him and from their neighbors who volunteered in the same locality. The unit commander saw himself separated from the organization he had created, or had perfected; it went to regiment, brigade and division. (vol. 1, 232)

148th Regiment Strength Return for October, 1917

The regiment with the exception of Co. K. was doing guard duty at Camp Sherman, Chillicothe, Ohio until October 8th, 1917, at which date it entrained for Camp Sheridan. Detrained at Camp Sheridan, Alabama on the morning of October 11th,

1917. Has been following the drill schedules
furnished by Headquarters, 37th Division.

"K" Company was doing guard duty at Fairfield,
Ohio (The Wright Aviation Field) until October
26th, 1917, at which date it entrained for Camp
Sheridan, Ala. Detrained at Camp Sheridan,
Alabama October 28, 1917. Has been following the
usual course of drill prescribed.

The regiment with the exception of K.
Co. received Telegraphic Instructions from
Headquarters, Central Department, Chicago,
Illinois to entrain on the 8th of October.

Company K. received Telegraphic Instructions
from Headquarters, Central Department, Chicago,
Ill to entrain on the 26th of October.

Found in *The 37th Division in the World War*

The infantry division consisted of a division headquarters,
two infantry brigades, a field artillery brigade, a machine gun
battalion, a regiment of engineers, a field signal battalion,
train headquarters and military police, ammunition, supply, engineer and sanitary trains, an aggregate strength of
979 commissioned officers and 28,050 enlisted men. There
were 1,306 enlisted men in various medical organizations,
170 in the ordnance department, 51 veterinary, while aggregate enlisted men numbered 27,071, of which number
25,391 were classed as combatants. The division carried
with it, 1,854 draft horses, 2,032 riding horses, 2,550 draft
mules, fifty-three pack mules, eighty-two riding mules, thirteen four-mule ambulances, 399 one-mule combat carts,
twenty-four one-mule medical carts, 101 two-mule ration
carts, eighteen two-horse battery reel carts, eleven six-horse
regimental and battalion reel carts, 98 one-mule water carts,
104 four-mule rolling kitchens, fourteen six-horse battery

wagons, 175 four-mule or four-horse combat wagons, two six-horse combined storage and battery wagons, 109 four-mule ration and baggage wagons, four two-horse spring wagons, fourteen six-horse store wagons, 238 bicycles, six trailmobile water carts, thirty trailmobile rolling kitchens, forty-one motor ambulances, 1,209 motor cars, 319 motorcycles, four two and one-half ton tractors, sixty five-ton tractors, 262 cargo trucks, 218 ammunition trucks, eight artillery repair trucks, three equipment repair trucks, six reel and fire control trucks, nine repair trucks, seven light repair trucks, twenty-five supply trucks, twenty-three tank trucks, four telephone trucks, three wireless trucks, and 216 caissons. The arms borne by the division, under these tables of organization, consisted of 17,667 rifles, 11,903 pistols, 1,506 rifle grenade discharges, fifty three-inch or seventy-five millimeter guns, twelve one-pounders, thirty-six anti-air craft machine guns, 224 heavy machine guns, twenty-four six-inch or 155 millimeter howitzers, 36 trench mortars, and—reverting to the simplest of all weapons—1,920 trench knives. (vol. 1, 306-307)

Gallipolis Daily Tribune, October 19, 1917

NEWS FROM COMPANY F

The plan to disband the Seventh Ohio, of which Co. F is a part, is being carried out.

Lieuts. Barlow and [Harold] Mackenzie and most of the company were transferred to Co. F, 148th U.S. Infantry.

Several corporals were assigned to the headquarters company of the 148th and Sergeants Lewis, Pinkerman, and John Oliver were placed in Company C of the same regiment. Capt. Houck, First Sergeant Adams, Supply Sergeant Broyles, Mess Sergeant Cromley, Musician Mayes, the three cooks, the two artificers and the five remaining duty Sergeants are still nonassigned.

Several men received promotions and will hold their rank wherever they go. Corporals Gillian and Thomas were promoted to Sergeants; Privates Burton, Neighbors, Mayes, Stormont, Craft, Hill, Walters, and

Musician Broyles were made corporals; Private Chas. Lewis was made artificer; Private Hugh Walker was also appointed corporal.

Roscoe Rutherford and Roy Johnston are in the base hospital with the measles, but are getting along as well as can be expected. Merl Vance who accidentally shot himself in the leg is improving rapidly.

Company F Strength Return for October, 1917

[Company F] moved from Camp Sherman, Chillicothe Ohio Oct 8th 1917 arrived Camp Sheridan, Montgomery Alabama Oct 11 1917. Robert T. Coughlin died of gun shot wound Oct 20 1917. Harold Moorehouse enlisted as private Oct 8th 1917. 8 corporals, 25 privates 1st class, 17 privates, 2 cooks transferred from 19th Training Company Depot Brigade Division Special Order 59 Oct 26/17. 1st Sergeant Adams, Bugler Mayes, Cook Snyder attached per Div. SO 59 Oct 26/17 from 19th Training Company Depot Brigade....

2nd Lieut. Alfred M. Barlow, National Guard; Camp Sheridan; Transferred from 19th Training Company, Depot Brigade SO 59, Oct. 26, 1917, per Headquarters 37th Division.

Gallipolis Daily Tribune, October 20, 1917

CO. F SOLDIERS

Transferred at Camp Sheridan.
Merl Vance's Leg Amputated.

Mr. Walter Brothers, a former Corporal in Co. F returned home from Camp Sheridan in Alabama Friday evening. Walter went down with the Company hoping to pass an examination but failed, due to defective eye sight and greatly to his disappointment.

He was near private Merl Vance when he accidentally shot himself. Young Vance suffered much pain and loss of blood, but he was rushed to a hospital and his leg amputated just below the hip. He will be sent home as soon as he is able to travel.

The soldier boys, generally speaking, are in fine condition, but loth to be separated which now looks probable.

Mr. Brothers states there are over 24,000 men in Camp Sheridan which contains 15 square miles of grounds, and which is, in his opinion, a long was ahead of Camp Sherman at Chillicothe.

The following members of Co. F have been transferred to the Eighth Regiment of Infantry: George Craft, Darwin Chevealier, Richard Cliff, Emmit Davidson, Seth Lyons, George Plantz, George Rose, Custer Smith, and William Smith.

The following members of Co. F were transferred to the Heavy Artillery: Emmit Daniels, Homer Duncan, James Evans, Lavinus Farley, William Hawley, Charles Jeffers, Harold Landthorn, Ora Montgomery, Charles Rathburn, James Saunders, Stanley Thomas, Jesse White, Ira White, Edward Woodward, Marine Watts, and Emmit Walters.

Gallipolis Daily Tribune, October 20, 1917

TWENTY-FIVE MORE

Men Taken From F Company at Camp Sheridan.

Mrs. H. E. Houck has received word from Captain Houck than 25 more of his men from F Company have been transferred and their places were filled with foreigners. They are mostly Dagoes and it is a hard job to train them.

To readers seventy-five and more years later, slandering comments concerning "Dagoes" seem peculiar and stupid, if not downright abhorrent. But the Gallipolis of WWI was an isolated community—and as racist and xenophobic as even were the "sophisticated" parts of the United States of that time. Young Skip Barlow was no better than his community: occasional racist comments, as will be apparent, appear in his letters. Only some years after the war would he atone at all for his ignorance, fighting to keep the Ku Klux Klan out of the Ohio American Legion (see chapter 13 for details on the speech he gave).

STATE OF OHIO
THE ADJUTANT GENERAL'S OFFICE
COLUMBUS

Nov. 7, 1917.

TO WHOM IT MAY CONCERN:

The records of this office show that,
            ALFRED M. BARLOW
enlisted in Co. F 7th Inf. O.N.G. May 22, 1913;
Discharged June 14, 1913, by reason of removal
from Company Station; re-enlisted Co. D 7th Ohio
Inf. June 15, 1916; Appointed Sergt.; Mustered out
with Co. Dec 21, 1916; Re-enlisted Co. F 7th Ohio
Inf. March 31, 1917; Discharged April 4, 1917;
Commissioned 2nd Lieut. and placed on duty with
Co. F 7th Ohio Inf. April 4, 1917; Mustered into
U.S. Service July 26, 1917; Discharged from O.N.G.
Aug. 5, 1917, by reason of being drafted into the
Armies of the U.S. per G.O. 21 A.G.D.

                        Geo S. Wood
                        The Adjutant General.

Found in *The 37th Division in the World War*

Organization of division headquarters was in itself a complicated affair. The major general, of course, was in command. There were right officers on general staff duty, a colonel, a lieutenant colonel, a captain, a first and a second lieutenant.

Under the division adjutant, who was a lieutenant colonel, were two majors or captains, a first and a second lieutenant. The inspector was a lieutenant colonel. The quartermaster was a lieutenant colonel, and had under him, two majors or captains, two first and one second lieutenants. The medical department and chaplains had a lieutenant colonel, two captains or majors and four captains, first or second lieutenants. The ordnance department was under a lieutenant colonel. The judge advocate's department had a lieutenant colonel and a major or a captain. The signal officer was a lieutenant colonel. The veterinary service was in charge of a major or captain and a captain, first or second lieutenant. The headquarters troop, numbering 122 men, was under a captain, a first and a second lieutenant. Five aides and aerial observers were assigned to the division commander. (vol. 1, 314-315)

LIEUTENANT COLONEL, E.P. WALSER

CHAPLAIN, S.L. MARTIN

SOCIAL CENTER
SEVENTH OHIO INFANTRY HEADQUARTERS

MOBILIZATION CAMP

Camp Sheridan Ala

Co K 148 Inf

Thursday Nov. 14, 1917

Dear Mamma and Grandma,

I have not your letter at hand but will try to answer it anyway. I have been made a 1st lieut, and assigned to K Co. 148 Inf. Harold's job was nothing of an honor. It comes in rotation every so many days. I have it today. I am simply Officer of the Day. The name is larger than anything else. We have to inspect the regiment as to sanitation & I must inspect the guards between 1 & 3 tonight. Then I must inspect the guard at the guard house tomorrow about 9:30 in the morning. I have a house here all to my self. It is 9x9 & 6 feet to the eaves. This gives me lots of room. I bought it from a Major for $10. I am going to be pretty close this month. I hope I don't over draw. If you can keep some money in the bank until after the first do so. I have to pay $12 for the colonel's horse. After this month I'll get $166.67 a month. Then I'll save quick cause my expenses won't be any more than they are now. Next month I'll send you my money I want paid for debts and you can pay them. I got an issue overcoat & had it fixed up and it cost me $9.50 for coat & $11 to be altered which makes $20.20 a lot less than half price. I've been invited out to dinner several times and have met many interesting people.

Sunday Nov. 18,

Your letter came this morning. The abbreviation for lieutenant is LIEUT.

Just after dinner today I was vaccinated and received my second para-typhoid injection. This will probably make me very sick soon. It will last only 24 hrs. thou. Tell all the folks I would like to write but that I have very little time. We formerly had Wed. & Sat. afternoons off but now we have officers school at that time so we have practically all our time taken up.

I will send you my O.V. [Ohio Valley] bank book and you can keep it there. My leggings have not yet arrived. Please give The Tribune my new address. I have received only two papers.

I saw Mr & Mrs Switzer. I don't know how much I have in the bank by this time. Next month I will put part of my money here. I'm afraid to check out any now I've had so many expenses. I've had to buy lots of books that have cost a heap.

Giver Earnest my regards and tell him I wish him all success. Harold is only about one hundred feet from me. Jarvises note must be in the bank or in the money drawer, or rather paper drawer in the writing desk. Maybe it was turned into the bank with the rest of the checks.

Have you heard from the pension yet? It must be a great worry for you to be delayed so long but it will be sure some time.

We will probably not go to France before February at least.

Be sure Mama and have your teeth and glasses fixed as soon as possible. Make arrangements with Dr. Vanden as soon as he comes home to save you a date. He will probably be pretty busy.

Give everyone my best.

With love,

Alfred

P.S. It is nice & warm. I have everything opened up. It is now 4 p.m.

Found in *The 37ᵗʰ Division in the World War*

An infantry brigade, as planned according to the new tables, consisted of two infantry regiments numbering 7,536 men and officers, and of a machine gun battalion numbering 739, a total of 8,078 combatants, which, with the addition of chaplains, medical department ordnance and veterinary department units, brought the total to 8,469. The infantry regiment consisted of 3,720 enlisted men and 112 officers. Each such regiment had a headquarters company commanded by a captain with a first lieutenant as second in command. The band section was in charge of a second lieutenant, as was the signal platoon. The sappers and bombers platoon had a first and second lieutenant, the pioneer platoon a second, and the one pounder gun platoon a first lieutenant, a total of eight commissioned officers. Forty-two men, consisting of the regimental sergeant major, the battalion sergeants major (three) the first sergeant, two color sergeants, mess, supply and stable sergeants, six duty sergeants, eight corporals, six cooks, four mechanics, seven wagoners, a horse shoer made up the first section. There were twenty-nine in the orderly or second section, and forty-nine in the band; fifty-one in the first telephone section of the signal platoon, ten in the second section assigned to headquarters, and fifteen in the third section assigned to the three battalions, or a total of seventy-six. There were nine sappers, thirty-nine bombers, fifty-four in the pioneer platoon, a total of 336 in the company. The supply company had 164 enlisted men, a captain, two first lieutenants and a second lieutenant. The machine gun company had a captain, two first lieutenants and three second lieutenants, and 172 enlisted men, and was armed with sixteen heavy machine guns and 178 pistols. The rifle or line companies of an infantry regiment consisted of 250 enlisted men, a captain, three first lieutenants and two second lieutenants. There were twenty in company headquarters, of whom two were the captain and the first lieutenant, who was second in command of the company. The first and fourth platoons were commanded by first lieutenants, and the second and third, by second lieutenants. Each platoon had its headquarters consisting of the lieutenant in command, a sergeant and four privates, armed with rifles who became vitally important as runners, charged with the heavy burden of helping to maintain communications. There were four sections in each platoon; twelve men in the hand bombers under two corporals, nine in the rifle grenadiers, seventeen in the third section known as riflemen, and fifteen in the fourth section, known as automatic riflemen, a total of fifty-eight. In each company were thirty rifle grenade dischargers, seventy-three pistols, sixteen automatic rifles, 235 rifles and forty trench knives. (vol. 1, 306-311)

Company K Strength Return for November, 1917

    Company on Regimental Guard Duty, November 11, `17, and Nov. 24, `17. Followed the usual Training Schedule, November 1, `17 to November 30, `17. . . .
    2nd Lieut. Alfred M. Barlow Infantry National Guard; Camp Sheridan, Ala; Assigned to Co. K from Co. F., Special Order 287.

Found in *The Thirty-Seventh Division*

Although [...] many men and officers had known military service extending over a period of months or years with the national guard, they were in the minority. The training of the division started first on the theory that discipline must be perfected, and corollary to this, was the never-ending emphasis upon the importance of saluting and acknowledging soldierly bearing.[...]

Hours each day (excepting Saturday and Sundays) were spent by the infantry in executing close order drill. Schedules outlining the movements to be practiced by squad, platoon, company and battalion were issued; they indicated exactly the drill to be given for every moment of the drill period and no deviation was permitted. Hour after hour, units went through the manual of arms, and day after day.   (vol. 1, 316-319)

Gallipolis Daily Tribune, November 17, 1917

CAMP SHERIDAN PLANS

Include Making Ohioans Into Complete "Fighting Division."

Montgomery, Ala., November 16.--Ohio soldiers will be formed into one of the most complete fighting units ever assembled in this country by the plans now being carried out at Camp Sheridan. When the Thirty seventh Division leaves Montgomery it will be a complete fighting unit, with the exception of battleplanes, and it is believed machines and aviators will be attached just as soon as the division once "gets over."

The men this week are working with the bayonet and rifle, and probably Monday morning will go into "No Man's Land" to learn the latest mode of trench warfare under instruction and guidance of the French officers now with the division. "No Man's Land," just southeast of the camp proper, is about completed, and when the troops get into action on it they will be fight-

ing over ground resembling the real battle front, just as much as time, inge-
nuity and money can make it.

Work with bombs will have a big part in the grueling struggle when
the troops get "over there," and on "No Man's Land" here the Ohioans will
get their practice in hurling the deadly little bombs which have made trench
warfare the most bloody in the history of the world. The men will start out
with dummy bombs and later will work with the real thing, learning just
how to hurl the little missiles with the most deadly effect.

The Ohio boys at Camp Sheridan are just being brought to a realization that there will be no furloughs before the "go across." That means there
will be no Thanksgiving or Christmas holidays at home. It means that their
thought of loved ones and home comforts is getting deeper and deeper; that
the privilege of writing letters and enjoying the movies and entertainments,
the athletic students and the educational classes at the "Y" is being more
and more appreciated; that the only touch of home left to them is that provided by the Red Triangle.

Found in *The 37th Division in the World War*

Chief among the organized agencies administering to the
welfare of the soldiers, must be listed the Y.M.C.A. With the
first arrival of Ohio troops, two small tents were pitched until
permanent buildings could be erected. About ten thousand
dollars per month was expended in Y.M.C.A. activities. Fifty
men were almost constantly employed to make life a little more
pleasant for the men. Ministers, physical directors, educators
and business men gave up remunerative employment to help
in the great cause. Ten "Y" huts were constructed, including
the Coliseum and buildings at the Rifle Range, Aviation Field
and Remount Depot. The total monthly expenditure necessary to keep up the activities of the larger buildings amounted
to about $400. In this was included the cost of stationery—a
million sheets of which were given out monthly—motion picture shows, athletic goods, outside entertainments, testa-

ments, etc. Over four hundred thousand calls each month were made on the Red Triangle. (vol. 1, 235-236)

148th Infantry Regiment Strength Return for November 1917

The regiment as a whole performed the intensive drill schedule prescribed by the Division Commander, i.e., close order and extended order drill, bayonet practice, bombing and trench work. The Regiment under the direction of Lieutenant Colonel K. I. Best has been constructing a Bombing Field with... trenches, etc. for the regiment. The 1st Battalion marched out to the Artillery Range for construction work on the trenches on the 27th of Nov. The 2nd and 3rd Battalions marched out on the 28th of November.

Found in *The 37ᵗʰ Division in the World War*

In December, 1917, many of the officers and men were looking forward to the holidays when families were planning to come to Montgomery to be with them. It had been announced that those desiring to do so would be granted a four-day leave to stay in Montgomery—from Saturday until Christmas which came on Tuesday. The Montgomery Chamber of Commerce co-operated with officials from the camp to make housing arrangements of all visitors. And then there was great excitement, and much changing of plans when General Treat announced a tentative plan to grant furloughs for all men of Camp Sheridan who desired to return to Ohio for the holidays, and who could pay for their transportation. This happiness proved to be short-lived. The War Department upon investigation, found that the return of so many men would literally swamp railroads, and transportation through the United States was already becoming a serious problem. It was therefore necessary for General Treat to recall his former decision, and those whose families must remain in Ohio, looked forward to a dismal Christmas. (vol. 1, 324)

Camp Sheridan Ala

Co A Detention Camps
Dec. 12, 1917

Dear Mamma & Grandma,

I certainly am not here for treatment. I am one of the officers of the camp. I have charge of building walls and roads and give lectures on bayoneting, bombing, how to judge distances, set sights and so forth.

I am very sorry to hear of grandmas illness. I do hope she gets better soon.

Tonight I am on guard and must be up until midnight. We have a lot of inspections to make.

The men here have venereal diseases, and are confined to this particular part of the camps.

Please look up my acct at the Ohio Valley. I am endorsing a check for $35. I am going to pay Halliday the $24 for my rain coat & trench coat. I don't know what I would have done without them.

I have another lieutenant in with me. We have made a regular shack 9 x 12. We have lots of room and a little wood. He has a tea set and alcohol stove. He is a fine man an actor and Christian Scientist. Isn't that peculiar.

It is now 11:15 p.m. Harold has just left. I expect to soon receive my commission as 1st lieut. I am only acting now.

We are not going to get to go home for Xmas. I am hard up anyway.

I hope you sell the farm.

Will the $35 be enough. I'll get my money on time next turn & I'll send it about Jan 1st. I can use a sweater or two when I go over. See if Bess Hudlins has the yarn for cousin Nellie Henlong & pay Bess for the yarn. Address me here. With lots of love,

Alfred

P.S. I just sent my pay down to a bank here. I will bank here from now on. I owe here 84.85. This clears me up. I bought a pair of shoes, underclothes, cotton pants & other little things. I'll send you a check and next month will try to pay the bank $50. I think if I were you I would buy war savings stamps if I had any change I didn't want but you better keep always $200 subject to check, you may need it. I need only socks now. I have enough sweaters. I do hope you have a good time. You certainly deserve it.

Why can't the girls come down to Montgomery & stay over Sunday some time? I'd love to have them. I'll always write business on a separate sheet. It's 9:30 now & I'll have to write until 12 at least.

Lots of love

Alfred

Check will be in my next letter. If you need more let me know.

Found in *The 37ᵗʰ Division in the World War*

Tall, soldierly, distinguished in appearance and bearing, General Treat made a vivid impression. He was born in Dexter, Maine, 30th December, 1859, and was 58 years old when he took command at Camp Sheridan. He was appointed to West Point from his Congressional district in 1878 and was graduated four years later...

Most of General Treat's service had been with the artillery. He went to Cuba during the Spanish American war, serving as adjutant general on the staff of General Wallace Randolph, commander of a field artillery brigade; he was present at the surrender of Santiago, and was with the artillery at San Juan Hill. (vol. 1, 220)

Headquarters, 37th Division,

                          Camp Sheridan, Alabama,
                             December 20, 1917.

Special Orders,)
)
  No. 115   )

   ...

    7. The following named officers are hereby relieved from special duty at the Detention Camp, and will report to the Commanding Officers of their respective organizations, for duty:
    Captain Smith Pothour, Inf., N.G., attached   134th Machine Gun Battalion,
    Captain Hiram E. Houck, Inf., N.G., attached to   Division Headquarters
    Captain Bert Aldrich, Inf., N.G., attached to   135 Machine Gun Battalion,
    1st Lieut. John Unkefer, Inf., N.G., 146th Infantry
    2nd Lieut. Alfred M. Barlow, Inf., N.G., 148th Infantry,
    2nd Lieut. William E. Jenkins, Inf., R.C., attached to   148th Infantry.

       By command of Major General Treat:

                 Dana T. Merrill,
                 Lt. Colonel, Infantry, N. A.,
                 Chief of Staff

Found in *The 37ᵗʰ Division in the World War*

Colonel Merrill was born in Maine on 15ᵗʰ October, 1876, attended public schools and was graduated from the University of Maine with the degree of Bachelor of Science in 1898. His military career began when he enlisted as a private in Company H of the First Maine Volunteer Infantry on 11ᵗʰ May, 1898. He was commissioned second lieutenant of the Twelfth U.S. Infantry on 18ᵗʰ September of that year and proceeded to the Philippines with that regiment, where he served during the insurrection from 15ᵗʰ May, 1899, to 15ᵗʰ May, 1902. He was a Distinguished Graduate of the Army School of the Line in 1908, and of the Army Staff College in 1909. He subsequently served in the Panama Canal Zone for three years as a captain in the Tenth U.S. Infantry. When the World War started, he was on duty in Washington and was detailed on the General Staff on 4ᵗʰ June, 1916. He was designated Chief of Staff of the Thirty-seventh Division on 16ᵗʰ August, 1917, and served in that capacity until the armistice was signed.... (vol. 1, 223)

148th Infantry Regiment Strength Return for December, 1917

The regiment as a whole closely followed the drill schedules published by Division Headquarters. It participated in the two March Pasts before the Commanding General of the 37th Division and before Gov. James Cox. The regiment as a whole marched to the Artillery range for construction work on the following days. 12/4/17-12/8/17-12/15/17 and 12/18/17. The three Battalions of the 148th Infantry marched to the Division Training Grounds on the following dates each respectively: 12/27/17-12/28/17 and 12/29/17.

The morale and appearance of the personnel of the
regiment was good....

   [2nd Lieutenant Alfred Barlow] Special Duty
Detention Camp 11/21/17 to 12/20/17. Resigned
as 2nd Lieutenant 12/14/17 to accept commission
as 1st Lieutenant.... Assigned to 148th, 37th
Division. Assigned to Co. K... --Platoon Command
School, Infantry School of Arms.

Found in *The 37ᵗʰ Division in the World War*

   Discipline tightened, too. Orders were issued to the effect that men must "fall in" under arms at the reveille formation, and inspectors were sent out through the camp to make
proper checks. General Treat announced censorship rules
governing newspaper correspondents on duty at the camp. In
the future, there could be no information published relative to
movements of troops or individuals from the camp. No reference could be made to any specific forms of training which
the division was undergoing. Information relative to arrivals
of troops or individuals could not be made public; a division
censor was placed in control.

   Greater emphasis was placed upon the necessity for observing military courtesy, particularly as regards saluting.
Orders were issued (26ᵗʰ December, 1917), to be effective 10ᵗʰ
January following, that particular attention should be given
to saluting commissioned officers and superiors, and to returning the salutes of subordinates and enlisted men. (vol.
1, 344)

   On 10ᵗʰ January General Treat issued a restriction order
against soldiers going into Montgomery because of a number
of smallpox cases which had appeared in the city. This dismal order broke all social activities outside the camp for the
rest of the month. It did not, however, prevent the thoughtful

Montgomery people from bringing their entertainment in to the boys, and the Montgomery Music Club presented a number of programs during the month at the Coliseum and Base Hospital.

The Y.M.C.A. and the Knights of Columbus redoubled their efforts to furnish entertaining movies, and athletic events while the camp was under restriction order. The camp was scored for available vaudeville material which was to be organized into a regular circuit to play at all Y.M.C.A. huts and the camp Coliseum. (vol. 1, 242)

Smallpox? I wonder if the real cause wasn't the crowded detention camp where Skip was posted and victims of another type of pox were held? Still, smallpox is mentioned elsewhere as the reason for the restriction.

Headquarters 37th Division,
Camp Sheridan, Alabama,
January 12, 1918

Special Orders,)
No. 12.   )

. . .

7.   1st Lieutenant Alfred M. Barlow, 148th Infantry, is hereby detailed on special duty at the Detention Camp, and will report to the Commanding Officer thereof.

8.   Four days after the arrival of Lieutenant Barlow at the Detention Camp, 2nd Lieutenant Ralph M. Mork, Inf. R.C., attached to the 148th Infantry, will be relieved from duty at the

Detention Camps, and will report to his Commanding Officer for duty.

By command of Major General Treat:

Dana T. Merrill
Lt. Col., Infantry, N.A.
Chief of Staff

Sunday January 13, 1918

Dear Mama & Grandma,

Received your letter the other day and was certainly glad to get it. I received the things from Aunt Grace and they certainly are appreciated. I can't have too many wool things. I need them right now. The weather here is cold. The ground freezes a little only but it is a penetrating disagreeable damp cold. I am very comfortably situations and have things conveniently arranged.

I wrote to Aunt G. right away.

We are in quarantine now but I'll see about the casserole as soon as I am allowed to go down to town. We can't now as there is smallpox in town.

My life is insured in the government just as Harold's is. You will get $50 per mo. for 20 years or rather $48 a month.

My school is only one of a dozen or more. I hear the training period has been extended 18 weeks. That would make us leave June 1st. I don't suppose we will leave before that.

I expect to send you a check for $100 the first of February, out of that please pay $5 or so to Moore & Merriman. I owe each a little. I'll attend to the bank later and tell you when to call for the policy.

I paid a lot of bills this month & had a check for $15 made out Dec. 26 come back on me. I had to pay $1.75 protest charges. Always keep some money on hand. Now I have had only $4 for the last week and it must run me to the end of the month.

If my accounts are correct I have over drawn again about $5. Please go right over to the phone and call up Herbert H and see how I stand and tell him to take the money from your acct. if mine is over drawn.

Most of my bills here are paid now and I'll have money coming in from now on.

Be sure and call him up right away.

From the rest of the $100 I send pay part to Wetherholt and tell him I expect to send you $25 a month there after. Or rather tell him you expect to pay him $25 a month there after.

Have you seen Mrs. Hayward yet?

Why don't you write Waggoner. He said he would take it and he has used it for nothing.

How is that nigger coming on.

I am being very saving as I must have about $200 worth of new equipment.

Please give everyone my very best, and Earnest & Ester my love.

Be sure and call up Herbert. I hope you both keep well.

With lots of love,
Alfred

P.S. I see Harold every day.

Here again, the racism exhibited is more the product of the time than any failing on Skip's part. He wasn't being intentionally cruel, simply thoughtless. Given the current climate in America, it was actually tempting to elide this and other racist comments. That, however, would be a re-writing of history and a betrayal of the purpose of this work, to portray the life in a World War I infantry division as fully as possible in words of the time.

148th Infantry Regiment Strength Return for January, 1918

January 9th, 1918. Twenty six enlisted men of the 148th Infantry were selected to attend the Officers Training Camp at Ison Springs, Texas. The Battalions of the 148th took the course on the Bayonet Grounds preparatory to going on the Rifle Range: 1st Battalion Jan 10th: 2nd Battalion Jan. 14; 3rd Battalion Jan 21st, 1918. The 3rd Battalion marched to the Divisional Training Grounds for construction work on the trenches January 17th, 1918. Forty two enlisted men transferred to the 148th Infantry from the 136th Machine Gun Battalion. Thirty eight men transferred to the 136th Machine Gun Battalion from the 148th on Jan. 20th, 1918. Prohibited from visiting Montgomery, Ala. Jan. 8th by reason Small Pox in that city. Paid by the Supply Officer of the 148th on Jan 22nd, 1918. Jan. 16th 1st Battalion Marches to the Rifle Range, returns Jan. 23rd. 2nd Battalion marches to the Rifle Range Jan 23 returns Jan 29 1918. 3rd Battalion marches to the Rifle Range Jan 29 1918, still on its tour of duty there. Two deaths in the 148th Infantry during the month of January. Sgt Lyman Doane, Co. L. appendicitis: and Patrick Maloney, Pvt, Co. K. pneumonia resulting from measles. Nineteen enlisted men of the 148th Inf. transferred to the 41st Engineers, Washington, DC.... Thirty three enlisted men transferred to the Motor Mech. Regt. Camp Hancock, Augusta, Ga.

Camp Sheridan Ala

Co K 148 Inf.
Sun Jan 20, 1917 [sic]

Dear Mamma & Grandma,

Just this morning I received your letter of Dec. 23 last. It is rather late to answer it now but I will try to nevertheless.

I certainly thank you for the yarn I received the mitts and the sweater and they certainly do come in handy. When we just have on shirts I wear both sweaters underneath.

I had a fine time Christmas. I took communion in the morning and then went to Kenton's for dinner. Two weeks ago today I was to Rev. McQueens who is the rector of the Church of Holy Comforter. The week before that I was to Lehe's. I've seen Miss Jean Lehe several times, her sister Mrs. Screws is the wife of Col. Screws of the Alabama regiment in the Rainbow Division. Now we are not allowed to go to town because of the quarantine. It seems there is smallpox in Montgomery. It's just a few cases thou. Montgomery feels pretty bad cause the soldiers spent a lot of money there. My school finished up yesterday. It was very interesting.

I hope Grandma is entirely well by this time. Do you want sugar badly. I think I can send you some if you do, be sure and let me know. That is after I get paid. I have only 7 cents now. I paid too many debts all at once. Pleas let me know immediately how I stand at the bank & if over drawn cover it until Feb. 1st. Telephone now at Camish. Where is Earnest's store located?

Love to all.
Write soon
Alfred

P.S. Did you get my last letter.

P.S. I don't get any paper so please subscribe for the weekly Tribune again.

AMB

Company K Strength Return for January, 1918

Continuing Daily eight hour extensive training, close and extended order drill-12 mile hike to Divisional Training Grounds for construction work 1/17/18-15 mile hike to Divisional Rifle Range for target practice 1/29/18. Refresher schools evenings from 6.30 to 7.30 P.M. Company at Infantry School of Arms preparatory to Range practice 1/21/18 to 1/26/18....

1st Lt. Alfred M. Barlow; Infantry National Guard Camp Sheridan, Alabama; 1/1/18 to 1/14/18 routine duty with Company. 1/14/18 to 1/31/18 Special Duty Detention Camp, Paragraph 7 Special Order 12, 37th Division 1/12/18.

Alfred M. Barlow 1st Lt. attending Platoon Commanders Course of Instructors Course in Infantry School of Arms beginning Dec 31/17.

Alfred M. Barlow, 1st Lt. Infantry School of Arms 1/1/18 to 1/12/18.

Camp Sheridan Ala

Co K 148 Inf.
Monday Jan 21, '17 [sic]

Dear Mamma & Grandma,

I just this evening received your mail which was written Jan. 6, 1917 [sic]. You can not expect me to get your letters unless you address them correctly. You must remember that this is a camp of about 30,000 men. Please be careful here after. Today I received a note from Aunt Grace saying that Thomas had been killed in or rather by a railroad. I suppose he was in the automobile. Just think one is about as safe in the army as out. I shall write to Aunt Mattie tonite. I never received anything from Minnie but a letter. I will write her too. I am too busy to think. I scarcely have time to think. I haven't been to town for three weeks.

John's deed for Wagoner is so far as I know at the O.V. Bank. The colored man was to pay to your acct $5 per mo. to The Commercial Bank. Ask Kerr if he has. Please see about my account at the O.V. bank.

I shall send you $25 for Wetherholt and some for Moore & Merriman. Telephone and ask how much I owe them.

How much coal have you? Save it and use as much gas as possible.

I have no one girl in Montgomery. I'll get debts paid first from now on I get $166.67 per mo. It costs me $1 a day for just board. Fuel & washing are high. Laundry $2 some weeks. Write soon about my money in O.V. Bank. I have only 7 cents.

> *Love,*
> *Alfred*

P.S. It is Tuesday now I have been so busy I have not been able to even seal up and send your letter. I am glad you got that much from the hay.

My work is very hard and I am tired out. Tell me details of Thomas's death. It shocked me greatly. I am oh so tired. It is 9:30 pm now. I have to study a great deal. I get paid about the 1st. I will send money to you to pay some at least to Merriman, Moore & G.H. Kerr. Please call them up if it's not too much trouble and ask them the amount I owe them. I know nothing of John's deed if it is not in the bank. Does the nigger pay?

If you can sell the farm do it. If not we can afford to keep it I reckon. We might live there some summer but I'd never own another cow or chicken or even a horse. I am sure glad you are in town.

> *Love*
> *Alfred*

News from the family was sometimes tragic for many of the soldiers at Camp Sheridan—or anywhere in the military, for that matter. In this case, it was information that Skip's first cousin, Thomas McGuire, had been hit by a train and killed while shoveling snow from Chicago railroad tracks soon after being drafted himself. The letter from his Aunt Grace mentioned below would be the one telling Skip's mother of Thomas's death. Skip's mother Eva's other sister, Mattie McGuire, was Thomas's mother. She survived her son by more than half a century, dying in 1974, just short of her 110th birthday. Her daughter, Martha Riddle, could still find tears for her lost brother as late as 1985.

"With the Colors"

Camp Sheridan Ala
Co K 148 Inf
Feb. 3, 1918

Dear Mamma & Grandma,

I received your letter today enclosing that from Aunt Grace which I am returning. I wrote Aunt Mattie and received a letter from Cousin Grace [probably meant to be "Cousin Martha"].

I have received my check but I forgot about my insurance & so did not get quite so much as I expected. As soon as I can get to a check I will send you one for ($55) fifty five dollars. Go slow on paying bills. My house is all paid for here and I now owe (here) only about $35 after I pay what I will this time.

I hope to be paid up here & there next time.

Don't tell this

{I do not expect we will leave here before the middle of

{March or the first of April.

I would of the $55 keep $35 pay Moore, Merriman, C.L. Kerr, & The Bankrupt Store $5 each. And tell them I'll settle up next time. Find out how much I still owe.

How much do we still owe Wetherholt?

I'm glad you are getting things fixed up.

Do not take any more water out of the cellar.

I have a man work for me--make my bed get my wood and water, sweep clean, and fix my shoes. I pay him $5 per month. I thus have that much more time for study and it certainly takes a lot.

Please ask Frank Beall if I can get a pair of no. 11 hip boots and send back the boots I got from him. I have not used them at all. If he hasn't the boots it will be all right for I will probably need both high and low boots.

I am out to the

Friday Feb. 6,

I am back in camp now. I was out to the rifle range. There I shot both the kinds of automatic rifles now used by the French and the British.

It is now twenty minutes of ten. I have just returned from a lecture by a British colonel.

In a moment or two Harold will be down and we will study together for an examination he will have tomorrow. Here he is now.

Love to all,

Alfred.

P.S. I hope my check is at the bank please telephone and see.

148th Infantry Regiment Strength Return for February, 1918

3rd Battalion returned from rifle range Feb. 5, 1918. The regiment less the 3rd Battalion participated in a Brigade Maneuver. Route - Out the upper Wetumpka Road to within one half mile of Judkins Ferry and returned. Distance covered - 12 miles. Inspected by the Commanding General, Chief of Staff and Division Inspector on the regimental drill field Feb. 7th and 8th, 1918. The officers and non commissioned officers attended a lecture on Discipline delivered by Colonel Applin of the British Mission, on Feb. 8, 1918. 1st Lieutenant J.F. Stewart and Sergeant J.H. Saumby, British Mission, attached to the 148th Infantry Feb. 14, 1918.

The Field and Company Officers attended tactical walks during the month. The regiment as a whole followed closely drill schedules as published by Headquarters, 37th Division. Headquarters Company, Supply Company and men in Line Companies who did not take course at Rifle Range marched to the Rifle Range Feb. 13, 1918, returned Feb. 20, 1918.

The health, discipline and morale of this organization was as a whole excellent for the month.

Dear Mama & Grandma,

I am so sorry the casserole was broken. If you don't get a crock to fit let me know & I'll see what I can do.

I've had to buy an other uniform. It cost $60 and is no better than the one I had only winter weight. Some of them cost from $85 to $100. I am sending $35. I am sorry it is so little. Next month I'll draw $166.67. Tell me what Wetherholt said. We will try and pay him $25 next month. I heard from Mame Berriage's friend but have been too busy to even write yet. I don't think I can go to where she lives.

I am going to a platoon commanders school now. It started today and I like it fine. We learn how to fight with the new weapons. It will be under French officers. When you cash this see how much I have in the bank.

I saw Mrs. Will Hayward yesterday.

> *With lost of love,*
> *Alfred*

P.S. I've had my life insured in your favor for ($10,000) ten thousand dollars.

Company K Strength Return for February, 1918

At Divisional Rifle range, target practice, 2/1/18 to 2/5/18. 15 mile hike from Rifle Range 2/5/18. Continuation of daily eight hour close and extended order drill. Platoon, Company, Battalion and Regimental attacks with problems therein. Trench warfare, bayonet and grenade practice. Non Commissioned refresher and pistol schools 6.30 to 7.30 P.M. Signal practice, semaphore, wig wag and its use in open and trench warfare....

1st Lieutenant Alfred M. Barlow, Infantry National Guard, Camp Sheridan, Alabama, Relieved of Special Duty Detention Camp... 2/9/18. 2/9/18 to 2/28/18 routine duty with Company. Infantry School Arms, Grenade Section 2/18/18 to 2/28/18.

Found in *The 37th Division in the World War*

The division, with its 28,050 men and officers, had a greater population than Adams county in 1920; greater than Ashland county, or Brown, Carroll, Champaign, Clinton, Defiance, Delaware, Fayette, Fulton, Gallia, Geauga, Greene, Harrison, Henry, Highland, Holmes, Jackson, Madison, Medina, Meigs, Mercer, Monroe, Morrow, Ottawa, Paulding, Pickaway, Pike, Preble, Putnam, Shelby, Union, Vinton, Williams or Wyandot; and greater than the combined populations of Pike and Vinton counties, within a few hundred of as great as the combined populations of Carroll and Geauga, or of Holmes and Morgan, or of Morrow and Vinton counties. The 17,567 rifles carried by the division would have armed more than twice as many men and women as cast a vote in Adams county in 1922, or in Brown county; nearly three times as many as voted in Carroll county, nearly four times as many as voted in Geauga, twice the number who voted in Monroe, Morgan or Morrow, Noble,

Ottawa or Paulding, Pike or Wyandot, or more, by several hundred, in each of fifty-eight out of eighty-eight counties of Ohio. (vol. 1, 315)

On 19th February, it was grimly announced that all enlisted men in the division were to be given numbers; a somber forecast of the time when the round aluminum disks were to be relied upon for identification purposes when so many who wore them would not speak again. (vol. 1, 364)

Chapter Three

Found in *The 37ᵗʰ Division in the World War*

The early training was greatly influenced by extensive trench warfare exercises, which was particularly emphasized at first in War Department instructions. Early in 1918 these instructions were revoked, as a result of a recommendation of A.E.F., and exercises and training in open warfare were substituted. The details of training, although at first controlled by schedules from division headquarters, were later on properly left to brigade and organization commanders. The general scheme was to pass progressively through the training of the individual, squad, platoon, company, battalion, regiment, brigade and division, and to have suitable and appropriate tactical exercises for all units from the battalion to the division, as well as exercises involving the combined arms, such as the support of infantry by artillery. At the same time the technical arms, such as the engineers, medical, ordnance and trains, had similar progressive programs, but with more technical work on the lines under which they could be expected to operate in France. Leadership for small units was a direct objective. (vol. 1, 320)

"With the Colors"

Camp Sheridan Ala
Co K 148 Inf.
Mar. 1, 1918

Dear Mama & Grandma,
    I expect you think I'm dead but I'm not. I have been going to grenade school. I had my examination this morning.

Saturday

I expect to go to a school on Field Fortifications which will start Monday.

I must write a very short letter as I want you to get the check as soon as possible. I am awfully sorry I over drew last month. It shall not happen again. I now owe less than I ever have. I now have within $25 or so all the equipment I need to go over.

I am sending you a check for $50. I am paying some to the bank too. I now owe less than ever. Things are coming along fine. I am paying as fast as I can. I bought a clothing roll for $7.60 and a bedding roll for $16. I took my second degree in Masonry & hope to be thru with it soon.

Please find out how much money I had left over from last month and let me know. As soon as I get straightened up I will send you so much and bank the rest here.

I hope you are both well. I keep too busy to think. If you want to go to Chicago, I would go. I'll send you never less than $35 a month and I want to send $50 a month for your own use.

It is like Spring here. Peach trees and shrubs have been blooming for two weeks. Use gas in place of coal and save your coal as much as possible.

I don't get the Tribune any more haven't since Christmas. I wish you would send the weekly to me.

What do you hear from the pension. I would write Switzer again if I were you. I hope you get it before I go over.

I don't think we will leave Montgomery for a month or six weeks and it may be some time then we will be at the port of debarkation.

I am hoping for an increase of $36 per mo.

If I make good I think I can make a captaincy within a year. I wish you would go to Chicago. We are making preparations to leave here but we will not leave before the time I said.

Be sure and let me know about my bank account. I owe Moore, Merriman, Bankrupt Store, Kerr, Drug Store & Beall for the boots. The boots are too small so I will send this back don't pay him for them.

My watch tells me I have still 10 minutes. I leave more time than I thought.

I will write more often now.

Where is Earnest's store?

Pay just a little to each one. I don't owe Moore anything. I just owe the bank.

Be sure and tell me how much money I had in the bank when they received my this month's check.

> *Loads and loads of love,*
>
> *Write soon,*
>
> *Alfred*

P.S. Some of the insurance papers are here but not all.

You will get yours in time. I didn't take mine out until the last minute in order to save expenses.

Found in *The 37th Division in the World War*

The training for warfare of this vast number was a task that would seem overwhelming in its immensity. It was necessary first of all, to ground each one of the men in the fundamentals of army discipline and then to teach each one the specialized and particular duty and work he had been selected to perform, whether it be firing a rifle or a field piece or a machine gun; bombing, digging trenches or first aid, or administering a field hospital; and there were many duties in which the same instruction was required for all, or for a great percentage. (vol. 1, 315-316)

Camp Sheridan
Montgomery, Ala.

Co K 148 Inf.
March 11, 1918

Dear Mamma & Grandma,

Your last letter came today. I am so sorry to hear that you are ill. I do hope you continue to get better and that grandma you get well quick too.

How glad I am that you have your pension. It certainly does take a load off my mind. Money matters have troubled me quite a bit lately. I made out a note to the bank when I renewed covering Moore's bill also. Now if you will not cash the check I sent you this month I will pay some on it and then I'll soon be able to pay off the rest. I would always try to keep $100 in the bank subject to check. I expect to always send you $50 a month and after I get the bank paid I won't owe anything at all.

I will write Bankrupt's a check tonite so that is thru with.

It's been a long pull, but we've made it.

If this money I send you accumulates always keep this $100 but the rest of it I would put in Liberty Bonds.

Tonight I received a sweater and two pair of socks from Aunt Mattie. It is so kind of her. I have her sweater on now. I can never get too many sox.

I see by your letter you cashed my check. Well, I'll go ahead and pay the bank anyway and you let me know how much I over draw. I will certainly make it up. Please if you are able to telephone in and find out what I have to date and in my next letter I shall tell you how much I would use. I expect to send the bank a check for $35 tonite I will also write Aunt Mattie. I've lots of letters to write but I go to school every nite until 8:30 and don't get back much before 9. It is 9:30 p.m. now. I do not think from present indications that we will leave Montgomery before June 1st or possibly later. We will probably stay at the port for some time then.

I am as much settled as I ever will be until this war is over and more so. I would like the Tribune. I will write to the editor tonite. I have in a round about way got one copy. I have just the same chance getting it as Grandma would if she lived in Chicago and it was sent to her M.M. Browne Chicago, Ill. You know my address and I can't see why you gave them what you did. This much of the subscription has been wasted.

The paper has been sent to camp and that's all. They can't waste time looking up people's address for 2nd class mail. If it had been a letter I would probably have received it.

I'm so dog dead tired. I'll leave to write to Aunt Mattie tomorrow.

I continually am glad about the pension. Be sure and let me know how you are and write me real soon.

> *With lots of love,*
> *Alfred.*

Found in *The 37ᵗʰ Division in the World War*

On 12ᵗʰ March, members of the Cincinnati Reds were entertained at Y.M.C.A. building No. 56. The band of the 147ᵗʰ Infantry Regiment played selections. Individual players of the team were introduced to the soldiers by Col. Galbraith. Boxing and wrestling matches completed the evening's entertainment. (vol. 1, 323)

Important members of the Reds team who might have appeared were star centerfielder Edd Roush, who had hit .341 in 1917, Sherry Magee, who switched between the outfield and first base and who had hit .321 after coming over from the Boston Braves during the season, thirdbaseman Heinie Groh (.314), and pitchers Fred Toney (24 wins) and Pete Schneider (20 wins).

```
                    TRENCH ORDERS
For Officers     37th DIVISION     18th March, 1918.

1.   One officer per company will always be
on duty.  The length of the tour of duty will
```

be determined by the number of officers with
organizations.

2.   The officer on duty will be responsible
for preparing a report of his tour of duty and
forwarding same through the Company Commander
to Battalion Headquarters. Reports of unusual
circumstances will be made to Company Commanders
who will report to Battalion Commanders. (See
pages 137 to 140 Infantry Drill Regulations and
pages 156 to 166 Manual for N.C.O. and Privates of
Infantry).

3.   Patrols will never be sent out without
definite orders as to what is required of them.
      A definite mission.
      Exact point of departure.
      Exact point to re-enter trench if
            circumstances permit.
      Signal to be used for recognition at night,
      Inform them of all other patrols that are
            out.
            Etc.
All listening posts and Sentries will be warned
regarding patrols, working parties, etc. in front,
signals of recognition, etc.

4.   Breech covers will be kept on rifles, when
provided, except when men are actually on duty
as sentries and their reliefs. Rifles and pistols
always loaded (except in U.S.) and locked, chamber
empty, except sentries who will have chamber
loaded and locked.

5.   All men will under ordinary conditions be
paraded twice in 24 hours as follows:-
            One hour before day break.

One hour before night fall.

Careful inspection of all weapons and ammunition, clothing and equipment will be made at these times.

After morning parade and before evening parade, rifles and pistols will be thoroughly cleaned and oiled.

6.   Company commanders will insure that every man knows his exact place in case of attack, bombardment or gas attack. Frequent tests will be made by day and night to insure that this is thoroughly understood.

7.   Carriers and messengers and litter bearers will be identified by special arm-brassard (left arm)

Carriers	white (handkerchiefs)
Messenger	red
Red Cross	

8.   Bayonets will always be fixed on front line trenches.

9.   (a) In very cold weather sentries will occasionally work the bolt handle up and down to prevent the striker from freezing.

(b) For same reason, in cold weather men will sleep with their rifles close to the body.

(c) All loading will be from the belt or bandolier. No ammunition must ever be placed on ground or parapet.

10. Wounded and sick men, if able to walk wear their equipment and carry their arms.
The rifle and ordnance equipment of men disabled who are unable to carry them also unserviceable

ordnance equipment will be sent to the Regimental
Ordnance Officer. Similarly, quartermaster corps
equipment will be sent to the Regimental Quarter
Master.

11. (a) All work on fire and cover trenches will
be carried out by the garrison of these trenches
assisted if necessary by the garrison of the
support and reserve trenches.

        (b) All work in rear of cover trenches
will be done by the garrison of the support and
reserve trenches.

        (c) If possible working parties will
consist of complete units.

        (d) Work on trenches will be done only
on orders from the Engineer Officer, Officer in
charge and the Commanding Officer in charge will
be responsible that this is done in a satisfactory
manner.

12. A covering party will always be provided for
working parties outside the front trench.

13. (a) Parties at work between the front and
reserve trenches may stack or ground arms.

        (b) Working parties out in front of the
fire trench will carry their rifle on the sling.

        (c) Every man on duty in the trenches
will be fully armed at all times. The balance
of the garrison may keep their arms in arm racks
during the day; at night their arms will always be
close at hand for immediate use.

14. (a) The importance of strict attention to
sanitation will be impressed upon all ranks.

        (b) All dry refuse, cigarette stumps,
burned matches (fire to be carefully extinguished)

to be placed in empty sacks, one of which will be
provided for each squad sector. The contents will
be emptied once a day.

(c) Latrines will be carefully policed.
Toilet paper will be provided in boxes near
latrines. These boxes will be kept closed.
Organizations will provide their own toilet paper.

(d) Organization surgeons will inspect
all trenches morning and night accompanied by the
Battalion and Company Commanders.

15. (a) A time table will be drawn up by each
Company commander and Commanding Officer, Machine
Gun Company. allotting hours of guard duty, work,
rest and meals, so as to equally distribute same.

(b) Working parties will be properly
organized. Definite tasks assigned. Each
Commanding Officer of a working party should know
what work is expected from his party before hour
appointed to commence, so that no time is wasted
in getting to work.

(c) Unless it can not be avoided, men
should never be taken for sentry duty without
having had a reasonable period of rest. When
this can not be done report will be made to the
Battalion Commander.

16. Company Commanders will make proper entries
in Trench Log Books each day using form pasted
under front cover.
He will also keep the Trench Store Book turning
over all trench stores to his successor obtaining
his receipt thereforin the book after checking all
stores.
Both books will be turned over to his successor,
receipts therefore being taken opposite the
entries, the officer being relieved certifying

as to the correctness of the statement and the
relieving officer signing the receipt. Commanding
Officers are personally responsible for all trench
stores.

17. (a) Ration parties will be provided from the
supports or reserves for carrying rations, water,
etc. to front line trenches.
(b) They will be made up of complete
units.
(c) Company Mess Sergeants will
accompany all ration parties and report them to
the Company Commander.
(d) They will be fully armed and make as
little noise as possible.
(e) Unused rations will be returned to
the ration part.
(f) Waste in any form will be
prohibited.
(g) Arrangements will be made that soup
or some hot drink is served between midnight and 4
A.M.

18. No man will leave the trenches without
permission from an officer. This order will be
made known to all ranks.
Each man will be shown the location of latrines.

19. One man per platoon and one for each Company
Headquarters will be selected for duty as guides
and will thoroughly familiarize themselves
regarding the entire system of trenches and names
of same. All officers must know the shortest
route from their own Headquarters to those of the
Company on their flanks and to their own Battalion
Headquarters. Their plan of action should embrace
what they will do in case a whole or part of

adjacent sectors are taken. They should know the main salients or the line and location of machine guns of other sectors which protect their own sector by enfilading fire.

20. After leaving the rendezvous there will be no talking or smoking until arrived in the trenches.

21. The troops being relieved will not leave the trenches until the relieving troops are in position, new sentries posted, trench stores and trench log book turned over and receipt taken. Platoon Commanders will at once examine all firing positions and assure themselves that each man can fire on the foot of the nearest wire entanglement. Examine ammunition and grenade stores.
When trenches are fully occupied and relief completed, that fact will be reported to Battalion Headquarters by Company Commander who in turn will report to Regimental Commander.
Men will stand at post and not be dismissed until the Company Commander has received reports from Platoon Commanders that everything is in order, sentries posted, etc.

22.   Instructions for Working Parties.
       Working party from (organization)
       Officers
       N.C.O.
       Privates
       Rendezvous.   Time
Guide will be furnished by
Tools: No.   Spades
                No.   Axes
                No.   Wire Cutters
                No.   Picks

```
                    No.         Hatchets
To be drawn from
   Stores:                      Sand Bags
                                Wire Rolls
                                Stoves
To be drawn from
Instruction on work from
Character of work
Location
Time of starting
Time of stopping
```

23. All non-commissioned officers will be
especially trained in obstacle wiring.

24. Alarm signals will be arranged in case of
gas attack. (See pages 56 to 60 Confidential Memo
Specimens of British Trench Orders, # 590)

By command of Major General Treat:

Dana T. Merrill
        Lt. Col., General Staff,
            Chief of Staff.

Found in *The 37ᵗʰ Division in the World War*

Schools for—it seemed—everybody, were established; for
cooks and horseshoers, bakers and buglers. They included
the infantry schools of small arms, the school for artillery
sergeants and farriers, for mess sergeants, company mechanics, supply officers and supply sergeants, bandsmen, school
of equitation, engineers school, hygiene and sanitary school,
divisional staff school, school for surplus officers, for the intelligence section, for liaison officers, infantry brigade school,

machine gun battalion, and regimental officers machine gun school, and infantry company officers school.

The infantry school of arms was in command of Lieutenant Colonel Carl I. Best, 148th Infantry, and consisted of the small arms department including a hand grenade and rifle grenade section, rifle and pistol section, automatic rifle section, and light machine gun section. (vol. 1, 338-339)

Headquarters 37th Division,
Camp Sheridan, Alabama,
March 18, 1918.

Memorandum Orders,   )

)

     No. 52   )

1. The following letter from the War Department, A.G.O., dated March 9, 1918, is published for the information and guidance of all concerned:

"The attention of all commanding officers is called to their responsibility in case of casual officers or enlisted men being attached to their commands of providing such activity, continuance of training, courses of instruction, etc., as will best secure their well being, further the interests of the Government and avoid interference with orders or instructions specifically governing such casuals."

2. The following letter from the War Department, A.G.O., dated March 13, 1918, is published for the information and guidance of all concerned:

"Our recent campaign to insure the officers and enlisted men of the service was crowned with most gratifying results. We accomplished even more than we had expected, and this was due to a very large degree to the hearty cooperation of the commanding officers and of those who were charged with the actual work in the various commands. But we must not feel that our task has been completed, for the great problem before us now is to see that no officer or enlisted man allows his policy to lapse. This question must be given the same attention and interest as was given your original efforts to insure all in your command.

"It is realized that there will be some and possibly many who may have a tendency to lose interest and let their policy lapse. Such cases should be given immediate attention and every proper effort made to convince the party how important it is to keep up his insurance, not only for the protection of his family, but for his own protection and benefit should he become disabled."

By command of Major General Treat:

R. E. Fraile,
Major, A.G.R.C.,
Acting Adjutant.

Regimental Strength Return for March, 1918

This regiment furnished guards for the division stockade on the 6th, 11th, 18th and 22nd of March. March 4th, 1918 - Regimental Maneuver - Each company acting as Advance Guard for a Battalion. March 7th, 1918, First and Second

Battalions marched to Division Pistol range for construction purposes. March 8th, 1918, Third battalion marched to Division Pistol Range for construction purposes. March 13, 1918, Sixty men of this regiment placed under quarantine for over-seas duty. March 18, 1918, Fourteen men transferred to the 19th Engineers, Camp Merritt, N.J.... Marched to Artillery range for 8 hour tour of duty in Trenches, from 4:00 P.M. to 12:00 Midnight. Second Battalion occupied trenches from 8:00 A.M. to 4:00 P.M. on March 22 1918. Mar. 27, 1918, Battalion exercises and trench warfare problem, First Battalion A.M., P.M. - First Battalion - Open Warfare Problem. Mar. 29, 1918 - A.M. - Second Battalion, Open Warfare Problem. P.M. - Third Battalion, Open Warfare Problem. The appearance, discipline and morale of this regiment for the entire month was excellent.

Found in *The 37ᵗʰ Division in the World War*

A census taken at camp (23rd March) showed that twenty-seven religious creeds were represented in the division, while nearly two thousand confessed to having no sectarian preference whatever. There were 5,227 Methodists, 4,231 Roman Catholics, 2,537 Presbyterians, 1,738 Baptists, 1,150 Lutherans, 1,080 Church of Christ, 1,054 Episcopalians, 690 Congregationalists, 468 United Brethren, 398 Reformed, 239 Christian, 231 Church of Christ Scientist, 98 Unitarian, 98 Universalist, 84 Evangelical, 36 New Thought, 27 Spiritualist, 27 Quaker, eight Seventh Day Adventist, seven Dunkards, three Swedenborgian, three Latter Day Saints, three Salvation Army, three Free Thinkers, one Epicurean, on Mohammedan, and 302 Jewish. (vol. 1, 316)

Company K Strength Return for March, 1918

```
    1st Lt Alfred M. Barlow, Inf. NG Camp Sheridan,
A, Three weeks course, Field Fortification Sec.,
Inf. School of Arms.
```

Camp Sheridan Ala

Co K 148 Inf
Apr. 3, '18

Dear Mamma and All,

It is now 3:45 p.m. and one of the hotter days we have had. The sun is just boiling down but the nights are cool.

I am so glad you are with Aunt Mattie than I had planned on going home. I don't think I will now until later. How I would like to go to G. about two days and then come on to Chicago and from there straight here.

Harold is here now. It is almost impossible to write because I am disturbed so much.

I finished my school of Field Fortifications and I am now attending a Gas Defense School. I almost have the writers cramp I write so much. We take notes practically all day and tonight I will have to be up away late to copy notes and take the examination tomorrow.

My school ends tomorrow something tells me.

It is nine o'clock now. I was about to say I thought that if I did not get to come now I would not get to come at all. In the intermission I have been putting thru my application for leave. I got as far as the Regimental Adjutant and he said the full quota of the regiment was on leave and that I could not get mine until the 17th or 18th. I don't know if I will try then or not. What do you think about it?

Please give Aunt Mattie my thanks for asking me. I received a letter from Morley the other day. Tell him I will write him soon.

With lots of love to all,

Alfred

P.S. I am invited down to a house party below here over Sunday the 10th. Please tell Aunts Lydia & Emma I will write them soon but I'm so tired I have had a headache for 3 or 4 days maybe the gas causes it.

Headquarters 37th Division,
Camp Sheridan, Alabama,
April 4, 1918.

Memorandum Orders,   )

)

    No. 61   )

1.   In accordance with instructions from the War Department, Supply Officers of all organizations will collect and separate all waste paper as outlined below. Paper will be collected by Reclamation Officer.

    (a)   Corrugated Paper Cartons (Cut open on sides and tied flat in bundles).
    (b)   Kraft Paper (in bags or receptacles).
    (c)   Magazines (tied securely in bundles).
    (d)   Mixed Papers (in bags or receptacles).
    (e)   Newspapers, Folded flat, (tied securely in bundles).

    By command of Major General Treat:

R. E. Fraile,
Major, A.G.R.C.,
Acting Adjutant.

Found in *The 37ᵗʰ Division in the World War*

On 6th April, the first anniversary of the entrance of the United States in the World War, the Thirty-seventh Division

paraded for the first time in Montgomery. The occasion was
the opening of the Third Liberty Load drive, and elaborate
preparations were made for the event. The men were in the
very prime of condition, and they had the added incentive of
a determination to make the handsomest possible showing
before the people of Montgomery whose own Alabama troops
had paraded before them so proudly before leaving the south.
The parade started promptly at nine o'clock, and was led by
Major General Treat, and his staff. (vol. 1, 252-255)

```
                    Hq. 74th Inf. Brig., 37th Div.,
                         Camp Sheridan, Alabama,
                              April      1918.
```

MEMORANDUM ORDERS

    No. 19.

1.   In addition to the information furnished by
Training Memorandum, Div. Hq., April 13, 1918,
weekly Training Schedule, Div., Hq., April 12,
1918, and Training Memorandum No. 63, Hq.. 37th
Div., April 14, 1918, the following is published.

    The route to be followed is as follows:
    Base Hospital - Upper Wetumpka Road - Cook's
Road - To Wares Perry Road - thence east via
Tippecanoe to Luzelle - thence south via Mt. Meigs
to Taylor's Field.
    Fourth day - Taylor's Field, via Carter Hill
Road, to Owen P. Water's Farm.
    Fifth day - Return to Camp Sheridan.

2.   First day's camp will be where Wares
Ferry Road crosses Eight Mile Creek, on Walter
Brassell's property. Bread and fresh meat will be

obtained by the Supply wagons as they pass through the junction of Wares Ferry Road and Seaboard Air Line. Supplies of bread and fresh meat for second day's camp will be obtained by supply wagons as they pass through Scotia, just south of Mt. Meigs. The camp for the second day will be just north of Aviation Field on Joel Thornton's property. Third day - troops will remain in camp. Fourth day - March will be resumed via Carter Hill Road and camp will be made on Owen P. Water's property at Baldwin Slough. Bread and fresh meat will be obtained at Holts' Crossing of the Georgia Central Railroad.

3. Organization commanders during the entire march will see that no straggling is allowed. Also that each man is restrained from drinking water out of his canteen until necessity requires. Each soldier should carry a lunch and should not be allowed to eat that lunch until ordered to do so by his regimental or detachment commander. For soldiers to eat all their lunch and drink all the water out of their canteens before a march is practically started is a reflection on the discipline of the command and the knowledge of requirements in the field by the company officers.

The usual sanitary regulations will be enforced during the entire march. Sinks will be dug daily and covered before leaving camp in the morning. Organization commanders will be held responsible that the vacated camp will present a neat appearance.

Officers and men will be prohibited from drinking water which has not been declared sanitary by the surgeon. When ordered by the surgeon all drinking water will be boiled. In each camp instructions will be posted indicating

the drinking water, where the stock are to be
watered, and where bathing will be permitted.

4.   Greatest care must be taken not to cross
plowed fields or in any way injure growing crops.

5.   Each organization should send an officer ahead
of the command into camp with orders to report
to the Brigade Adjutant for information such as
location of his camp, water supply, fuel, etc.

6.   Each officer will be required to carry his
usual equipment, including note-book, lead pencil,
compass, etc., and Supply Officers must be prepared
to furnish suitable paper for making sketches.

7.   Inspections will be made by each organization
commander to see that orders with reference to
baggage, size of bundles, etc., are obeyed. Any
violation of these orders will be reported to
Brigade Headquarters.

8.   The outpost commander's order and his sketch
position will be turned in to Brigade Headquarters
as soon as completed and will be turned over to
the Chief of Staff, 37th Div., on the return of
the Brigade to Camp Sheridan.

9.   Organization commanders will have a practice
drill in packing their field wagons prior to the
march.

                By command of Brigadier General Gaston:

                            G. D. Light,
                      Major, Adj. Gen., N.G.
                         Brig. Adj.

Found in *The 37ʰ Division in the World War*

From the first there was an attempt to arouse pride and patriotism through frequent ceremonies and parades. An emphasis was placed upon physical training. Standards that were fixed required each man to be able to "chin" himself on the horizontal bar ten times, to life a sixty pound weight over his head with each hand, to run a hundred yards in fifteen seconds and a half mile in four minutes, to run and jump eight feet, to cover a fifty foot course in which were included three four-foot ditches and three three-foot hurdles, to vault a fence five and one-half feet high, to scale a seven foot wall, to climb a twenty-foot rope in twenty seconds, to excavate a cubic foot of hard earth with pick and shovel in an hour and a half, to march twenty miles in twelve hours, carrying full equipment and ammunition, rifles and belts, to make a forced march of six miles in one hour, double timing for short distances and dropping then into a fast walk; boxing, and wrestling were taught in their fundamentals. The men were urged to harden themselves so they could sustain aimed rifle fire at the rate of eight shots a minute for ten minutes. (vol. 1, 318-319)

Gallipolis Daily Tribune, April 12, 1918

INFANTRY TO GO

Ohio National Guard at Camp Sheridan in the List.

Washington, April 11.--The infantry units of the federalized Ohio National Guard, Camp Sheridan, Ala., are to be rushed to France as speedily as possible to help repel the big German drive on the western front, under a new plan of the general staff.

They are to be fitted in with British or French troops, wherever needed or wherever they can be used to best advantage.

The artillery and other troops will remain at Camp Sheridan for further training. When they are sent over seas later they will be reunited with the infantry units into a division organization, after which all will take their place on the line as the Ohio division of federalized guardsmen, according to the plan.

France has been called upon to aid in hastening the movement of American troops across the sea by sending additional officers for the training camps in the United States. General Vignal, military attache of the French embassy, after a conference tonight with Major General March, acting chief of staff, cabled his government, suggesting that any officers that can be spared be detailed for duty in America.

```
                              Headquarters 37th Division,
                                 Camp Sheridan, Alabama,
                                        April 17, 1918.
Memorandum Orders,              )

                                )

     No. 69                     )
```

2.   Report indicates that there is considerable manure on the roads in and near the camp and on the drill grounds. Organization commanders will at once take steps to keep the streets within the limit of their commands, as well as drill areas, free from manure.

The Sanitary Inspector will arrange for the police of such areas and roads as are not specifically assigned to organizations. He will likewise assume charge of the unoccupied camps and take proper steps to clean and close latrines not in use. The Quartermaster's Department will furnish the necessary material.

Attention again is invited to the necessity for measures being taken to combat the fly menace. Fly traps will be constructed by each organization and placed in use in and around kitchens and stables. The Quartermaster's Department will furnish the necessary material for this purpose,

the traps to be constructed by troops. Fly paper
will be issued by the Quartermaster Department.
Enlisted men detailed in the kitchens and dining
rooms will be provided with fly swatters and
instructed to keep these places free from flies.
There are still kitchens in this camp on which the
ventilator has been raised but which have not as
yet been properly screened.

By command of Major General Treat:

R. E. Fraile,
Major, A.G.R.C.,
Acting Adjutant.

Headquarters 37th Division,
Camp Sheridan, Alabama,
April 21, 1918.

Memorandum Orders,   )
)
   No. 72   )

1. (a) Attention is directed to the provisions
of paragraph IV, General Orders, No. 17, War
Department, February 13, 1918, which is as
follows:

"1.   Commanding officers of posts, camps,
cantonments, and other stations of the Army
will cause the finger prints to be made of
all officers of their commands on special form
provided for the purpose.

    2.   Finger-print records of officers now in the service will be forwarded to The Adjutant General of the Army, together with a list of officers of the command, whether present or absent, whose finger-print records have not been made, with reason therefor.

    3.   Commanders of departments and other places not covered by paragraph 1 will require officers at their headquarters or under their immediate command to have their finger prints made and will forward the records to The Adjutant General of the Army.

    4.   Finger prints of officers hereafter entering the service will be made and forwarded as soon as practicable after original appointment, or in the case of reserve officers as soon as practicable after being called into active service."

(b)   Identification Record Cards of Officer are now being distributed to all organizations. These cards will be prepared under supervision of the organization surgeon at the earliest practicable date, and sent to these Headquarters with the list referred to in subparagraph 2, above.

By command of Major General Treat:

R. E. Fraile,
Major, A.G.R.C.,
Acting Adjutant.

Headquarters 37th Division,
Camp Sheridan, Alabama,
April 21, 1918.

Memorandum Orders,   )
)
     No. 72   )

2.   (a)   A clinic for the treatment of venereal
cases will be established by the Division Surgeon
in the southeast half of the Detention Camp
Infirmary.

     (b)   Commanding officers of all
organizations are enjoined to compel the
attendance of all enlisted men who have been
requested by the medical officers in charge of the
clinic to appear for treatment at specified times.

     (c)   The following schedule for
treatment at the clinic is announced:

          (1)   New venereal cases and those
cases marked "no duty" will report during the
A. M. hours at times to be specified by the
officers in charge of the clinic.

          (2)   Chronic cases (those under
training): 3:00 PM - All troops in the Camp
north of Western Railroad of Alabama (Field
Artillery Brigade, 112th Engineers, 112th
Field Signal Battalion, 37th Headquarters
Troop, Military Police and Trains). 6:00
PM - All troops south of Western Railroad
of Alabama (Infantry Brigades, 134th Machine

Gun Battalion, Detention Camps, Engineer
Regiments and casuals).

By command of Major General Treat:

R. E. Fraile,
Major, A.G.R.C.,
Acting Adjutant.

Headquarters 37th Division,
Camp Sheridan, Alabama,
April 23, 1918.

Memorandum Orders,   )
)
     No. 74.   )

1. The following communication from The Adjutant
General of the Army, date April 19, 1918, is
published for the information and guidance of all
concerned:

"1.   On January 11, 1918, the Secretary
of War directed that troops en route to
France would compile lists separately for
each supply department, showing shortages in
their equipment and have same ready for Base
Commander upon disembarkation.
2.   Recent advice from General Pershing
indicates that the foregoing instructions are
not being complied with. It is absolutely
necessary that troops en route to France
compile lists showing types and quantities

of their equipment and present same to Base Commander on disembarkation.

    3.   The Secretary of War directs that all concerned be advised that the foregoing instructions will be strictly adhered to."

2. Graduates from the Third Officers' Training Camp, who have been recommended for commission, will wear a strip of white cloth, 2 inches long and 1/2 inch wide, to be worn on the lower left sleeve of the service coat, with the lower edge thereof parallel to and 3 inches from the lower end of the sleeve.

By command of Major General Treat:

R. E. Fraile,
Major, A.G.R.C.
Acting Adjutant.

Headquarters 37th Division,
Camp Sheridan, Alabama,
April 25, 1918.

Memorandum Orders,   )
)
   No. 75.   )

1.   (a) The following telegram from The Adjutant General of the Army, dated April 24, 1918, is published for the information and guidance of the members of this command:

"President of the United States has appointed Friday, April 26th, as Liberty

Day and has requested people of the United States to pledge anew their financial support to sustain Nation's Cause and that patriotic demonstrations be held this day will be observed at all Army Posts and by all Army Commands in appropriate manner. Patriotic program will be prepared and will include public reading of President's Message of April 18th. Enlisted men on Liberty Day will be relieved from all duties not demanded by maintenance of discipline and carrying out of military program. Liberty Bond Officers of Departments and Tactical Divisions in limits United States will forward by mail reports of celebration."

Friday, April 26, 1918, will be observed as a holiday and the drill program suspended for the day.

(b)   The following officers are charged with the preparation of appropriate programs for their command which will be held at 10:00 A.M., at which time the President's message of April 18th will be read and appropriate speeches and music provided in the programs.

(1)   Commanding General,
        62nd Field Artillery Brigade,
        62nd Field Artillery Brigade and
            attached units.

(2)   Commanding Officer, 112th Engineers,
        112th Engineers,
        112th Engineer Train,
        112th Supply Train,
        Ordnance Depot Company Number 128.

(3)   Commanding Officer, 112 Train
          Headquarters & Military Police
      Division Headquarters,
      112th Military Police,
      112th Field Signal Battalion,
      112th Sanitary Train.

(4)   Commanding General, 73rd Infantry
          Brigade.
      134th Machine Gun Battalion.

(5)   Commanding Officer, 74th Infantry
          Brigade, and attached units at
          Aviation Grounds.

(6)   Commanding Officer, 22nd Engineers,
          22nd, 46th and 47th Engineers.

(7)   Commanding Officer, Base Hospital, Base
          Hospital.

The troops of the Camp Quartermaster's
Detachment will attend the ceremonies prepared by
the Commanding Officer, 112th Engineers.

By command of Brigadier General Gaston:

R. E. Fraile,
Major, A.G.R.C.,
Acting Adjutant.

Hq. 74th Inf. Brig.,
Owen P. Water's Farm,
27 April 1918. 10:00 P.M.

Field Orders
        No. 8.
Troops.

1. The enemy is reported to be marching in strong force on MONTGOMERY from the south. Division Headquarters still at CAMP SHERIDAN.

(a) Advance Guard Major A, commanding, 1st Bn., 147th Inf.

2. This Brigade will rejoin the Division tomorrow.

(b) Main Body in Order of March.

147th Inf., less one Bn.
136th M.G. Bn.
148th Inf., less one co.

3. a. The Advance Guard will clear the line of outposts at 7:45 A.M. tomorrow and march by the most direct route to CAMP SHERIDAN.

b. The Main Body will follow the Advance Guard at a distance of 500 yds.

(c) Detachment,

c. Usual orders reference 112th F.S.Bn. liason.

(d) Detachment of Ambulance Co.

d. Detachment of Ambulance Co., will follow at the rear of Main Body.

(e)   Rear Guard,   One Co., 148th Inf.
                       Capt. A, commanding,
                    4. The Field Train will
                       follow the Main Body at closed
                       distances in the following
                       order:
                             Ration Section,
                             Baggage Section,
                             Forage Section,
                             Detachment of Field
                             Hospital Unit.
                    5. Messages to the head of the
                       Main Body.

                              J. A. GASTON
                         Brigadier General,
                              Comdg.

Dictated to officers detailed
to receive orders.
Copy to Division Commander.

Company K Strength Return for April, 1918

   Daily 6 1/2 hr drill in trench warfare;
company, battalion, regimental and divisional
combat problems. On 15 mile hike with Regiment
4/2/18. On 8 mile hike with Division to
Montgomery and return with review by C.G. 4/6/18.
6 mile hike to Div Training grounds 4/11/18; acted
as attacking party (repulsed); occupied trenches
8 hours 4/12/18; 6 mile hike to Camp evening
4/12/18. 5 day hike to Taylor Aviation Field
and return 4/24/18 to 4/28/18 (with Brigade).
Distance marched about 38 m. Non Com's Refresher

School evenings 6.30 to 7.30; Signal practice, wig
wag, semaphore, etc....
     1st Lt. Alfred K. Barlow, Inf. NG Camp
Sheridan, A Gas Defense Course.... 10 day leave
of absence.... Routine with company 4/1/18 to
4/15/18 Bayonet Section I.S.A. 4/16/18 to 4/23/
18.... On 10 days leave since 4/24/18....

Gallipolis Daily Tribune, April 27, 1918

Lieut. Barlow Here.

   Lieut. Alfred Barlow arrived here Friday afternoon from Camp
Sheridan on a few days visit. He is looking exceedingly well and enjoys
life in the big camp. He reports all our boys well.
   Lieut. Barlow came here to visit his mother before going to France but
found Mrs. Barlow to be in Chicago on a visit. He will go on to Chicago to
visit her before returning to Camp.
   Lieut. Barlow is making a fine record for himself in the army.

                         Headquarters 37th Division,
                           Camp Sheridan, Alabama,
                             April 29, 1918.

Memorandum Orders,   )
)
     No. 79.   )

2.   (a) Hot weather may be expected very soon.
This command will go into cotton khaki uniform
at an early date, to be announced later. Officers
will be required to wear cotton khaki uniform when
the command goes into khaki. It is recommended
that officers take immediate steps to purchase,
from the Quartermaster or elsewhere, such small

quantity of cotton khaki uniform as they may deem necessary. As the supply is limited, these purchases should be made at once.

(b)   Organization commanders will draw such amount of cotton khaki as will insure each man having two pairs of cotton breeches.   One of these pairs should be of new issue, and used for social purposes.   Requisitions for cotton blouses may be submitted at the same time.   As there is only a limited supply of the latter, the Quartermaster will reduce issues pro-rata in accordance with the supply on hand.   No cotton O. D. shirts will be issued in lieu of flannel, nor will such shirts be worn without authority from these Headquarters.

(c)   Clothing made of Gabardine cloth is hereby authorized, except for formations.   The wearing of Gabardine cloth uniforms is prohibited at all formations.

(d)   Woolen clothing, when no longer worn, will be collected by organization commanders, and that which requires cleaning and repairing will be turned over to the proper supply officer, who in turn will make arrangements with the Reclamation Division for necessary repairs and cleaning, in accordance with instructions to supply officers.

(e)   Letter from the Depot Quartermaster, Atlanta, Ga., states that hereafter breeches, wool, coasts, wool, shoes, field, shelter tents, half, poles and tent pins necessary to fully equip troops ordered overseas will be furnished at the Port of Embarkation.   Those now on hand in the Quartermaster Warehouse here will be issued only to troops on priority, and when the present stock is exhausted, no replenishment will be made until further orders.

By command of Brigadier General Gaston:

R. E. Fraile,
Major, A.G.R.C.,
Acting Adjutant.

148th Infantry Regiment Strength Return for April, 1918

April 2, 1918, 150 men transferred to Camp Wadsworth, Spartansburg, S.C. April 5, 18, First Division Maneuver. April 6, 1918. The Division paraded through Montgomery, Ala in connection with the Third Liberty Loan. April 10, 1918, the Regiment went to the Divisional Training Area (Artillery Trenches) returning 4:00 P.M., April 11, 1918. April 24, 1918, the Regiment less the 1st Bn. which was at the Rifle Range participated in a five day march made by the 74th Brigade. Objective Taylor's Field. Distance - 37 miles. The health and condition of the men on this march was excellent. Weather - good.

Chapter Four

Headquarters 37th Division,
Camp Sheridan, Alabama,
May 2, 1918.

Memorandum Orders,   )
)
   No. 82.   )

1.   The following policy with reference to
punishments of enlisted men is published for the
information and guidance of all concerned. Any
orders conflicting with this policy are revoked:

(a)   Attention is invited to Par. 333, Manual
for Courts-Martial, 1917. This authorizes company
commanders to give punishments for minor offenses
in certain cases, and should dispense with many
trials by courts-martial.

(b)   It is believed that the confinement
of old offenders with young soldiers is very
injurious to the latter. The Stockade will be
used only for prisoners serving sentence, or
awaiting trial, or result of sentence, by General
Courts-Martial. Men who are drunk should be
promptly confined and held in close confinement
until sober; otherwise the officer whose duty
it is to confine the soldier practically become
responsible for actions of the soldier committed
while the soldier is mentally irresponsible.
Drunken soldiers need not necessarily be placed
in the Stockade and will not be sent there if

there is any other suitable place in the regiment
or detachment where they can be closely confined.
In an organization commander has charges against
a soldier which in his opinion justify trial
by general court-martial, the soldier should
be confined in the Stockade. No charges will be
referred to a general court-martial unless in
the opinion of these Headquarters the probable
sentence will be dishonorable discharge and
confinement for at least a year at Leavenworth
or elsewhere. All other charges should be
referred to either special or summary courts, and
the sentence awarded will be served within the
regiment or detachment.

   (c) It is believed that having a large
number of prisoners in a regimental guardhouse
is useless, and injurious to the discipline and
morale of the command. In almost every case it
will be found that soldiers sentenced to short
terms of confinement and hard labor can be much
better taken care of by the company commander
having the soldier confined to the limits of the
company under the supervision of a provost non-
commissioned officer during the day, and the
noncommissioned officer in charge of quarters
during the night.

               By command of Brigadier General Gaston:

                         R. E. Fraile,
                           Major, A.G.R.C.,
                           Acting Adjutant.

Found in *The 37th Division in the World War*

On Sunday morning, 5th May, the 37th Division, unbeknown to itself, entered a new and what was to prove to be the final phase of the role it was to enact on this side of the Atlantic as a part of the great armies the United States was calling together, training, and sending into battle across the water. The warm, bright Sunday dawned much as those which had gone before; men awoke to the delightful knowledge that reveille did not follow quite as swiftly on taps as was its custom weekday mornings. There was that Sunday air of rather lazy and leisurely cleaning up; the bugles blew church call, and bands played less insistently than for evening parades. But division headquarters received word from the Adjutant General of the Army that Major General Charles S. Farnsworth had been assigned to command the 37th; he was expected to arrive in camp within a few days, and he reached Montgomery on the afternoon of 8th May.

General Farnsworth was born 29th October, 1862, in Lycoming county, Pennsylvania, and received his early education in the public schools. In 1883 he was appointed to West Point from Clarion, Pennsylvania, and was graduated four years later. He entered service as a commissioned officer in that branch of which he was later to act as chief, the infantry, and served in the 25th, the 7th and in the 18th, moving about through the Dakotas, Montana, Colorado, Cuba, Michigan, Alaska, Washington, Kansas, California, the Philippines, Texas, Mexico, and Oklahoma. During the Spanish American War he was division quartermaster of General Lawton's division, which was then a part of the Fifth Army Corps which carried the campaign against Santiago and captured that city. When that task was accomplished, he was appointed aide to General Chaffee, another soldier Ohio gave to the country for the struggle of 1898, and accompanied him to Havana. In the summer of 1899 he commanded an infantry company that was a part of the first expedition the United States sent to Alaska, and assisted in building Forts Gibbon and Egbert and the Alaskan telegraph system. When General Pershing led the punitive expedition into Mexico in 1916, General Farnsworth was on duty at El Paso, Texas. He led his regiment, the Sixteenth U.S. Infantry, during the first three months of the campaign, when it formed a part of General Pershing's forces. (vol. 1, 383-384)

```
                            Headquarters 37th Division,
                               Camp Sheridan, Alabama,
                                        May 5, 1918.
Memorandum Orders,           )
                             )
     No. 84.                 )
```

1. Practice will be taken up during Monday and Tuesday drill periods and by drills after 3:00 P.M., in marching troops with <u>music</u> in preparation for a Division Review on Wednesday afternoon at 2:00 P.M.

Attention will be given to: -

(a) Keeping step in unit.

(b) Marching with left foot in step with music.

(c) Dress of lines.

(d) Duties of officers and N.C.O.'s as file closers.

(e) Practice in eyes right.

(f) Proper band cadence

(g) Short snappy march step.

By command of Brigadier General Gaston:

R. E. Fraile,
Major, A.G.R.C.,
Acting Adjutant.

Found in *The 37th Division in the World War*

Hours each day (excepting Saturday and Sundays) were spent by the infantry in executing close order drill. Schedules outlining the movements to be practiced by squad, platoon, company and battalion were issued; they indicated exactly the drill to be given for every moment of the drill period and no deviation was permitted. Hour after hour, units went through the manual of arms, and day after day, until precision and exactness were attained; until the movements were executed with that "snap" that is the mark of a well drilled body of men. (vol. 1, 321)

```
                         Headquarters 37th Division,
                           Camp Sheridan, Alabama,
                                    May 6, 1918.

Memorandum Orders,            )
                              )
     No. 85.                  )
```

1. Pursuant to telegraphic instructions Quartermaster General, April 30, 1918, the following allowance of clothing will be issued to troops:-

```
        1 coat, cotton
        2 breeches, cotton, pair
        1 shirt, flannel
        1 shirt, cotton
        1 leggins, pair
        2 stockings, light wool, pair
        3 stockings, cotton pair
        1 hat, service
        1 belt, waist
        1 shoes, marching pair
```

```
        1 shoes, russet pair, until stock
exhausted, then additional pair shoes, marching.
        1 slicker
        3 blankets, three pound
        1 bag, barrack
        1 bed sack
        1 coat, blue denim
        1 trousers, blue denim
          Undershirts and drawers - instructions
          later.

    2.  Company and battery commanders will
designate an enlisted man to make weekly
collections of overdue books borrowed from the
Camp Library

        By command of Brigadier General Gaston:

                    R. E. Fraile,
                    Major, A.G.R.C.,
                    Acting Adjutant.
```

Camp Sheridan

Montgomery, Ala.

Co K 148 Inf

May 6, 1918

Dear Aunt Mattie & Uncle Tom,

It is now 10:20 p.m. and I am just getting to write my first letter since my return. We are especially busy as we are getting ready to go to the rifle range. Wednesday I must tell you of how I spent my evening when I left you and my return trip. I went into Studebakers when I left you intending to go to some musical show that I saw billed but instead saw the play the program of which I enclose.

Everything about it was to my unsophisticated mind most unusual. Everything to use the modern interpretation of the word was far from "popular." It was if I may use the term distinctly high browish. The play was excellent. I do hope you may see it. It was most unusual.

In Cincy visited Fort Stewart. Was to dinner at Bontets' twice. My train left at ten so until ten I went to a dance at the University with Judith and Joe. I had a grand time arriving in Montgomery at 7 p.m. Saturday.

I shall surely never forget my trip to Chicago and I wish to thank you both for the grand times I had.

Please tell Mamma I shall probably write her tomorrow nite.

With lots of love to you all,

Alfred.

Headquarters 37th Division,
Camp Sheridan, Alabama,
May 11, 1918.

Memorandum Orders,   )
)
      No. 88.   )

     1.   All pistols, calibre .45, holsters, extra magazines, pistol belts and magazine pockets in the possession of any unit of the Division will be immediately turned in to the Camp Ordnance Officer.
     2.   The 37th Division "will be filled to authorized strength from men received in the April draft". Requisitions for equipment and supplies will be made accordingly.
     3.   The following telegram from The Adjutant General of the army, dated May 10, 1918, is published for the information of all concerned:

"Repeat following to all troops under your
command colon quote General Pershing has issued
the following order to all units of the American
Expeditionary Forces in France colon May eighth to
all Commanding Officers colon I wish every officer
and soldier in the American Expeditionary Forces
would write a letter home on Mothers Day this is
a little for each one to do but these letters will
carry back our courage and our affection to the
patriotic women whose love and prayers inspire
us and cheer us on to victory Pershing unquote
The Secretary of War most heartily approves the
foregoing and desires to urge upon every officer
and soldier in the Army that he emulate the
example of the soldiers in France by writing a
letter home on Mothers Day May twelfth."

By command of Major General Farnsworth:

R. E. Fraile,
Major, A.G.R.C.,
Acting Adjutant.

Found in *The 37ᵗʰ Division*

The men learned the care of their field equipment upon
which, one day, they were to depend for their very existence;
they learned how to care for the rifle, nomenclature, setting of
sights, aiming, the "trigger squeeze," adjustment of the sling,
the proper firing positions, loading, range finding, and bayonet fighting. Squad, platoon and company for hour after hour
went through "open order" drill, practice in guard duty and in
signaling; in practice marches by day and by night, in making and breaking camp, in individual cooking, and in carrying
and communicating messages. They were taught the use of
the gas mask and were drilled to regard the disagreeable head

gear as their "best friend." They were taught how to throw hand grenades; men who developed skill in rifle practice were trained for "snipers," and learned the use of cover in stalking the enemy, and the art of camouflage. Other specialists were taught the automatic rifle, the trench mortar, or the machine gun and pistol. Officers from the division were detailed to attend various schools and bring back with them the latest developments to be communicated in the various schools established and operated throughout the division. (vol. 1, 321-322)

                                Headquarters 37th Division,
                                   Camp Sheridan, Alabama,
                                          May 13, 1918.

Memorandum Orders,   )
)
    No. 89.   )

        1.   OFFICERS' EQUIPMENT AND CONTAINERS
THEREFOR.

    (a)   The following list of equipment,
compiled from various War Department orders,
circulars, and letters, is prescribed for the
officers of the 37th Division of overseas service.

    (b)   ALL officers are hereby directed to
provide themselves with the required articles
during the week ending May 18th. It is suggested
that the articles required to be in the possession
of the officers be carried as indicated in
the various columns of the table, and that
such articles marked "optional" as the officer
decides to take be carried in the five containers

mentioned, to fill the vacant space which will be
left after prescribed articles have been inserted.

   (c) The following list of articles are
required:

NOTE: Items marked (d) are for dismounted officers
only.
       Items marked (m) are for mounted officers
only.

   ["1": 'Carried on person'
   "2": 'Trunk locker'
   "3": 'Clothing Roll'
   "4": 'Suitcase'
   "5": 'Bedding Roll'--the following has been extensively reformatted for
these pages]

1 Bedding roll, canvas	5
1 Cot, folding, canvas	5
4 Blankets	5
1 Comforter	5
1 Mattress or bed sack	5
1 Shelter Tent, complete	5
1 Wash basin, canvas or rubber	5
1 Bucket, canvas or rubber	5
1 Flashlight, electric	3
Extra batteries	2
1 Haversack and pack carrier	d1
1 Canteen with cover	m1
1 Cup	m1
1 Knife, fork and spoon	m1
1 Meat can	m1
1 Bacon can	m1
1 Condiment can	m1
1 Pistol	1
1 Holster, pistol	1

```
1 Belt, pistol                            1
1 Hat, service, with hat cord
     sewed on                             1
1 Necktie, black                          1
1 Pair Russet Shoes                       dm1
2 Extra magazines, pistol                 1
21 Cartridges, ball                       1
1 First aid packet                        1
1 First aid pouch                         1
1 Field glasses                           1
1 Compass (preferably with
     illuminated dial)                    1
1 Watch                                   1
1 Whistle                                 1
1 Message Blank Book                      1
1 Note book                              1
6 Pencils                                 2
1 Fountain Pen                            1
2 Identification tags                     1
2 Tapes for identification tags           1
  Trunk locker, (or steamer trunk
     same size as trunk locker)
     One or more according to
     personal baggage allowance.          2
1 Clothing roll                           3
1 Cap                                     2
6 Towels, 4 hand and  2 bath              2,3
1 Overcoat, regulation                    5
1 Slicker or rain coat with
     detachable lining of wool         {lin-
     or fleece, or Trench Coat,        {ing
     (English)                            1
2 O.D. Woolen uniforms, 1 heavy
     and 1 light                          1,2
3 O.D. Shirts, flannel                    1,2
4 Linen shirts with detachable
     cuffs                                4
```

12 Collars	4
6 Cuffs, prs.	4
1 Belt, waist	4
2 Prs. Shoes, heavy, hobnailed marching, or trench boots	2,5
2 Prs. Leggins	1,5
2 Prs. Gloves, woolen or riding	1,4
Toilet articles - several cakes of soap and sale water soap, hair and tooth brushes, razor, etc.	3,5
2 Pajamas, heavy	2,3
2 Pajamas, light	4
2 Shoe polish, packages	2,4
4 Prs. extra shoe laces	3
12 Handkerchiefs -(Some O.D.)	2,4
Official books and papers	2
4 Suits underclothing, 2 cotton and 2 heavy wool	1,3,4
1 Woolen Helmet	2
12 pairs socks, 6 heavy and 6 light wool	1,2,3,4
1 Dispatch case, by Staff Officers and those whose duties may require its use	m1
1 Spurs	m1
1 Riding boots	m1

(d)   The following is a list of articles, the possession of which is optional with each officer. Officers who have been overseas have suggested them as desirable provided the baggage allowance of the officer will permit them to be taken.

1 Pillow - Air pillow recommended
1 Camp chair, folding
1 Tub, rubber or canvas

```
1 Light, gasoline (Preferable), or oil
  Paper and envelopes
2 O.D. Shirts, cotton
1 Vest, leather or flannel
1 Belt, Sam Browne (Optional until arrival abroad)
1 Pair shoes, russet, for wear under arctic
    overshoes
1 Pair arctic overshoes
1 Leather portfolio - for officers carrying papers
1 Sleeveless sweater
1 Moccasins, reaching to ankle, large enough to
    wear with 2 pr. wool stockings and to be worn
    inside of rubber boots
1 Pr. Rubber Boots, hip
1 Housewife
1 Sponge                                          1
1 Bag for soiled clothing                         1
1 Pair wool puttees                               1
```

By command of Major General Farnsworth:

R. E. Fraile,
Major, A.G.R.C.,
Acting Adjutant.

One of the joys of going through papers such as those of the 37th Division housed in the National Archives in Washington, DC is the occasional double-take… such as the inclusion of "1 Housewife" under optional articles to take overseas. It's possible, of course, that another meaning was intended, but the common one is certainly the more delightful.

Camp Sheridan
Montgomery, Ala.
Co K 148 Inf

May 16

Dear Mamma,

Our heavy baggage leaves Sunday for over-seas. We leave in a few days for a concentration camp and then for port of embarkation.

We have to buy loads of equipment for over-seas service. I've paid the Ohio Valley Bank the hundred dollars.

If you can send me a hundred dollars please do so <u>at once</u>. I may not need to use it but I hate to feel as I do now. I have many things to buy and have practically nothing. If you can make it more than a hundred do it. I'll leave to spend about $200 but I will try to get as much as possible in Europe.

Some must be bought here. I am working early & late. I am dog dead tired. I can hardly hold a pen.

Please write immediately & if you leave no checks tell me what bank to draw on and for how much. Address me here. Mail will be forwarded if I leave.

With lots of love,

Alfred.

```
                              Headquarters 37th Division,
                                 Camp Sheridan, Alabama,
                                      May 17, 1918.


Memorandum Orders,          )
                            )
     No. 92.                )


     1.  All officers and organizations in this
camp who have been furnished with documents from
```

Divisional Headquarters, either confidential, secret, or Manuals, will at once turn it, neatly boxed, to Division Headquarters all copies which will not be taken with the organization or in the personal baggage of officers.

One officer from each regiment or separate organization will be designated to collect these documents and pamphlets. The greatest care will be taken that no secret or confidential document is thrown away or placed where it may be of service for any unlawful purpose.

2. The following telegram from The Adjutant General of the Army, dated May 16, 1918, is published for the information and guidance of all concerned:

"By order of President Italian Flag will be displayed on all buildings under your control on May Twenty Fourth, the Anniversary of entrance of Italy into the War."

3. The following telegram from the Commanding General, Port of Embarkation, Hoboken, N. J., dated May 16, 1918, is published for the information and guidance of all concerned:

"Baggage of officers below the grade of General Officer is limited to one bedding roll, one trunk locker, and one piece of hand baggage,- horse equipment in addition."

By command of Major General Farnsworth:

R. E. Fraile,
Major, A.G.R.C.,
Acting Adjutant.

Headquarters 37th Division,
Camp Sheridan, Alabama,
May 18, 1918.

Memorandum Orders,   )
)
    No. 93.   )

1. The following telegram from The Adjutant General of the Army is published for the information and strict compliance of all concerned:

"When units are ordered away from your camp War Department orders direct you will see that every officer leaving your command is equipped with officer's qualification card, also 3 x 5 locator card, latter in duplicate. Also every enlisted man shall be equipped with Qualification Record Card, also 3 x 5 locator card, latter in duplicate, to comply with request of General Pershing and directed by the Ward Department."

2. Aliens over twenty-one (21) years of age of undoubted loyalty to the United States, born in Germany, Austria, Turkey or Bulgaria, and who are to be naturalized, will be send to Division Headquarters at 1:00 P.M., Sunday, May 19, 1918.

The detachment from each regiment or separate unit will report under a commissioned officer who will have the recommendation of the immediate commanding officer of each man.

Aliens born in allied or neutral countries will be cared for in a subsequent order.

By command of Major General Farnsworth:

R. E. Fraile,
Major, A.G.R.C.,
Acting Adjutant.

Headquarters 37th Division,
Camp Sheridan, Alabama,
May 19, 1918.

Memorandum Orders,   )
)
    No. 94.   )

1.   (a) The Camp site will be carefully policed, firewood, empty boxes, etc., piled in an orderly and uniform manner.

(b) The area in front of the kitchens, about the garbage racks and platform will be free from any food particles. Dry sand will be sprinkled on ground where garbage has been spilt. Empty garbage cans will be thoroughly cleansed inside and out.

(c) Kitchens and mess halls will be cleaned in the proper manner and no food of any description will be left in them, leaving the iceboxes thoroughly cleansed and empty.

(d) Tent floors will be thoroughly scrubbed.

(e) Bath houses will be thoroughly scrubbed and policed in and underneath them to insure that no discarded articles of clothing be left there.

(f) Latrine pits will be treated liberally with crude oil and mortar black, seats will be scrubbed, and the lids nailed down with a single nail before leaving.

(g) Stables will be swept with great care, corrals and picket lines carefully policed and sprinkled with lime, and the manure hauled to the designated dumps.

(h) All picket lines will be burned over when abandoned.

(i) All drainage ditches will be cleared of any rubbish or other material which would interfere with the free drainage of the camp site.

(j) All paper and other combustible rubbish, including tea and coffee grounds, and tin cans will be burned in the incinerators and the latter will be thoroughly flattened before removal to the rubbish dumps.

(k) Regimental and separate organization commanders will not vacate their camp sites until they certify in writing to these Headquarters that the provisions of this order have been complied with.

(l) The camp will be inspected by Division Headquarters.

By command of Major General Farnsworth:

R. E. Fraile,
Major, A.G.R.C.,
Acting Adjutant.

Camp Sheridan Ala
Co L 148 Inf.

May 23, 1918

Dear Mamma,

We leave here tomorrow for Camp Lee Virginia. I received your letter with check for $100 last night. I have already drawn on you for $50. I can send you $50 the first of the month.

When you sent the $100 did you know I had signed your name to a $50 check.

Some of the boys are spending $200 or $300 at a clip. I am sending the insurance receipt for my last endowment insurance. I get about $16 a month more on the other side. I must leave now must do some packing.

I am not need to get very much except a pair of leggins and a pair of dress shoes.

Write me here right away. If you haven't enough will send you back $50.

Have a couple of street car tickets & stamps in here.

With lots of love,
Alfred

Camp Lee Virginia

May 27 1918

Dear Mamma,

We left Camp Sheridan Friday about 3:30 p.m. and arrived here yesterday a little after dinner.

Our trip up was rather uneventful. We sang, read magazines and slept.

We stopped at Augusta, Ga. and exercised by marching up to the center of town where we stacked arms and fell out for about thirty minutes. Georgia does not seem so fertile as Alabama. I rather think I like Alabama better. We stopped at Florence, Ga. for supper. Here as elsewhere along the way very typically pretty Southern girls met the trains and gave the soldiers coffee and cigarettes. They had plenty of each but it was a pleasure to receive them at their hands.

Camp Lee is I understand a two division camp. It is certainly an immense affair.
There are very few troops here besides ourselves. It is being fast filled by drafted men
however now are at present in civilian clothes. They are a most ungainly looking lot.
I imagine most of them are Southern mountaineers.

We live in barracks here. Every thing is fine--baths and everything convenient. This
was for the "National Army" and we were only "Volunteers."

The sun here is scathingly hot and because we go over soon we must wear wool.

When we get the new men we will drill them 12 hours a day. At first they will be
drilled separately then together. Thus they will learn from our men.

Petersburg is three miles from camp. We have street cars. I have not been to town
yet. We are near the center of camp. Theater, Y.M.C.A. and head quarters are all
near. Richmond the capital is only twenty miles away. I hope to get up there some
time soon. It's 10:30 p.m. and I'm almost asleep.

We certainly do work hard.

With lost of love,

Alfred

P.S. I received your letter today. I am now in Co. L. This change will be permanent.
I like the captain and all the officers. This is the first time I've really been satisfied.
My but I'm lucky. Every captain and 1st lieutenant in the regiment was transferred.

Dear Mamma,

I am writing my letter on the other sheet. This is for you alone.

By all means go to Denver this summer. I will send you $25 as soon as I get
my check and I think I can send $25 more, later in the month.

I may be able to send $50 right away. I want to save $125 to pay the 1st
Nat Bank next September. I've paid the interest up to then.

Harold Mackenzie was up before a board and was discharged. This
happened or rather he heard today. He is going to join the Marines. He is selling his
things.

According to Harold Mackenzie's son, Harold opted out of the Army because he did not want to be an officer. He had been charged by his family with responsibility for one of the younger men in Company F. When he was reprimanded for fraternizing with enlisted personnel after having diner with that soldier (named John Oliver, subsequently killed in action), Mackenzie requested a discharge so that he could enlist as a common soldier. He did not feel he could make the distinctions between ranks required of him. He did in fact enlist in the Marines, served in France, and was honorably discharged as a sergeant. He later became a Lutheran Minister in Gallipolis, as did his son after him.

```
                          Headquarters 37th Division,
                          Camp Lee, Petersburg, Va.,
                                      May 28, 1918.
Special Orders,       )
                      )
    No. 148.          )


1.    A board of officers, to consist of -
      Brigadier General Charles X. Zimerman, N.A.
      Colonel Sanford B. Stanbery, N.G., 145th
            Inf.,
      Lt. Col. Paul L. McCook, N.A., Inf.
            Replacement Camp,
      Lt. Col. Florence S. Van Gorder, N.G., 145th
            Infantry.


is appointed under the provisions of Section 9,
Act of May 18, 1917, to examine into and report
upon the capacity, qualifications, conduct, and
efficiency of such officers as may be ordered to
appear before it.  In case any officer is not
recommended for discharge from the service of the
United States, the board will recommend, after
consideration of his occupation, service and
qualifications, both before and after entering the
```

service of the United States, the branch of the
service for which he is best fitted.

Captain Frank X. Frebis, N.G., 37th
Headquarters Troop, will act as Recorder of the
Board.

By command of Major General Farnsworth:

Dana T. Merrill
Lt. Colonel, General Staff,
Chief of Staff.

Headquarters 37th Division,
Camp Lee, Virginia,
May 28, 1918.

Special Orders,   )
)
    No. 148.   )

2.   Pursuant to telegraphic notification from
the Adjutant General of the Army, May 25, 1918,
First Lieutenant Albert H. Mackenzie, N.G., 148th
Infantry, is honorably discharged from
the service of the United States, as of that date.
First Lieutenant Albert H. Mackenzie was mustered
into Federal service at Gallipolis, Ohio.

By command of Major General Farnsworth:

Dana T. Merrill
Lt. Colonel, General Staff,
Chief of Staff.

148th Regiment Strength Return for May, 1918

Division Review, with Major General Farnsworth, reviewing, May 5th, 1918. First Field Inspection, May 4th, 1918. 74th Brigade pitched camp, with the Officers of the 147th Infantry inspecting the 148th Infantry, vice versa. Divisional practice march. Distance covered, 10 3/4 miles, heavy marching order. May 19th, 1918 the regiment marched to the Rifle Range for two days practice; returning May 21st, 1918. May 24th, 1918 the regiment entrained at Vandiver Park Station, Camp Sheridan, Ala, for Camp Lee Petersburg, Va. Arrived at Camp Lee and detrained May 26th, 1918. The work of training recruits and securing equipment for a war strength regiment being rushed to completion.

Alfred M. Barlow, 1st Lieut; Absent) Trans to Co. A 148th Inf.... date May 17/18.

Alfred Barlow 1st Lt Trans Co A. to Co L.... May 20th, 1918. Routine duty the entire month.

Found in *The 37ᵗʰ Division in the World War*

When the time came to move the Thirty-Seventh overseas it had been divided into two groups. The first consisted of Division Headquarters, Headquarters Troop, the 134th Machine Gun Battalion, the 73rd Infantry Brigade, the 74th Infantry Brigade, the 112th Field Signal Battalion and the 112th Engineers. The second group consisted of the 62nd Field Artillery Brigade, the 112th Train Headquarters and the Military Police, the 112th Supply Train, the 112th Sanitary Train, and the 112th Ammunition Train. The first group had entrained at Camp Sheridan for Camp Lee 20th May-25th May; and the second for Camp Upton, 14th June-17th June. From the day on which the division was thus divided at Alabama, it was never reunited as a combat unit. (vol. 2, 19)

Company L Strength Return for May, 1918

```
Condition of the Organization at Midnight on
the Last Day of May, 1918:
    6 officers present
    0 officers absent
    118 enlisted men present
    2 enlisted men absent
```

148th Infantry Regiment War Diary

```
Entire regiment less third battalion and
a detail of Officers and men from the Sanitary
Detachment, embarked on the USS Susquehanna.
```

[postcard dated June 22, 1918]

Camp Lee Virginia
Col L 148 Inf
June 19, 1918

Dear Mamma,

This is probably the last letter I will write from here. We leave soon. I can't say exactly where from or when. The most of our work is done now. I've been auditing with several others the paper work of the regiment, so to bed any where up to 3:30 a.m. Will leave a card on this side saying "I have arrived safely." It will be posted as soon as I land as when they telegraph we have arrived it will be mailed.

Lots of love,

Alfred

Found in *The 37ᵗʰ Division in the World War*

On 23ʳᵈ June the remaining units sailed from Newport News in a convoy of the transports, Patria, Re d'Italia, Pocahontas, Susquehanna, Duc d'Aosta and Caserta; with this convoy the South Dakota, Gregory, Huntington and Fairfax went as escorts; the Leviathan was unescorted, but moved out of the harbor with four destroyers circling around her and a dirigible overhead. The latter soon dropped behind and when morning came, the destroyers had likewise turned back.

The Duca D'Aosta would arrive in Europe July 15th with the 26 officers and 718 men of the 3rd Battalion, including Lieutenant Barlow, on board.

On Board July 4, 1918

Dear Mamma and Grandma,

When we first embarked I jotted down several impressions I wished to tell you of while they were yet fresh in my mind but now I find that I cannot find my book.

This is our thirteenth day on board and our twelfth day out. We expect to arrive tomorrow about 7 a.m. thou we may not get dis embarked before noon.

Like Paul I cannot tell where we embarked than it was not New York. We have three thousand seventy three soldiers on board. This is an Italian liner. The officers and crew with the exception of the waiters for the officers mess are Italians. I like the officers very much. They are very interesting to talk to especially the second officer who was torpedoed once and has several other interesting experiences.

When we first started the sea was about like Lake Michigan was when I was in Chicago. When in the state room you could hardly tell the boat was moving but never the less even slight as the motion was it soon began to make its self manifest. The fishes were well taken care of the first two or three days, but most of the men soon recovered althou some had relapses two or three days ago when we had a little storm. I was Officer of the Day at the time and had to be all over the ship especially at night to see that no lights were showing and that the men did not smoke below decks. The wind and rain were terrific while they lasted but the wind did not last long enough to cause many big waves.

I saw several large black fins or tails of fish and was told they were porpoises. One day too we saw many flying fish and they particularly impressed me. They do not simply jump out of the water as our fish do in the river but seem to travel parallel to and about six inches from the water for from ten to twelve feet at a stretch.

Its rather monotonous on board. I give the men physical exercise almost two hours a day and conduct non-commissioned officers school about the same length of time. The rest of the time I read, play cards and sleep.

Yesterday I finished King Lear. It had never particularly impressed me previously. I certainly appreciate it now however almost if not quite as much as Hamlet. Grandma I've read Edmund Dantis too thou I consider it far inferior to "The Black Tulip," and the series beginning with "The Three Musketeers."

Another lieutenant and myself have a rather commodious state room with "fresh" running water. Some of the officers were not so fortunate and are posted several in a room while several second lieutenants have second class quarters.

I have heard that most of the men write exceptionally sentimental letters while in France. I now know why. Practically everything else is forbidden. My letters are due to be very uninteresting. Be careful to get my address right it will be--

Co L 148th inf.

A.E.F.

via New York

The AEF is of course American Expeditionary Force. This will be forwarded.

With lots of love,

Alfred.

[marked by hand: "OK, Estel L. Stewart Capt 148 Inf"]

<u>*Personal*</u>

July 4, 1918

Dear Mamma,

The other letter is to show to Aunt Mattie & Grace et cet. and this is for you.

I sent you a box by freight from Camp Sheridan. It was the big wooden box. I sent it to Earnest C. Have you received it yet. From Camp Lee I sent you a small package--the old bedding roll and some clothes I can use when I come back. In the big box were some things belonging to Harold which please have his folks come and get. The big box was shipped collect so you pay Earnest for it. I have about $50 in the O.V. Bank. You draw that what ever it is and use it as I can't use it now.

I have as I told you on a post card from Camp Lee allotted $100 a month to you, beginning with this month July. That is the government at Washington will take $100 a month out of my pay and send it to you direct. You should get your first $100 about the 1st of August. In case you do not let me know. It may be late the first month but it will be prompt once it gets started. If you don't find much to my credit in the bank and are short of money let me know and I will send you some right away. I may any way. The boots I bought at Frank Beall are in the box & shipped to Earnest. If he won't take them pay him and maybe Earnest can get rid of them for you.

I've got so much to say I can hardly think of it all. We are in the most dangerous part of the ocean now. We have about 200 miles to go. I probably will not see any fighting for some time.

You had better keep this letter as what I have to say is advice only but it may be my last as I shall try to avoid business but I should like to get it all out of my system at once.

In September my note will be due at the 1st Nat. Bank. Pay that.

Tell me how much you get from my acct. at the O.V. Bank.

Make it small if you wish, but always have that available. <u>Next</u>

<u>Keep $200 (when you get things squared up of course. This is surplus money I'm speaking of) in the savings department of the O.V. Bank you get 4% interest and in case of emergency it is available.</u>

Get a <u>good refrigerator</u> and have it large enough.   *Get ice regularly & milk.*

Have the barn roof torn off and boards bought (good boards) and leave the boards now on torn off and have it re-sheeted leaving no cracks. Then buy some guaranteed 3-ply paper like we used at the farm and have it put in good condition. Have the front porch at the farm fixed up. Have it roofed and have the wood work so fixed that it will not deteriorate. Have the porch painted. This needs it bad. If not fixed it will go to pieces soon. A stitch in time saves nine.

As soon as possible if $60 a month is enough from me start an account in each of the Building & Loan associations of $5 a week each. That will make altogether $40 a month.

I've packed most of my writing paper where I can't get at it and that is the reason for this variation. You notice I am writing two letters one personal and the other you can send around. You can show it to Mr. Sibley if you wish.

I don't know whether I would sell the farm or not even if it don't bring in anything. Don't try to improve it but keep it from deteriorating. How is the sweet clover? I hope you have not let Williams plow it up. Make him be careful of the trees. By the way I think I owe $3 at his garage. I wish you would see. I am sure I do. Please pay it.

I would like to buy the Edwards place if we could get it reasonable. I would buy the place down next the road too if I could get it right. I wouldn't expect to make anything much but if I'd ever farm there again I'd have lots of land for pasture.

{As soon as I get a chance I'll write to and go and see

{Cousin Morley.

Please tell me how you are fixed financially! I want you to be all right. How much pension do you get.

I'd like to have enough after the war to have you have all you want then I would marry Judy.

I suppose because of the war granite or marble is pretty high now. I want to put a tomb stone on papa's grave some time. For the present before I can do it myself when you get able put up a foot marker with his name and date on it like this diagram. It may cost $25 or so.

Marion S. Barlow

1839-1917

granite
ground surface
concrete

It is on a part of the Lanning lot is it not! Is there any more room there? I may need some of it for my own personal use.

Hire a machine or something but go out to the farm occasionally. Tell me what crops are in what fields. I do hope you are both well. Loads of love,

Alfred.

[Marked by hand: "*OK, Estel L. Stewart, Capt., 148 Inf*]

Morley Browne, Skip's second cousin, lived in England. Skip wouldn't see him until after the war was over see Chapter Eleven.

Chapter Five

Found in *The 37ᵗʰ Division in the World War*

The Third Battle of the Aisne (26ᵗʰ May-18ᵗʰ July) had been begun before the first element of the Thirty-seventh Division had left America (18ᵗʰ June) and it had ended before the last elements had reached France (21ˢᵗ July).

As the Ohio Division was arriving in France [German General Erich von] Ludendorf was planning his next offensive which was to sweep the German forces beyond the Marne toward Paris, and cut the Paris-Nancy railroad; and striking east between Prunay and the Argonne would divide the French front; he would then march on to Paris down the valley of the Marne, at the same time attacking at Ypres, breaking through the Amiens-Montdidier front and descending on Paris from the north; he would cut the forces of [General Douglas] Haig off from those of [Marshal Henri-Philippe] Petain and break the latter in two. (vol. 2, 10)

The Stars and Stripes, France, July 5, 1918

THE A.E.F. TO AMERICA--JULY 4, 1918

On this anniversary of our independence, the officers and men of the American Expeditionary Forces on the battlefields of France renew their pledges of fealty and devotion to our cause and country. The resolve of our forefathers that all men and all peoples shall be free is their resolve. It is quickened by sympathy for an invaded people of kindred ideals and the war challenge of an arrogant enemy. It is fortified by the united support of the American people.

(Signed)   PERSHING

The Stars and Stripes, France, July 5, 1918

THE WEEK'S BATTLE LINE

The week ending Wednesday, July 3, though marked by no major engagement, has seen a series of raids and reconnaissances on the western front, including the Italian line, made on the grand scale.

The reconnaissances in at least three instances were smashing local attacks in force, each of which, brilliantly executed, won back appreciable slices of ground, captured important points of vantage or assault, and made a considerable number of prisoners.

On Friday the British advanced on a three and a half mile front east of Nieppe Forest to an average depth of nearly a mile, taking 450 prisoners.

The same day the French, south of the Aisne, pushed into the German lines on a front of four and a half miles to a depth, in some points, of a mile and a quarter. Their prisoners totaled 1060. Vigorously counter-attacked by the enemy during the next two days, they everywhere maintained their new positions. On Sunday, the French won the high ground near Villers Cotterets in a half-mile advance, making 275 prisoners.

The third reconnaissance in force was the attack by American troops Monday in the sector northwest of Chateau-Thierry. Our advance reached a depth of a kilometer along a three kilometer front, inflicted heavy losses on the enemy, and gained 500 prisoners.

On Saturday an American raid near Montdidier made 36 prisoners. Hostile raids near Chateau-Thierry and the Vosges were repulsed by our fire. The Italians have continued their assaults on the defeated Austrian Army, and their prisoners now total over 20,000. Washington has announced the presence of American troops in Italy and adds that more will be sent if they are needed.

Allied airmen on the western front have put in an active week, with American pilots sharing in bombardment and combat honors.

148th Infantry Regiment War Diary for July 5, 1918

```
Dropped anchor in harbor at Brest, France.
Debarked in lighters part of regiment remaining
with ship to unload.  Marched four miles to Camp
```

Pontenezen where third battalion and Med Detail
rejoined regiment.   107 officers/3037 men.

Found in *The 37ᵗʰ Division in the World War*

The lighters came alongside the Duc d'Aosta at 6:45 p.m.
At 7:15 p.m. the transfer was complete and the lighter reached
the dock at 8:00 p.m. The men came ashore as fast as facilities would permit; companies and detachments were formed
and the troops marched to the first rest camp at Pontenezen
Barracks, where they arrived at 10:00 p.m. [vol. 2, 31]

The American Red Cross provided postcards for informing families that
soldiers had made the crossing in safety. Barlow's, like the rest (due to needs
of military secrecy) had no date on it and needed no stamp. Hand-written,
instead, was "Soldier's Mail," canceled with "Soldier's Mail, Mail Censor, U.S.
Army Base":

Mrs. M.S. Barlow

1066 First Ave.

Gallipolis

Ohio

Arrived safely over seas.

Alfred.

[Stamp: "Held until safe arrival of steamer; Then mailed. Censor."]

74th Regiment War Diary

Regiment marched to Brest (by Battalions) [from Pontenezen, 4 km away] and entrained in three sections. Heavy marching order. Travel rations issued to men for three days.

Headquarters 37th Division,
American E. F.
4, July, 18.

BULLETIN No. 22

1. Billets of all officers concerned in the Division will be marked by a sign showing the name and rank of the officer billeted therein.

2. The Provost Marshal will arrange with the Commanding Officers of organizations for signs along highways in this area indicating the organization in each area and signs on the roads indicating in which direction the particular organization is billeted.

3. All Headquarters, including Staff establishments at Division Headquarters, will be open from 7:00 A.M. continuously until 9:30 P.M. daily. A commissioned officer, or a <u>responsible</u> Field Clerk or noncommissioned officer, will always be on duty during this period.

4. Until further orders, the authorized headgear for this area is the campaign hat. Overseas caps will not be worn. This applies to Billeting officers and other ranks.

5. (a) Target practice will commence at the earliest available moment on ranges which will be arranged for by Brigade, Regimental and Battalion Commanders for this purpose in connection with the French Mission. The officers of the French Mission will arrange for the ground after its suitability for Target practice has been determined by officers of this Division who will use the course.

(b) Attention is invited to the requirements of the Program of Training that the unamended qualification course of Small Arms Firing will be used as given on page 59 Small Arms Firing Manual, 1913, corrected to April 15, 1917, headed "Regular Courses". This course includes Instruction Practice, Qualification Course and Record Practice Qualification Course.

(c) Each organization will keep a record of the total score on each range for each man firing for the Instruction and Record Courses. Record Course will be fired for Instruction purposes and not for Qualification purposes. The greatest attention will be given to the detail of competent coaches on the firing line.

(d) The instructional pamphlets issued from these Headquarters today are the property of the organizations to which distributed and not to individual officers. These pamphlets, together with the Drill Regulations and Manuals, form the

basis of training in the subjects covered and as
set forth in the program of training, 1st phase,
for the 37th Division. Attention is particularly
invited to the necessity for a thorough school
course in the publications designated in the
program of training, which, supplemented by Field
Service Regulations, Drill Regulations and Manuals
furnish a complete guide of training for the units
of this Division.

6. General Headquarters, American
Expeditionary Forces, July 2, 1918 American
Official communiqué 9 P.M. yesterday afternoon
in the Chateau Thierry region our Infantry
with effective co-operation from our batteries
stormed the village of Vaux de Bois de la roche
and the neighboring woods. The attack was made
in co-operation with the French on our right
who advanced their lines on hill 209; our own
positions were advanced on a front in a mile and a
half to a depth of 1000 yards. The enemy's losses
in killed and wounded were heavy his regiment
holding the sector attacked offered obstinate
resistance and was practically annihilated. Our
losses were relatively light. A German counter-
attack made early this morning was entirely
repulsed. The enemy again suffered severely
and left additional prisoners in our hands. The
prisoners captured in the attack and counter-
attack number over 800 and includes six officers.
This increases the total of prisoners taken by
our troops in this vicinity during the last month
to nearly 1200. The material captured by our
troops in yesterday afternoon's operations include
trench mortars and over 60 machine guns. The day
passed quietly at other points. American aviation
squadrons cooperated with our troops in the action

northwest of Chateau Thierry.   3 of our aviators
did not return.

By command of Major General Farnsworth:

Official: Dana T. Merrill,
                    L. Colonel, General Staff,
                       Chief of Staff.

R. E. Fraile,
Major, A.G.R.C.
Adjutant.

(FOR OFFICIAL CIRCULATION ONLY)
                    Headquarters 37th Division,
                       American E. F.
                          9, July, 18.

   1.   The Division Signal Officer will cause
the Standard Time received by telegraph to be
sent out by telephone at 12:00 noon daily to the
Headquarters of each organization, where it will
be transmitted to all organizations.
        He will at the same time, either
personally or through a representative, give
the correct time to the heads of the several
Departments on or near 12:00 noon daily.   This
will include the Commanding Officer, Headquarters
Troop.

   2.   REGULATIONS FOR WRITING, MAILING AND
CENSORING MAIL IN THE 37TH DIVISION

        (a)   The post office at the 37th Division
Headquarters has been designated Army Post Office
No. 763 and all mail addressed to personnel in

this Division should carry "A.P.O. No. 763" as a part of the soldier's address.

(b)   Inside the letter and at the bottom of the last page should be written the name, rank, company, regiment and A.P.O. No. 763.

(c)   In the upper right had corner of the envelope, underneath the words "Soldier's mail", write the letters "O.A.S." (on active service).

(d)   If the letter is written in a foreign language, print the name of the language in English at the top of the first page and forward unsealed.

(e)   A letter to you should be addressed as follows:

```
| Corp. John Webster,              |
|                                  |
| Co. "A", 145th Infantry,         |
|                                  |
| A.P.O. No.  763                  |
|                                  |
|    American E.F.                 |
```

(f)   When the letter is completed it should be given to the officer designated as censor for the company or detachment to which the writer belongs, who will censor communications at once and write the words "Censored by", under which is written name and rank, diagonally across the lower left hand corner of the envelope.

(g)   After the communication is censored by the company or detachment censor, it will be forwarded to the regimental post office, where the regimental censor will stamp each communication with the prescribed stamp: - "passed as censored". Mail of separate organizations, entitled to censor stamp, shall be handled exactly as prescribed above.

     (h) Regimental censor will forward all mail promptly to the 37th Division Post Office, (A. P. O. No. 763).

     (i) An officer is privileged to censor his own mail by writing the words "censored by" and writing his name and rank in the lower left hand corner of the envelope, turning same into the regimental post office, where it will be cancelled and forwarded by regimental censor.

     (j) A rule for censoring mail is generally stated as "say nothing that will be of any value to the enemy". Mention of names of towns, dates of troop movements, names of railroads, conditions of troops, etc., are prohibited....

TRAINING

     3. In all tactical exercises it is essential that officers and enlisted men be fully acquainted with the problem, and the steps being taken to carry it out. Nothing is more important than the full and complete interest of the entire command. To this end, in all tactical exercises, officers will explain the problem to their organizations, and will concisely state the part the particular organization takes in its execution. Thereafter, advantage will be taken of every opportunity to keep the organization acquainted with the progress

```
of the exercise.  This is as important in training
as it is on the field of battle....

          By command of Major General Farnsworth:
Official:                    Dana T. Merrill,
                    L. Colonel, General Staff,
                        Chief of Staff.
R. E. Fraile,
Major, A.G.R.C.
Adjutant.
```

The Stars and Stripes, France, July 5, 1918

THE SCISSORS VS. THE PEN

(This pamphlet was prepared by an unreserved buck who joined the colors to make the w. s. for d. [the world safe for democracy], but remained to have his innermost thoughts cut to hellandone by a lot of Reserve Shavetails--such as the one that wrote in here not long ago about the correspondents of the A.E.F.)

1.--Lieutenant Ogleburg is stricter than a Sunday school superintendent with a lot of young folks out on the annual picnic. He learned the censorship regulations by heart when they were first issued, and they have grown in on him. The way he wants you to write letters he doesn't want to have your family or your girls know you're in the Army at all, or that there's a war going on. If you write about going on guard he says you mustn't say that you do two hours on and four hours off. He probably figures it out that if the Germans knew that they'd lam over a lot of shells from an airplane just the time the relief was going around.

2.--Lieutenant Plattisdan is even worse. Besides clipping the military stuff out of your letters--thus raising hob with the stuff on the other side-- he takes it into his hands to correct your grammar, to dot your i's and cross your t's for you. That might come in handy if you were writing to a professor or somebody that was educated, but if you're writing to a girl what good does it do you? Besides, the only chance a soldier has to be sloppy, to give his mind rest and not bother about being correct is when he's writing letters; so why not let him go the limit?

3.--Lieutenant Uphank has a trick of refusing to cut things out but calling you into his billet, showing you what's wrong or what he thinks is wrong, and then asking you to re-write it with the hush-stuff left out. He says that's by far the better way, because then the folks when they get your letters don't think they're being cheated out of any inside dope on the war, but believe they're getting all there is to be got. But the result is that you never get round to rewriting the letter and the first thing you know you get a letter from you're [sic] old man wanting to know why the hell you don't write.

4.--Lieutenant Yap-Devens has one main hip on censoring the criticism of superior officers. To give an illustration Bill Bronley, in my shack, was rushing the same girl I was back in the States, and I didn't know how to come back at him. Finally I wrote to the girl's married sister and said that Bill was a big cheese. The first thing I knew the Loot had me on the carpet. "What for?" says I. "Criticism of superior officer," says he. It seems I'd forgot all along that Bill was a first-class private.

5.--Lieutenant Dix is a suspicious son-of-a-gun. If you throw any French phrases--even innocent ones like *cognac*--just to let the girl know you're making progress with the language and customs of the country, he calls you in and wants to know where you got it. I always thought a censor was supposed to be like a father confessor; that he wouldn't give you away no matter what a lot of stuff you told him--but not so. He says that all mail matter written in a foreign language can't be handled by him, but has got to go down to the base censor. Result: I can't practice up writing what little French I know, and have the fun of showing it off. Just as if the lieutenant didn't have brains enough to translate *cognac*.

6.--But Lieutenant Lee-Meade is the best one of the bunch. I'm his orderly, so he knows me well enough to know I don't know anything, much less any military information, and couldn't spell the name of the town we're in, much less pronounce it. So when I hand him a letter of mine he says, "Sure there isn't any rough stuff in that?" "Sure, lieutenant," says I. "Sure now?" he says, "because if there is they'll be coming back on me." "There isn't a thing I wouldn't tell my own mother," says I (the letter being written to her). So he says "Awri," and puts his John Hancock on the last page and on the envelope and off she goes in time to catch the afternoon mail load. If there were more loots like him there'd be a lot more letters written in the A.E.F.

Found in *The Thirty-Seventh Division*

During the period from 8th July-11th July the 74th Brigade, entraining at Brest, arrived at the Bourmont training area. Brigade Headquarters locating at Damblain....

Gradually, the various units of the division which were to serve together thence forward were thus collected in the Bourmont area and as each unit arrived it was assigned to a village and entered upon the prescribed course of training. When finally assembled in this area the units of the division were located as follows:

...

Chaumont-La-Ville--Third Battalion, 148th Infantry, and 112th Engineer Train.

...

As soon as a unit arrived in the training area, it was familiarized with the rules that were to govern its conduct in the new and strange environment.... The first bulletin issued from the newly established Division Headquarters at Bourmont on 30th June set forth a list of calls to govern, excepting on Sundays and holidays. The routine established was:

Reveille...5:30 A.M.
Assembly...5:45 A.M.
Mess...6:30 A.M.
Sick Call...7:00 A.M.
Drill..7:30 A.M.
Mess...12:00 Noon
Drill..1:30 P.M.
Mess...5:30 P.M.

Retreat and Inspection................6:30 P.M.
Call to Quarters..........................9:15 P.M.
Taps...9:30 P.M.

Leaves and furloughs... could not be granted in the division prior to 10th October. There were directions concerning the uniform, motor vehicle accidents, the speed of motor vehicles, trench-foot, hunting privileges, promotions of the fit and elimination of the unfit, absence without leave; the method of dating correspondence, the clothing and equipment of enlisted men sent to hospital, the disposal of effects and reports of deaths, wounded and missing, the care of automatic arms, machine guns and rifles, and replacement requisitions.

Attention was directed to orders regarding cutting of trees and brush and obedience to the laws of France, to rations for traveling parties, to the disposal of unserviceable clothing, to disturbing bee hives, to fires in billets and barns, to bread and sugar tickets, to the care of footwear, to the use of automobile headlights in the presence of airplanes, to gas defense, and to the care of animals....

Troops billeted in one town were not permitted to visit another town without a written pass to be given only for important reasons. A strict censorship over mail was maintained. No orders or letters could contain names of towns in the area; and the greatest care was to be exercised in the protection of orders and instructions issued; all copies were to be held strictly confidential, and all waste paper from offices must be burned under proper supervision. (vol. 2, 33-39)

Gallipolis Daily Tribune, July 12, 1918

Boys of F. Company Over There.

The Gallipolis boys of the old F Company are safe in Europe. Cards are being received to that effect by mothers and friends.

The Stars and Stripes, France, July 12, 1918

FRANCE TO THE A.E.F--JULY 14, 1918

France celebrates on July 14 her national independence, as the Americans observed theirs July 4. On these two solemn days, American and French hearts beat in unison. All feel that the moment approaches when, thanks to their common efforts, the defeat of Germany will allow all the free nations to celebrate at last the independence of the world.

July 11, 1918 (Signed)   J. JOFFRE

Found in *The 37ᵗʰ Division in the World War*

By the time the Thirty-seventh Division reached France the training policy for the A.E.F. had been well established. The first infantry camp was at Gondrecourt, another one organized around Neufchateau; and others later in the vicinity of Dijon, Toul, St. Dizier and Jorgany twenty-one in number when hostilities ceased....

Base sections had been established at St. Nazaire, Bordeaux, Naute-Brest, and LeHavre, and a regulating station at Is-sur-Tille. Between the zone of the bases and that of the advance, and intermediate section was established to regulate shipments from the former to the latter. Depots were located at Selles-sur-Cher, Gievres and Songy; a station for repair parts at Tour, Chateauroux and Nevers; refrigeration and cold storage posts at Tours, Gievres, Blois and Orleans; bakeries at Dijon and Gievres; advance depts. And repair shops and Mehun, Foecy, Gievres and Romorantin. Hospitals were established in all the above localities. The stage was almost completely set for the last act. (vol. 2, 17-18)

The Stars and Stripes, France, July 12, 1918

PAYDAY A MONTH WILL BE ASSURED UNDER NEW PLAN

Some Money for Every Man in Whole A.E.F. Every Thirty Days

AMOUNT NOT YET DECIDED

System Will Not Affect Those for Whom Ghost Now Walks Regularly

-----

A pay system will soon be adopted in the A.E.F. by which every man will receive every 30 days some of the money due him.

What this plan will be, just how it will operate, how much of his pay a soldier will be allowed per month, these and other details cannot now be announced. But it can be stated with certainty that a new plan will be put in operation, and that there will never be again, once that plan is in operation, a soldier in the whole A.E.F. who has gone without any money at all for more than the customary month which everyone has to wait.

The new play will not interfere with men who are not fortunate enough to be so situated that their pay comes around regularly, month after month, with only a few days' fluctuation of the date one way or another.

Details Not Announced

It is not now possible to announce how closely, if at all, the new plan will follow the one outlined in this newspaper a few weeks ago, when the fact that official steps toward a revision of the pay system were being definitely taken was first made known to the Army.

The men who will benefit by the once-a-month-sure plan are, of course, a relatively small proportion of the whole A.E.F. Now that the million mark has been reached, that proportion, however small it may be, is growing all the time.

Wounded men make up a good part of the number. A wounded man means a service record temporarily strayed, and a misplaced service record, under the present plan, means no money. Men newly arrived from the

States are also apt to be moneyless for a varying period under present pay methods. But the payless payday is to be a thing of the past.

Found in *The 37th Division in the World War*

On Sunday, 14th July, some elements of the Thirty-seventh Division were already billeted in their training area in France; others were hurrying there on troop trains, and still others were on the high seas. Paris, that morning, heard the roar of guns and the Germans went over the top in a rush that carried them past the Marne, between Chateau Thierry and Dormans, and the second battle of the Marne was on. It was to end in a dismal defeat for the enemy, leaving his western flank crumpled, his lines of communication destroyed, and depriving him once and for all time, of the initiative. (vol. 2, 10-11)

Stars and Stripes, France, July 12, 1918

CAN YANKS WEAR CROIX DE GUERRE?

Statutes Say Foreign Decorations Must Go to State Department

CONSTITUTION BANS GIFTS

But Are They Going to Come Off?
Ask the Man Who Already Owns One

When the first Croix de Guerre were bestowed upon American soldiers, everybody was happy--especially the men who had won them. And then some killjoy came along and spilled the beans.

"It's agin the law," he said, pointing to Sections 3268 and 3269, page 4461, volume four, United States Compiled Statues.

Sections three two and so forth state that decorations from foreign Governments have to be tendered to the State Department. The inference is that the State Department turns them over to the person they are intended for by whoever gives them.

But that isn't the worst. A Compiled Statute is only a compiled statute, but now along comes the Constitution of the United States, the same constitution that gave Congress the right to levy armies and declare war, and says, in Article II, Section 2, Paragraph 2:

No Presents or Emoluments

"No title of nobility shall be granted by the United States: And not person holding any office of profit or trust under them shall, without the consent of Congress, accept of any present, emolument, office, or title, of any kind whatever, from any king, prince, or foreign state."

Do the Croix de Guerre come off? Hold! The reprieve! On March 26, 1918, there was introduced in Congress a resolution which will grant to all members of the military and naval forces of the United States authority to accept decorations conferred upon them by any of the Governments of the Allies. This resolution was in accordance with a recommendation made by the Commander-in-Chief, A.E.F., when the first Croix de Guerre were awarded.

That resolution, at last reports, was awaiting passage. There is, of course, not the slightest doubt that it will eventually pass.

But until then--is anybody going to fly in the face of the Constitution by continuing to wear the Croix de Guerre? Our answer is that, if anybody does, and if the Supreme Courts hears about it, it will remark what a fine day it is, forget for a couple of seconds that there is such a thing as the Constitution, and say, "Next!"

Found in *The 37ᵗʰ Division in the World War*

Gradually, the various units of the division which were to serve together thence forward were thus collected in the Bourmont area and as each unit arrived it was assigned to a village and entered upon the prescribed course of training. When finally assembled in this area the units of the division were located as follows:

...

Chaumont-La-Vine—Third Battalion, 148th Infantry, and 112th Engineer Train.

...

It was during this training period that Brig. General William P. Jackson joined the Division, to take command on 21st July of the organization he was destined to lead so bravely and efficiently throughout the remainder of the war. He relieved Colonel Galbraith, who had been in temporary command of the brigade since the unit left the United States, and who now returned to his own organization, the 147th Infantry. (vol. 2, 33-35)

The Stars and Stripes, France, July 19, 1918

YANKS BATTLE GRIMLY AGAINST HUN HORDES IN FIFTH OFFENSIVE

Americans Part of Target in Major Operation for First Time

FINE WORK BELOW MARNE

Artillerymen at Last Get Chance to See Foe and Fire at Him Point Blank

-----

AVIATORS IN CURTAIN RAISER

Bag of Prisoners Includes Complete Battalion Staff Stranded on Southern Bank of River

-----

The fifth German offensive of 1918, after a month of costly delay, was finally launched on the evening of France's national holiday, launched last Sunday night, by more than 40 of the best divisions the German high command could muster on a 50 mile front that stretched from Chateau-Thierry up around the stubborn citadel of Rheims and eastward into Champagne.

The next morning at dawn the German infantry began its dogged advance. The setting of the same sun that looked down on that advance saw the Allied forces pushing the Germans back through the slight reaches of territory that they had gained in the impetus of their first rush.

The great drive was broken the day it began. By the end of the first 48 hours of fighting the offensive bore many of the earmarks of an historic check. By the time the greatest depth of the hostile advance was no more than five miles, and that was a narrow indentation in the unbroken Allied front.

A Grand Style Operation

The offensive was a major, grant style operation comparable in scale to the biggest efforts the enemy had put forth in this decisive year, but, in the sense that all German drives in the west are either a drive for Paris or a drive for the Channel ports, this was a preparatory rather than a direct thrust. It appeared at the outset as an effort to pinch out their Rheims salient as by a pair of giant forceps, establish a base of operations on the Marne and so prepare the path that leads to France's capital.

The fifth offensive was notable for the utter lack of the element of surprise. For two weeks the evidence accumulated by aviators and every other form of scout a modern army knows pointed to Champagne as the scene of the long delayed drive. Therefore, the Allies were ready, and the advance was met with such immediate resistance that counter-attacks were in progress at some points before the first day was gone.

French, Italian and American troops met the onslaught, and the British aviators in great numbers shared in the fighting that is done in the skies.

Part of Vast Target

This was the first time since the war began that American troops have been part of the target of a major offensive. Some few American soldiers were thrown into a gap during the later progress of the big March drive, and American troops in numbers that counted jumped into the fight which halted the Germans in the first days of June in and around Chateau-Thierry. But here were Americans ready and waiting.

They were in the thick of some of the most desperate and spectacular fighting on the whole stretch, some of the most desperate and spectacular fighting American soldiers have ever known. The prisoners captured by them in the first 48 hours, according to a rough, unofficial guess, numbered about 1,200.

No American troops came in for more violent fighting than those repre-sented in that stretch of the line to the south and west of Rheims--the stretch from Chateau-Thierry to Dormans along the Marne. The battle line was the river itself, and the Germans had to cross it first.

They crossed it. They go badly messed up doing it and afterward. And on Wednesday night the American communiqué announced:--

"In the Marne sector our troops have entirely regained possession of the south bank of the river."

Infantry Comes at Dawn

The Germans prepared the way with a bombardment of high-explo-sives, shrapnel, mustard gas and other poisons, and compared with fighting against such an attack, walking boldly into an outpouring from rifles and machine guns is like a holiday excursion. Then at dawn came the Hun in-fantry swarming across the narrow, smooth-flowing, curving stream on 50 or 60 swiftly slung pontoon bridges. As they crossed, the Allied artillery opened fire against them, the machine gun bearing airplanes swooped down on them, and they were met on our side by men ready and primed for hand-to-hand fighting.

There was plenty of use for rifles and for fists in the confused and stub-born battle that followed on the southern band of the Marne. By sundown on Tuesday the Americans had pushed back to the river's edge the enemy troops that had taken territory in their sector of the battlefield and had left on their side only a few scattered detachments of Boche infantry and ma-chine gunners.

Sticks to River's Edge

It would scarcely be the nicest military accuracy to describe the American action at this point as a counter-attack. As it looked Wednesday morning, it seemed rather the successful outcome of a swaying, unremitting contest of their own ground by Yankees into whom the rushing enemy had infiltrated, now by eights, now by companies, now by battalions.

Thus it can be said of one American battalion that it never left the river's edge at all, though at one time it hung on alone with Germans all around. And it can be said of one German battalion that, after infiltrating according to the approved and this time not very happy German method, it collected in a ravine and so was all together when it came time to surrender to the surrounding Yankees, who sent to the rear the entire battalion, major, staff and all.

In this swaying battle, Americans would be taken prisoner and then re-captured by their own pals before the enemy could make off with them.

The heavy toll of dead and wounded exacted from the enemy by the waiting Allies was heavy not only because they were waiting, but because the Germans, in almost all of their advance, had difficult territory to nego-tiate.

In crossing the Marne between Chateau-Thierry and Dormans, they had to move over an unprotected flat into waiting guns. The American ar-tillery, entering a war in which the artillery has been doomed for the most part to the dismal and unsatisfactory business of shooting day in and day out at a distant and unseen foe--firing forever at a mathematical point--was here suddenly presented with the opportunity of firing point blank. It made the most of it.

Five Defend Bridge

When the artillery chronicle comes to be written, there will have to be a page set aside for the story of the call for volunteers to take a field piece right down to the water's edge and use it as you would a rifle against the German host, racing across a bridge at that point. Of the many volunteers, five were picked, and they wrought a mighty damage before they them-selves--all of them--were killed.

The artillery story will tell, too, of an American regiment arriving on the scene with batteries of heavies and going into action under fire.

The Air Service, too, must have an honored chapter in history of the battle that began in the early hours of July 15. Not only had American avi-ators played a memorable part in the advance reconnaissance which robbed the offensive of every atom of surprise, but they supported the ground workers in every daylight hour, riddling the German concentrations and de-fending their own.

And the cavalry. For in this battle mounted American cavalry made their first appearance on the western front. They were only six strong, six rough-riding enlisted men who carried messages when all wires were down, went on with their work through a tornado of fire, charging through gas clouds with ducked heads, going on with their messages afoot when, as hap-pened to two of them, their horses were shot down under them.

It is difficult for anyone who has been in contact with the troops fight-ing south of the Marne to write temperately and with fine national modesty of the spirit shown by the troops--a spirit that would thrill a hundred million hearts back home and that fulfilled its promise to all those who hoped and prayed and believed that the Yankee of the generation would go on to a world battlefield and show himself a good soldier.

As They Reached the Hospital

That spirit had a chance for expression in the hand-to-hand fighting reminiscent of the battles of the pioneer forefathers. But it expressed itself in a thousand ways, and never more eloquently than at the field hospital where ambulance after ambulance brought up its load of wounded--fearfully wounded, who persisted in grinning and rattling away with exuberant boyish satisfaction till the doctors who worked over them could not speak for the lumps in their throats and the proud mist in their eyes.

Always, as the wounded were lifted out, you could hear them explaining to all within earshot that they had to five or ten or 20 Fritzes before a Fritz got them.

One man with a badly hurt leg will be around again before long, but this did not interest him. He wanted the litter boys to understand that, with the aid of a well-placed machine gun, he had done for 250 Germans before a German did for him.

One Youngster with his back shot to pieces lay on a stretcher with his wounds invisible to the passerby and to each one he volunteered the information that there was nothing the matter with him and that, if he could horn a cigarette off any guy around there, he would go back to the front on the next ambulance. He died before the day was done.

Wanted Quick Transfer

One man waited just long enough for a piece of shrapnel to be pried out of an ugly wound in his leg to bide his time until the doctors should be engrossed in another case, when he sneaked out of the first aid station and made tracks for his outfit, then in the thick of things, as well he knew. That is why no hospital appealed to him.

A young Infantry lieutenant, whose leg was shot away below the knee, begged the field surgeons who dressed him to transfer him immediately to the Artillery so that he could go on with his business of killing Germans. They reminded him that such a transfer was out of the power of anyone at the moment, but they promised him that his days in the Army were not over yet. And the promise cheered him mightily, as you could see by the smile he wore when they carried him to the waiting ambulance.

It scarcely abated that spirit any to learn, as the vast spreading tidings told many of the men on Tuesday, that a German had wantonly bombed an American hospital the night before. The world was carried to the very front by many a Signal Corps man and many a tuck train worker. It helped.

That spirit glowed through all ranks and through every branch of the service. The colonel who made trip after trip to his dugout carrying the wounded boys of his own command in his enormous arms and the Q.M. truck master who, while guiding his train under cover, was shot through the leg by a low-swooping German plane and then drove his motorcycle 15 kilometers to a field hospital before he fainted--they were made of the same stuff, those two.

Everybody in It

So was the chaplain who shouldered a pick and dug graves in the broiling sun all day long. So was the little flat-footed unruly private who had been tried, as last resort, in the medical detachment of one Infantry regiment and who, when the first aid station where he was working was blown to pieces and when he found he was the only person there not disabled, managed somehow to crawl out and, after an almost miraculous journey through a downpour of shells and shrapnel, to give the news and bring back aid.

So were all the litter boys, who worked like Trojans, the hospital men who toiled grimly over the patients brought in to them, the Signal Corps men who lay on their bellies mending wires while the shells poured down all around them--went on mending wires while the men on either side were hit and put out of business.

Against them were young Germans, shock troops for the most part, but in all the netful of prisoners drawn in to headquarters by the French and the Americans, there was noted a lower morale and a feebler enthusiasm than any batch of German prisoners have shown since the excitement began on March 21.

Some of the prisoners were taken in strange ways. One group of eight Americans were caught, herded together and marched to the rear. Midway in their course they suddenly overpowered their captors, took them prisoner and brought them back to America, plus several others casually picked up en route. One very young American was across the Marne when he escaped from his drowsy guard. He armed himself handsomely with the automatic of a dead German officer, and, thus fortified, swam the river and rejoined his outfit.

In some placed, the French and Americans were so mingled as to ear the phrase Franco-American troops, and in one little hillside graveyard the Italians who were playing the role of grave-diggers for the moment alternated the graves--one French, one American, one French, one American, and so on across the sunlit field, keeping the alliance to the very end.

The right wing of the German offensive did not reach west of Chateau-Thierry, but, until the infantry started to move last Monday at dawn, its exact limits could not have been guessed. At least the aerial and artillery activity reached that far and, therefore, when Monday morning came, the Americans there were on their toes.

They were bound to defend their neatly won village of Vaux, and when all that visited them afoot proved to be merely a German patrol, they gave it a savage reception, took prisoner what was left of it and celebrated the day by pushing their won line several hundred meters ahead of where it had rested for a fortnight and more.

The Stars and Stripes, France, July 19, 1918

NEED ANY PAJAMAS?
ASK YOUR COLONEL

Regimental or Higher Commander Must O.K. Package Requests

If you want a set of Mark Twain, 5,000 cork-tipped cigarettes, a fur coat and a bathing suit shipped you by your aunt in Evanston, Ill., there is no use asking the captain to approve the request. The power of granting approval in such cases is now taken from the company commander and placed in the hands of the regimental or higher commander. A War Department bulletin from Washington has done the deed.

Thus have new duties been devised to while away the colonel's leisure hours.

The bulletin on the subject of packages from home further explains that the same restrictions apply to express and freight shipments as to parcel post. None of these agencies may accept Aunt Lucy's package unless the request bearing at least a colonel's signature is presented with it.

Furthermore, the War Department order warns the colonels and higher that they must not approve requests for supplies that could be obtained by the need soldier in France.

Two points are not covered by the bulletins. What about stray units that have no colonels? And what about Christmas?

Found in *The 37ᵗʰ Division in the World War*

Troops billeted in one town were not permitted to visit another town without a written pass to be given only for important reasons. A strict censorship over mail was maintained. No orders or letters could contain names of towns in the area; and the greatest care was to be exercised in the protection of orders and instructions issued; all copes were to be held strictly confidential, and all waste paper from office must be burned under proper supervision. (vol. 2, 39)

3rd Battalion War Diary for July 21, 1918

```
Companies I, K, L, M, Medical at Chaumont
la Ville. 2 days rations with troops. 2 days
rations in supply train. Daily routine, rifle,
grenade, gas, etc. 18 officers, 820 men. Weather:
clear. Roads: good. Health: excellent.
```

Found in *The 37ᵗʰ Division in the World War*

Campaign hats were ordered turned in, and the overseas cap and wrapped leggings at last were authorized. Enlisted men were ordered to place all their personal property in barracks bags which were to be stored. Beginning Sunday, 21ˢᵗ July, all men were ordered to carry steel helmets and gas masks and to wear cartridge belts filled with ammunition when more than twenty-five yards away from billets or barracks; officers and enlisted men leaving the towns in which they were billeted were required to carry their arms; working parties were required to carry gas masks, helmets, arms and ammunition. (vol. 2, 49)

148th Infantry Regiment War Diary for July 22, 1918

```
    Regiment following daily classes in Gas,
Grenade and Target practice.
```

Found in *The 37ʰ Division in the World War*

Training of the division... came to an abrupt and unexpected halt....

Field order No. 1, Headquarters. 37th Division, A. E. F., France, 21st July, 1918, 2:00 P.M. brought the news:

"This division (less detached units) moves to another area."

"Movement by rail--exception: all motor transport by marching, under orders to be issued later."

"Entraining will begin 22nd July, 1918.... "

"Entraining stations--Bourmont, Breuvannes and Damblain."

"Duration of journey, about 16 hours."...

Thus did the training of the division come to a sudden termination and thus was the organization by formal notice propelled forward into the line, the goal upon which minds if not eyes had been fixed for so many tedious months. (vol. 2, 69-71)

148th Regiment War Diary for July 24, 1918

Entire Regiment (by Battalion) marched to rail heads Area #3 and entrained last section leaving at 2.22 AM.

The regiment moved, on this day, from Chaumont la Ville to Breuvannes.

ON ACTIVE SERVICE

WITH THE

American EXPEDITIONARY FORCE

July 24 1918

Dear Mamma,

I have not heard from you but hardly expect to for a while yet. I am well and everything is well with me. I am very busy. I can speak French much better than I thought I could and am improving rapidly. I know enough now to "get by" anywhere. My French is poor but I understand some and can make myself understood. I am staying in the same house with a school teacher and we give each other lessons.

I expect we will move again soon and then it may be some time before you hear from me.

My pen is broken. Please get me a small Conelin or other self filling pen at Moore and send it to me. A small pen to be carried loose in my pocket.

You are the only person I have written to since I have been in France.

Here the weather is always like a cool summer day at home. The land and scenery are the same as at home. It is a remarkable similarity. This pen is so bad I can hardly write.

Tell everyone I will write when I can.

With lots of love,
                                              Alfred

Censored A M Barlow 1st Lt. Inf. N.G.

148th Infantry Regiment War Diary for July 25, 1918

Colonel Lynch assigned to Command Regiment.
Entire Regiment detrained Area #2 and marched
to Billets, Battalion billeting in different
towns.

3rd Battalion War Diary for July 25, 1918

From railhead to Clezentaine.   Routine at
Clezentaine.   2 day rations with troops.   18
officers, 820 men.   Weather: good.   Roads: good.
Health: good.

(CONFIDENTIAL - NOT TO BE TAKEN INTO FRONT LINE
TRENCHES.)
                          Headquarters 37th Division,
                                   American E. F.
                                     25, July, 18.

BULLETIN No. 37

    1.   Particular attention will be given
to aggressive action on the part of our troops
now about to enter into the line.   The spirit
of the offensive in the form of completely
dominating what is known as "No Man's Land" must

be encouraged. It is necessary that all parts of the enemy's positions not strongly held by them be over-run by our reconnoitering and combat patrols.

2.   In every platoon in the Division special attention must be given to instruction in patrolling, which must include the use of cover, the writing of messages, and the rendering of reports. Patrols must be taught to be aggressive and alert at all times. It is expected that every platoon placed in either the first, second, or third lines, will have a number of men in it who know all trenches, paths, roads and wires that radiate in any direction from the platoon.

3.   Every man must be instructed in and have thorough understanding of the method of giving alarm by sentries and patrols. Actual practice in giving the alarm is the only sure means of knowing that the methods are understood.

4.   As one of the measures to achieve this end, it is suggested that in each platoon there be organized a special scouting detachment of from 6 to 10 selected men, men who are fearless, skillful in the use of their areas, resolute in combat. Groups of this nature, carefully trained in scouting, bombing and with the rifle, cannot fail to not only overcome small detachments of the enemy which may be encountered, but to hold their own against large patrols should occasion require it.

5.   Officers going in advance of the line of regimental headquarters will remove Sam Browne belts and carry side arms.

6.   LIAISON.

The greatest attention will be paid
to liaison with troops to front, rear and flanks.
The Division Commander and members of his Staff
will frequently test the liaison of units in all
directions.

7.   Commanders must constantly practice
liaison within the organizations as well as with
adjoining organizations. This training in liaison
must be a matter of night as well as day training.
The maintenance of liaison within the billeting
area is valuable training that will fully repay
the efforts when the test in the trenches comes.
Make it a point to keep the troops on your right
or left constantly informed of everything that
goes on in your area. Reports received from
areas will be investigated and if found to be
true, transmitted to the adjoining areas. The
information may be in the nature of news or it may
be in the nature of information as to terrain or
other military matters.

8.   Liaison officers and non-commissioned
officers must be furnished with means of
communication. This means may be any one of
the many that are now in common use for the
transmission of information. Do not trust to a
single means of communications. Send frequent
messages and in them always give two things:
(a) the hour of sending; (b) the hour when the
action reported about took place. All men must
be instructed in liaison between aeroplanes and
infantry.

9.   Test all means of liaison at least once per day.

10.   Avoid all assemblages of men when within two miles of the hostile artillery. This rule can only be enforced when the men have had preliminary instruction and training beyond the range of artillery and have become accustomed to the precaution. Covered places for instruction can be found in almost any area on the roads and openings in the woods. The artillery will probably not fire upon groups of men unless the men can be seen from balloons, aeroplanes, or other observation stations. When in any of the front lines the danger spots are usually: (1) places of assembly for meals; (2) places where cooking and fatigue are being done; (3) cross roads and road forks; (4) assembly places such as bulletin boards, stores, amusement places, etc. in towns.

11.   Every man must be impressed with the necessity of not exposing himself unnecessarily. We will all believe that each one is brave until he proves the contrary so there is no necessity of any one exposing himself to prove that he is not afraid. Unnecessary exposure may mean, and will usual mean, not simply injury to himself, but injury to other members of his command or to members of the command that follows his own.

12.   When men are assembled for instruction, meals, fatigue, or other duty, outlooks will be posted to watch for aeroplanes. Upon an aeroplane being sighted the outlook will give the alarm and all men will at once take cover in the shade and remain perfectly quiet until the aeroplane has disappeared. No men, other than the guard

detailed, will be permitted to look toward the
aeroplane.

13. Machine guns and automatic rifle
positions which annoy our platoons <u>must</u> be
accurately located.

14. Every man in every platoon must know at
all times exactly where his platoon and company
headquarters are located and how to reach them
under cover and also how to reach them by the
quickest route. Every man must know the direction
toward the enemy and the place that he is to
specially observe. Every man must know to what
place the roads, paths, and trenches leading away
from his platoon area lead to. To teach these
things it will usually be necessary to write out
the names and show them to the men. Few men can
remember the names of places unless they have seen
the name written out. Every company officer and
non-commissioned officer will be expected to be
familiar with all parts of no-man's land in front
of his company. This knowledge must be acquired
by the officers and non-commissioned officers going
out (after notifying adjacent organizations) with
reconnoitering parties of two to five men. The
gaining of this knowledge should be begun as soon
as the platoon enters the sector. Failure to
begin to get this knowledge at once will be looked
upon with suspicion.

15. As soon as any company is placed in
a front line the company and platoon commanders
will begin to make their plans for <u>a raid</u> upon
the enemy trenches, but such raids will <u>never</u> be
carried out until the plans have been approved by
the Division Commander.

16.   During day time only sufficient sentinels
to properly watch the front will be posted.   There
must be economy of men to save them for night
duty.

17.   The occupation of observation line
trenches should usually be especially light during
night and during fogs.

18.   Every man in the platoon should know how
to give the alarm in case of approach of a hostile
patrol, in case of a hostile raid, in case of a
hostile attack, and in case of gas.

19.   If artillery is bombarded with gas it
will at once notify the infantry because such
bombardment may be indication of an attack.   A
similar rule applies to the infantry when it
receives bombardments.

20.   Every abandoned or partially abandoned
village in front lines will be carefully searched
for Germans at least twice daily, to wit:
immediately after day break and again in time
to complete the search before dark.   During this
search necessary arrangements must be made to
support the searching parties and to prevent by
fire, other than that of the searching party, the
retirement of any enemy who may have been hiding
in the village.

21.   In the front line do not use the
telephone unless the messages are coded, or
immanent danger requires the use of the 'phone
without code.   Telephone discipline must be
maintained among the telephone operators.   It

is equally important that telephone discipline
be deeply instilled into all persons who use the
telephone.

22. When platoons or higher organizations
occupy first positions they will designate men
whose duty it will be to open and place across the
roads and trails, and tie in place, the accordions
(wire loops) that have been placed for that
purpose.

23. When a shell strikes the ground near
men, every one should instantly drop to the
ground. The fragments of the shell fly outward
and upward. Frequently there is plenty of time to
drop before the fragments leave the shell hole and
thus the dropping close to the ground may save the
lives of those near.

24. In the German attack on June 12, 1918,
on the French near the Aisne the following was
observed:
(a) The French reserves were able to
locate the points being fired upon and thus enabled
to march around those points and take their proper
positions with little loss.
(b) The targets against which the enemy
fired were usually cross roads, villages, ravines,
or places reported by their aeroplanes as occupied
by troops.
(c) The Germans removed prisoners,
especially officers and enlisted men of special
intelligence, to comfortable quarters (frequently
in hotels) where the prisoners were allowed to
live together in rooms in which were concealed
dictographs for the purpose of recording

their private conversation and thus obtaining information.

ACTION IN CASE OF CAPTURE

25. If by fortunes of war some of our men are captured by the enemy, it is necessary that they know how to act in order to keep from disclosing valuable military information.

Remember that there are two sorts of men in every army. A large percentage of men are brave soldiers, who would no more give information away to betray their country than they would fly. These are not the men we fear. The men we fear are those of a weak character. If you are captured it is only necessary for you to give your name and rank. Outside of this, answer nothing. If you must talk, then the following answers by a German prisoner are good examples of what to say: "It was dark and we did not know the road; we slept in a village, but do not know the name; the wires were all right, but we paid no attention to them; we knew there were dugouts, but did not know how many steps, etc." The other method is best, refuse to talk. If you do, and give the enemy information, you are traitors to your country and worse than all, traitors to your own pals.

CLEANLINESS

26. Cleanliness of person and clothing, neatness and orderliness of clothing and equipment, and military courtesies, are even more important when in the front line trenches than when in the training area. They must therefore receive the constant attention of all officers and non-commissioned officers. Remember that

lice will not inhabit clothing and persons that
are constantly being cleaned and cared for.   It
is said that in some commands "influenza" is a
polite word to cover the less aristocratic world
"lousiness".

GAS

27.   Gas discipline, which includes exact
obedience to all orders and thoughtfulness in
taking precautions against gas, is very important
now.

28.   In an operation recently conducted in
a certain division,... about 350 men raided a
portion of the enemy's works lying in the bottom
of a valley. As a part of the operation, the
artillery heavily gassed with phosgene a ruined
village lying in the same valley and about 1000
meters from the area raided. A seven mile an
hour wind blew directly from the village gassed
to the position raided. Within eight or nine
hours after the raiding party returned, over 200
gas casualties developed, many of them serious.
The odor of the phosgene was apparently smothered
in the fumes caused by the artillery box barrage
around the raiding party and the presence of the
gas was not suspected though many men were made
very sick, vomiting and gasping, during the raid.

29.   The need for the intelligent study
and application of the principles governing the
use of gas in attack and defense, and of the
principles governing the use of gas in attack and
defense, and of the principles governing defensive
measures against gas, as well as the need of close

liaison between gas officers and their respective commanders, is apparent.

30.   Each platoon must have a gas noncommissioned officer who must be specially trained to inspect the masks and who will be held responsible that they are inspected.

31.   Every gas mask must be inspected by a competent inspector each day. The inspection should include the canister, for a few drops of rain or a few drops of water properly placed by a German sympathizer, or a few pin pricks, may render a mask useless and result in a casualty.

32.   Sign posts will be posted by battalion commanders on all roads and paths leading to the front to show the beginning of the gas alert zone. These signs are orders to place the gas mask in the alert position.

33.   The gas drill by battalions training in the third positions from the front will include daily gas alarms using the various gas alarm devices that are used in the most advanced lines.

34.   The German yellow cross shell, which seems to be much dreaded, has a black body with a double yellow cross on it (that is, one upright bar and two cross bars, called the Lorraine Cross). It is filled with poison gas (Yprite, two quarts) and it makes a sound on passing just like any other shell and its fragments produce the same effect as another shell, therefore it cannot be recognized by the noise of passing or by the noise of its explosion.

35. The chief function of collective or
dug-out protection against gas is to provide a
place where the men may rest in safety from gas
without the discomfort and fatigue of wearing
the respirator. This purpose is defeated if the
men are ordered to come out of dug-outs on the
sounding of the gas alarm. Such an order should
only be issued in the case where the dug-out is
not gas-proof and in the front line where the
possibility of attack must be met. Even here the
number of men turned out should be the minimum
necessary.

36. It has been the policy of the enemy to
wear out their opponents by prolonged gas shell
bombardments preceding an attack. If the men are
forced to wear their respirators for several hours
they become tired and their resistance is cut
down. On the other hand, if they have proper dugout protection they may rest and sleep in perfect
safety from gas during the preliminary bombardment
and thus save their strength to meet the assault
when it comes. Men in the forward areas except
those on duty should sleep in the dug-out, keeping
always a sentry on guard at the entrance of each
to lower the blankets in case of a gas alarm.

37. SUPPLIES IN ENEMY TERRITORY.

        Supplies found in territory vacated
by our enemies or captured from our enemies
are the property of the Allied Governments and
must not be distributed by troops excepting by
orders of general officers. This applied whether
the property belonged formerly to the French
Government or to the German.

No helmet, insignia or document of any kind, found or won in combat, will be retained by any officer or enlisted man.

38.   The taking of such supplies and their appropriation for the use of individuals or for the use of organizations except as specifically provided in orders from the American E. E. is one of the most serious of military offenses.   It is expected that no offenses of this kind will be committed by any member of the 37th Division. Should such pillage be brought to the notice of any officer or noncommissioned officer it is his duty to immediately stop the action, report it to higher authority, and take necessary steps to prevent a recurrence.   By means of lectures and conferences every man of the Division must be impressed with the consciousness of his duty in this respect and taught to exercise his utmost energy to prevent such practices and maintain the honor of the American Army, of the 37th Division, and of his particular unit.   It should be impressed upon the men that the usual punishment by court-martial for such action is death.

39.   The material pertaining to aircraft brought down within the sector will not be disturbed in any way; it will be protected from depredation until taken in charge by proper authority.

40.   In advances commanders must see that supply officers specially detailed closely follow the advancing lines to take charge of all property encountered and to provide for the issue of provisions and forage captured.   This will require details of men to assist the officers who will

organize the party so that the property will be
guarded and issued equitably. It will be his
duty to co-operate with commanding officers in
maintaining the strictest order and discipline in
and about the places where stores are found.

SECRECY IN OPERATIONS

41. Military matters will not be discussed
in public places or at any time or place with
civilians. The enemy gains much information
through injudicious remarks dropped by officers and
enlisted men, and frequently dresses his agents in
the uniform of the United States or Allied officers
or soldiers to accomplish his ends.

42. Prompt report will be made to the
Intelligence Officer of any civilian seeking
military information or of anyone whose actions
are suspicious.

43. Questions which, if overheard, might be
of value to the enemy, will not be discussed in
front line trenches. The enemy has an elaborate
listening-in system and it will be safe to
presume that he picks up most of the conversations
indulged in close to his lines.

44. Maps or sketches will not be marked so
as to show our own or allied positions.
No document, map or letter will be
carried into front line trench which might be of
value to the enemy if captured. One of the most
valuable sources of information is the address of
a letter received by a soldier.

No document or insignia which, if captured or found by the enemy might disclose information, will be carried on patrol, raiding party or attacking unit. Patrols and raiding parties will be inspected by commanders sending them out, to see that no such articles are worn or carried.

45. Attention is invited to the following training which must be entered upon at the earliest practicable moment:

(a) Intensive Training in Gas - quickness in adjusting masks and in practice wearing masks for long periods.

(b) Practice for Hand Bombers and Rifle Grenadiers.

(c) Training of Automatic Rifle teams.

(d) Practice in all methods of Signaling and Liaison including instruction in the use of rockets, and signals of all characters.

(e) Previous training memorandums will be carefully examined and a study made of such data pertaining to present conditions.

46. THIS TRAINING MEMORANDUM WILL BE <u>STUDIES</u> IN CLASSES BY ALL OFFICERS AND NONCOMMISSIONED OFFICERS IN THIS DIVISION. IT WILL FURTHERMORE BE READ TO ASSEMBLED PLATOONS. IT WILL SERVE AS A BASIS FOR INSPECTION OF TROOPS.

By command of Major General Farnsworth:

Official: Dana T. Merrill,
                     L. Colonel, General Staff,
                          Chief of Staff.
R. E. Fraile,

Major, A.G.R.C.
Adjutant.

Note:-   Distribution to all officers and
additional copies, as indicated below, to each
infantry regiment (proportionate distribution
to separate battalions and other units) for
distribution to platoon sergeants.
Additional copies:

```
60 - Each Infantry Regiment.
10 - 134th M. G. Bn.
20 - 135th M. G. Bn.
20 - 136th M. G. Bn.
30 - 112th Engineers
 4 - 112th Engineer Train
20 - 112th Field Signal Bn.
10 - 112th Supply Train
20 - 112th Supply Train
 8 - 112th Military Police
 4 - Headquarters Troop
 2 - Each Sanitary Squad
 2 - Each Brigade Headquarters.
```

The Stars and Stripes, France, July 26, 1918

REAL MAIL TRAINS WORKING FOR A.E.F.; OTHERS TO FOLLOW

Delivery in Some Cases Cut from Two Days to Two Hours

SPEEDIER TRIP TO STATES

M.P.E.S. Officer Goes Home to Instruct Troops in Intricacies of Army Addresses

-----

Real railway mail trains, with the sorting of the precious envelopes and packages going on while the mail is being rushed to its destination, are now actualities in the A.E.F.

Already there are in operation railway mail trains between Tours and G.H.Q., from one of the base ports through Tours to Paris, and from two of the base ports to Tours, where the Central Post Office, A.E.F., is located. And there will be more to follow, notably one direct between Paris and G.H.Q.

Each one of these mail speeding devices comprises a postal car, an express car, and two bulk cars, with three men to each crew. Strong along the sides of the cars are sacks, one for each station on the route, and the letters are sorted and thrown into those sacks in time for them to be thrown off at their proper destinations. The system is almost exactly like that employed on the railway mail trains in the United States.

From Two Days to Two Hours

The value of these trains is primarily for mail within the A.E.F. It is estimated that, in certain instances, the time needed to get a letter from one point in France to another will be cut down from two days to two hours. That will make for the speeding up of official correspondence--even including the kind that goes "through channels"--and will enable the average A.E.F. man to get in closer and quicker touch with his pals in other units, or with his old unit if he is detached from it, in hospital or otherwise.

The new system will also help in hustling mail to the States, and in that connection it is proposed soon to establish a mail train running from Nantes, in the S.O.S., through to one of the base ports in the near future, with more to follow. So at last it looks as if Dad wouldn't have to cable, "No mail in six weeks. Mother much worried," the way he used to--that is, if Dad is the cabling kind.

Mail from the States will be generally accelerated by the speeding-up process applied to the other two kinds of mail.

Always a Rush Job

Unloading a mail boat at a base port is always an emergency or rush job, inasmuch as the postal authorities have nothing but a general hunch as to when the boat is to come in. When one does come in they bend all hands to the job, get the mail sorted as speedily as they can, and shoot it along the line, even to the uttermost regulating stations up front. To protect that mail in transit, to see that it doesn't go A.W.O.L. or get strayed from the unit for which it was intended, one man of the M.P.E.S. rides in every car of first class mail that is loaded at a port and shot up to a regulating station. Soon there will be also a man for every car of second class mail.

Transfer clerks have also been placed at every station in France where mail is to be distributed to units of the A.E.F. situated in that area. The duty of the transfer clerk is to receive the mail sacks dropped off at his center and see to its distribution to the various A.P.O's lying in his domain.

In case his station is at a railway junction, he sees to the transfer of sacks from the main line on which the railway mail train runs to the lines that will reach the A.P.O.'s that he serves. His is a new profession in the A.E.F.--that of postmaster and enlisted man combined.

Telling Them How Back Home

To facilitate still further the hastening of mail from the States to the fighting forces, an officer of the M.P.E.S. has been sent back to the old country for the express purpose of instructing the troops that are coming over in the necessary postal arrangements which they must make in order to give their home folks their correct addresses in France. This officer is also collaborating with the Federal postal authorities in the interest of more accurate sorting of mail before it is put on the shops, and in speeding the getting-over process generally.

Every effort is being made to see that the casual officer or man detached from his unit gets his mail in fair time and gets it all. As soon as the Central Records Office gets personnel enough o keep a record of each man up to the second, this will be a mere matter of minutes in noting the new address on the envelope.

The Stars and Stripes, France, July 26, 1918

YANKS HAVE SHARE IN GREAT VICTORY OF ALLIED ARMS

Germans' "Peace Offensive" Turned from Failure Into Disaster

ENEMY USES 60 DIVISIONS

Americans South of Soissons and Along Marne Push Foe On Into Deep Pockets

-----

On July 15, the Germans, under the generalship of Ludendorff, launched on a front of 120 kilometers their fifth great offensive of 1918--the biggest and most ambitious move they had undertaken since the drive of March 21.

They called it, and they taught their troops to call it, their Friedensturm or Peace Offensive. By that very name they promised their patient people a final blow of such force that the Allies would be driven to accept a German peace.

Ten days later the fight was still on. In those ten days more than 60 German divisions had been engaged and badly mauled. More than 30,000 German soldiers had vanished as prisoners, behind the advancing Allied lines. Between 400 and 500 German cannon had been taken and a great mass of German material had either been seized by our troops or destroyed hopelessly in the disordered German retreat.

Despite a most bitter resistance, victorious Allied armies were still advancing over reconquered territory. The proud citadel of Rheims not only had not been taken; it stood safer than ever. And the threat of a march on Paris was indefinitely postponed.

Initiative Passes to Allies

Above all, the initiative had passed to the Allies. Only a fortnight before, the German military critics had been boasting that the enfeebled Allies could never resume the initiative. "And," they explained, "whoever says initiative, says victory."

Ten days after the launching of the German offensive on which enemy military leaders had spend a month in preparation and on which they based such high hopes, the Crown Prince found some 40 divisions of his army caught in a narrow land steadily narrowing pocket--what was left of the bold salient he had thrust down between Soissons and Rheims in May. On three sides of this pocket, French, British, Italian and American troops were attacking, pounding mercilessly on German lines that had already receded at some places to a depth of 14 kilometers.

This pocket is almost as difficult to leave as it is dangerous to occupy, for a large part of its densely crowded area is swept by the Allied artillery, and its railroad line from Soissons to Chateau-Thierry was soon crossed and cut by the advancing Franco-American troops.

Narrow Path Through Center

This left only a narrow, insufficient path down the center of the pocket--at best a pitiably insufficient corridor for the easy withdrawal or for the reinforcement and adequate supply of the pocketed divisions, and now a corridor incessantly bombarded by the French, British and American aviators.

As the news of the turn of the tide reached Berlin, the observers at that deluded capital cheered themselves up by expatiating on the fact that, in the first rush of their drive, they had succeeded in crossing the Marne and establishing a strong bridge-head on its southern bank. Their journals dwelt lovingly on that fact in their issues of July 19.

The very next day, the last living uncaptured German had vanished from the southern bank of the Marne, and the pontoon bridges swung across its waters during the next two days were Allied bridges. At many places the anvil chorus of the bridge layers were played by the hammers of the American Engineers.

On Sunday, French and American soldiers were marching through the ruins of Chateau-Thierry and the American communiqué of Tuesday night told how our troops that were swarming over the Marne had gained possession of Jaurgonne, the little village whose walls witnessed some of the most savage encounters of that first June day when the hurrying Yankees took a hand in the fighting in this sector.

Failure Becomes Disaster

It was on July 18 that what had appeared up to then to be merely an historic German failure was turned with dramatic swiftness into an historic German disaster.

It was on July 18, while Ludendorff was trying as best he could to make something out of the small success he had gained between Rheims and the Marne, that General Foch suddenly appeared on the front between Soissons and Chateau-Thierry with an unexpected army of French and American troops.

In making this attack on a 28-mile front, much was sacrificed for the sake of surprise. Over bad roads, through nights of storm and blackness, troops were hurried to that sector and plunged into the counter-offensive without an hour's delay--without any artillery preparation. Some of our own troops gained the front line only just in time to go over the top at the appointed hour. Some, caught in the jam of traffic on the congested roads, had to double time to reach the line in time.

Swept Off Their Feet

Such 11th hour warnings as the enemy may have had did not lead him to expect, apparently, that the attack would come so soon or that it would ever come in such force.

The mass of Germans swept off their feet, the great quantity of guns and other material captured, the German officers and German men caught--literally--napping in their dugouts, the complete absence of any dangerous and poisonous traps left in the wake of their disordered retreat--all these things testified to the surprise that the Allied strategy achieved.

The fighting that followed was on a larger scale, was crowned with more spectacular success and was fraught with consequences of greater historical import than any fighting in which Yankee troops had shared since the war began. It was the first appearance of the American soldier in a major Allied offensive. It was the first major Allied offensive since the arrival of the A.E.F.

At many points in the line which dipped down from Soissons to Chateau-Thierry and up from there to Rheims, American units were engaged. They were in the thick of it. Where they were, the fighting was hottest.

Exultant and Swift Advance

The advance of the Infantry was exultant and swift. With tanks ahead of them and their own guns behind them, they went down over the top singing. Up hill and down, across fields, across streams, across ravines, the Infantry raced, driving the enemy before them, moving so fast that the machine guns couldn't keep up with them. They set a fearful pace for those following loyally with ammunition and supplies.

The various American regimental and brigade P.C.'s, the field hospitals and the other points which serve and trail behind the doughboys had the novel and exhilarating experience of moving forward three times in 48 hours. The unsung toilers of the Signal Corps, what with the pace of the

Infantry and the thunder of the barrage, found wiring in the forward area an impossible task during the first few days.

Messages had to be sped on their way by the T.P.S. or ground telegraphy, and by that ancient and honorable institution--the runner on the battle-field. The runners covered themselves with glory and one of them made spectacular distances by capturing a German bicycle and taking it for his own.

The craving for speed was contagious, and many a time when a French cavalryman would fall, you would see a Yankee made a leap for the horse, mount it at a running jump land go charging ahead with a strange, heathen-ish battle-cry all his own.

Enemy's Guns Used

German battery commanders were seized and sent to the rear. When a Yankee gun would be put out of business, a new German gun and German ammunition would be pressed into service in its place, and there were enough unharmed German guns and unexploded German ammunition left behind in the retreat to keep busy all the extra artillerymen the Americans could muster.

As the pressure was applied on the western side of the pocket, so it was applied also from the south and the east, and the yielding enemy withdrew from Chateau-Thierry on the morning of the 21st.

The French and American troops that moved through the town that day and the next found the French and American flags flying from the mai-rie. Here and there in the ruined streets an American canteen or a fragment of olive drab wood was found as mute mementoes of the men who died in those streets that first day the German offensive was halted in early June.

Found in *The 37th Division in the World War*

If one were to picture himself the Baccarat Sector as an orderly, symmetrical system of regularly, neatly arranged, cleanly chiseled trenches, fenced in by barbed wire barri-ers, and facing squarely a similar system occupied by the enemy, he would have a totally erroneous conception of the conditions under which the Thirty-seventh found itself oper-ating. So thinly held was the front line, for example, that it was easily possible to wander through the confusing maze of trenches and out into No Man's Land without realizing that the limit had been passed. All, or at least nearly all, of the trenches were in a poor state of repair. The wire likewise was inadequately maintained. The distance across No Man's Land varied from a few meters to one kilometer or sometimes to one and one-half kilometers.

...

A quiet sector; but the quietude was of a sort with which the Thirty-seventh had been totally unfamiliar. The tranquillity prevailing in the sector seemed to consist in nightly air raids during which German planes flew over the lines and dropped bombs at Baccarat, at Azerailles, at Neufmaisons, and around other villages and points in the sector. It seemed to consist in shelling of now this position and now that one, sometimes by day, sometimes by night. It consisted of raids against our lines by parties varying in size from a few men to a platoon. It consisted in calling for barrages against such attacks, in fighting them off with machine gun fire, automatic rifle fire, rifles, bayonets and hand grenades. It consisted in daily reconnaissance flights over our lines by German planes, and in combating them with anti-aircraft artillery. (vol. 2, 105-107)

The Stars and Stripes, France, July 26, 1918

ALONG THE FIGHTING FRONT FROM SOISSONS TO BELOW THE MARNE

In its first drive an American platoon, after advancing several kilometers, came into possession of a building which had been a German regimental headquarters. Personal effects scattered about, a half-cooked meal, maps and documents on tables and in racks told of the precipitate departure of the commander and his staff.

In the room which had been the office of the commandant was a dead dog. Attached to his collar was a metal tube. In the tube was a message calling for assistance from a German machine gun nest which, at the time of reading, had long since fallen into American hands.

The dog, trained as a message bearer, had been dispatched with the call for help, had been struck by a shell fragment, as was evidenced by a would in his side, and had struggled on to the headquarters, only to find it abandoned. He will be remembered and respected by the American platoon as one servant of the Kaiser who nobly did his duty and died.

A private of the buck species was watching a plane duel in the skies.

"Quite a sight," said a voice beside him, and his head nearly dropped off when he saw that it belonged to the general commanding the division.

There is a story in that same division, about the same general, which describes how he was seen one day recently walking along and chatting with a top sergeant. This shows that a use has at last been found for top sergeants.

That division did its share and paid its price for the doing, when it helped to drive the Hun back across the Marne. That night someone softly opened the general's door, and then as softly closed it. And the word went around that he sat with his face buried in his hands, and his frame quivering with sobs.

A long line of German prisoners, four abreast, in which were some Germans who admitted riding frontward not many weeks ago in trains bearing the placard, "Nach Paris," marched southward along a dusty French road in charge of a detachment of Americans from the unit which had captured them. The population of each succeeding village turned out to see the procession, watching it for the most part in silence, but always with a smile for the American guards.

There was one diminutive French soldier who stood exuberantly at a corner where the line turned.

"*Tout droit a Paris*," he explained, "tout droit"--which is the French road direction for straight ahead.

But the Germans couldn't see the joke.

Burly, dirty, whiskered, all in, but enthusiastic, a sergeant recounted the exploits of his platoon to his colonel.

His was a tale of the Boche infantry met and bested, of machine gun nests cleaned up at the point of the bayonet, of Germans killed and Germans captured.

"Makes a fellow feel pretty good, doesn't it?" observed the colonel.

"Yes, and it makes a fellow feel pretty glad that he's on this side , too, sir," said the sergeant.

An M.P. was standing in the doorway of the hotel de ville. It had been a quiet day, as days go a little way behind the lines. And just then the quietness came to an abrupt end, for a shell landed outside the hotel de ville, and the force of it knocked the M.P. down.

The M.P. got up and sniffed. He smelled gas.

The gas alarm was the bell in the village church. The M.P. ran to the church. While he was running another shell landed close enough to send him sprawling again.

Once more he got up, and this time made the church without any further Charlie Chaplin incidents. And he began to ring the bell like all getout. He hadn't been ringing it long before a shell hit the belfry, put the bell out of business, and blew the M.P. all the way back to the altar.

He got up, ran out of the church, stumbled on a man who had been stunned and took him into a dugout.

It was all in the day's work. And to prove how very workaday it all was, the M.P.'s name happens to have been Smith--Private Smith.

All kinds of things happen to helmets, and almost as many kinds of things happen to canteens. A cavalryman who was relaying messages had a piece of shrapnel related to him that flattened his canteen like a pancake. He was wearing the canteen on his hip at the time, so he didn't mind the water's running down all over his pants.

"And then I ran into some gas," he said. "We got through it all right, both of us. Of course, it didn't bother the horse, because he's got more room for it in his lungs."

Easy come, easy go.

One of the German regiments opposite the Americans, the members of which are, by this time, probably listed as "missing, believed prisoner," had just been paid when the curtain went down on their activity in *la guerre*.

Exactly 48 hours after the Germans marched before their paymaster and got their pay, they marched before an American officer, who relieved them of the modest collection of marks, pfennings, and other things they had received.

American regulations for the handling of prisoners provide that all money shall be taken from them and placed in a fund which is devoted to the common needs of prisoners.

Rules specify that no P.G. shall be deprived of his personal effects-- Iron Crosses and the like--but almost any captured German is willing to sacrifice anything he has for real tobacco.

When one Boche arrived before the examining officer and was told to empty his pockets, he laud out five partly filled sacks of American makin's, and not much else. For it he had traded off an Iron Cross, his helmet, a trench knife, and all the buttons he could spare.

A certain American private wasn't satisfied, however, with any modest, vest pocket souvenirs of the battle. Nothing would do for him, he explained, but a German machine gun.

After his unit was relieved he went to a salvage pile, selected a weapon in good order, and carried it, in addition to his full pack and rifle, all the long, weary kilometers back to *repos*.

It was not until after he had arrived that he discovered it was a French and not a German gun he had seized. We won't repeat his remarks when he made the discovery.

The composition of the perfect M.P. is as follows: Suspicion, 90 per cent; more suspicion, 10 per cent; total, 100 per cent and then some. All men, according to the M.P. at the front, are created equally suspicious characters. Rank, or the lack of it, mean absolutely nothing.

If you have any doubts, you can ask a certain French lieutenant colonel who is attached to a certain American divisions. He was going along a road toward the front when an M.P. stopped him. Most people do get stopped.

The colonel tried to explain, but the M.P. simply couldn't see him, and the colonel was at the end of his wits and his language. As a last resort he sent for his orderly, who happened to be a little Irishman of the combative variety common to the A.E.F.

The little Irishman came flying over the roads, via motor, and cleared his superior in short order. But if it hadn't been for the little Irishman, there is no telling where the French colonel would be now.

All of which goes to prove that no officer is a hero to his dog-robber.

A cavalryman who was doing Paul Revere work between a headquarters and the line tied his horse to a tree and proceeded on foot to his destination, where things were rather hot.

While he was gone things began to grow rather hot around that tree, too. He has pretty good evidence that they did, anyway. For when he returned, there was a gaping hole in the earth where the horse had stood. A bit of rope dangling from the tree.

Be he a private or a general, "writing home" usually occupies the first leisure minutes of a soldier just out of action.

Parked near the headquarters of a unit back from the line was an impressive limousine, and in it sat a major general, pounding on the keys of a small portable typewriter held on his lap. He had sought the privacy of his automobile to write home.

The Q.M. Corps had fallen down on the job. It is rather tough to have to admit this, but it is proved by the fact that the mahogany Louis Quatorze writing desks ordered for individual soldiers with brass studded legs--the desks, of course--have never shown up.

So everybody uses the next best thing--a 20-gallon gasoline can, preferably empty. It sometimes rolls off your knees when you are trying to write on it, but otherwise it's O.K.

When he reached the gas hospital he was in a state of extraordinary good humor.

"What are you so happy about," they asked him.

"That's easy," he replied between smiles. "I'm going to get some clean underwear."

How much stuff does a Yank take into the line? It all depends on the Yank.

In one squad you will see a man carrying full pack, including extra shoes and overcoat, and wearing a whole strung of corned Willie cans much as a Fiji Islander wears a loin cloth. Another man in the same squad will go up minus his blouse, and carrying only a blanket, gas mask and helmet.

Nothing makes an American soldier prouder of his organization than being in action with it. Any man up front will tell you that his platoon is the best in the company, that his company is the best in the regiment, and his regiment is the best in the Army--that the artillery of his division is infallible and the officers are unbeatable. The colonel always comes in for praise.

"Our colonel," said one doughboy, "may be stout and not much for height, but you ought to soldier under him. He's a regular fellow. Why, he's the kind of a guy that if he was in the ranks would make a good private!"

Which is about the highest tribute a private can pay to his colonel.

A French officer stood on a hilltop south of the Marne and trained his glasses on the field where Yank and Boche were having it out.

As he looked he smiled. For through the smoke he could see doubled Yankee fists finding their desired target on the tips of Hun noses and the points of Hun jaws.

He belonged to that five per cent slice of the Army that doesn't smoke. His unit was stationed in a wood, and as he had all the Yankee's skill with a pocket knife, he whittled himself a pipe in his spare time. Now he smokes. If the chance of war had stationed him in a marble quarry, he would probably have turned into a sculptor.

One of the regiments which took part in the "Soissons push" was relieved in the line just after nightfall, marched back, and established camp at the edge of a peaceful village. About 1 o'clock the next afternoon the soldiers awoke, partook of a late breakfast of coffee, bread and beans, and began to talk it over.

At 1:30 the bandmaster called his command together and marched it to headquarters to serenade the colonel. They started with "Over There," with the accent on "We won't be back till it's over." Everybody at headquarters sang the refrain, including the colonel.

"But," said the colonel, at the conclusion of the piece, "if you want to serenade somebody, serenade the men. Come on, and I'll go with you."

With the colonel marching at its head, the band made the round of the regiment, serenading each battalion in turn.

"This is my party," said the colonel, "for the best regiment of fighting men in the world."

The farther you get into France--in other words, the nearer you get to the front,--the less French you hear. That explains why the headquarters troop top was discouraged.

"I've been in France three months," he said, "and I only know seven words of French. And I was in Mexico two months, and learned ten words of Spanish."

The colonel had led them into the fight, and it was the colonel's all-seeing eye which noticed that the little 18-year-old private had been gassed.

"Get back!" he shouted. "You've done your bit--get back!"

So the little private dutifully got back. On the way he passed a farm. In a shed were six Boches whom the fight had swept past without noticing.

Their hands went up in a jiffy. When the little private reported at the dressing station for treatment, the six were still with him.

Your M.P. must escort the prisoners to the rear, and there has been quite a lot of this job lately up Chateau-Thierry way. One captured lieutenant got quite a way down the road with a pistol hidden on him, and, in a moment of irritation at the guying he was getting from 50 of his own men who were goose-stepping cheerfully into bondage with him, he took a pot shot at the M.P.

The M.P. was wounded, but not disabled, and a pistol duel followed: in another moment there was one less Prussian junker in this vale of tears. The outcome was greeted with unaffected delight by all the other prisoners, who were reveling in the first chance to speak their minds that they had had in all their days.

One burly and bristling exemplar of German militarism with Captains knots on his shoulder and an iron cross on his chest was included in a recent bag of prisoners. He was indignant, to say the least, at the time of his capture, and the mood intensified as he was marched back to the intelligence officer.

He hadn't heard the questioning officer speak more than five words of German before he burst into the conversation.

"Do you allow privates to call officers by their first names in this Army?" he demanded witheringly.

"Why?" asked the officer.

"Well, this pig," said the Boche, "called me Heinie every time he addressed me."

A German lieutenant came before the officer who was listing and tagging prisoners.

"What's your name?" he was asked.

"Johannes Jacobi."

"Any relation to Willhelm Jacobi?" asked the American officer.

"A brother," said the Boche in surprise.

"Well, if you look around when you get there, you'll find him in the prisoners' pen. We got him, too."

The doughboys in the push south of Soissons have the greatest respect for the French tanks that went over the top with them and almost a love for their game little French operators. From the outset the Yanks and the tanks worked well together.

"The tank I was with saved my life five times," said one admiring soldier, "and if I ever run across the Frenchman who was operating the machine gun on the nigh side I'm going right up and kiss him French fashion, whiskers and all."

A lanky private was detailed to take a captured German artillery officer to regimental headquarters. He had progressed about half a mile when the American noticed that his charge was tearing up some papers he evidently didn't want to get into American hands and scattering the pieces along the road.

"Ain't you the cute cuss?" said the American. "Now you just go back and pick them all up."

The officer may not have understood the instructions, but he did the gestures which accompanied them, and he complied. He spent the next half-hour painstakingly gathering the fragments of a map which, when pasted together, showed all the Boche artillery positions in his sector.

If the open fighting that some of the troops are undergoing keeps up we will have to invent some new slang. They still speak of going over the top, but it isn't satisfactory because, as a matter of fact, there sometimes isn't any top for the reason that there isn't any trench--or not much of a trench, anyhow.

"Going out after 'em" has been used. Anybody got any other suggestions?

Found in *The 37ᵗʰ Division in the World War*

On 27ᵗʰ July Field Orders No. 2, Hq. 37ᵗʰ Division, 27ᵗʰ July, 1918, 5:00 P.M. announced that the division would relieve the 77ᵗʰ Division. This order specified that the... 148ᵗʰ [Infantry replaced] the 308ᵗʰ.... The order further directed that "when our battalions occupy the first position the battalions of the 77ᵗʰ Division will withdraw two platoons (less grenade throwers, rifle grenadiers and automatic riflemen) for each company. The remainder of their personnel will be amalgamated with our first line battalions." (vol. 2, 74)

148th Regiment War Diary for July 27, 1918

Regimental Command group moved forward to third line. 1st Battalion moved forward marching during the night and taking cover at day break. Air raid at night lasting about twenty minutes before All Clear sounded. Balance of Regiment on Gas defense work, range, grenade etc.

148th Regiment War Diary for July 30, 1918

Aeroplane raided surrounding villages dropping
two bombs and using Machine Gun fire, circling
over village, raid lasting about 30 minutes. Anti
aircraft guns active. All clear sounded at 11.30
PM. Headquarters to march to Fontenoy to "STONE"
light marching order, condition of men excellent.

3rd Battalion War Diary for July 30, 1918

Position #3, Clezentaine. 17 officers, 714
enlisted men. Routine duty entire sector.
Weather: clear. Roads: good. Health: excellent.

Company L Strength Return for July, 1918

    4 officers present
    2 officers absent
  202 enlisted men present
   18 enlisted men absent
    . . .
    Alfred M. Barlow 1st Lt; Special Duty Town
Mayor (village of Clezentaine).

148th Infantry Regiment Strength Return for July, 1918
. . .
Officers
148th Regiment:
Col. James A. Lynch
Lt. Col. Karl I. Best
Major Leon E. Smith
Major William L. Marlin
. . .

Co. L:
Capt. Estel L. Stewart
1st Lt. Alfred M. Barlow
1st. Lt. George F. Wunder
1st. Lt. Nathan S. Clark
2nd Lt. George J. Waterhouse
2nd Lt. Thomas J. Weaver

Chapter Six

Found in *The 37ʰ Division in the World War*

Battalions ordered to move were directed to send forward billeting parties to their destinations. Troop movements were to be made under cover of darkness and troops were to be bivouacked under cover of woods and remain under cover in daytime.

The relief was ordered, at 9:30 A.M., per F.O. No. 3, Hq. 37th Division A.E.F., 31 July, 1918.

This order directed that, on the night of August 2-3, the 1st and 2nd Battalions of the 145th Infantry and 147th Infantry should relieve the 308th and 306th Infantry, respectively, in the first, or front line and in the second, or support line positions. At the same time, the Third Battalions of the 145th Infantry and of the 147th Infantry and the 148th Infantry were ordered to move forward to the Reserve or Meurthe Positions at Bertichamps, Grande Boivre and Gelacourt, respectively. On the night of the 3rd and 4th August the 1st and 2nd Battalions of the 146th Infantry and 148th Infantry were to relieve the 307th Infantry and 305th Infantry in the first and second positions.

The First Battalion, 148th Infantry, entered the front line trenches on 28th August, as the First Battalion, 305th Infantry moved out. (vol. 2, 76-77)

(FOR OFFICIAL CIRCULATION ONLY)

Hq. 37th Division,
American E. F.,
1 August, 18.

BULLETIN NO. 44.

1. Inspection by the Commanding General of the units of this Division shows clearly that

the provisions of existing orders respecting
inspections, cleanliness and orderliness of
billets, protective measures against gas and
bombing, are not carried out in all organizations
of this Division. The Commanding General directs
me to state that all of these have been the
subject of orders from these Headquarters and
contained in the current series of bulletins,
the bulletin of yesterday particularly calling
attention to the necessity for taking cover
against bombing and requiring officers and men
to enter and remain within shelters during the
continuance of bombing or gas attacks.

      Wherever casualties occur in this Division
resulting from bombing or gas, an investigation
will be made from these Headquarters and, where
it is shown that proper protective measures have
not been taken by responsible officers and non-
commissioned officers, action will be taken against
the negligent parties.

<u>BARRAGES</u>

      2.   (a) In the normal case, barrage
"A" (the barrage in front of the most advanced
outguards, also called "normal Barrage") will
be required before barrages "B" and "C" (the
barrages in front of the lines of resistance).
It may happen, however, that through error or on
account of exceptional circumstances a call for
two barrages (A and B, A and C, or B and C) may be
received by the artillery at about the same time.
In such case, it being impracticable to lay down
both barrages, the order of priority of barrages
will be as follows: (1) barrage "A", (2) barrage
"B", (3) barrage "C".

      (b) The barrage signals are published
by Divisional or higher authority.

(c)　When a barrage is called for, the artillery continues to fire for ten minutes unless directed otherwise.　If the infantry which the artillery is supporting desires the barrage to continue longer than ten minutes there must be a second call for the barrage.　This call may be by rocket signal after the completion of the first barrage, or it may be by telephone during or after the first barrage.

(d)　The artillery sends to each infantry battalion headquarters in the front line an officer for liaison purposes.　This officer must be furnished by the infantry battalion commander with an interpreter, who must be prepared to report to the liaison officer at 8:00 A.M., August 2nd.　It is the duty of this liaison officer to verify by phone a rocket signal for a barrage. It is also his duty to supervise the work of the French artillery non-commissioned officer furnished front line companies and to assist in every way the co-ordination of the work of infantry and artillery.

(e)　The French artillery also furnished one non-commissioned officer to each battalion in the front line.　Each of these non-commissioned officers must be furnished an interpreter by the battalion commander and must be given all the fire signals and informed of lines of communication. These interpreters must be prepared to report to the non-commissioned officers at 8:00 A.M., August 2nd.

(f)　Each infantry unit, no matter how small, that has authority to call for a barrage must have a permanent detail for handling rockets and other artillery signals.　The men of this detail must be so arranged that one or more will be always present at the unit to give the signals.

No other men will be permitted to handle the
rockets or give the artillery signals when men of
the permanent detail are present. Signals calling
for barrage will be given only on the order of a
commissioned officer.

(g)   Counter preparation fire by
artillery is the artillery fire delivered in front
of the location of the normal barrage and before
the normal barrage occurs. It is intended to
demoralize the enemy's organizations that are
forming for the assault. Counter preparation
fire will be asked for only by battalion or higher
commanders.

(h)   There is a different kind of rocket
for each different kind of barrage. In order that
our artillery may not fire upon our own men it is
very important that there be no mistake made in
the kind of rocket used for signal. Therefore
all commanders will at once cause rockets to
be inspected, sorted, and placed in proper
places so that there will be no probability of
an error being made in rocket signals. It will
be exceptional when there will be necessity for
having more than one kind of rocket on the same
line. Under no circumstances should the different
kinds of rockets be kept in the same receptacles
or in receptacles that are near each other.

3.   The attention of all is called to the
importance of accuracy in making intelligence
reports. Where observers or others report
occurrences as taking place in a certain
town or along a certain road or in any other
certain vicinity when, as a matter of fact, the
occurrences are taking place in some other town,
on some other road, or in some other vicinity,
all higher commanders are likely to be misled and

there may result orders which will entail losses of life or material of our trips, and failure to destroy enemy activity or material.

4. Anti-Tank rifles and their ammunition which may be taken on the Army front, will be sent to the 2nd Bureau of the 8th Army (French). The Bureau advises that rewards as follows will be given for such rifles and their ammunition:-

> 100 Francs for the first rifle sent
> to the 2nd Bureau,
> 50 Francs for additional rifles,
> 5 Francs each for the first 25
> cartridges,
> 2 Francs each for the following
> 50 cartridges.

5. Huts that have been previously used for ammunition by the VIth Army Corps (French), and which may now be vacant, are not available for use for the shelter of any kind of stores by organizations of the 37th Division.

By command of Major General Farnsworth:

Official:

Dana T. Merrill,
L. Colonel, General Staff,
Chief of Staff.

R. E. Fraile,
Major, A.G.R.C.
Adjutant.

Aug. 1, 1918

Dear Mamma and all,

Everything is well with me. Do you get your money from the government. I hope you do. If you once get it it will come steady after that. This is my third letter. I have not heard from you. My address is

Don't put more on.

> *Lt. A M Barlow*
> *Co L 148 Inf*
> *Amer. E. F.*

Via New York

It is quite cool here. I'm coming along quite well with my French. The lady I am billeted with has two daughters who are school teachers and have both been graduated from Normal school

I am enclosing some stamps as letters are free now.

I could write very interesting things if it were permitted.

Just to think in America I slept on a cot now I am sleeping in a bed with a big room to myself and the room costs me 10 cents a day and the government pays 20 cents.

I turn my rations over to these people and buy some things extra and have fine meals. --for the present.

In about two or three months I expect to get a leave of absence and then I will go to England if possible.

We have for breakfast only scalded milk but with sugar. Big meal at eleven and another at 7 or 7:30 p.m. It does not get dark until about ten o'clock.

This is probably the last time I'll have a chance to write for a month.

With lots of love,

Write soon,

Alfred

P.S. I have not heard from you yet.

Censored A M Barlow 1st Lt Inf N.G.

3rd Battalion War Diary for August 2, 1918

Enemy artillery active about 3:00 am until 4:30 am - shrapnel bursting in our vicinity.
Following movements took place:
Company K, from position at Vaxainville to Hablainville.
Company I, from position in Bois Bouvroye to Pettonville.
2 days rations, 5 days forage with troops. 10 officers and 632 men available for all duty. Weather: cloudy-breezes. Roads: dry and hard. Health:excellent.

The Stars and Stripes, France, August 2, 1918

YANKEES HUMBLE GERMANY'S BEST IN OURCQ BATTLE

Prussian Guard Is Driven from Sergy in Hand to Hand Fighting

FORD RIVER TO MEET FOE

Ammunition Dumps Seized, Guns Turned on Hun--You Can Bathe in the Marne Now

-----

The end of July, the end of the fortnight which launched the grandiose offensive of the Crown Prince saw the Germans fighting more and more stubbornly in an ever narrowing pocket between Soissons and Rheims, fighting no longer on the Marne, but on the Ourcq, with Fere-en-Tardenois, the main crossroads of the pocket, reached, seized and held by the forces of the Allies.

The German offensive, which began badly, halted and then turned into a German retreat, had, in the course of a fortnight between characterized by the greatest capture of guns and ammunition the Allies have ever made on the western front and the deepest Allied advance in battle since the first Battle of the Marne.

The same historic fortnight confirmed the reports that Allied forces had taken a foothold on the White Sea, and that 10,000 kilometers from Chateau-Thierry Japanese troops were entering the war by way of far Siberia, two rallying points for all who hate and fear the German in that vast domain which was once the realm of the Romanoffs.

And word comes from Milan of the jubilant acclaim with which American troops were received in the streets of that Italian city as they marched through on their way to the Piave front.

August 2, 1918--and all's well.

News of the turn in the tide of events has slowly seeped into startled Germany, and even the official note of explanations makes illuminating reading. From its text, as set forth in the *Frankfort Gazette* and other

Boche journals, this paragraph is not without its interest to the Yankee fighting man:

"Thus the destructive power of our enemies is far from being broken. The enemy is using reserves to which are being added daily American troops of which we should not underestimate the fighting worth."

Ourcq Another Antietam

The fighting worth of a good many American units was being tested by the Germans in the savage engagements fought from the beginning of this week, and the Ourcq has taken its place in pages of American history as another Antietam. Speaking at a dinner in Paris on Monday night, M. Andre Tardieu, High Commissioner from the French Republic in Washington, said to his hosts:

"Today on the Ourcq an American division beat the first division of the Prussian Guard."

That was describing in a sentence the climax of ten days of fighting-- ten days in which Yankee troops pursued the Germans over a torn and reeking countryside, pushing ahead in some places as far and as fast as 15 kilometers in three days.

It was ten days of fighting against stubborn rearguards and nests of machine guns. What it means to clean up a forest with snipers in many a tree and every thicket deadly with a hidden machine gun, only those can tell who have lived through such memories as the Bois de Trugy and the capture of Epieds.

The Stars and Stripes, France, August 2, 1918

CROIX DE GUERRE NOW LEGALLY WORN

President Approves Bill Giving A.E.F. Right to Decoration

Decorations bestowed on American soldiers by the Governments of any nation at war with the Central Powers may now be worn without violating any law of the United States.

The Army Appropriation bill, as approved by the President last month, gives the specific permission demanded by the Constitution of the United States before foreign decorations may be worn.

The bill also stipulates that American citizens who have received since August 1, 1914, decorations for distinguished service in the armies or in connection with the filed service of the nations at war with Germany shall be permitted to wear those decorations on entering the military service of the United States.

This act, among other things, allows men who have been awarded the Croix de Guerre by the French Government to wear it without flying in the face of the constitution. It also permits General Pershing to wear the Grand Cross of the Order of the Bath bestowed on him by Great Britain.

The Stars and Stripes, France, August 2, 1918

AMERICAN UNITS EAST OF RHEIMS DID THEIR SHARE

Less Spectacular Part of Battle Even More Complete Check

HUNS HALTED IN TRACKS

Yankees Get in Great Work With Bayonet During Vain Thrust for Chalons

-----

When, on the morning of July 15, the long-delayed German offensive was launched on both sides of unyielding Rheims, the world's searchlight swung along the line and settled at that point where, furiously resisted by Fanco-Yanko Infantry and Artillery, the enemy slung his score of bridges and swarmed across the Marne.

There was movement there, movement and visible crisis, and the watching world was so intent that it scarcely noticed what was happening east of Rheims. It scarcely noticed what was happening because nothing happened. Twenty-five picked divisions from the armies of the Crown

Prince flung themselves triumphantly against 35 kilometers of the Allied line. And nothing happened.

As surf dashes against a granite breakwater, so this huge, confident German army dashed against the Allied line. It is back where it started from, with 50,000 casualties to charge up to profit and loss. In the opinion of officers high in the French staff, this was the severest defeat either side had suffered on the western front in three years. It made possible the counter-offensive which was sprung three days later on the salient between Rheims and Soissons.

There is not a shadow of doubt that the Germans expected as swift an advance as they had experienced in their big thrusts in March and in May. But this time there were two elements present which had not been present in March and in May. One element was the exact advance knowledge that the French command possessed as to the place, the force and even the hour of the offensive. The other element was the American soldier--in great numbers.

The Yanks Drop In

That Champagne sector was commanded by General Gouraud, him they call the lion of the Argonne. He was the youngest general France had in August, 1914. One arm is gone now, one hip is shattered and the wound stripes on his sleeve are five. There were Americans among the troops who received his now famous order announcing that the offensive was at hand and that there should be no weakening. There was none.

The Americans had just dropped in. An unending stream of them had been passing by, bound for another job elsewhere, and it was a little as though the general had come out to his gate and said:

"Hello, Americans. If you're looking for a fight, there's going to be one here pretty soon. Come in and take a hand."

And they did. They got there just in time. They found themselves in one of the oldest and most perfect defensive positions on the front, a land so netted with trenches for a depth of many kilometers that it is like a wrinkled old face. There are so many of them and their web is so intricate that it is difficult to say of any line that is marks the second or third or fourth trench.

As the known hour on the night of July 14 approached, the Allied artillery got ready. Fifteen minutes before zero it began a startling and deadly

fire which caught in their forward area the German divisions packed densely there for the intended advance.

Unforgettable Bayonet Work

Our fire kept them from going back and they had not yet received the
order to go forward. Thus caught, they were so badly mauled that one division had to be withdrawn incapacitated at the last moment.

Then at the appointed hour the German barrage dropped its rain of
death into our first line. But that first line was empty. General Gouraud had
quietly drawn all his forces backward to an intermediate position--a kilometer or so behind--and there they waited for the oncoming Germans, who did
not know where they were.

When meet they did, the fight that followed was fierce beyond any
power or words to tell. As far as the American units were concerned--and
particularly was this true of one regiment among them--there was precious
little shooting, but such bayonet work as the men who saw and did it will
never forget.

The battle line swayed a little. Here and there, the Germans pushed
their way in, only to be pushed bloodily out again. It was a scrimmage inde-
scribable, a fight to a standstill, and once when a party of Germans made off
with a knot of French prisoners, a party of Yanks went howling after them
and came back with the whole crew, German and French both.

The Men Who Waited for Death

That offensive on the line east of Rheims began at 4.17 on the morning of July 15. By 11 o'clock on the same morning, the Champagne offensive was over--definitely, completely finished. It had gained nothing, unless you count that strip of evacuated trench that was vacated before they
started. Since then, at his ease and without meeting any resistance whatever, General Gouraud has quietly taken the greater part of it back.

And the Germans had expected to be in Chalons that same night--
Chalons, a good 20 miles to the south. The captured orders show not only
that they were to be there that night, but show, too, the officer personnel appointed to administer the town and distribute its rich food and wine stores
to the triumphant army.

No Nearer Than Before

The Germans are now no nearer Chalons than they were the day they
started, and if you leave it to any of the Americans who helped bar their path
to tell the reasons, you will first have to hear their glowing account of the

French machine gunners, who did not leave the first line trench at all, but stayed there alone to confuse the advance and cut to pieces as many of the Huns as they could before their own turn came, as come it surely would.

One of these machine gunners was not killed, but captured. Later he escaped. His brothers in arms welcomed back the dirtiest, hairiest, tiredest, happiest poilu you ever saw, and they stopped all proceedings then and there to put another decoration on his already magnificent bosom.

The Stars and Stripes, France, August 2, 1918

ALL MAIL DELAYS NOT P.S.'S FAULT

Incorrect Addresses Large Factor on Holding Up Deliveries

"E.F., N.Y." IS NOT ENOUGH

Neither Is "Company E, U.S. Infantry"--157 John Smiths Licking Huns
-----

Incorrectly addressed mail is contributing its share to the difficulties of delivering letters and packages to the members of the A.E.F.

Twenty-one per cent of the mail arriving in France in June for American soldiers--a total of 700,000 letters and 65,000 sacks of paper mail was insufficiently or improperly addressed, according to statistics compiled by the postal service. Instead of being sent direct to its ultimate destination from the distributing stations at the base ports, it had to be forwarded to the Central Post Office at St. Pierre des Corps, near Tours, where clerks went through directories of the A.E.F., readdressed it, and forward it to the men for whom, in their judgment, it was intended.

This task is a difficult one because there is hardly a name in the A.E.F. now which is not duplicated several times. There are, for example, 157 John Smiths, 105 Henry Browns, 94 James Wilsons, 52 Henry Jacksons, and 41 William Blacks serving under General Pershing against the Huns.

"Company J, Pershing's Army"

The letter addressed, "Private John Foster, Company J, Pershing's Army" and the one addressed Private Carmelo Abiss, E.F., New York," probably will reach their rightful owners, but it will take time. Four-fifths of the misaddressed 21 per cent received in June was addressed merely "Somewhere in France" or "A.E.F.," with no company or regimental designation.

The postal service declares that much confusion would be avoided and much labor saved by observing these rules:

"Notify all from whom you expect mail of your address immediately.

"Have your mail addressed to you regiment and company, or, if you are on detached service and have a permanent station, to the office or branch of the service to which you are attacked, with the A.P.O. number.

"If you have recently changed stations, notify the Central Post Office, St. Pierre des Corps, of your new address on cards which may be obtained at any A.P.O.

The Correct Form
"The following form of address should be used:
>Sergt. John Smith,
>>Co. A, 95th Regt. Infantry,
>>>American Ex. Forces
>A.P.O. (May be given if desired.)

--or if on detached service and permanently stationed:
>Corporal John Smith,
>>Q.M. Corps,
>>A.P.O. ---."

Here are some examples of improperly addressed mail for which the postal service now is seeking owners:
>Mr. Bennie Hill, colored,
>>Colored Regiment,
>>>Somewhere in France.
>Mr. Geff Patrick,
>>Moxhlehugg 1st Lt.,
>>>Soldiers' Mail.
>Mr. Stewart Apaulding,
>>Military Mail, Foreign Service,
>>>Passed by Censor, A.E.F.,
>>>>New York.

Private Howard E. Donegan,
Company E, U.S. Infantry.

Stars and Stripes, France, August 2, 1918

WAR AS THEY'RE WAGING IT SOMEWHERE SOUTH OF SOISSONS

An American lying wounded in a wheat field was somewhat taken aback by the spectacle, in slow and stately approach, of a German officer. He was magnificent with medals and he wore a monocle.

Every once in a while his impressiveness was spoiled by a nervous turn of the head and the suspicion of a squirm--just as if someone were tickling his tail with a bayonet.

Someone was, for looking beyond, the wounded American saw a great, big, husky American negro prancing along, showing every tooth in his head.

"Hi-yi, boss," he called out jubilantly, "Ah don' know what Ah's got, but Ah's bringin' it along!"

Mess sergeants are just the same, whether they're in Kansas City, Missouri, or Chateau-Thierry, France--always suspicious that the whole Army is trying to edge in on their company mess.

The beans ran low--which will indicate the gravity of the situation--in a company that was having its first hot meal out of the lines.

"Three hundred and seventeen men I've fed," finally exploded the mess sergeant. "Three hundred and seventeen! And when we went into line we were only 250 strong. You'd think a company would lose when it's fighting, but it don't. It *gains*."

The American regiments that share in the avalanche which fell on the German line between Soissons and Chateau-Thierry are groaning under the weight of the souvenirs.

Nearly every man wears a "Gott Mit Uns" buckle on his belt till you would think it was a Q.M. issue on which regulations insisted. Nearly every man carried a German watch, many of them handsome watches shielded by metal trench cases. One doughboy had 14 watches--"time to burn," as he waggishly put it.

Some brandish Luger pistols, and the lucky ones can be seen these days staring into the distance through fine German field glasses and trying to look as much like generals as possible. But the prizes are Iron Crosses. Every Yankee wants to win the Iron Cross in a manner not contemplated by the Kaiser.

While the Franko-Yanko troops were chasing the Germans between the Aisne and the Ourcq, the generals were happily counting the stocks of ammunition and the hundreds of guns that were falling into their hands. But the hungry doughboy, lean from three days on iron rations and not too much of that, was happily devouring the food supplies they found in many a hastily abandoned dugout.

Never before in its history did the American Army eat so much weiner and pumpernickel as it did that great day

-----

In the midst of the battle one young lieutenant, running into a pal of his, showed him under the flap of his pocket a little gold brooch.

"If anything should happen to me," he said, "try to get hold of this pin, will you, and when you get time ship it back home to my mother."

The other promised, and the lieutenant went his way. He had not gone 20 feet when he was struck by a shell and killed instantly. The pin is on its way to America.

The captain looked suspiciously at his left trench-shoe

"A machine gun bullet went through the heel near the Marne," he said, "and yesterday another went straight across my foot between the sole and my stocking. It didn't do more than scorch me. But if they hit this darned shoe again, I'm going to get a new pair. They seem to think I'm Achilles."

A tattered doughboy, too new from battle to have been either shaved or deloused, was exhibiting an ornate and ugly revolver he had taken from a German officer.

"I'd like to have that," said an Artilleryman. "Us guys are so far behind we never get a chance at any good souvenirs like that."

"Take it," said the Infantryman, "it's yours."

"Why," demanded the Infantryman's buddy afterward, "did you give that revolver away?"

"Aw," said the doughboy, "we'll be going over the top again in a week or so, and I'll have a chance to get all I want."

To those who hung about France through a long, monotonous winter of wondering if the American Army would ever get started, there is something startling in the occasional discovery of a young Infantryman who sailed from New York as late as June 12 and yet went over the top with the veterans on July 18.

On a dusty roadside near the front of a line of empty trucks were halted at various rakish angles, their wheels caked with mud. The drivers snored in the seats or lay stretched on in the wheatfield alongside. Everything was still save for the distant boom of the guns and finally the rat-a-tat-tat, not of a masked machine gun, but of an unseen typewriter.

A passerby trailed the sound to the interior of one of the trucks and within saw a soldier sitting in the throes of composition, his bandaged foot resting on a sack of oats.

"You poor stiff, do they make you do paper work way up here?"

"Paper work, hell!" he replied affably. "I'm writing a letter to my girl."

One young lieutenant who was grazed three times by shrapnel was finally so badly wounded in the leg that he had to be carried to the first aid station. Later, he was put into the first truck going to the rear, and when he saw them lifting in a friend of his who had collapsed from shell-shock, he volunteered to hold him in his arms.

The lieutenant got his fifth wound when a shell came out of space and struck and killed his friend as he was cradling him.

Listing prisoners is always interesting work.

Ernst Herman wore the insignia of an aspirant. In his pockets he had the epaulets of a second lieutenant. His period of probation over, he was to have become a lieutenant the next day. Had he been captured 12 hours later, he would have been an officer and--he wouldn't have had to work all the time he remains in captivity.

"Kaiser," said the next prisoner when asked his name.

"Holy Smoke!" exclaimed the doughboy who brought him in, "I've captured the main show."

"Kaiser," repeated the prisoner, "Conrad Kaiser, and I'm 36 years old."

Up to the time that Germany's dwindling man-power caused the military finger to beckon him, Kaiser had been a college professor.

"Will they send us to America?" asked the next prisoner, an artillery captain. He was told that "they" wouldn't, and expressed regret.

"I had decided to go to America after the war anyhow," he explained. "There is nothing more for me in Germany. My father and mother were killed by an air bomb and my two brothers died in action. I'm the only one of the family left."

The American ambulance sections attacked to the French Army are the boys that have the pets, it's so easy for them to carry a mascot around. But one of the sections has had bad luck with theirs. Now they have a puppy chosen because its coat is a perfect olive drab.

They have tried dogs before and angoras. They have tried foxes. One was named Minna and was run over. One was named Pinard and died a quarter of an hour after they had bought them from a poilu. They had paid 15 francs for him. Too expensive, they thought--a franc a minute.

It must be admitted that Pinard died of drinking cognac. That the moral of that is---

-----

This didn't happen to an American, but it made some Americans gasp, and boosted the blue coats one more notch in their estimation.

A French balloon observer was attached to an American unit. For four days he went up in his bulby sausage and remained there unperturbed by whistling shells, directing the fire of American batteries. On the fifth day a German airplane dived from a low cloud with its machine gun going. The balloon dissolved in flame and smoke, and the observer took to his parachute.

The Boche airman, not content with destroying the sausage, pursued the Frenchman as he floated down, pumping bullets at the outspread umbrella. And the Frenchman coolly drew his revolver and answered the Boche's fire.

Stars and Stripes, France, August 2, 1918

LEMONADE SERVED ON EDGE OF BATTLE

Salvation Army Beverage Helps to Quell Fever of Wounded

MOSQUITO NETTING, TOO

And the War Doughnut Is Present in Force, Just As You'd Expect

-----

When the wiping out of the Soissons-Rheims salient becomes a mere incident in the growing list of German victories that might have been, there will probably be no item better remembered by men who were wounded while on that little job than the item of lemonade.

One division in particular will thank the Salvation Army with pocket-books open for the carload of juicy yellow Italian fruit that happened to be near enough to Soissons and to Chateau-Thierry to make a real Yank drink for Yank wounded available in the thick of things.

The S.A. had been looking forward to hot weather, drive or no drive, and they were getting ready to substitute real lemonade, with rinds and everything, for the old reliable chocolate or the doubtful pinard. The water supply was none too good, and when a man is hit, he wants something to drink as soon as he can get to it.

Everybody to the Barrels

So when the doughboys and the Artillery and the Signal Corps began sending representatives back to visit the dressing stations, the Salvation Army came to the fore with those Italian lemons, beaucoup sugar and barrels of clean, cold water which they brought up on a Ford delivery truck. Every Yank that got within range of that lemon threw away his cigarette and made a dive for his tin cup.

The doctors say that a good many who couldn't walk, and who couldn't make a dive for their own share, are going to live and go back to the States because they got a drink that killed their fever when they needed it most. Lemonade is a lifesaver to wound-fevered men, and this particular lot turned some good tricks for the surgeons.

Another thing that was imported for use in the emergency was mosquito netting. When the need for protection against flies was apparent at the evacuation hospitals and dressing stations, the Salvation lassies sent to Paris and got all they could.

Then, too, the doughnut batteries more than scored on this latest strategic retreat of Fritz. Two little Salvation lassies fed 28 lost, hungry doughboys in a bunch, less than six hours after first starting their refreshment station. Battle smoke could not blot out the cheerful smell of frying nor shellfire drive away the allure of the unctuous sinker.

"They came up like camions, unlimbered like 75s and were in action in nothing flat," said one grinning Artilleryman. Which is what a Franco-Yank might call "some liaison."

Found in *The 37ᵗʰ Division in the World War*

The Thirty-seventh was ordered to hold the Baccarat sector, the eastern limits of which were those of the eastern limits of the army corps zone and was located about three kilometers within the Vosges mountains. The western boundary ran through the Herberviller, included Pettonville, Hablainville, the eastern half of Azerailles, Glenville, Fonteney-le-Joute, Domtail and St. Pierremont. It was, approximately, a line joining the junction of the Vezouse and Blette rivers with the junction of the Rau, Baxerupte and Meurthe rivers. (Vol. 2, 91)

3rd Battalion War Diary for August 2, 1918

```
     Battalion marched from Fonteury to Gelacourt.
9 kilometers.  Condition [of] men good [on]
arriving Gelacourt 1:30 A.M....
```

Found in *The 37th Division in the World War*

The command of the sector was to pass to Major General Farnsworth at 8:00 A.M. on 4th August. The command of the east zone would pass at the same hour to Brig. General Zimmerman with Headquarters at Neuf-Maisons; that of the west zone to Brig. Gen. Jackson with Headquarters at Merviller.

The command of the sub-sectors Badonviller and Montigny would pass to Colonel Stanbery (145th Infantry) and Colonel Galbraith (147th Infantry) respectively at midnight, 2nd and 3rd August. The command of the two sub-sectors, St. Pole and De-le-Blette would pass to Colonel Weybrecht (146th Infantry) and Colonel Lynch (148th Infantry) at midnight, 3rd and 4th August. (vol. 2, 78)

(FOR OFFICIAL CIRCULATION ONLY)

Hq. 37th Division,
American E. F.,
4 August, 18.

BULLETIN NO. 47.

1.   The following communication from General Headquarters, A. E. F., July 31, 1918, is published for the information and guidance of all concerned:-

"1.   Advices received from the War Department indicate that numerous requests for articles to be sent to members of the A.E.F. are still being received in the U.S., that are not approved by an officer of regimental or higher rank.

. . .

3.   Approval for shipment of any articles from the U.S. shall be limited to such things as are absolutely essential and that cannot be obtained in France through the Supply Departments, Red Cross, Y.M.C.A., Salvation Army or from civilian sources."

2.   (a) The Sanitary Inspector has been directed to secure and turn over Lister bags which will be maintained constantly filled with chlorinated water at a point easily available to all troops passing through the towns in which you are located.
(b) The chlorination of this water will be made by a Sanitary Assistant assigned for duty with each Town Major. Town Majors will be held responsible for the maintenance and operation of this order.
(c) Troops are forbidden to use any but chlorinated water and great care will be taken to see that all water provided for the use of troops, in water carts or other means, is properly chlorinated.

3.   A Motor Dispatch Service is maintained between these Headquarters, Neufchateau and Chaumont. Mail to be sent to any of these points will be delivered to Message Center, this Division.

4.   Platoons will at once inspect to see that all their men have the required two days reserve rations. They will be held responsible for the immediate replacement of missing rations and for disciplinary measures that will prevent loss or use of the reserve rations. Company commanders will inspect their companies for

reserve rations between August 10th and 12th, and report to battalion commanders any shortages of reserve rations in their companies.

5.   (a)   When gas officers take over responsibility for gas defense appliances within the areas occupied by their respective organizations, they will promptly see that all dugouts therein which purport to be protected against gas are actually gas-proof. They will remove curtains from dugouts which are imperfectly protected. The protection of such dugouts will be perfected as soon as possible.

(b)   Regimental Gas Officers of Infantry Regiments will prepare and submit to Division Gas Officer as soon as possible lists of -

(1)   Protected dugouts within the area occupied by their organizations,

(2)   Dugouts which should be protected, in order of urgency of need.

The map reference of each dugout so mentioned will be given. Other Gas Officers will submit similar lists for such parts of their areas as the Regimental Gas Officers of Infantry Regiments are not responsible for. The gas proofing of dugouts is done by the Engineers.

(c)   Gas Officers will see that the curtain of protected dugouts are always wet and that all measures necessary for the collective protection of their organizations are taken.

(d)   Gas Officers and N.C.O.'s will see that within their organizations every sentry who goes on duty knows the methods by which cloud, projector and shell gas attacks may be recognized and the action to be taken in each case. Sentries will be cautioned against giving unwarranted alarms, but care will be taken to avoid the

development of a conservatism that would lead
to delay in sounding the alarm in case of actual
attack.

(e) Gas officers will impart to all
ranks within their organizations the information
that the enemy frequently launches gas attacks
against new divisions, and that these attacks
occur particularly during relief. They will
see that the strictest gas discipline will be
maintained and that all necessary measures are
taken to safe-guard their organizations against
gas.

(f) Regimental Gas Officers and Gas
Officers of separate organization will draw their
anti-gas supplies for their organizations through
the Divisional Gas Officer from the division gas
dump.

(g) In the event of any projector
attack or a gas shell attack of any considerable
importance (more than fifty shells) Division
Headquarters will be notified as promptly as
possible. The time, nature of attack, map
reference and organization attacked will be
stated.

6. Dead animals will be delivered by the
organization to which they belong, in escort
wagons, to burial grounds up the road Baccarat-
Glonville, in a field on the left side of the road,
approximately two (2) kilometers from Baccarat.
At this place the animals are skinned by Frenchmen
who are on duty at that place. The organization
concerned will furnish a detail of two (2) men to
bury the carcass. The Division Veterinarian will
be notified at once upon the death of animals.

7.   (a)   The sounding of horns, whistles, or other instruments making noises in any way similar to gas alarms is prohibited on or in advance of the Azerailles-Baccarat-Raon road. All enlisted men, as well as officers, are hereby directed to stop and hold in the nearest town any vehicles violating this order, reporting the detention at once to Division Headquarters.

(b)   Commanding officers of organizations equipped with motor transportation will see that each and every driver is instructed on this particular point and they will furnish Division Headquarters, through channels, with a certificate that every driver has been so instructed. This report will be made not later than noon August 6th.

(c)   Traffic regulations are being violated in this area. The normal speed for trucks will be 8 miles an hour, for motorcycles 20 miles an hour, except in the city of Baccarat and passing though towns, when they will conform to the posted speed limits. All motor vehicles will comply with traffic regulations. The Military Police will summarily arrest violators of this order.

By command of Major General Farnsworth:

Official: Dana T. Merrill,
                              L. Colonel, General Staff,
                                 Chief of Staff.

R. E. Fraile,
Major, A.G.R.C.
Adjutant.

Found in *The 37ᵗʰ Division in the World War*

In single file the line of shadows pushed forward through the narrow passageway that twisted and doubled back upon itself. The hob nailed soles of the army shoes seemed to make a terrific amount of noise. Occasionally a smothered oath testified that a loose section of duck-boarding had pivoted upward when its end was stepped upon by a trooper the other end rising and delivering a smashing blow on the soldier's chest. Now and then whispered commands to "cut out that noise" were heard when some luckless individual brushed his pack against the wall of the trench, causing his mess equipment to rattle. Whenever a flare rose upward from the German lines, bathing the wastes of No Man's Land and the trenches with a bright calcium glare, the line would halt and stand motionless until the light had died away. From time to time small groups were detached from the main body and took their various assigned positions in observation posts, combat positions or in the support positions. Midnight found men of the regiment standing in the first line trenches, with their eyes trying to see through the wall of darkness that enshrouded the barbed wire and debris of No Man's Land. An automatic rifle was in position, ready to spout forth rain of death and piles of hand grenades nearby were within easy reach, should it be necessary to repel an attack.

In the dugouts that sheltered the platoon command posts a rack of pyrotechnics gave means of sending into the night the rockets, previously designated as calling for a barrage or warning against a gas attack. To those whose lot it was to endure that first night's vigil in the trenches the memory of the hours of nerve-racking expectancy of an attack will forever remain vivid. At intervals a staccato burst of fire from some automatic rifle would shatter the stillness as some nervous soldier imagining that he saw a movement in the barbed wire promptly sent a dozen bullets in the general direction of the supposed enemy. But nothing happened. (vol. 2, 83-84)

3rd Battalion War Diary for August 9, 1918

```
Regular schedule to include problems in
platoon attack 2:30 P.M. to 8:30 P.M., using blank
rifle cartridges and live hand and rifle grenades.
Automatic rifle practice was conducted on short
range constructed by the Battalion.  2 days
rations with troops.  11 officers/652 men available
for all duty.  Weather: cloudy - light rain.
Roads: wet but hard.  Health: excellent.
```

The Stars and Stripes, France, August 9, 1918

MUMPS LEADS IN DISEASES THAT HIT 131,075 IN FRANCE

But Whole Army Loses Less Than Three Per Cent of Working Time

-----

DISEASE KILLS ONLY 923

Tuberculosis Scores Low, Trench Foot Near Bottom, Measles Almost Last

-----

This was a pretty healthy Army during its first year in France. Up to June 1, it might have, with all the people in it, lost 62,714,000 days' work through being sick in hospital or in quarters. But it didn't come anywhere near that; it lost only 1,481,000 days through sickness--or, to be banker like and exact, it lost only 2.377 per cent of its working time.

In all, during that first year in France, the A.E.F. had 131,075 cases of sickness reported; and out of that number only 923 died, or less than one per cent of the sick men, 84.36 per cent were returned to duty, usually with their original units; 15.55 were "otherwise disposed of"--which means put into other lines of work, sent for corrective treatment (as in the case of the flat-foot school), or discharged.

Of the total time lost by illness, the A.E.F.'s medical authorities can trace 32.44 per cent of it to communicable diseases, such as mumps, measles and scarlet fever. To respiratory disorders, such as pneumonia, they can trace 19.20 per cent of the day-wastage.

As for the individual diseases, mumps--good old cheek-puffing, childhood haunting mumps--was the worst offender, taking more toll of the A.E.F.'s huskies than any other malady. Bronchitis is the second highest, and the venereal complaints came in a bad third.

Fourth came the laryngitis-pharyngitis-tonsillitis group; fifth, lobar pneumonia; sixth, measles; seventh, tuberculosis (which, by the way, claimed only 300 out of the total sick); eighth, arthritis and synovitis; ninth, rheumatic fever; and tenth, otitis media, which--if you don't know, and nobody can blame you for not knowing, for we had to look it up ourselves--is something that happens to your ears.

Other Itises in Toll, Too

Going in order, down the list, the following ailments took their toll, beginning with the eleventh, hernia:

The so-called bowel-group (enteritis, colitis, gastritis); bronchial pneumonia; scarletina; the "not diagnosed cases" (their number brings them in at this point); pleurisy; skin diseased; hemorrhoids; flat feet; valvular distention of the heart; diphtheria and the diphtheria carriers; heart diseases other than the valvular troubles; mental diseases; scabies.

Then there follow more names of complaints hard names and rare names, which it will do little good to call here. Suffice it to say that trench-foot is well down toward the bottom of the list in respect to the number of men it laid up; that the German measles is even lower still; and--above all--that dysentery, bane of all armies in the field ever since year One, is the second from the end.

All of which would seem to prove to the layman-soldier that, notwithstanding the rigors of that first winter of ours in France, notwithstanding the fact that we were new to the country and its several varieties of climate, notwithstanding the fact that we had to make practically all our own sanitary provisions and everything, we were a pretty healthy and able-to-be-about bunch of citizens.

The Stars and Stripes, France, August 9, 1918

PAY BOOKS OCTOBER 1

The pay book, which this newspaper forecast in its issue of June 7, has come.

Beginning October 1, they will be used to provide pay for men on detached service, in hospital, in leave areas, or whenever the soldier's record, pay card, or other data needed to prepare a payroll is not available.

Organization commanders will on receipt of the G.O. outlining the pay book, prepare requisitions for the books showing the strength of their commands.

Soldiers arriving for duty with the A.E.F. will be paid on payrolls for all unpaid periods to include the month in which they left the United States, and individual pay books will be opened for them on the first day of the succeeding month.

The Stars and Stripes, France, August 9, 1918

NEW SERVICE RECORD IF YOURS IS LOST

Inquiry Must First Be Made at Central Record Office

If your service record is lost, and if search at the Central Records Office, near Tours, fails to bring it to light, then you are not called on to look any further for it--or rather, your C.O. isn't called on to. Get a new one.

Service records of soldiers dropped from the rolls, according to G.H.Q. Bulletin 49, and assigned to replacement organizations, are sent to the Central Records Office. Accordingly, when a soldier reports to an organization minus his service record, commanders should apply directly to that office.

If the record is not there, an application for a new one must be made according to Paragraph 9 on the first sheet of the service record form. This states that in case a service record is lost, a report of the fact must be made to the Adjutant General of the Army, who will start a new one. It will go first to the depot where the soldier enlisted, and then follow his own military career until it catches up, all commanding officers he has had making the appropriate entries.

The Stars and Stripes, France, August 9, 1918

CANNED LAIT IS FIXER

[BY CABLE TO THE STARS AND STRIPES]

AMERICA, Aug. 8.--If your G.H.Q. suddenly pleads with you to have some malted milk, here is the reason. A malted milk company found with an improper surplus of flour has settled with the Government food board by donating $50,000 worth of its product to the Army and Navy.

You may also get beans. New York State's food conservation bureau sobbingly announces that 125,000 bushels of beans will go where bad beans go if you don't get busy eating them.

The Stars and Stripes, France, August 9, 1918

56,000,000 SOCKS IN UNCLE'S WAR OUTFIT

Ten Million Breeches Also Figure in Bill for Army to April 1

[BY CABLE TO THE STARS AND STRIPES]

AMERICA, Aug. 8.--Only after a careful revision and report by the Board of Review of the General Staff will contracts by let on the "cost plus percentage" plan hereafter.

Figures have been published by the War Department showing that Uncle Sam has purchased uniform equipment alone, up to April 1, in the following large quantities; 55,958,000 woollen socks, 10,507,000 woollen breeches, 8,000,000 woollen coats, 5,377,000 overcoats, 4,337,000 puttees, 191,000 overseas caps.

Motor equipment purchased included 17,988 motor trucks, 3,420 passenger cars, and 9,860 motor ambulances.

There have also been drafted into service horses and mules to the number of 366, 392.

The Stars and Stripes, France, August 9, 1918

VEGETABLES ABOUND IN MANY MESS HALLS

Permanent Camps Enjoy Garden Delectables and Save Tonnage

Radishes, green onions, lettuce and half a dozen other summer delectables have been for several weeks on the menus of most of the troops in the A.E.F. that are stationed at permanent camps. The amateur farmers of the S.O.S., who in their idle time last spring set out war gardens, are reaping the fruits--or, rather, the vegetables--of their endeavor.

Gardens at practically all the base hospitals, where convalescents did their trick with the hoe before returning to active duty, have turned out highly successful. Fresh vegetables in abundance supplement the regular rations. The same is true of the casual and rest camps, where troops passing through devoted their spare time to working the gardens for the benefit of future tenants, and of the various depots where organizations are permanently stationed.

With the bulk of the harvest yet to come in the line of potatoes, corn and more substantial vegetables, the war gardens already have produced an appreciable supply of food, thereby saving a valuable amount of ship tonnage for the transport of other supplies.

Found in *The 37th Division in the World War*

During the time the division occupied the sector, battalions rotated in the front line, in the support, and in the reserve line. The routine of one relief was much the same as another. Officers made the preliminary reconnaissance; trench maps and plans of defense were turned over; guides met the incoming battalion as it stumbled forward in such darkness as only the foothills of the Vosges could provide and outgoing battalions went back to such recreation, rest and relaxation as digging trenches in the support line, or delousing, washing and drilling in the reserve line.

Reliefs, as noted in the division war diary, took place as follows:

...

Second Battalion, 148th Infantry, by Third Battalion, 148th Infantry, 11th August.

...

Third Battalion, 148th Infantry, by First Battalion, 148th Infantry, 31st August. (vol. 2, 160-163)

3rd Battalion War Diary for August 11, 1918

```
     Tactical firing and range problems with
the use of specialities -- automatic rifles and
grenades.  Moved from Gelacourt to Pettonville,
leaving at 8:30 pm -- arriving 10:20 pm.  Distance
6 kilometers....  2 days rations with troops.  10
officer and 636 enlisted men available for all
duty.  Weather: clear and warm.  Roads: hard and
dry.  Health: excellent.
```

3rd Battalion War Diary for August 12, 1918

```
Routine duty in second position....
```

Adj. #110
(FOR OFFICIAL CIRCULATION ONLY)

Hq. 37th Division,
American E. F.,
13 August, 18.

BULLETIN NO. 55.

1.   From August 5th to August 12th,
inclusive, thirteen men of the Division have
been wounded. Of these thirteen, nine of the
wounds have been accidental. This indicates
carelessness, and possibly in some cases lack
of discipline in organizations, and failure
of officers to observe and correct careless and
dangerous practices going on in their commands.
Organization commanders will take precautions
which will prevent these accidental woundings,
most of which are from careless use of fire arms.

2.   The inspection of trenches by officers
detailed from Division Headquarters shows that
more time should be spent by officers in explaining
situations to their men and also in instructing
them as to how to recognize friends and enemies.

3.   Rockets in poor condition must be turned
in at once and good ones obtained. The poor ones
will be used at the Division Center of Instruction
for instruction purposes.

4.   So much of section (b), Par. 1, Bulletin
50, Headquarters 37th Division, 8 August, 1918, as
requires enlisted men, when arriving in Baccarat,
to leave their <u>helmets</u> with the Military Police,
is revoked.

5.   Organizations will render to Division Ordnance Officer semi-monthly reports as of the 15th and last day of each month, showing the amount of Ordnance equipment on hand and all shortages of same.

Sufficient blank forms for Infantry and Machine Gun Companies will be furnished upon application to Division Ordnance Officer, so that reports will be uniform.

By command of Major General Farnsworth:

Dana T. Merrill,
Colonel, General Staff
Chief of Staff.

Official:

R. E. Fraile,
Adjutant General,
Division Adjutant.

Found in *The 37ᵗʰ Division in the World War*

Lieut. Wilton C. Rood, Battalion Adjutant on duty with Major Southam, left headquarters on a personal reconnaissance.... He examined the rifles of Corporal George Hadnett and Private Pasqual Digiacome. Both bayonets were bloody. Hadnett had bayoneted two Germans and shot a third at a close range, Lt. Reed reported. The equipment of our dead men was examined. None of it was missing. One of the rifles was loaded and locked; this probably belonged to Private Digiacome who had fought with grenades. Outside the posts the ground which had been fought over was clearly marked. There were a dozen "big pools of blood from twelve to thirty inches in diameter; two trenches leading to German lines were trailed with blood. On one we found a hat and on the trench leading to the corner of the woods I found the rifle with two cartridges in it.... The Germans evidently took the shelter to be the entrance to a dugout. A potato masher grenade had been exploded in it. The hat lay just outside the entrance. The entire place showed evidence of a hand to hand conflict."...

In forwarding the report of the raid, Col. Stanbery called particular attention to the brave and gallant action of Corporal Hadnett and Private Digiacome who withstood fifty or more Germans, evidently killing or wounding many of them. The two men were the first soldiers of the division to receive the Distinguished Service Cross. (vol. 2, 150-151)

Distinguished Service Cross Citation
Pasquale Digiacome
Private, Company F, 145th Infantry

For extraordinary heroism in action east of Baccarat, France, August 15, 1918 . He was one of four men who successfully held a small advanced post against a raid of 80 of the enemy. Two of the defenders were killed, but the staunch work of the others drove off the raiders. He engaged in a hand-to-hand encounter with the assailants with hand grenades and his rifle.

Distinguished Service Cross Citation
George Hadnett
Corporal, Company F, 145th Infantry

For extraordinary heroism in action east of Baccarat, France, August 15, 1918. He was in command of a small advance post which was successfully held by three men and himself against a raid by 80 of the enemy. Two of his party were killed, but the staunch defense of the others drove off the raiders. He personally killed three of the enemy in hand-to-hand fighting.

Adj. #136.
<u>(FOR OFFICIAL CIRCULATION ONLY)</u>

Hq. 37th Division,
American E. F.,
15 August, 18.

BULLETIN NO. 57.

    1.   PATROLLING

        Patrols must leave by P.P. designated in plan of patrol and return by P.P. also given in plan of proposed patrol. Circumstances may arise where the points of departure and return may have to be somewhat changed, but these should be infrequent.

        The points of exit and entrance for patrols should be changed, - never using the same points frequently. Patrol leaders must always bear in mind their mission - a combat patrol is out to fight - an ambuscade patrol is to fight and capture prisoners, and a reconnoitering patrol is out for information and only fights in self defense. Foolhardiness is not permissible, but aggressiveness is essential. Patrol leaders must, before going out, have several plans for accomplishing their mission. A patrol started out and was not able to get through the wire and patrol was called off, while if an alternative plan had been formulated, it might have been possible to continue the patrol, to an ultimate success.

        All members of patrols should have night reading compasses, - at least the patrol leader and his assistants, - and compass directions given to all the patrol both for out trip and for in trip. Attention is called to the fact that the steel helmet is liable to influence the needle of the compass, also the illuminated dial (as with the watch) may give away the patrol's position.

2.   Attention is invited to Bulletin No. 54,
G.H.Q.A.E.F., August 7, 1918, relative to Venereal
Diseases, the provisions of which will be strictly
complied with.

All Commanding Officers, and particularly
the Military Police, are enjoined to enforce
the provisions of Paragraph 3 (H) relative to
the placing of houses of prostitution as well as
saloons indulging in improper sale of intoxicants
to members of the American E. F., as "off limits".
When necessary, guards will be posted to enforce
this order.

3.   Attention is invited to G.O. 130,
G.H.Q.A.E.F., August 6, 1918, as follows -
Paragraph 8, sub-paragraph (a) G.O. No. 40, c.s.,
these headquarters, is amended to read as follows:
"(a) An immediate report of the death of an
officer, soldier or civilian attached to or serving
with the American Expeditionary Forces, stating
name, army serial number, rank, organization,
cause, place, date and, if possible, hour of
death, whether or not in line of duty, and whether
or not result of own misconduct. This report will
be sent by means of telegraph or runner without
delay to the immediate commanding officer, or if
in a hospital by the commanding officer thereof,
to the adjutant of the next higher administrative
commander. These reports will be consolidated
by the adjutants of divisions, S.O.S. sections,
or higher commands, as at 5:00 o'clock p.m.
each day and telegraphed to the Central Records
Division, A.G.D., A.P.O. 717, providing the total
casualties for the day do not exceed ten. If
the total casualties exceed ten, the consolidated
report will be compiled at such hour as to meet

the requirements of the courier service, and
forwarded by courier. An extract report showing
officers killed, seriously wounded or missing will
be sent by telegraph. For the present reports
will not be forwarded to the Adjutant General of
an Army or Corps except by commanding officers of
army or corps organizations not forming a part
of the division. Officer and soldiers captured,
missing or wounded in action will be reported in
similar manner, wounded being classified as serious
or slight, and the report will show whether the
officer or soldier is entitled to a wound chevron.
        The last sub-paragraph of Par. 14, G.O.
No. 100 is amended accordingly."

        4.   In accordance with advice from the
French Corps Commander, warning is again given as
to the danger from gas shells. Since the Germans
mix gas with high explosive shells and with
shrapnel, the only safe plan when shells begin to
fall in the neighborhood is to put on the mask and
wear it....

                By command of Major General Farnsworth:

                            Dana T. Merrill,
                     Colonel, General Staff
                         Chief of Staff.
Official:

R. E. Fraile,
Adjutant General,
Division Adjutant.
Adj. #166.

Hq. 37th Division,
American E. F.,
16 August, 18.

BULLETIN NO. 58.

1.   The following instructions relative
to construction of trenches in this sector will
govern:

        (a)   The Division Engineer will direct
the commander of the engineer battalion in each of
the two brigade sectors to report to the infantry
brigade commander as his technical advisor.
This duty of the battalion commander will be in
addition to his regimental and battalion duties.
Other engineers will assist the infantry only when
detailed by the Division Engineer upon request by
the brigade sector engineer. Such requests should
be confined to those for men to locate by stakes,
wire, tapes, etc. the Trenches and bayous called
for by the plan of defense....
        2.   It has come to the attention of these
Headquarters that officers and men are filling
canteens and drinking water from springs and water
supply before it has either been chlorinated or
boiled, in violation of the provisions of Par.
3, sub-par. (b), Bulletin No. 45, Headquarters
37th Division, 2 August, 18. This is a dangerous
proceeding and contrary to the best advice from
the Army and Corps Headquarters; both of these
headquarters having advised that the water supply
of this sector is unfit for drinking unless it has
been chlorinated or boiled....
        5.   All messages of a secret nature sent
by pigeons will be coded. Pigeon messages must

```
not disclose organizations or locations by being
sent uncoded.  Practice messages will be marked
"practice".
```

```
          By command of Major General Farnsworth:
```

```
                    Dana T. Merrill,
                Colonel, General Staff
                  Chief of Staff.
Official:
R. E. Fraile,
Adjutant General,
Division Adjutant.
```

The Stars and Stripes, France, August 16, 1918

FIRST ARMY, A.E.F., IS NOW IN FIELD

General Pershing in Command: 2,500,000 Yanks Here by End of Year

-----

The First Army, American Expeditionary Forces, is formed and in the field. The announcement, made during the week, represents the most important step in the organization of the A.E.F. which has been taken in its year and a quarter of existence.

General Pershing has taken direct command of the First Army. This command will be in addition to his duties as Commander-in-Chief of the whole A.E.F. The corps commanders announced to date are Major Generals Liggett, Bullard, Bundy, Reed and Wright.

The divisions composing the army corps, which in turn compose the First Army, have undergone preliminary training and seen active service in sectors which were not exactly quiet.

The announcement of the First Army's formation came on the same day that the Senate Military Affairs Committee was informed that a million and a half American soldiers were now actually in France, and that the War Department expected to continue sending troops at the rate of 250,000 a month to the end of the year. This means that more than 2,500,000 American soldiers should be in France on or soon after December 31, 1918.

G-3   FIRST ARMY, A. E. F.,
                             Neufchateau, August 17, 1918.

     1.   The First Army assumes command of the American troops in this area tomorrow morning, the 18th instant.

     2.   The troops concerned are:
           Army troops of the First Army
           I Corps, consisting of corps troops, and the 5th,
                82nd, 90th, 42nd Divisions
           IV Corps, consisting of corps troops, and the 1st,
                2d, 4th, 89th, 37th Divisions
           V Corps, consisting of corps troops, and the 3d,
                33d, 35th, 78th, 26th and 80th Divisions
           VI Corps, consisting of 79th and 91st Divisions

     3. A complete order of battle will be furnished by G-1 when completed.

                              R. McCleave,
Colonel, General Staff,   G-3.

The Stars and Stripes, France, August 16, 1918

ALONG THE FIGHTING FRONT

The chaplains from two Yankee regiments that had stormed the slope above Ourcq came wearily back at sundown from the task of burying their dead. They were two much uplifted men, and their eyes were shining as they made their brief but eloquent report.

"In all that battlefield," they said, "we found, without a single exception, that every one of those boys died crouching forward, died with his face toward Germany."

When, as happens often in the rush of open warfare, the airplanes are transformed into the most mobile of all artillery and sweep down to pour machine gun bullets into the unsheltered infantry of the enemy, they become targets for the crack rifle shot. A shot that reaches the head or heart of the low-flying assailant will do the trick.

The trick has been done a good many times. When, if ever again, there comes a lull in the bouncing war, it may be possible to assemble the data and announce how many German planes have been brought to earth this summer by Yankee rifles.

Or, better still, by Yankee riflemen, for on several occasions, officers and men at regimental and divisional headquarters dropped their work, grabbed up Roche rifles that had just been confiscated from prisoners and dashed out into the open to take a few pot shots.

A wounded officer from among the gallant French lancers had just been carried into a Yankee field hospital to have his dressing changed. He was full of compliments and curiosity about the dashing contingent that had fought at his regiment's left.

"A lot of them are mounted troops by this time," he explained, "for when our men would be shot from their horses, these youngsters would give one running jump and gallop ahead as cavalry. I believe they are your soldiers from Montezuma. At least, when they advanced this morning, they were all singing 'From the halls of Montezuma to the shores of Tripoli.' *C'est epatant, ca!*"

A former sergeant who had just been busted and who carried fresh in his mind the melancholy memories of court martial, was lifted wounded from the ambulance at the field hospital. He was grinning from ear to ear.

"Well," he said, "here's one stripe they can't take away from me, damn 'em."

The generation of American mothers that have trained their boys to care for their teeth as the people of no other country do would glow with pride if they could trek up in the wake of our Army in Action and see the whole rear area dotted at sunrise with Yankee soldiers, just out of battle, and every man brushing his teeth. Often most of his possessions have been jettisoned in the rush of the advance.

And now abideth these three, the rifle, the shovel, and the tooth-brush. And the greatest of these--

-----

Than Seringes, the village the Yanks captured on July 29, there is only one more battered town in all the area between the Marne and the Vesle. That is Vaux. Seringes had been held by the enemy for a good two months; his signs were on the buildings, his lettering on the guide-posts, his dead filled the village church yard. There the Yanks found buried many of the Boches who had died on July 15, the first day of the ill-starred offensive the Crown Prince wishes he had never made. They had been carried back as far as Seringes and buried in a church yard which the Germans never dreamed they would have to give up. "Hier ruht,...," "Es Sterben furs Vaterland" and so on. Of the church, only a shell is left, with two cherubs hanging uncertainly over the shattered altar and, as though still quickened by the vibrations of the guns that thundered there a little time ago, the altar-lamp swinging to and fro above the desolation.

There is no room in this or any other paper to list all the runners who distinguished themselves in the Second Battle of the Marne, but one name shall be set down because the name is Irish Stock, and he is.

How perplexing, sometimes, is the runner's task in the war of movement you can guess from the fact that one regiment P.C. just south of the Ourcq moved three times in one day--three moves within the area of a single, heavily shelled village. They were wise moves, for each of the abandoned headquarters was destroyed by gunfire--one two hours, on half an hour, one 15 minutes after the colonel had moved on.

One regiment, in the first swift advance of General Mangin's Army, got part of a night's rest in a forest. Their own general, speeding past them at daybreak, noticed that every man had seized the breathing spell not only to sleep but to wash, brush up and shave. They looked snappy in the morning sunlight. The general said nothing, but his eyes gleamed his appreciation. He is tremendously proud of them. He ought to be.

He was a battling boxer from south Boston before the war and somewhere between Soissons and Rheims the Germans shot him through the chest. He was being carried from the regimental aid station in a litter when he spied another wounded man from his company lying to one side waiting his turn. The boxer raised such an uproar that they had to let him get off and try to walk while his pal was carried back. The doctors said it would be impossible for him to walk. He walked.

At a battered street corner of a badly demolished French town an American captain stood watching three American doughboys swinging up the road.

"Here comes the greatest men in the world," he said, "just the plain, everyday privates. They are the gamest lot I ever saw. Why, I almost cry every time I think of these kids.

"See those three coming up? Well, if a German regiment should turn the corner and start their way, do you suppose they would break and run? No an inch. They'd stand right where they are, unsling their rifles and begin firing, killing all they could until the last one of them was shot down.

"I know, for I've seen them do things that took just as much nerve. You can't beat 'em anywhere."

During the German retreat the enemy's last rearguard action was made by hostile planes that flew back over the American lines.

One of these planes was flying over a big field in the direction of a French town where American troops were stationed. At the edge of this town an American machine gunner had his machine well camouflaged, waiting for just such a target. Just as the German flyer got half-way across the field, the American opened fire from his hidden position.

"Did you get him?" his captain asked a trifle later.

"No, sir," answered the gunner, "but I must have scared him a bit, because he dropped all three of his bombs together out in this vacant field and beat it back about as fast as a bullet could travel."

Another German plane, swooping around a farmhouse, was startled and soon driven away by very accurate rifle fire. At least the firing was accurate enough to convince Fritz that he was in no safe neighborhood.

But he didn't know that the rifle was being handled by a lieutenant colonel in the American Army, who, enraged at the audacity of the hostile bird-man, grabbed the weapon and soon had the "supremacy of the air" in that particular locality well under control.

One lieutenant found the full meaning of the famous phrase, "The command is 'Forward.'"

While serving in the advance, he received official notification that he was to report for a certain duty back in the S.O.S. He had found no great trouble in moving forward for over a week. But in starting back he was forced to wait around in the rain with his bedding roll all ready for nearly three days before he could locate any sign of a conveyance leading to the rear.

An Artillery officer, who had been a fairly well-known golfer and a keen enthusiast back home, was looking out across a rolling plain that only recently had been heavily pounded by heavy shell fire.

"I've seen some well-trapped courses," he said, "but I must say this is the best bunker course I've ever run across. There's a pit every 20 feet. Par here must be about 200."

A heavy rain was beating down upon a woods where an American company was resting. It was just after daybreak when an observer, walking by, looked in. The rain was pouring and the trees were dripping a young flood, but every member of the company was still sleeping, dry as dust, for each squad had built itself a canopy from innumerable square boxes that had been discovered in this section.

"Where did they happen to find these boxes?" some one asked.

"German ammunition left behind," as the reply. "Every box you see is full of German rifle bullets. They make the greatest little rain sheds in the world."

Frine is his name. At least that is the corruption of an Italian moniker which the top sergeant found too difficult to decipher. He wrote it Frine, for short. The boys in Company B.---Inf. call him Friday.

Private Frine is (or was) an automatic gunner, and was in the big push of July 18. With his company he went forward in the region west of Chateau-Thierry. He had often boasted what he would do to the Boche if he got a chance but such boasts are often made, and nobody pays a great deal of attention to them. But Friday got his chance, and made the best of it.

His company was held up by a German machine gun, mounted in a tree. The company had halted and was beginning to maneuver to flank the Boche. The method apparently seemed too slow for Friday. Or his brain may have been a bit feverish and sized up the situation from a warped viewpoint, for he already had two bullets in his left shoulder. He had been told to go to the rear, but he held doggedly on. He hadn't got his Boche yet.

Before anyone realized what was happening Friday was up and moving at a rapid gait straight at the tree supporting the Germans, while the gun barked at him. He never faltered, and he reached the tree without further hurt. Under it he fired his pistol twice. (He had left his automatic rifle behind when he made the dash, for the 19 pounds of it do not facilitate speed.) One German reeled over, and the other was only too willing to yell "Kamerad." Down he came, lugging the Maxim, and was marched back to the company by Friday. Company B resumed its advance, and Private Frine was now willing to go to the rear.

He had got his Boche.

Three Yanks found themselves in a shell-hole 50 yards from a German machine gun. Two of them had painful head wounds. They were so thirsty they were choking.

It was up to someone to get out and cut the canteens from two good Germans who lay between the shell-hole and the machine guns.

"You stay here," said the old regular to his bunkie," because you've got a wife. I'm going to pray and go out and get that water."

The fire flew from the clump of bush as he drew near the coveted canteen, but it flew high. He got back with the water.

```
Field Order No. 2                  August 18, 1918
```

Pursuant to Memo Order #38... a relief of the S/S La BLETTE will be accomplished on the nights of 21/22 and 22/23 August, 1918 as follows:-

NIGHT OF 21/22 AUGUST:

(A) 1st Position:- 3rd Bn. will relieve the 2nd Bn....

To secure continuity, the following personnel will remain in each position, after the relief is completed, as follows:-
    1 Officer with each company for 72 hours.
    1 Sergeant with each platoon for 72 hours.
    1 N.C.O. (additional) who is familiar with the patrols
        with each company for 72 hours.
    1 Member of each Auto Rifle Team for 72 hours....
    Battalion Commanders will arrange for the necessary preliminary reconnaissances, advance billeting parties, guide and will make suitable arrangements with the Supply Officer regarding the proper distribution of rations and transportation of baggage for each movement.....
                        by order of Colonel Lynch

From *Service with the Fighting Man: An Account of the Work of the American Young Men's Christian Assocations in the World War* edited by William Howard Taft

A secretary with the 37th Division wrote:

'I took the Khaki Trio and their folding organ Wednesday, August 20, 1918, up on the ration train with me, reached battalion headquarters at 10 p.m. and gave our first concert in a dugout to eighteen men. We spent the rest of the night at the guard house, sleeping in bunks, hammocks, and on the floor with rats running all over us. Got up early next morning, gave our first concert at 6 a.m., then started up the trenches, stopping wherever we found a platoon of soldiers, gave them a concert, and put on our fifth and last concert for the day at 3 p.m. at the farthest outpost on the edge of No Man's Land... '

```
   Adj. #258.
(FOR OFFICIAL CIRCULATION ONLY)

BULLETIN NO. 62.                    Hq. 37th Division,
                                   American E. F.,
                                    20 August, 18,


      1.    The spying activities of the enemy
have been proved to be going on lately and the
greater part of their work is done in the French
or some Allied uniform.  It is necessary to watch
carefully the railroad trains while they are being
made up in the stations.
            Any soldier or citizen should be able
to explain very plainly his reasons for being at
a certain point at any particular time and when
questioned, should be able to prove his identity;
otherwise he will be arrested.
            The real identity of soldiers of all
ranks must be established and when soldiers
```

are questioned, they must submit willingly and display identifications. All officers will furnish identifications whenever requested to do so by the Military Police or other military authorities; if they refuse, they will be arrested.

2. An American Division has, in the past few days, had a large number of casualties from gas. The French authorities have informed us that the Americans placed the masks on promptly and properly, but that they then remained in the low ground which had been gassed. The result was many unnecessary casualties. Commanding officers will caution every man in their organizations repeatedly as to precautions necessary to avoid gas casualties and will include in their instructions explanation of the fact that the gases are all heavier than air and therefore settle in low places and therefore than troops subjected to gas should as soon as practicable seek high ground or high places in the buildings occupied by them.

3. The attention of all brigade and regimental commanders is called to the following extracts from instructions given by the commander of the Eastern Group of Armies, to which the 37th Division is now attached:
(1) "The battalions of the first line must be trained in falling back. It is very important to have the men understand that it is a maneuver and not a retreat."
(2) "As soon as the bombardment begins, everybody must put on the gas mask."
(3) "Work on shelter for horses and men and organization of positions must be hastened."

(4) "Alarm practice will take place at the end of each month, the execution and movement being under control."

4. Riding horses may be kept at any point, day or night, in the Division sector where their services as mounts are required. This will be regulated by Brigade Commanders. There has been no orders issued from Division Headquarters prohibiting the use of horses in advance of a certain line.

5. So much of sub-paragraph (b), Par. 3, Bulletin No. 45, these Headquarters, 2 August, 1918, as states that glass tubes of hypochlorite of lime for chlorinating water will be issued by the Division Medical Supply Officer, is amended to read that these tubes will be issued by the Unit Supply Officers. This article is now furnished by the Quartermaster Department instead of the Medical Department.

6. The French Gendarmerie (Military Police) often ask information of a confidential or secret nature. This may be by order of Military authority or on their own initiative. Every person in the American service of whom enquiries are made, should make sure that he is not dealing with a German spy in the uniform of a French Gendarme.
     Each officer of the French Gendarmerie carries an identification card, each Sergeant and Gendarme carries an identification disc and if they belong to the Territorial Gendarmerie, an identification paper called "Bulletin of Service."

7. General Orders of the VIII French Army prescribe the hours of opening of the cafes, restaurants, and wine shops to troops in the territories of the armies as follows:

> From April 15 to September 15:
> > Open from 10:30 A.M. to 1:00 P.M.
> > Open from 5:50 P.M. to 9:00 P.M.
> From September 15 to April 15:
> > Open from 10:30 A.M. to 1:00 P.M.
> > Open from 5:00 P.M. to 8:00 P.M.
> Violators of this law will be dealt with

as follows:

> > 1st Offense - Close to the troops
> > for 15 days
> > 2nd Offense - Close to the troops
> > for 30 days
> > 3rd Offense - Close completely for
> > 15 days
> > 4th Offense - Close indefinitely.
> > The Town-Majors will
> > see that this is
> > strictly complied
> > with.

8. Requisitions for motor equipment and supplies must be made out in regular requisition form (4 copies) and sent to the office of the Motor Transport Officer by Tuesday of each week for delivery on Wednesday of the following week.

> By Command of Major General Farnsworth:

> > Dana T. Merrill,
> > Colonel, General Staff,
> > Chief of Staff.

Adj. #290.
(FOR OFFICIAL CIRCULATION ONLY)

BULLETIN NO. 63.   Hq. 37th Division,
                                        American E. F.,

                                     21 August, 18,

    1. Reports of patrols seem to indicate that
patrol leaders are failing to realize the value of
surprise - of delivering the first blow. Absolute
surprise should be counted as equal to doubling
the strength of the patrol. Therefore patrols
of any size less than a hundred men should not
hesitate to open fire on a patrol double its size
every time that it is possible to open fire or
attack in any way as a surprise.
    The Corps Commander says: "Reconnaissance
patrols must penetrate and must push on to the
line of resistance and must at the same time bring
back prisoners or papers taken from enemy dead.
It is important that all patrols should go on
until they come in contact with the enemy. The
General commanding the Army Corps considers it of
the greatest importance that these reconnaissance
patrols be executed at regular intervals, and
urges officers of all ranks to see to it that
effective results be quickly obtained. We can
no longer at the present time remain content with
negative information."

    2. DIRECTIONS FOR CARRYING OUT TESTS FOR
CHLORINATION OF WATER.
            (a) The dropping bottle is graduated in
10 c.c. and 30 c.c. Fill to 10 c.c. mark with 50%
K.I. Fill to 30 c.c. mark with the other solution

which contains 5% soluble starch and 1% zinc sulfate.

   (b) Thirty minutes after treatment test as follows; Fill mess cup within on inch of the top with the treated water. Add 10 drops of solution from dropping bottle, stir, and wait one minute. A distinct blue should appear if chlorination has been successful and contains a residual content of free chlorine of not less than one-tenth part per million. Viewed in a good light any case in which there is doubt should be regarded as negative.

  3. The following is reported from an adjoining sector:

   The opening of a gate in a communicating trench by our troops caused the explosion of a small mine or other trap laid on the firing step by the Germans. Several men were injured.

   Attention is invited to the necessity of taking precautions in this respect.

   By command of Major General Farnsworth:

       Dana T. Merrill,
     Colonel, General Staff,
      Chief of Staff.

3rd Battalion War Diary for August 22, 1918

  Moved from second position to first position on night of 21-22 August. Reported to Commanding Officer, 148th Infantry at 2:27 am 22nd August that all reliefs were complete. This movement

in compliance with Field Order #2, Headquarters,
148th Infantry, 18 August 1918.

2 days rations, 5 days forage with troops. 10
officers and 568 enlisted men available for all
duty. Weather: clear; warm. Roads: hard and dry.
Health: excellent.

3rd Battalion War Diary for August 23, 1918

Routine duty in first position. An aeroplane
shot down at about 10:00 am. Plane understood to
be German, and fell in vicinity of Herberviller.

2 days rations, 5 days forage with troops.
14 officers and 617 men available for all duty.
Weather: clear-warm. Roads: hard and dry.
Weather: excellent.

The Stars and Stripes, France, August 23, 1918

ISSUES GLASSES HERE TO BENEFIT TIRED A.E.F. EYES

Optical Ingenuity Produces Aluminum Framed O.D. Spectacles

SPECIAL GAS MASK LENSES

Window Panes to Be Replaced by Your Own Particular Style of Vision Straighteners

-----

Three thousand doughboys are wearing new glasses whose frames look
as if they were made of platinum.. But it isn't platinum. It's the stuff that
keeps the Liberty motor light--aluminum.

The doughboys started wearing the glasses only a few weeks ago. They are of the new standard pattern designed for the rough usage of the Army--and they look it. They're as military as a bayonet, and apparently almost as unbreakable. And the doughboys are for them. No more writing back home for that prescription and the extra pair.

The glasses are put together in France by American soldiers, ground and polished out of American glass on American motor-driven machinery. The aluminum frame incloses two round lenses--a sort of port hole window effect. The templets--the things that hook onto the ears--are little cables, the twisting of the wires being very obvious. But they're warranted not to rust.

Enough to Go Around

And the best part about it is that they're free--although a man can only have one pair issued at a time. And there will be enough to go around. The spectacle makers for the Army are going to stay on the job while the doughboys go on breaking their old ones, and needing new ones as their eyes grow dull from hunting flannel lizards, body turtles and Germans.

In a certain populous region of France there's a barrack-like building full of filing cabinets, sergeants, buck privates, and polishing and grinding machines. Into that room come packing cases full of wrapped and cushioned squares of rough glass and spectacle frames.

Out of that room go spectacles by the hundreds with lenses of the best optical glass obtainable--glass that scientists have made to filter out the glaring, eye-tiring lights of the spectrum, ground to the measurements that the medical officers took down when they gave that latest of army "shots," the shot of atrophine or belladonna, at the same time they looked with their instruments into the insides of the soldiers' eyes.

Skill and Patriotism

The making of soldiers' glasses is only one more of those accomplishments that make Uncle Sam's war effort. He didn't have much to start with, beyond professional skill and patriotism, when he began his war optical plans. The peace time spectacle makers of the United States had fallen into the habit of using German optical glass, because it was good, but mostly because it was cheap. Some they had bought from England. Optical glass wasn't made on a commercial scale in the States.

Optical glass requires a special sand, special formulae, and special processes. Of course better spectacles were manufactured in the States than anywhere in the world, but even here supremacy was limited. Because even the polishing had depended on the use of an abrasive known as Turkish emery. And early in the war a boat loaded with enough of this emery to supply the spectacle makers of the States for several years had been lost.

But we had to have those glasses. American science and mechanics combined. Pittsburgh, Rochester and Corning, N.Y. proved, what they had contended right along, that they could make optical glass as good as any, and out of sand from the West. The polishers declared their independence of Turkish emery by substituting a member of the carborundum family. The aluminum frame and non-corrosive wire templet were designed to stand rough usage.

Eight Units at Work

Captain F. H. Edmonds of Washington organized and brought to France the first optical manufacturing unit. The men who are at work over the motor-driven grinding and polishing machines in the A.E.F. shop were all drawn from the best of the manufacturers' benches back home.

There are now eight optical units attached to base hospitals and they are in charge of oculists ranking high in their profession. The number of these units is being increased.

As a side line the central shop is supplying spectacles of dark glass for doughboys who have been gassed and those needing them after the injections of atrophine or belladonna.

And there is another side-line, largely experimental so far. Men wearing glasses lose a few seconds jerking off the glasses before they jump into their gas masks. Many of these men have considerable difficulty in seeing without their glasses. So now gas masks are to be made with lenses ground to the wearers' needs. There are difficulties, but the optical men say they will be beaten.

Supplying Artificial Eyes

One of the most important jobs the optical men are handling is the supplying of artificial eyes to the wounded. Thousands of eyes of all sizes, shapes and colors are in stock at the A.E.F. manufacturing plant. When a eye is required for a wounded man at a base hospital, an approximate description of the eye--the details of color, size and shape--is sent, and the optical men dispatch a selection of artificial eyes to the hospital There a surgeon completes the work of matching and fitting the new eye. On some cases the wounded come to the plant to have to selection made there. In practically every case, it is almost impossible to identify the eye that has been fitted, for in color, motion and all it seems to correspond to the good eye opposite.

The Stars and Stripes, France, August 23, 1918

SOAP AND WATER FOR MESS ARTISTS

Personal Cleanliness Urged for Everyone in Army

"The United States Army triumphed over preventable disease in the tropics. The lessons learned there must be applied here and now."

With that statement, Bulletin 57, just issued by G.H.Q., proceeds to lay down the law about a few simple matters of health which some men in some units seem to have overlooked.

Cooks must keep their finger nails cut short and cleaned. They must scrub their hands with hot water and soap before entering the kitchen. And everybody, whether cook or captain, must be extremely mindful about washing the hands carefully after visiting the latrine.

"Personal cleanliness is still our most reliable protection against disease," says the bulletin, which will be read to every outfit at the first formation after its receipt, again after two weeks, and then as often as changes in personnel make it necessary to let the new men in on it.

Adj. #366.
(FOR OFFICIAL CIRCULATION ONLY)

BULLETIN NO. 66.   Hq. 37th Division,
                                    American E. F.,
                                    24 August, 18,

TREATMENT OF GERMAN PRISONERS.

    1.   The German Press, undoubtedly inspired, is at present claiming that in recent battles some detachments of American soldiers, in the progress of the battle, refused to give quarter to detachments of German soldiers not guilty of treachery, after resistance had ceased and offer was made to surrender. This campaign is being waged in the German Press for the purpose of increasing the power of resistance of German soldiers by instilling in their minds the idea that they will be killed if they attempt to surrender. The Commander-in-Chief desires in this connection to impress upon all officers and enlisted men the policy of the United States in this respect, which is that an offer to surrender on the part of enemy soldiers not guilty of treacherous conduct will be accepted and these soldiers given food, shelter and protection, strictly as laid down according to the laws and customs of war on land set forth on our Field Service Regulations.

    This paragraph will be read to every officer and enlisted man in this Division and its provisions will be strictly complied with.

2.   Daily instruction in gas training and discipline will be given in every organization and to every individual of this command.   Inspections will be instituted by Division Headquarters to determine the state of gas discipline and training in this command.

3.   In all cases of arrest by the Military Police, where Provost Marshal reports are sent to organization commanders, these reports will be forwarded promptly by the organization commanders to the office of the Division Judge Advocate, with notation of action taken.

By command of Major General Farnsworth:

Dana T. Merrill,
Colonel, General Staff.
Chief of Staff.

3rd Battalion War Diary for August 27, 1918

Routine duty in first position.   Activity normal.   Gas alarm at 20:45 o'clock 26, August; all clear at 22:00 o'clock.   No gas in this sector.   Repair work on wire and duck boards in this position.
2 days rations and 5 days forage with troops.   12 officers and 604 men available for all duty.   Weather: clear; cool.   Roads: hard and dry. Health: excellent.

Adj. #437.

(FOR OFFICIAL CIRCULATION ONLY)

Hq. 37th Division,
American E. F.,
27 August, 18.

BULLETIN NO. 68.

1.   The Division Commander informs all members of the Division that the first man to take an AUSTRIAN prisoner will be especially commended. The capture of an Austrian prisoner at the present time is an honor that all the organizations, French and American, in this part of the country are keenly competing for.

2.   Par. 6, Bulletin No. 35, Par. 5, Bulletin No. 37, and Par. 3, Bulletin No. 46, all Headquarters 37th Division, in-so-far as they have reference to side, arms, ammunition, gas masks, and helmets, are rescinded and the following substituted therefore:
        (a)   All officers and enlisted men in advance of the Route Nationale No. 59 (Azerailles-Bertichamps road) when leaving their camps or towns, whether on or off duty, will carry arms. They will carry or wear the steel helmet and gas mask whenever they are not in their billets.
        (b)   Officers going in advance of regimental headquarters will remove Sam Browne belts and wear other belts, or will remove the shoulder strap of the Sam Browne belt.
        (c)   Commanders of each billet, camp or town will designate limits beyond which no officer or enlisted man shall go without arms and

ammunition.   Commanders will mark by appropriate
signs the above-described limits.   Working and
carrying parties will always have their arms,
ammunition, masks and helmets by their side ready
for instant use....

   4.   Pistols needing repairs will
be collected by the Supply Officer of each
organization.   A list of the pistols by numbers
and, if possible, a statement of the broken parts,
will be prepared and delivered with same.
      A truck will call at each organization
on Saturday, August 31, for these pistols which
will be repaired and returned.
      Broken pistols which have been
previously repaired will be returned on Saturday,
August 31.

      By command of Major General Farnsworth:

            Dana T. Merrill,
            Colonel, General Staff
            Chief of Staff.
Official:

R. E. Fraile,
Adjutant General,
Division Adjutant.

Stars and Stripes, France, August 30, 1918

U.S. FOR EVERYONE, SAYS NEW ORDER FROM PRESIDENT

All other Distinctive Names to Be Dropped for Land Forces

APPLIES TO COMMISSIONS

Rule That Concerned Officers Is Broadened to Affect Everyone in O.D.

The military land forces of the United States will hereafter be known solely as the United States Army. All other distinctive names, such as National Guard, National Army, Regular Army, Reserve Corps, and any and all others, will be dropped. The announcement in made in a general order by the President.

It means that the insignia U.S. will be worn by all enlisted and commissioned members of the Army.

Announcement was made three weeks ago in a War Department cablegram that officers would hereafter wear only the U.S., as stated in this newspaper. The new order broadens this rule to apply to everyone in O.D.

Commissions in the Regular or National Army, National Guard or Reserve corps will hereafter be regarded as commissions in the United States Army--permanent, provisional or temporary, as stated in the conditions under which the commissions were issued.

In line with this step, provisional and temporary appointments in the grade of second lieutenant and temporary promotions in the Regular Army and appointments in the Reserve Corps will be discontinued during the war.

Embodies in G.H.Q. Bulletin

The President's order, as embodies in Bulletin No. 59, G.H.Q., A.E.F., follows in full:--

"This country has but one army, the United States Army. It includes all the land forces in the service of the United States. These forces, however raised, lose their identity in that of the United States of America. Distinctive appellations, such as the Regular Army, Reserve Corps, National Guard and National Army, heretofore employed in administration and command, will be discontinued, and the single term, the United States Army, will be exclusively used.

"Orders having reference to the United States Army as divided into separate and component forces of distinct origin, or assuming or contemplating such a division, are to that extent revoked.

"The insignia now prescribed for the Regular Army shall hereafter be worn by the United States Army.

Commissions in the U.S.A.

"All effective commissions purporting to be, and described therein as, commissions in the Regular Army, National Army, National Guard or the Reserve Corps shall hereafter be held to be, and regarded as, commissions in the United States Army, permanent, provisional or temporary, as fixed by the conditions of their issue; and all such commissions are hereby amended accordingly.

"Hereafter during the period of the existing emergency all commissions of officers shall be in the United States Army and its corps, departments and arms of the service thereof, and shall, as the law may provide, be permanent, for a term or for the period of the emergency. And hereafter during the period of the existing emergency provisional and temporary appointments in the grade of second lieutenant and temporary promotions in the Regular Army and appointments in the Reserve shall be discontinued.

"While the number of commissions in each grade and in each corps, department and arm of the service shall be kept within the limits fixed by law, officers shall be assigned, without reference to the term of their commission, solely in the interest of the service; and officers and enlisted me will be transferred from one organization to another as the interest of the service may require.

"Except as otherwise provided by law, promotion in the United States Army shall be by selection. Permanent promotions in the Regular Army shall continue to be made as prescribed by law."

Stars and Stripes, France, August 30, 1918

VILLAGES LINKED IN RECORD TIME BY RAILWAY UNIT

Seven Hours, Three Minutes, Sees 2.68 miles of Track Laid

-----

135 MEN FOREGO SMOKES

Director General of Railroads Himself Cables President--But Not for Help

-----

While the units that had been engaged in the recent fighting were blissfully enjoying a well-earned rest, 135 members of the first company of Railway Engineers to arrive in France celebrated that victory by establishing what is believed to be a new track laying record, completing 2.69 miles of narrow gauge railway in seven hours and three minutes.

The work marked the completion of an important railway line from one French town to another, upon which the company had been working for several weeks. Officers present when the record was made were outspoken in their conviction that the gang could have easily completed four miles during the full working day of 12 hours had there been further track to lay in that sector.

A captain and a lieutenant were in charge of the detail. All necessary materials for the job had to be brought up from behind, two 60 cm. steam locomotives pushing the rail cars forward as soon as a section of track was spiked down. Two motor trucks were used for hauling ties.

The amount of material handled gives more than a hint of the magnitude of the task and the tremendous amount of labor involved--approximately 105 tons of steel rails, 7100 ties, 1830 pairs of fishplates, 8 kegs of bolts and 37 kegs of spikes, making a total of over 230 tons.

"Nous le faisons toujours," replied the captain when complimented upon the showing made by the company. "We always do it" is, by the way, the motto of the company although the bucks usually use the free translation, "We produce the goods."

"We Produce the Goods"

The company had been producing the goods in France for 13 months, erecting warehouses, surveying, laying track, grading, stringing pipe lines, building barracks, installing electric lights, constructing railroad yards, operating everything from 15 ton cranes to Ford ambulances, remodeling hospitals--in short, performing all the manifold and endless duties of Yank Engineers. Assignment to the construction of a light railway line was a welcome change, and the work was pushed in a way that earned the commendation of superior officers.

Then came news of the Chateau-Thierry drive.

Determined not to let the Infantry get too far ahead, the men redoubled their efforts. Each day brought a better report of the amount of track laid. The grading details. working several miles ahead, finished their end of the job and drove their mules back to the base camp. They maintained that even Heinie assisted in the work by loosening the stony ground of lots by means of occasional loads of hate. These were dropped under cover of darkness, so that the men sometimes woke in the morning to discover that some unintentionally kind fairy had partly completed the work ahead. One day the steel detail completed two miles of track, but even then the bunch was not satisfied.

"The doughboys will be in Berlin before we reach the Rhine at this rate," commented one buck private. "We'll have to lay four kilometers a day."

"That ees impossible," remarked the French interpreter.

"Impossible, hell," rejoined the buck.

Cable to the President

Next day the men laid 12,360 feet of track, a performance that so pleased the Director General of Railroads, who was present, that he sent a cable to President Wilson commending the company. The interpreter no longer spoke of impossibilities.

The captain believed that the men could do even better, so he called a conference of the sergeants and, after telling them of his plans, regaled them with several selections from Kipling. When the company assembled on the morning of the big day, the C.O. told them that he wanted the job finished by supper time.

"What's the use of working until supper time?" piped a voice from the rear rank. "Let's finish the job by noon and get a half day off."

Tracks were laid that morning at an average rate of 33 feet to the minute. Train crews rushed the material over the lines as fast as the rails could be loaded on the cars. One gang worked ahead stringing ties, another unloaded the rails and threw them quickly into place. As soon as one section was completed the rail car was pushed ahead. When one car became unruly and decided to leave the track, it was pushed out of the way by sheer man power.

Speed, speed, and then some more speed, without even a pause to roll a cigarette. The track seemed to go forward by leaps and bounds, especially when the gang caught sight of the truck that carried the mess waiting at the end of the line. At 1:33 p.m. the lieutenant, who had been giving a lift on the rails, threw his hat in the air and yelled, "Finn!"

"Seven hours and three minutes," announced the captain. "Some birds."

The "birds" did not hear him. They were racing for the truck where "Sammie," who can make even bread pudding palatable, was shouting, "Come an' get it!"

Everyone was pleased, including Spike, the hard-boiled wild board mascot, who strutted around as if claiming credit for any new records made in that neck of the woods. The captain congratulated the lieutenant, who passed on the congratulations without sending them through the proper military channels. The mess sergeant showed his appreciation by serving canned salmon and canned potatoes instead of the usual canned charlie horse and canned tomatoes.

But the men in the company aren't satisfied. They believe that they can lay five miles of track a day.

"Nous le faisons toujours," declare the bucks.

Stars and Stripes, France, August 30, 1918

SERVICE STRIPES TO DATE FROM ARRIVAL

Time Spent on Transport Is No Longer to Be Counted

The computation of time for the wearing of the gold service chevron will in future be made from the date of arrival at a French, British or other European port, according to a cablegram from Washington just received at G.H.Q.

In the past this time has been reckoned from the date on which the transport left United States territorial waters. Now, instead of counting from the first day out, we shall have to count from our first day in.

Stars and Stripes, France, August 30, 1918

OUTLOOK IS DARK FOR XMAS PARCELS

But Chief Postmaster Has Not Given Up All Hope Yet

Just what will be done about Christmas packages for the A.E.F.?

That's the big question the chief postmaster down at Tours is trying to thresh out. The chief likes Christmas packages just as well as anybody does, and he has used up many sheets of good bond paper trying to figure it out.

If every man in the A.E.F. is allowed a five-pound package for Christmas from home, it would require 700 cars a day for ten days to transport the gifts from the base ports to the ultimate consumers in the S.O.S. and the Z. of A.

The railroads of France are doing their level best these days to supply and feed the Allied Armies, and a spare car is almost a thing of the past. But if there is any way of delivering Christmas packages to the A.E.F., the chief postmaster says he is going to find it.

Under the present conditions, however, such prospects look dark.

S-E-C-R-E-T   S-E-C-R-E-T
                 DAILY OPERATION REPORT.
                     148th Infantry.
                 29 to 30 August 1918.
                     Noon to Noon.

I.   ACTIVITY:
      (a) Infantry-(Including Patrols)
            Our Own Troops:------Usual Liaison
                  Patrols.
A reconnaissance patrol of 1 officer 10 other
ranks, to reconnoiter enemy wire and enemy Machine
Guns in vicinity of 431.15/195.80. Mission
accomplished. No Machine guns found in that
vicinity, enemy wire in bad condition, apparently
from shell fire.
            Enemy:--------------Nothing to report.
      (b) Machine Guns:
            Our Own:------------Nothing to report.
            Enemy:--------------20:20 -- 6 bursts,
                  target unknown from Clair Bois.
2:23 -- 4 bursts from Clair Bois, target unknown.
2:31 to-4:50 two bursts from Domevre, target P.P.
5 -- 430.64/195.75
      (c) Trench Cannon (Trench Mortars, Stokes
Mortars, and One-Pounders.)
            Our own:-Trench Mortars:-3 rounds fired,
target 431.00/196.00, time 22:00, gun position
430.70/195.60, Mission Decoy.
                  One Pounders:-16 rounds fired,
target 430.90/196.67, position 429.80/195.50
            Enemy:--------------Nothing to report.
      (d) Artillery:
            Our own:-----------Approximately 130
shots fired at enemy position.
            Enemy:--------------17:00 to 17:15 -- 11
shots from Verdenal, target Bois Bouvroye.

(e) Aeronautics:
  Aeroplanes:
  Our Own:------------One plane circled over Hablainville at 14:00. Another plane over Hablainville at 8:00.
  Enemy:--------------Nothing to report.
  Balloons:
  Our own:-----------Nothing to report.
  Enemy:--------------Nothing to report.
(f) Casualties:
  Killed:------------None.
Wounded:------------Pvt. Cassen Nole, Co. H. 148th Inf. suspected self-inflicted wounds.
  Gassed:------------None.
(g) Movements of Troops (Reliefs, etc.)
  Our Own:-----------Nothing to report.
  Enemy:--------------Nothing to report.
(h) Work done by Command:
  1st Position:-------Building of saps, improvement of duck boards and signal racks.
  2nd Position:-------General improvements of old trenches, 15204 Cu. Ft. of dirt excavated.
(i) Miscellaneous:-------Nothing to report.
(j) General Impression of the Day:----Normal.

    James A. Lynch
    Colonel, N.A.
    Commanding. 148th Inf.

3rd Battalion War Diary for September 1, 1918

Relieved from duty in 1st position. Marched to delousing station at Merville.

2 days rations and 5 days forage with troops.
Weather: clear and warm.   Roads: hard and dry.
Health: excellent.

Chapter Seven

3rd Battalion War Diary for September 2, 1918

March table: Company M from Merviller to Gelacourt, 8 kilometers. Company I from Merviller to Bois de Bouvroy, 4 kilometers. Companies K and L from Merviller to Vaxenville, 4-1/2 kilometers.

Routine duty in second position.

2 days rations and 5 days forage in supply train. 14 officers and 620 men available for all duty. Weather: clear and warm. Roads: hard and dry. Health: excellent.

FIRST ARMY, A.E.F.,
OFFICE OF THE CHIEF OF STAFF,
Ligny-en-Barrois, Meuse, September 4, 1918

MEMORANDUM FOR: General Pershing

1. In connection with our conversation this morning the following are my views relating to the concentration of our forces to the north:

The forces available may be divided into three classes, based on the period of availability.

First Class: Available before attack on St-Mihiel and not associated with that attack.

III Corps Headquarters.

32nd Division. Now near Soissons, Probably in fair shape, has artillery.

28th Division. On the Vesle. Poor shape, has artillery.

77th Division. On the Vesle. Fair shape, has
     artillery.
29th Division. Belfort. No artillery.
92d Division. St-Die. No artillery.
37th Division. Baccarat. No artillery.
36th Division. 13th Training Area.
     (Bar-sur-Aube) Has no artillery.
79th Division. Prauthoy. No artillery.
33d Division. Ligny-en-Barrois. Has
     Artillery.

Second Class: Available in estimated time of five
days after the attack on St-Mihiel.
     80th Division. Stainville. No artillery.
     35th Division. Vicinity of Liverdun. Has
          artillery.
     91st Division. Vicinity of Toul. Has no
          artillery.

Third Class: Available after the attack has
stabilized.
     4th Division. Reserve of V Corps. Has
          artillery.
     82nd Division. In line east of Moselle. Has
          artillery.

In addition a minimum of two other divisions
complete, one brigade of artillery, and two corps
headquarters (I and V).

2. The foregoing scheme will give us the
following:
     A. Immediately available, one corps
headquarters, 9 divisions, of which there will
be 4 divisional artilleries. The time when these
divisions can arrive is dependent, except in
the case of the 36th and 33d, upon their relief

by French troops as they all occupy sectors at the present time. When their relief, etc., is accomplished we should be able to take over a front of four divisions and have in reserve, 5 divisions.

      B. Available after the attack on St-Mihiel stabilizes, seven additional divisions with six divisional artilleries. My estimate is that these divisions can be moved around the 20th instant. We should therefore have available about between the 20th and 25th instant a total of 16 divisions with 10 divisional artilleries.

      3. The plan I propose is as follows:
The 33d Division to be sent at once into sector west of the Meuse under the French Second Army. III Corps Headquarters to proceed at once to take command of the sector of the 33d Division. The divisions mentioned under the first class above to be sent without delay to report to the III Corps Headquarters where they will gradually take over part of the line. This will be the first step in the concentration. After the attack on the St-Mihiel salient I propose that the IV Corps Headquarters be expanded into an army headquarters and take over the line between the French Second Army and the Moselle. The I and V Corps Headquarters to be sent at once to the line west of the Meuse and, as soon as they can be relieved, the seven divisions involved in the attack on St-Mihiel to be sent to report to these two corps headquarters. In the meantime, First Army headquarters will turn over the defense of the salient to the Second Army Headquarters and proceed to carry out the attack to the north. In reference to this last part another solution is to have two corps headquarter take

over the defense of the sector at St-Mihiel and to
continue to function under First Army Headquarter.
This scheme contemplates leaving the IV Corps
Headquarters in the salient and for a new corps
headquarter to be sent in to relieve the I Corps
Headquarters. This also has in mind that an army
headquarters would be instituted without delay
using the IV Corps Headquarters as a nucleus.

    4. If the foregoing is approved, steps
should be taken at once by G. H. Q. to provide
the additional corps headquarters and to provide
for the relief of the III Corps and the various
American divisions now in sectors and not engaged
in the St-Mihiel attack.
    Note: I have already wired G. H. Q. concerning
the relief of the III Corps Headquarters, and I
will see the Commander, French Second Army this
afternoon and arrange with him in accordance with
the above plan.

                                    H. A. Drum,
                              Chief of Staff.

SECRET   SECRET
                  DAILY OPERATION REPORT.
                     148th Infantry.
                  3 Sept. 4 Sept. 1918.
                     Noon to Noon.
I. ACTIVITY:
    (a) Infantry-(including patrols:--USUAL
liaison patrols.

    A reconnaissance patrol of 1 officer and 14
other ranks, to reconnoiter enemy's wire from
431.55/195.75 to 432.00/196.00, left P.P. #3
(431.25/195.25) at 9:15 and arrived at 431.64/

195.50 at 23:20, where two large groups of enemy
(approximately 20 in each group) were sighted.
The patrol observed them for a short time until
certain of their presence, then withdrew to P.P.
#3 (431.25/195.25) to give warning to outguard.
The patrol leader gave above information to
commander of C.G. #1, who passed the information
to the units on the right and left, also to C.
G. at P.A. Babal. The patrol was held at P.P. #3
in readiness for any possible attack for about an
hour.

A wiring party, to repair damage done by
enemy patrol of previous night, was delayed from
21:00 to 23:30 by supposed enemy patrol sighted
in front of P.P. #5 (430.64/195.75) where wire
was to be repaired. Sharp activity on part
of all arms took place for approximately five
minutes, after which the garrison, wiring party
and covering party of 1 officer and approximately
20 men, remained quiet in observation. Nothing
developed so the covering part was posted at edge
of enemy's wire opposite the P.P. and the working
party began their task. Intermittent Machine Gun
fire, somewhat enfilade, from the right, delayed
the wiring party, who continued their work until
about 0:30 when enemy trench mortar shells began
bursting all along edge of woods in this vicinity
and over the P.P. The wiring part left the
position followed by the covering part and the
garrison of the post, who closed the trenches and
passages as they left. The bombardment lasted
for about five minutes. The Garrison of P.P.
#4 was strengthened by addition of two more men
and P.P. #5 was again occupied, by twelve men,
and two trench mortars held in readiness. No
indication of enemy entrance into trenches or P.P.
Approximately 30 shells were fired by the enemy.

The following casualties were reported:
Private Ferch, Co. A. 148th Inf.,- several slight
wounds on left wrist and head from grenade or
debris from trench mortar shelling.
Private Koesterer, Co. C. 148th Inf. severely
wounded in left thigh and abdomen by grenade or
mortar shrapnel. Also left thumb and forefinger.
Private Wardlow, Hqtrs. Co., 148th Inf. slight
bayonet wound in right thigh, probably accidental.
Corporal Richmond, Hqtrs. Co., 148th Inf., slight
grenade wound in right thigh.

No Machine Gun activity to report except
almost continuous auto rifle fire from P.P. #3
(431.20/195.20) and 4 (431.17/195.51) in direction
of Domevre.

In 1st Position, general work, policing of
trenches and dugouts, and repair of duckboards.
10 Cu. Ft. earth removed, and trenches widened.
Wire repaired in front of P.P. #5 (430.64/195.75).

In 2nd Position, 9134 Cu. Ft. of earth
excavated. General improvements in trenches and
dugouts.

September 4, 1918   *Co L 148 Inf*
Be sure and get   *Amer. E.F.*
the address right   *A.P.O 763.*

Dear Mamma,
    Yesterday and day before yesterday I received your two letters dated July 22
and Aug. 8. If you have the address as I have it here I will get them sooner I think.
The A.P.O. is American Post Office 763. This saves much time if it is on the letter.

I am glad you received the $100. It will come every month. I also sent you $50 by
a Y.M.C.A. which you should received as soon as you do this letter if not before. At
Montgomery just before I started away I lost a pocket book in which I had $100. I
didn't tell you before because I didn't want you to worry.

Now the $100 a month will come to you regularly and I will send you money whenever I can. I don't need much right now but I will have to buy a few things before winter. I am going to try to go to see Cousin Morley in England in two months. I will have been in France two months tomorrow. I have been up to the front line but am back now. We are shelled some by artillery.

I am sending you a point de Lunville lace collar. It cost a little over $5 here but I imagine would be $25 in America. The cross is the cross of Lorraine. I have seen them made. It is fine work and very hard on the eyes.

I do hope your nose is all right.

More tomorrow

September 10
I have been so busy and so tired at night that it's been some time since I wrote the first part of this letter. Since then I've sent you $50 more by the Y.M.C.A. This makes $100 in all.

From now on you may have no worry about finances. You will get $100 every month from the government direct. Then I will send you what money I can. I have now about 1000 Francs. A franc is about 20 cents so it makes about $200. If you need any more money let me know, and I will send it to you.

It's been raining and I was wet thru but I am all right now.

Write as often as you can for letters are welcome here as one gets rather lonesome.

Please give my love to all.
With lots of love,
Alfred

P.S. Please when you write use the abbreviation for lieutenant which is Lt.

Censored by A M Barlow 1st Lt N G Inf

The Stars and Stripes, France, September 6, 1918

2,000,000 LETTERS POORLY ADDRESSED

Figure Represents Third of One Week's Arrivals at Base Port

At one base port last week, in four shipments of mail, there were 4,000 sacks of letters, or 6,000,000 letters, for the A.E.F. One-third of those letters were not properly addressed, consequently George is wondering why Polly hasn't written.

With the proper addressing of mail, the M.P.E.S. plays on delivering all mail from 16 to 20 days from the time it is stamped at the New York post office. An A.E.F. mail train is now running between Paris and Chateau-Thierry, and more trains will be running between Paris and other parts of the Z. of A. in a short while.

It is planned to have a postal express service in working order by September 15.

A postal battalion , a separate unit the same as the Q.M.C. or the M.C. is being formed.

The Stars and Stripes, France, September 6, 1918

EVEN THE GENERAL WASN'T TOO BUSY

Little Ohio Boy Gets His Letter from "Place Across Ocean"

There are a thousand things which touch the heart of the American officer on the job with Uncle Sam in France. They are sometimes very little things.

A brigadier general with the A.E.F. was stationed at Camp Sheridan, Ala., last Christmas when he received a letter from a little Ohio boy, a very little fellow whose few scribbled words occupied four sheets of paper. He had read about wars and generals. He wanted to have a general write to him. He said he wanted to cheer for the soldier boys, and that the only way he could do it was by writing letters.

The general replied, saying that if bigger boys had as big a heart and as good a spirit as he the war would soon be ended. That was eight months ago.

The other day when duties with his troops were keeping the general unusually busy, a bundle of letters was handed him. On the top of the bundle was one from the little Ohio boy, whose home is in Shelby.

"I'm Too Small, They Say"

"It's been a long time since I have heard from you or from any other soldier," he wrote. "I l wish I could be where the soldiers are, but I can't. I'm too small, they say.

"But, please, general, won't you write me a letter while you are in France? I have never received a letter in all my life from France, or from any other place across the ocean."

Now in France soldiers pounce on mail bags. They devour letters whole. They do everything but eat letters. But usually they glance through each one in the pile which they might happen by a stroke of good fortune to receive at one time, see who it's from, get a rough idea of what's in it and pass on to the next one. Then, when a little leisure comes along, they go over each one carefully.

Brigadier generals do this as well as privates.

But this letter, coming as it did out of the silence of many months, made the general pause. He read further:

"I've never seen you, general, but I want you to come back home safe. But please don't come back, or let any of the boys come back, until they have licked the Kaiser. I know you're going to do it."

The general's stenographer was nearby.

"Take a letter to this little boy, St. Clair," he said, and began his dictation:

"'Faith will move mountains.'

"No, cross that out. Say, 'Faith like yours is going to help us win this war.'"

The Stars and Stripes, France, September 6, 1918

HOLELESS MACARONI SAVES TONNAGE, TOO

Vermicelli Now Shipped Instead to Nick Waste Out of Holds

The Army's food sharks and boat packers have just found a new way of nicking a couple of acres of waste air out of the solidly packed holds which bring the doughboys' rations to France.

The hole in the macaroni has been abolished.

The macaroni without a hole is as unnatural as a round, solid doughnut, so the holeless doughnut will be called by its rightful name, vermicelli. Company messes will soon see less of the rubber tubing and more of the angle-worm kind of stuff that on mess tables goes under the family name of "wiggles." It's only a question of shape and name, anyway. They're both made of the same things.

Incidentally, macaroni and vermicelli makers back in the States are said to be suffering from strained intellects due to the necessity of changing their formulae and manufacturing processes on account of the scarcity of wheat and the use of wheat substitutes.

The big thing is to obey the dictates of the Government food board and yet make macaroni, spaghetti and vermicelli that will hang together. Nothing annoys a macaroni eater more than to have three or four inches fall off the end of the string on the way to his mouth.

3d Section, General Staff
No. 9300

GENERAL HEADQUARTERS,
ARMIES OF THE NORTH AND NORTHEAST,
Provins, September 7, 1918

The General, Commander-in-Chief

To General Pershing, Commander-in-Chief, A. E. F.,
Chaumont

In course of our latest interviews you
requested:
First, the release of the American 37th,
92nd and 29th Divisions which are in sector on the
front of Lorraine and of the Vosges.
. . . .
In accordance with our agreement, the 3
American divisions in the east, specified above,
were to be released September 15, 18 and 20,
respectively.
. . . .
1. As concerns the American divisions in the
east, I intend to return the 37th Division to you
on September 15, as agreed.
. . . .

PETAIN.

S-E-C-R-E-T
Hq. 3rd Bn., 148th Infantry,
Amer. E. F., 9, Sept. 1918.

Field Order No. 4,
Par.1, Pursuant to R.F.O. 6, 7th Sept. 1918,
a relief of S/S La Blette will be accomplished as
follows:

Night of 12/13 September, 1918:

(a) 2nd Position C.R. 110-   (1) Co. M will
                                  relieve Co. B,
                                  (2) Co. K will
                                  relieve Co. F
                                  (3) Co. I- No
                                  change.
                                  (4) Co. L- No change

Night of 13/14 Sept. 1918:

(b) 2nd Position C.R. 110-   (1) Col A will
                                  relieve Co. M,
                                      (Pettonville
                                      forward
                                      Position.)
                                  (2) Co. M to
                                  Gelacourt after
                                  relief by Co. A,
                                  (3) 3rd B. Hq.
                                  remains at
                                  Vaxainville, (No
                                  movement.)

Par.2, Company Commanders of Companies K
and M will arrange for the necessary preliminary
reconnaissance, advance billeting parties,
guides, and will make suitable arrangements
with the Battalion Supply Officer for the proper
distribution of rations and transportation of
baggage for both movements, paying particular
attention to furnishing guides for the ration
carts.

Par.3, The above relief will be executed with
the utmost secrecy so as to prevent observance by
the enemy; all movements to be completed before

daylight.   FORMATION- Column of files on right side
of road.
      Par.4., Notification of completion of
relief on both nights will be sent to Battalion
Headquarters immediately; each notification to be
followed up at the earliest possible moment with
a report, sketch or tracing showing exact location
of each unit.

                        By order of Major Marlin
F.H. Hume,
1st Lt. 148th Inf.
Bn. Adjutant.

S-E-C-R-E-T   S-E-C-R-E-T

            DAILY OPERATION REPORT.
                148th Infantry
            8 Sept. to 9 Sept. 1918.
                Noon to Noon.

I.   ACTIVITY:-
      (a)   Infantry-(Including patrols.
            Usual Liaison Patrols with 75th French
Infantry.
      A reconnaissance patrol of 1 officer and
13 other ranks to reconnoiter enemy's wire and
positions at bridge 430.80/196.33. The patrol
found that the river gets broader as it approaches
Domevre. The enemy has two lines of wire from
the bridge to the P.S. Road, the outer band only
being in fair condition. The wire is stretched
across the river, making entrance by this means
impossible. There was no enemy activity in
vicinity of bridge W of Maison Detruite. All

flares come from farther south. They seem to have
poor flares since 6 out of 10 fired failed to light.
    Short bursts of Machine gun fire from 4:35 to
4:56 near Herbeviller.

    In the 1st Position, General improvement
of position. 108 duckboards laid, field of fire
cleared at Chauviret, and improvement of alternate
P.P's. 1012-1/2 Cu. Ft. of earth removed during
this period.

    In 2nd Position, improvement of trenches,
5840 cu. ft. of earth were removed.

II. AERONAUTICS:
    Aeroplanes:---Our own:---11:10 to 11:40 -
- one allied plane circled over Azerailles,
Hablainville, Migneville, crossing Boche line to
N.E. Returned same route.
    Balloons: - - Nothing to report.

III. Artillery:-
    Our own:- - - -

TIME	NO.	CAL.	TARGET	FROM	REMARKS
12:15	10	75	Bois de Pretres		
				Herbeviller	Registering
20:13 to					
20:20	33	120	Igney		
				Migneville	Harassing.
22:05	8	75	Clair Bois		
				Montigny.	Harassing.
3:05	5	75	Igney		
				Migneville	Harassing.

    Enemy:- - - -

TIME	NO.	CAL.	TARGET	FROM	REMARKS
12:20	40	77	Migneville		
				432.20/199.30	Harassing.
13:12	8	77	Bois Bouvroye		

```
                              Clair Bois      Registering
16:40        4    77 Migneville
                              430.30/197.50   Registering
23:25       20   105 432.60/192.70
                              438.50/198.20   Harassing.
22:15        5    77  S. edge Migneville
                              Clair Bois      Registering
```

IV. MACHINE GUNS:
        Our Own:- - - - - - -Nothing to report.
        Enemy:- - - - - - - -

```
TIME   TARGET                    FROM WHERE      BURSTS
22:00  P.P. #3 (432.20/195.20) Domevre            1
3:50   P.P. #7 (430.18/195.81) S.W. end Bois de
                               Pretres             1
```

V. GENERAL IMPRESSION OF THE DAY:---- Quiet with exception of heavy artillery activity.

        James A. Lynch
        Colonel, U. S. A.
        Comdg. 148th Inf.

Distinguished Service Cross Citation
Herman L. Hess
First Lieutenant, 148th Infantry

For extraordinary heroism in action near Cierges, France, September 9, 1918. Accompanied by a soldier, he made two trips through heavy machine-gun fire and rescued two wounded men who had been left lying in an exposed place when the battalion took up a new position.

Found in *The 37th Division in the World War*

On 12th September, the day before the newly formed First American Army attacked in the St. Mihiel Salient, the head-quarters of the Eighth (French) Army, General Gerard issued the orders that were to move the Thirty-seventh Division out of the sector and into another and livelier theatre of activity.

These orders recited:

"The 131st Division of Infantry (French, artillery excepted), will be directed beginning 12th September, in the morning, from the region of the Vosges to the rear part of the sector of Baccarat West. On its arrival in its new zone the 131st Division of Infantry will be under the orders of the general command-ing the Sixth (French) Army Corps. This division will relieve the Thirty-seventh D.I., U.S., in the Baccarat sector....

The end of the tour of duty in a "quiet sector" was in sight. None knew what the future held for him or for the divi-sion but all sensed that another milestone had been passed. Mobilization at the home stations, recruiting, the movements to Camp Sheridan, training, another step forward to Camp Less, and a short one to Hoboken or Newport News, embar-kation, the Atlantic, Brest or Havre, training again, and the trenches; and now what? [vol. 2, 163-164]

General Pershing was given the task of reducing this [St. Mihiel] salient and formed the First American Army which he commanded. On 12th September the attack was launched, and on the morning of 13th September, the salient was re-duced; .... The American Army, acting as a unit, under its own commanders, had proved its dependability.... The enemy no longer had a salient as an advanceguard on the western front while from the Scarpe to the Oise, the allies were press-ing close to the last German defenses.... In this final effort, American troops were again to act as a unit, under their own commanders and the Thirty-seventh Division was to play a varied role; it was to attack in the Meuse-Argonne, hold part of the St. Mihiel sector for a time, and then attack again in Belgium. [vol. 2, 172-173]

The Stars and Stripes, France, September 13, 1918

SUBSTITUTE HOME NOW ON PROGRAM FOR MEN OF A.E.F.

Would Provide Places in Army Centers to Meet American Girls

FIRST IN TOWN NEAR LINE

Dances, Card Games, Tea Would Be Enjoyed, Not to Mention Heart-to-Heart Talks

------

A cozy, inviting home-like house where lonesome doughboys will find friendly and charming American girls waiting to talk to them and make sandwiches for them and sing to them and dance with them around the phonograph--a series of such houses to be opened in all those French towns where Yankee soldiers crowd thickest--that is the proposal now being perfected by various organizations in and outside the Army.

They will not be Y.M.C.A. huts nor Y.W.C.A. huts nor "hostess houses," in the sense of that term as it has been used in the cantonments back in the States. The hope is to create something that will deserve the name of Substitute Home. The present plan is to open the first of these homes as an experiment in a town quite close to the front. It will be manned (laughter) by 12 American girls.

This house and all that may follow it is based on the realization that, in an army of young men from three to six thousand miles from home, there are times when there is nothing in the world a soldier needs and wants quite so much as just the chance to sit and talk with the kind of girl he used to call on in his own home town, that there is nothing that would do his pep and his immortal soul more good than just the chance once in a while, to drop into a pleasant house made friendly and pleasing to the eye by the artful hands of some gentle American women.

Card Games and Dances

There would be rooms to read in, rooms to write in. Probably there would be teas and ice cream parties. Certainly there would be card games and dances. Above all, there would be just such heart-to-heart talks as the wall of every veranda in America could tell if walls had ears.

There is no present intention of barring anybody from these hospitable houses. There is no reason why a man, just because he has been commissioned, should therefore be coldly received. But these hostesses will be blind to bars, and officers wishing to come to the party must spiritually hang their Sam Browne belts on the fence outside.

If the first house is a success and the plan unfolds throughout the A.E.F., there is no reason why the staff of each house should not be supplemented in any given afternoon by American girls who happen to be working in that vicinity.

In many a center there are charming nurses, telephone girls, Y.M.C.A. aids, Y.W.C.A. workers, Red Cross girls--such as the veterans of the Smith College Unit--a small army of devoted American women in France, many of whom have the gifts and the goodwill to play occasional hostess in such a house. In addition to those who might be summoned from America for the purpose, the houses would therefore do a big work if they did nothing else than provide places where the American soldiers and the American women in France might meet and talk together without any one's throwing a fit.

The Stars and Stripes, France, September 13, 1918

HERE'S THE HOYLE ON CENSORSHIP AS PLAYED IN A.E.F.

G.H.Q. Tells How German Hardware May or May Not Be Sent Home

RULES FOR LETTERS ALSO

Old Regulations Restated, New Ones Added in General Order Just Published

-----

All the latest dope on what you may and what you may not get past the censor is brought up to date for all concerned, which means everybody, in a new General Order, No. 146, hot from the G.H.Q. presses. Some of the more interesting restrictions and releases are here re-hashed.

Inasmuch as every doughboy fresh from the Soissons-Chateau-Thierry battlefield is laden with enough German hardware to open a store, the question of souvenirs has become a burning one.

All enemy property acquired under any circumstances whatever should be turned over at once to an Intelligence officer.

"Have a heart," says the outraged doughboy, who has just chased a fat German colonel for two kilometers for no other reason than because the girl across the street back home had casually expressed her desire for a Hussar's helmet. But, the order goes on to mollify him, if the trophy is not of value to the Intelligence Section, it will be returned to the sender. Such trophies may be of vast importance to the General Staff as giving identification not otherwise verified and information about new enemy equipment of value to our own supply and technical services.

Requires Written Approval

As for sending these souvenirs home. It is absolutely verboten to mail your father a German machine gun, even if you captured it yourself at the point of a bayonet. Indeed, trophies in general, are forbidden expect enemy helmets, caps, badges, numerals and buttons, and those only on approval by a field officer, such written approval to be contained in the package.

'There are other limitations on what you may send home in parcels. You may not send any necessities of life. You may not send any clothing, except gloves, handkerchiefs, laces and such trifles designated as gifts for the folks. And these can be sent only to the United States and Canada. You may not send Government property and you may not send explosives. Whatever desire you may have to send Aunt Lucy a hand grenade you must firmly suppress.

Then there's the question of photographs. All members of the A.E.F. are forbidden to take photographs unless photography is a part of their official duties. If you have a camera, you may keep it, but you must keep it unloaded in the bottom of your barrack bag. A perfectly beautiful picture of yourself may be mailed home every little while, provided the background is entirely non-committal.

These Are Also Barred

The familiar foxy trick of trying to smuggle letters home by returning officers, returning Y.M.C.A. secretaries or returning wounded is violently defendu. The sender and the bearers of such illicit missives are liable to dire punishment.

Certain inclosures are forbidden. Besides tell-tale photographs, photographic negatives, immoral post cards, naughty-naughty pictures, dirty poems, official papers, captured papers, maps and the like are also barred.

You may not write to a newspaper on any subject connected with military matters unless you have written permission from the Chief, G-2-D, G.H.Q., A.E.F. If an objectionable letter of yours is published back home without your knowledge, you are the goat nevertheless.

The order gives a few illustrations of what is considered dangerous information, to be rigorously excluded from all letters, diaries and other writings. You must not mention a place in the Z. of A. from which you are writing. You must make no reference to future operations, whether you know or are just guessing. You must not tittle-tattle about troop movements, armaments, defensive works, morale, supplies, railroad positions, road conditions, reserves, ammunition, supplies or effects of hostile fire. You must not give any information at all about aircraft, tanks chemical warfare and other technical services.

The Matter of Addresses

If you do not like our gallant Allies either individually or in lump, do not say so and don't particularize. If you think the general made a botch of his last operation, keep it dark. If you disapprove of the grub, stow it. If you think the top sergeant is a curious mixture of half-wit and thug, let no one guess it from your letters home.

Then there is the matter of addresses. If you are in the base or intermediate section of the S.O.S., you can give the town as your post office. But that is all. It doesn't take the lid off on all matters military going on thereabouts. If you are writing to some pal belonging to a loose organization in a town in the Z. of A. that has no Yankee post office, address him without mentioning the town. Then enclose than envelope in an outer envelope addressed to the C.O. Armee-Americaine, followed by the name of the town and department.

As for putting your own address and unit up in the upper left-hand corner--don't. Put your name, your rank and your branch of the service and no more. Put Corporal J. Marmaduke Archibald Doe, U.S. Marine Corps, but no more. Don't put 912th Regiment, U.S.M.C., Cologne, or anything so intimate and detailed as that.

The blue envelope is still a safeguard of privacy. But you may use only those blue envelopes issues by the Chief Q.M., A.E.F., and not of those azure substitutes that have been caught in the act. The certificate that the letters within are strictly non-military must be signed or the blue envelope is useless. It may contain as many letters as can be stuffed into it, but they must all be from one soldier.

No Limit on Number

There are certain passages in the order which govern less the letter-writers than their censors. There is a stern warning to all officers who may have tried or might be tempted to try to lessen the censorship work by discouraging or actually forbidding correspondence.

"Organization commanders," the order says, "will use every effort to cause the men of their commands to write regularly--at least once a week--to their parents or families. It is to be distinctly understood that there is no limit placed on the writing of letters. No commanding officer is to limit the number of letters."

An officer who comes across a letter written in a foreign language he understands may censor it; otherwise, it goes to the Base Censor, who is responsible for the military innocence of epistles couched in every tongue known since the Tower of Babel.

Examining officers may not write any remarks, sassy or otherwise, on letters they are censoring. If they ever tell any one the little private secrets their job discloses to them, they are flying in the face of a specific order and will probably be met with a punishment that has a kick in it.

Any letter referring to a casualty thereby passes out of the domain of all local censorship. It must be censored at the Central Records Office, A.G.D., A.P.O. 717, and should be there addressed.

The Stars and Stripes, France, September 13, 1918

OFFICERS MAY BUY UNIFORMS AT COST UNDER Q.M.C. PLAN

Army Depots to Sell Cloth and Supervise Work of Civilian Tailors

-----

READYMADES ON SALE, TOO

Style Changes Being Worked Out by Board Soon to Submit Its Findings to S.O.S. Chief

-----

A plan which originated within the General Purchasing Board of the Quartermaster Department whereby an officer need pay for his uniform only the cost of production is now being developed throughout France. This will so reduce the now familiar expense of commissioned finery that it will do away with one of the reasons why officers of the A.E.F. wish they weren't.

According to this plan, each Q.M. depot will have a tailoring system through which the officer can buy his cloth and then be fitted and outfitted on the spot. At each depot, civilian labor will be contracted for and the officer need add to the price of his cloth only his share of that labor cost.

Presumably neither the cost nor the method will be uniform throughout France, for the labor conditions will vary in different sections.

Work for French Tailors

In some cases, for example, the chances are that it will be more practical for the depot quartermaster to arrange with one or more of the local French tailors to make the uniforms at a fixed price, which price would be paid by the officer to the quartermaster who, in turn, would turn the money over to the tailors. Or, in some places, it will be simpler for the Army and the tailor to agree on a proper price, make that the standard and then let the officer in quest of raiment deal directly with the tailor. This is the system now in force in Paris, where an officer, if he goes to certain designated tailors, can have his cloth made into a suit at a charge of only 100 francs.

The quartermaster is also making arrangements to have on hand at an early date an adequate supply of ready-made uniforms for officers built that way.

It may well be that the officers will have to haunt the tailors soon in quest of alterations, for a board is now threshing out the problem of fall styles for officers and enlisted men. Is revision necessary? If so, in what respect?

All the burning questions of split tails, roll collars, bellows pockets and the like are now up for final consideration and the board will soon submit its recommendations to the Commanding General of the S.O.S.

The Stars and Stripes, France, September 13, 1918

COLOR CHANGES IN RULES FOR OFFICERS' CAPS

New Pipings Announced for Overseas Headgear in General Order

SAME CLOTH AS UNIFORM

Tank Service Gray, Chemical Blue and Yellow, Cavalry Yellow and Scarlet--Many Others

-----

G.H.Q. has come out with an announcement calculated to make American officers recognizable even when they have their rain coats on.

No longer will they be allowed to run around under headpieces that look as if they had been designed for the man who costumed the moving picture players in the war drama during our neutral days, and made the actor soldiers' uniforms on the Burbank system, so nobody's feelings would be hurt.

Here is the latest rule for officers' headgear, as set forth in G.O. 149:

For officers while serving with the A.E.F., the overseas cap will be the same model as that worn by soldiers, but the material will be similar to that of the officers' uniform, and will have piping showing at the edge of the flap as follows:

General Officers, gold.

General Staff, including officers attached to the General Staff or performing General Staff duties, gold and black in equal proportion.

Adjutant General's Department, dark blue.

Dark Blue, White Threads

Inspector General's Department, dark blue with white threads.

Judge Advocate General's Department, dark blue with light blue threads.

Quartermaster Corps, buff.

Ordnance Department, black with scarlet threads.

Signal Corps, orange with while threads.

Medical Department, maroon.

Air Service, green with black threads.

Corps of Engineers, scarlet with white threads.

Tank Service, gray.

Chemical Warfare Service. cobalt blue with yellow threads.

Corps of Interpreters, green with white threads.

Cavalry, including officers with headquarters troops of Infantry divisions and train headquarters of Cavalry divisions, yellow.

Artillery, including officers with ammunition trains and artillery parks, scarlet.

Infantry, including officers with train headquarters of Infantry divisions, light blue.

Machine Gun organizations, Infantry, light blue with scarlet threads.

Cavalry, yellow with scarlet threads.

Chaplains, black.

Field Clerks, black with silver threads.

Line officers detailed in a staff corps or department will wear cap with piping specified for corps or department in which detailed.

These caps will be sold by the Quartermaster Corps to officers.

The Stars and Stripes, France, September 13, 1918

NO SPEED LIMIT AT SHRAPNEL CORNER

Signboard at Death Bend Says: "Don't Stop to Think It Over"

Humor may have its place, but so far no one has arisen to say that the boundaries of that place do not include the first line trenches.

Up near the Vesle, at a point which isn't as near the front as it used to be, one of the main roadways, after stealing up a valley, runs out of concealment suddenly and rounds the exposed end of a hill. Until a few days ago this hill was under the direct and constant observation and fire of Boche guns. It was a bad place to be--as was attested by a sign hanging from the limb of a battered and denuded tree.

"DEATH BEND, FRANCE," announced the sign, "SHRAPNEL CORNER."

Below were these road directions:

"BLIGHTY"--with an arrow pointing toward the front--"3 kilometers."

"NOHUN"--with an arrow pointing rearwards--"5 kilometers."

"HOME"--with another arrow ditto--"5,000 kilometers."

"BUT DON'T," concluded the sign, "STOP HERE TO THINK IT OVER."

Found in *The 37th Division in the World War*

On 14th September, division headquarters learned the destination of the unit (but the information did not filter down to regiments) in the following telegram from First (American) Army Headquarters:

"The Thirty-seventh Division will proceed by rail; movement to begin morning 17th September, from present area to a new area, detraining at Robert Espagne, under arrangement to be made by G-4, First (American) Army.

"On arrival at Robert Espagne, Thirty-seventh Division is attached to Third Corps, U.S., and will be reported to

Commanding General, Second French Army, for orders...."
[vol. 2, 165]

From 3rd Battalion War Diary for September 14, 1918

    March table: Company L from Vaxainville at
21:30 to Valois at 3:30. 22 kilometers.
    Command moved to Valois.
    2 days rations and 5 days forage in supply
train. 17 officers and 636 men available for all
duty. Weather: fair and warmer. Roads: good.
Health: good.

From 148th Infantry Regiment War Diary for September 14, 1918

    After arrival in Moyen all troops cleaned
persons and equipment and spent the time in the
inspection of equipment.

G-3 No. 202   FIRST ARMY, A.E.F.,
SPECIAL ORDERS   September 15, 1918.

    The following telegraphic order, having been
issued September 15, 1918, is herein embodied for
record:
            1. Commanding General
                37th Division
                Baccarat
                G-3 Number 299. The 37th Division
will proceed by rail, movement to begin morning
September 17 from present area to a new area,
detraining at Robert-Espagne,... On arrival
at Robert-Espagne, 37th Division is attached
to American III Corps, and will be reported

to Commanding General, French Second Army, for
Orders....

By command of General Pershing:
                          H. A. Drum,
                    Chief of Staff.

Hill House Farm   Wadhurst

Sept 15. 18

Dear Cousin Eva --
I received your very welcome letter and I was pleased to hear you were all well.
I have been expecting to have some news of Alfred but have not yet heard anything
from him. Doubtless he is in France but I hope he is alright. There are a great many
of your soldiers in England but I do not expect they grant them leave to visit their
relatives. The fighting in France is very bad but as you doubtless have heard the
Allies are pushing the Germans back and a great many victories have been won. I
do not think the war will finish before next year. The winter months and the bad
weather, I think will prevent it. Tom, my youngest son, is in France, after coming
back from Palestine and has been home for 14 day leave. He was then looking very
well & fit. My eldest son Willie, he has been in England for 3 months from Malta
& Harold he is at home in the north of England. We are all doing what we can.
I have on the farm. I shall be glad when the war is over but I shall be very sorry
indeed to see it finished -- until we have conquered the Germans we do not want a
repetition of this either our selves or our Children in their time it must be finished for
all time and we in England have America to thank for their great help in the time
of need. I am sure the loses that your country will sustain will be immense but I do
hope that yours will come out alright but there is of course the danger. The hospital
opposite my house is full of wounded. I only wish I was younger. So that I could
out & help the Boys. Doing all I can to provide on my farm all I can in respect of
milk and vegetables.

I must close now with love to
your dear Mother & self from
your affectionate Cousin
Morley Browne

FIRST ARMY, A. E. F.,
OFFICE OF THE CHIEF OF STAFF,
Lygny-en-Barrois, September 16, 1918.

From: Chief of Staff, First Army

To: Commanding General, French Second Army

    1. For your information I have the honor
to inform you that the proposed distribution of
troops in the zone now occupied by the French
Second Army will be as follows... :
    ....
    V Corps - 79th Division, 37th Division, 91st
Division, with the 92nd Division in corps reserve.
The 29th Division to be used as army reserve will
also be assigned to this corps.
    ....
    2. It is requested that insofar as
practicable the troops be most conveniently placed
to be brought up into the above arrangement.

                                    H. A. Drum
                                  Chief of Staff.

                    Headquarters, 148th Infantry,
                    American Expeditionary Forces,
                            16 September, 1918.
Field Order
   No. 9

    1. Pursuant to F.O. 17 Headquarters 37th
Division 1918 this regiment moves to another area.
Movement being by rail.

2.   Entraining will begin on morning of 17 September....

3.   Entraining Stations: Garberville -- Moyen.

4.   Duration of journey, about 8 hours.

5.   Responsibility for this regiment entraining at stations rests with:
 a) Commanding Officer, 1st Battalion 148th Infantry
  for Garberville.
 b) Commanding Officer, 3rd Battalion 148th Infantry
  for Moyen.

6.   Every precaution will be taken to assure defense against aeroplanes, Machine Gun platoons will be attached to each train as indicated in entraining table. Platoons attached to each train leaving from each entraining point will be placed in position near railway stations before dusk, Sept. 16th and render necessary anti-aircraft protection during the entire period of entraining. Platoons first to arrive at detraining points will render necessary anti-aircraft protection during the entire period of detraining....

By order of Colonel James A. Lynch
R.F. Ohmer
Capt. 148th Inf.
Adjutant

From 3rd Battalion War Diary for September 17, 1918

March table: Company L from Vallois at 21:30
to Garberville at 24:00.   5 kilometers....
     Prepared for and marched to entraining point.
     2 days rations and 5 days forages in supply
train.   18 officers and 645 men available for all
duty.   Weather: rain and cloudy.   Roads: fair
conditions.   Health: good.

From 3rd Battalion War Diary for September 18, 1918

March table: Company L from Garberville at 2:
00 to Bar le Duc at 11:00.   130 kilometers....
     L Company and Battalion Headquarters
detrained at Mussey and marched 8 kilometers to
Bar le Duc.
     20 Officers and 646 men available for all
duty.   Weather: cloudy, some rain.   Roads: fair
condition.   Health: good.

                        Headquarters, 148th Infantry,
                     American Expeditionary Forces,
                           18th September 1918.

From: Commanding Officer, 148th Infantry.

To: Commanding General, 37th Division.

Subject: Location of Organizations.

          1.   The location of the different
organizations comprising the 148th Infantry are as
follows:

```
Regimental Headquarters.........Fains
Headquarters Company...........Fains
Machine Gun Company............Fains
Supply Company.................Fains
Sanitary Detachment............Fains
1st Battalion Hq...............Fains
       Cos. A,B,C,D............Fains
2nd Bn. Hq.....................Combles
       Cos. F,G,H..............Combles
3rd Bn. Hq.....................Bar le Duc
       Cos. L and M............Bar le Duc
       Cos. I and K............Veel
       Co. E...................Veel.
```

```
                    James A. Lynch
                    Colonel, USA.,
                    Comdg. 148th.
```

September 18, 1918   *Co L 148 Inf.*
                                                            Amer. E.F.
                                                            A.P.O. 763

Dear Mamma,

Your letter of Aug. 10 came the day before yesterday and your letter of Aug 20 came yesterday.

The package I sent from Camp Lee was by Adams Express. There was nothing in it of much value. I am glad you got the big box O.K. Was the little brown leather grip in the big box? I hope it was.

I wrote out a check some time ago on the Ohio Valley Bank for F100 which is about $20 so you had better leave a little there to cover it. I will write no more checks. I have been forty two days at the front but am back now. Don't know where I'm going. By this time you doubtless have the allotment of $100 from the government and the two $50 money orders I sent by the Y.M.C.A.

That will be $200 altogether during September. That will pay the insurance and leave about $150 over. This letter won't get to you before Oct. 1st and by that time you will have $100 more. I hope you get every thing you need for winter use gas it is a lot better than coal. Have plenty of covers and <u>leave the windows open</u> and you will not <u>catch cold</u>. Then you can light the gas and dress in the other room.

Thou I never remain in the same place long my address is always the same.

You can send the pen to this address and it will get to me O.K. Everyone is getting papers from home, it seems but me. Please have the weekly Tribune sent to me. It will get here all right if it is started right. I was with Capt. Tom Jones the other night and saw the only papers I've seen since I've been in France and for about 2 months before.

Night before last I ate supper in the same chateau in the same room at the same table and in the same chair the Emperor of Germany sat four years ago.

I have a very good "striker"--man who works for me. He packs and un packs my baggage and mends my clothes, keeps the buttons sewed on and every time I change shoes he washes them and polishes them.

I hope Grandma is better and that you have entirely recovered. I am very sorry I did not get to see Mildred & Laura as I had plenty of time and could just as well as not.

I am sorry to hear Uncle John has been ill but am glad to hear he is better.

Please give my regards to all.

       With lots of love,

             Alfred.

Censored by A M Barlow 1st Lt. Inf. N.G.

Found in *The 37ᵗʰ Division in the World War*

On 19th September, information issued from division headquarters to the effect that the division would move to still another "new area" by bus and its own transportation, starting at 4:00 P.M. the next day; billeting parties were to leave at 1:00 P.M. (vol. 2, 166)

Translation from the French, found in
The United States Army in the World War (The Center for Military History)

3d Section, General Staff   FRENCH SECOND ARMY,
No. 690/3   Laheycourt, September 19, 1918.

SPECIAL ORDER

1. At 8 a.m., September 21, 1918, the Generals commanding the American I, III, and V Army Corps will take over the command of their respective zones, designated by Memorandum No. 633/3. September 14, as amended by Memoranda No. 3,627/3, September 17, and No. 683/3, September 18.

2. III Army Corps, on the right. Headquarters: Rampont.

V Army Corps, in the center. Headquarters: Ville-sur-Cousances.

I Army Corps, on the left. Headquarters: Rarecourt.

3. a. On the same date, the disposition of the divisions assigned to the American III Army Corps, including those present in and marching to that zone, is as follows:

...

b. On the same date, the disposition of the divisions assigned to the American V Army Corps, including those present in and marching to that zone, is as follows:

....

(2) Center Sector: Held by the American 79th Division which will be relieved later by the American 37th Division which has arrived in its sector, with the exception of its artil-

lery, its mounted elements, and its trains. These elements will join its division the night of September 22/23.

....

Hirshauer,
General Commanding.

Translation from the French, found in
The United States Army in the World War

3d Section, General Staff   FRENCH SECOND ARMY,
No. 687/3   Laheycourt, September 19, 1918.

SPECIAL ORDER

1. The American 37th Division, detrained in the region of Robert-Espagne (Headquarters), will proceed, beginning the evening of September 20, to the zone of the American V Army Corps, where it is placed at the disposal of the latter.

....

By order:

FRANTZ,
Chief of Staff.
FIRST ARMY, A. E. F.,
Ligny-en-Barrios, September 19, 1918.

Annex No. 5, (Field Order No. 20)
(Operation Z)

PLAN OF EVACUATION OF SICK AND WOUNDED AND SUPPLY

    I.   EVACUATION OF SICK AND WOUNDED:
        . . . .
        (B)   V CORPS SECTOR AND ALL TROOPS
THEREIN:
        Seriously Wounded: Evacuation hospitals to be established at Froidos and Fleury-sur-Aire.

Slightly Wounded: Evacuation hospital at Vaubecourt, and excess to Bar-le-Duc, 1/2 of French H. O. E. and base hospital.

Gassed: Hospital to be established at Julvecourt.

Psychiatric Cases: Nubecourt.

Contagious Diseases: Annex of E. H. at Vaubecourt.

Normal Sick: To E. H. at Fleury-sur-Aire.

. . . .

II. EVACUATION OF ANIMALS:

All troops: To army animal evacuation stations at Heippes and Autrecourt.

III. RAILHEADS:

. . . .

V CORPS:

 79th Division - Rampont.
 37th Division - Rampont.
 91st Division - Froidos.
 32nd Division - Fleury.
 Corps troops - Froidos.

. . . .

There will be a reserve supply of rations and forage at each railhead. This will be used to replenish supply trains in the event of the failure of daily automatic supply train from regulation station.

All divisions must carry at all times the rations and forage called for in Par. 302, F. S. R.

IV. GASOLINE AND OIL SUPPLIES:

Gasoline and Oil Reserve: Fleury

Stations at: Vadelaincourt-Froidos. For reserve to be used in case automatic supply fails at any railhead.

V. ENGINEER SUPPLIES:

      Engineer parks at: Les Islettes
      Souhesmes

                        Dombasle

Rattentout

                        Aubreville

    VI. CHEMICAL WARFARE SUPPLIES:
      Chemical Warfare Park (Offensive) at:
Clermont
      Gas Park C: At Les Montairons, 3 kms.
south of Ancemont.
      Gas Park D: At Beauchamp Farm, 4 kms.
southeast of Les Islettes
    VII. SIGNAL CORPS SUPPLIES:
      Signal Corps Park C: At Souilly
    VIII. MEDICAL CORPS SUPPLIES:
      Medical Park C: At Souilly
      Medical Park D: At Vaubecourt
      Medical Park E: At Fleury
    IX. MACHINE GUN DEPOTS:
      Machine Gun Depots at: Nixeville
                      Les Islettes
                  Brahant-en-Argonne
    X.   MOTOR SUPPLY:
      Spar Parts, Motor: At Ferme Longues-
Roies, 2 kms. east of Triaucourt on Triaucourt-
Souilly Road.
     . . . .
    1. The supply of ammunition to the
antiaircraft artillery, French and American, will
be controlled by G-4, First Army, in accordance
with demands of the Chief of Artillery, First
Army.
    2. The corps munition officers will issue
on demand of army artillery units in their
corps areas such small arms ammunition as may be
demanded by these units.

3. Divisional munitions officers will issue on demand of antiaircraft units in their areas, 8-mm. Hotchkiss ammunition in strips up to 1,000 rounds per gun per day of firing.

4. Artillery reports will be made daily, closing at 6 p.m. Infantry reports will be made every ten days.

5. Attention is invited to instructions in letter from G-4, First Army, to corps commanders, on plan of ammunition supply, dated September 16, 1918.

By command of General Pershing:

H. A. DRUM,
Colonel,
Chief of Staff

From 3rd Battalion War Diary for September 20, 1918

March table: Company L from Bar le Duc at 18:30 to 65.30-13.50 [Recicourt]. 51 kilometers....
2 days rations and 5 days forage in supply train. 25 officers and 644 men available for all duty. Weather: colder-light rain. Roads: somewhat muddy. Health: good.

from 148th Infantry Regiment War Diary for September 20, 1918

The 148th moved by truck train from Faius, to reserve position Northeast of Verdun.

FIELD ORDERS   FIRST ARMY, A.E.F.,
No. 20   Ligny-en-Barrois,
                      September 20, 1918--3 p.m.

   ...
   1. (a) The enemy holds the front from
Clemery (east of the Moselle to the Aisne) as
follows:
          (1) Clemery to the Meuse inclusive.
          Thirteen division in line.
          Eleven divisions (estimated) in
reserve in vicinity of Metz.
          Of the foregoing divisions four are
being reconstituted.
          (2) The Meuse exclusive to the Aisne
inclusive.
          Five divisions in line.
          (3) The morale of all these divisions
is below normal.
          (b) The Allied Armies attack on the
front the Meuse exclusive to the Suippe exclusive:
          (1) Direction: Toward Mezieres.
          (2) Mission: To force the enemy from
the line of the Aisne.
          (3) Objectives: First, Dun-sur-Meuse-
--Grandpre---Challerange---Sommepy. Second,
Stenay---Le Chesne---Attigny---Rethel.
          (c) The French Fourth Army attacks
on the front La Harazee exclusive to the Suippe
exclusive and assists our army in the reduction of
the Argonne Forest by the capture of Binarville,
Lacon and Grand-Ham. The French XXXVIII Corps
will attack on the right of the French Fourth
Army.

The Stars and Stripes, France, September 20, 1918

HERE AND THERE IN THE S.O.S.

Worn shoes washed in big steamroller tubs the same as your collars are washed back home, and punctured and badly-wounded rubber boots patched and vulcanized by the methods the tire man uses in the garage these are two of the hurry-up ways in which the Army salvage plant at Blois is cutting time and labor in making old shoes and boots into new.

No other shoe plant in the world washes shoes in a laundry machine, the salvage men say. Soaking hardened shoes in oil vats is another new feature.

In repairing rubber boots, big-scale operations have produced more novel methods. For instance, there's the drying of boots after they have been thoroughly washed. The boots are placed, soles down, over hollow tubes out of which rush continuous blasts of hot air.

After all the torn parts have been cut away and the edges cleaned--perhaps the whole heel and half of the sole must be taken off--the boot is shoved on an iron last of exact size. Expert tire repair men then build up new fabric in the holes, using strips of raw rubber, and a molded heel if necessary. Then the boot is clamped in a steam-frame and baked until the new parts are as solid as the old.

Shoes that can't be repaired are not wasted. French girls shed their uppers into leather shoe strings, each shoe making seven or more strings.

There are machines, acting on the player-piano principle, in the hospital records department of the Chief Surgeon's office that have mechanical electric brains that tell infallibly just how many soldiers are in hospitals with mumps and influenza, or gunshot wounds of the arms and legs--tell just how many men are suffering from each disease, and how many have been wounded in each part of the anatomy.

Not only that, but the machines sort the names of the sick and wounded alphabetically, record changes in diagnosis and complications, tell the dates of admission and discharge from hospital, the total number of days in hospital, and whether sickness or injury was in line of duty. They tell a lot of other things, too.

The basis of the system is a record card printed something like a meal ticket or street car transfer. When the lists of the sick and wounded come to headquarters a card is made out for each man. French grubs run the cards through machines which punch little holes in all the ruled divisions for the card, the location of each hole definitely marking the number assigned to a disease or wounded, dates, names by the first four letters, and all the other data to be recorded.

The card contains 35 or more holes when finished. They look like a section of a player-piano roll. The punctured cards go to the electric tabulating machines, through which they run at fastest machine gun speed, little speedometer dials clicking up the figures sought.

After being tabulated the cards are run through machines which sort them alphabetically by name or according to any other information desired. For instance, this machine will sort out at one time the cards of all men with fractures of the arms or legs, wounds of the head, face, abdomen and chest, and a dozen other parts of the anatomy if desired.

Lieutenants who used to drive cream-colored underslung racers, and were in the habit of telling confidentially how "she'd make over 70 any time you stepped on her," won't have much chance to travel along French roads so fast that the poplar trees look like a wall.

The Sunbeams and Packards and Wintons of the A.E.F. have got to be mighty circumspect on the open roads and in the towns of the S.O.S. from now on. For the word has been passed round that M.P.'s on motor-cycles are flitting around the headquarters towns, and they're going to be just as rough as the township constable who used to build a new porch to his house out of one week's justice court fees.

Found in *The 37th Division in the World War*

The 145th bivouacked in the Bois de Recicourt, arriving 21st September. The 146th Infantry occupied the same woods, arriving 20th-21st-22nd September; the 147th in Verriere en Hesse and the Bois de Recicourt, arriving 21st-23rd September; and the 148th in the vicinity of Recicourt (21st September) and in the woods near the C.R. Hermont.

These units of the Thirty-seventh Division found themselves gradually working into positions in the Avocourt Sector, where they were to attack when the world's greatest battle should open along the western front. (vol 2, 169-170)

From 3rd Battalion War Diary for September 22, 1918

```
Routine duties second position.
2 days rations and 5 days forage in supply
train.  Weather: rain.  Roads: soft.  Health:
good.


Field Orders
    No. 10
Advance data for Attack

Formation upon departure:
Line of Battalions:-
Order:-         2nd Battalion. . . . Right
Battalion
                1st Battalion. . . . Left Battalion
                (Right of the Base Battalion)
Extension in depth as follows:

For each Battalion ----
    2 Companies in first line: Platoons in lozenge
formation.

Interval between Battalions in line -- 100 Meters
Distance in depth between Companies -- 300 Meters

Interval between Platoons in Line   -- 60 Meters
Distance between Platoons           -- 60 Meters

                By order of Colonel James A. Lynch
                    R.F. Ohmer
                    Capt. 148th Inf.
                    Adjutant
```

Field Order No. 11

Advance data for Attack Order.

1.   One way projector communications will be
established between battalion and Regiment. The
sending station will search from the receiving
station by directing its flash toward all prominent
points near the desired station and sending the
call letter several times. It will continue
to send that call letter until the call is
acknowledged by one red rocket. One second rocket
(message received) one white rocket (repeat).

2.   All radio T. F. S. and visual messages will
be coded as   follows:

          1.   By code book Mohawk.
          2.   List number one, Liaison for all
Arms, 78 and 79.
          3.   List No. 2   Table T.   (Table Q in
reserve).
          4.   Coordinate key No. 325.
          5.   Code names specified in Memorandum
Orders No. 70. Headquarters, 37th Division,
except that (Chris-Cross will be used for the
Division P. C.)

3.   Pigeons, 16 pigeons are assigned to each
regiment of infantry to be distributed as directed
by the Regimental Commander. These pigeons will
be delivered by the signal corps on "D" day minus
1 and will remain in possession of the regiments
until the final objective has been reached, unless
they have been used after all other means of
communication have failed.

4.   Regiment will establish a chain of runners between Brigade and Regimental Headquarters, and Regimental Hq. and Bn. Hq.

5.   Runners will carry messages in the right side breast pocket of the blouse and it will be the duty of any officer or men observing the runner that has become a casualty to search that pocket for the message and see that it is delivered to its destination.

6.   SIGNALS BY AEROPLANES TO GROUND: By fire works.
        "Where are you"   (for marking out line)
            1 cartridge of
                6 stars.
        "Understood"
            1 cartridge of
                2 stars.
        "Anti tank gun at this point"
            Yellow smoke.

7.   Signals from the ground:
            Signals from the ground to aeroplanes by fireworks.
        "Objective reached"
            Caterpillar rocket
        "Request for barrage fire"
            3 Star Cartridge
        "Friendly heavy artillery is firing on us"
            One star V.P. Cartridge followed
            by green parachute V.B. Cartridge.
        "We are going to advance, increase range"
            Rocket with green stars
        "We are here"
            Bengal white flare
        "Message Understood"
            1 red rocket

"Repeat signal or message"
    1 white rocket.
"One hour delay orders in
    Yellow smoke rocket
    execution of next phase"
        followed by a
        flag rocket.
    ....
The staking out of the 1st wave will be done
on demand of the infantry aeroplane which will use
the conventional signal (1 cartridge of 6 starts)

                    By order of Colonel James A. Lynch
                                R.F. Ohmer
                            Capt. 148th Inf.
                            Adjutant

Chapter Eight

Found in *The 37th Division in the World War*

The front to be occupied by the American Army was to be between the Meuse and the western edge of the Argonne forest. The army was to consist of three corps—the First under General Liggett, the Fifth under General Cameron and the Third under General Bullard. The divisions, from left to right, were the 77th, 28th, 35th, 91st, 37th, 79th, 4th, 80th, and 33rd....

Of the three army corps attacking, the Fifth was at the center; and of the three divisions in the Fifth Corps, the Thirty-seventh was at the center, as it moved into position on the night of 24th September....

Immediately in the center of the sector assigned the Thirty-seventh was the pile of crumbling stone that had once been Avocourt. Between Avocourt and the northern edge of the woods was Montfaucon. The right boundary line of the sector passed just to the left of the village. The left boundary line of the sector curved to include Ivoiry, about three kilometers west and about 800 meters to the north of Montfaucon. (vol. 2, 174)

Infantry brigade commanders were ordered to draw up their plans of attack including proposed dispositions, instructions and assignments and submit them to division headquarters at 11:00 A.M. on 25th September. The advance infantry regiments were to be formed with two battalions in the front line and one battalion in support. The remaining units of each brigade less that portion assigned to the divisional reserve, was to constitute a brigade reserve. The officer commanding the provisional infantry regiment detailed as divisional reserve, was to command the reserve and was ordered to place his troops in position in the Bois de Verrieres and the Bois de Chattancourt, six minutes before the attack.

These woods were several kilometers to the south of the front line positions.

Packs were to be turned over to regimental supply officers; and overcoats and slickers were to be made into rolls and carried instead of packs. Each rifleman was to carry an extra bandoleer of ammunition; all available rifle and hand grenades and entrenching tools were to be carried; canteens were to be filled and two days' reserve rations carried. A hot meal (which was to be the last for a long time to come) was served the men as near "H" hour as possible. (vol. 2, 181-182).

A pouring rain had preceded the Thirty-seventh into the Recicourt area. While it waited to attack, every leaf in the forests in which the division camped dripped water for three days and nights, without ceasing, it seemed;... But the weather cleared during the afternoon on 25th September. It was clear but dark as the units of the division found their way to their stations during the hours before midnight, although a heavy ground mist made movement through the woods very difficult. And it was clear when, at eleven-thirty, the heavy guns all along the front held by the First American Army flashed and roared the opening of the intensive artillery preparation. (vol. 2, 197-198)

From 3rd Battalion War Diary for September 26, 1918

Battalion as part of Divisional Reserve formed up at 67.33-13.20 for advance. MAP REFERENCE-"AVOCOURT #216."

All messages except those lost on field of battle attached.

2 days rations with troops. Weather: clear. Roads: poor (shell fire). Health: good.

William L Marlin
Major, 148th Infantry
Commanding, 3rd Battalion

Distinguished Service Cross Citation
Henry Hiser
Private, First Class, Company B, 136ᵗʰ Machine Gun Battalion

For extraordinary heroism in action near Avocourt, France, September 26, 1918. When the advance of his platoon was held up by fire from a hostile machine-gun nest, Private Hiser advanced alone ahead of the platoon, worked his way around the flank and rear, and single-handed killed the officer in command and a gunner and captured 15 prisoners, thereby enabling his platoon to advance.

Distinguished Service Cross Citation
Sam A. Andrews
First Lieutenant, 145ᵗʰ Infantry

For extraordinary heroism in action near Montfaucon, France, September 26, 1918. Lieut. Andrews displayed brilliant courage and leadership in leading his platoon against and capturing a strong enemy machine-gun nest. In this exploit he was killed, but his notable coolness and determination furnished an inspiration to his men.

Distinguished Service Cross Citation
Fred C. Redick
Captain, 146ᵗʰ Infantry

For extraordinary heroism in action near Montfaucon, France, September 26, 1918. Severely wounded in the head and leg while leading his company, he refused to go to the rear, though he was ordered to do so by the battalion commander and attending surgeon, continuing in the attack and inspiring his men by his conspicuous bravery.

From 37th Division War Diary for September 26, 1918

The Division went over the top at 5.30 A.M., September 26, 1918, 145th Infantry on right, 1st and 2nd Battalions in line with 3rd Battalion as regimental reserve.

1st Battalion, 146th Infantry, Brigade Reserve. 147th Infantry, 1st and 3rd Battalions, in line with 2nd Battalion as Regimental Reserve. 148th Infantry, 2nd and 3rd Battalions as Brigade Reserve - 3 Companies 135th Machine Gun Battalion operating with 73rd Brigade and 3 Companies 136th Machine Gun Battalion operating with 74th Brigade. The Division Reserve consisted of 1st Battalion, 148th Infantry and 2nd and 3rd Battalions 146th Infantry, and 134th Machine Gun Battalion. 113th Field Artillery attached to 73rd Brigade....
99th and 154th Aero Squadrons attached to 37th Division.

The Advance continued successfully during the day and the line settled for the night just north of Ravine de la Fuon about 3 kilometers north of Avocourt. The first prisoners began to arrive at Division cage... and during the day approximately 800 were captured, also quantities of ammunition, machine guns and some field pieces both light and heavy. The weather cleared from rain and fog and greatly assisted this day's operations.

989 Officers
25622 Men
Fair - Weather
Muddy - Roads
Excellent - Health
Trenches and bivouac.

Summer Waite,
Major, General Staff, Acting G-3.

Distinguished Service Cross Citation
Norris W. Gillette
Captain (then, First Lieutenant), Medical Corps, 148th Ambulance Company

For extraordinary heroism in action in Bois de Septsarges, near Montfaucon, France, September 26, 1918. While in command of a medical detachment working forward through the woods on the right flank of the 73rd Brigade Sector, Lieutenant Gillette encountered a large number of men in confusion who were without officers and under fire from enemy snipers located both at the edge of the woods and at a strong point on a knoll beyond it. By his remarkable courage and tact, and through the power of his inspiring heroic example, the scattered troops were reorganized into squad and platoon groups and took up a position from which they as part of a battalion later moved forward and drove the enemy from the woods and overcame the enemy's strong point.

Distinguished Service Cross Citation
Robert C. Bunge
Captain, 148th Infantry

For extraordinary heroism in action near Montfaucon, France, September 26, 1918. While in command of a combat liaison group operating between the 37th and 91st Divisions, and under heavy hostile artillery fire, Captain Bunge, although painfully wounded by a shell fragment and burned with gas, courageously remained in command of his company, maintained contact with the enemy, and directed the company movements. When the attack was continued on September 27 and his company was acting in the same capacity, while passing through a terrible hostile artillery barrage he received a serious fracture of the skull from enemy shell fragments, and refusing to be evacuated he tenaciously continued with his group. Later on the same day, while leading his company, he was again seriously wounded by shell fire, which necessitated his evacuation.

Distinguished Service Cross Citation
Charles C. Chambers
Lieutenant Colonel, Infantry Officers' Reserve Corp (then Major), 135ᵗʰ Machine Gun Battalion

For extraordinary heroism in action in Bois de Septsarges, near Montfaucon, France, September 26, 1918. While voluntarily going forward on a mission of establishing liaison between a front-line unit of his own division and the division on the right, Major Chambers encountered a large number of men falling back in confusion, badly disorganized and without leaders, as a result of a heavy artillery fire and machine-gun fire from pill boxes in the woods and from a strong point on the heights beyond. With the greatest energy, courage, and leadership, at a most critical time and under a heavy fire, he reorganized the scattered troops, put them in trenches, and later led them forward, overcoming a stubborn resistance from machine guns, drove the enemy from his position, reestablished the front line and accomplished his liaison mission. By his calmness, decision, and courage he inspired great confidence among the scattered and confused troops.

```
G-3 Section                        V ARMY CORPS, A.E.F.
No. 27      Ville-sur-Cousances, September 26, 1918


          12 Noon to 12 Noon, September 25/26


     1.   HOSTILE SITUATION AT BEGINNING OF DAY:
The enemy continued to exhibit increased activity
in his sector in the Argonne.  There has been a
```

considerable number of aerial reconnaissance, and heavy harassing fire.

2. INFORMATION RECEIVED OF ENEMY DURING DAY: Traffic and circulation on roads and railroads continued abnormal in the afternoon of the 25th and during the late afternoon several groups of soldiers of about 20 each were seen to enter trenches opposite west of our sector. Reconnoitering planes however at an earlier hour brought information that the enemy line was thinly held. The 37th Division has identified the enemy opposing them as the 157th Inf. Regt., 54th Foot Artillery Bn., and the 1st Guard Division. The 5th Guard Division is also reported as being directly in the rear of enemy's supports. Majority of prisoners taken did not know of presence of American troops opposite them.

3. HOSTILE MOVEMENTS, CHANGES AND CONDUCT DURING DAY: It may be generally stated that the principal movement of the enemy in the face of our attack has been one of rapid retirement. In a few local cases stubborn resistance in the form of machine-gun nests has been encountered, but those have been quickly overcome by our troops. Fires, demolitions, and explosions of dumps and stores, together with the destruction of the principal roads, indicate that the enemy has not yet reached the position decoded upon for serious defensive action. In many cases, owing to their rapid retirements, our forces were unable, at all times, to maintain contact, but during the late forenoon the pace of the retreat seems to have decreased. Up to noon, the 37th Division, the center unit of this corps, reported that they had met with very little hostile resistance. The opening of our

artillery preparation met with little response
from the enemy and even when our fire increased
their reaction was very feeble, being directed
principally upon Avocourt. At 5:50 a.m., a Boche
signal for barrage met with no response from
their batteries. The offensive brought to light
four new hostile balloons, Samogneux, Lissey,
Dun-sur-Meuse, and Milly. At 10:30 a.m., the
enemy opened some artillery fire on the Avocourt
Road, but no other hostile activity was observed
by a reconnoitering plane at this time. Main
approaches and roads to Montfaucon are barricaded
and hostile antiaircraft activity was encountered
here. However, later information just before noon
states that the town seems deserted
    . . . .
    5. OWN SITUATION AT BEGINNING OF DAY: Very
favorable for the successful exploitation of
operations planned. All infantry, artillery and
auxiliary units in place, and weather conditions
ideal.

    6. OWN CHANGES, MOVEMENTS AND ACTION DURING
DAY: The 32nd Division (corps reserve) under
orders from V Corps moved to Brahant-en-Argonne
area. Movement by marching started at 19 hours,
September 25, P. C. closed at Autrecourt at 6
o'clock the artillery preparation was commenced,
and was gradually increased in its intensity
during the night. The infantry advance started
at 5:30 under protection of a rolling barrage.
All units reported that attack started on time
and the right brigade of the 91st Division states
that both of its regiments reached enemy's front
line without casualties or opposition. Later
information from this division at 20 o'clock
established the left of their line in the Trachee

de la Salamandre with few casualties and with the capture of some guns. Our troops were observed along the northern edge of Bois de Montfaucon at 9:10 o'clock. About this time the division to the right of us was just south of Cuisy and tanks were on the line between Cheppy and Varennes, on our other flank. At 9:52 the 79th Division reports the movement of their P. C. to 15.3-71.2, 1 km. N.W. of Esnes. Mopping up operations are being carried on in Bois de Cheppy, Bois de Malancourt, and Bois de Montfaucon, and the small ravines within them. Conflicting reports have been received about the progress of our center division (37th), but indications are that its advance has been more hindered by the enemy than was the case in the two flank divisions. Artillery observers report that American troops were seen between Eclisfontaine and Epinonville. This is the most advanced detachment of which we have information. Excellent artillery preparation and barrage were most helpful in making the advance.... Few reports had been received of activity of tanks up to noon....

10. RESULT OF ACTION, OWN AND ENEMY: The attack has been successfully pushed by all divisions and a rough line of the front at noon may be said to run through Cuisy and Cheppy. Full reports, however, are not in and in many cases we have information that the advance is far beyond this line. Hostile ammunition dumps in vicinity of Montfaucon blown up.... The 37th Division has recorded over 400 prisoners at its P. C. at noon. Up to 9:10 a.m., the 79th Division had evacuated 150 prisoners in Esnes, with 2 machine guns captured.

. . .

```
     12.  ESTIMATION OF SITUATION:  All
indications point to an early attainment of the
corps objective.
     . . .
     14.  VISIBILITY, from poor to fair.  ROADS
(in enemy territory) destroyed.  MORALE,
excellent....

                         T. H. Emerson
                         Colonel, Engineers,
                         A. C. of S., G-3.
```

Gallantry in Action Citation
William S. Kelly
Private, First Class, Headquarters Company, 147th Infantry

For gallantry in action near Ivoiry, France, September 26, 1918, while assisting a wounded comrade to a place of safety under heavy enemy fire.

Distinguished Service Cross Citation
James V. Schairer
Private, Medical Detachment, 147th Infantry

For extraordinary heroism in action near Montfaucon, France, September 26, 1918. Seeing two men fall wounded, Pvt. Schairer immediately went to their assistance, unmindful of the extreme danger that he was exposed to, and after dragging the men to a shell hole administered effective first aid. A few days later he was killed in the performance of his duties.

Found in *The 37ᵗʰ Division in the World War*

Major William L. Marlin, commanding the Third Battalion of the 148ᵗʰ Infantry, gives the following account of the operations of that unit around Montfaucon on 26ᵗʰ September:

The order of battle of the 37ᵗʰ Division on the morning of September 26, 1918, was 73ʳᵈ Brigade on the right and 74ᵗʰ Brigade on the left. In the 73ʳᵈ Brigade the 145ᵗʰ Regiment of Infantry led the attack and in the 74ᵗʰ Brigade the 147ᵗʰ Infantry was in the front line. One battalion of the 146ᵗʰ Infantry was detailed to 73ʳᵈ Brigade reserve and two battalions to Division reserve. Two battalions of the 148ᵗʰ Infantry were detailed to 74ᵗʰ Brigade reserve and one battalion to Division reserve. My battalion, which was the Third Battalion of the 148ᵗʰ, was detailed to Division Reserve and reported to Colonel Pickering, Commander of the Division Reserve, on the night of the 25ᵗʰ of September at about eleven o'clock.

The Third Battalion of the 148ᵗʰ Infantry was the leading unit of the Division Reserve and followed the attack on the morning of the 26ᵗʰ, passing through Avocourt at about 9:00 A.M. The reserve caught up with the leading troops at the northern edge of the Bois de Montfaucon at about 4:00 P.M.

At about 5:00 P.M. of the 26ᵗʰ, the situation was as follows: "The 145ᵗʰ Infantry had reached the northern edge of the Bois de Montfaucon and the top of the slope just north of the woods. Montfaucon was still held by the enemy. The 79ᵗʰ Division had not yet advanced as far as the 37ᵗʰ. The front line had apparently reached as far north as the physical condition of the men in the attack would permit them to go. The head of the Division Reserve was at the cross roads at the northern end of the plank road through the Bois de Montfaucon. At this point a conference was held between General Farnsworth and Colonel Pickering. Major Moynahan, of the 146ᵗʰ Infantry, and myself were standing nearby.

General Farnsworth ordered Colonel Pickering to send the two leading battalions of the Division Reserve forward for an attack on Montfaucon. One battalion was to attach and seize

the hill just to the west of Montfaucon, while the other battalion was to attack the city from the southwest under cover
of this leading battalion. General Farnsworth endeavored to
secure artillery support for this attack, and the artillery were
to fire on Montfaucon until 5:45 P.M.

I led my battalion through the lines of the 145th Infantry,
reformed on the high ground just north of the Bois Montfaucon
and at about 5:45 P.M. launched the attack on the hill to the
west of the city. I instructed the Captain of the company on
the right to guide the right of his line on the machine gun
emplacement located just west of Montfaucon and on top of
the hill. My battalion went forward and received fire from
machine guns in the orchard west of Montfaucon, the machine gun emplacement on top of the hill and from the city of
Montfaucon. Pushing steadily forward we drove the Germans
out of the orchard, capturing an anti-aircraft battery and ammunition dump, including two guns, a major of artillery and
three others. The battalion gained the top of the hill just at
dark and rested and occupied the trenches constructed by the
Germans and protected by wire which ran east and west along
the ridge. Outpost groups were established and the Germans
who still occupied the machine gun emplacement were driven
out. (vol. 2, 255-256)

Capt. Thomas H. Morrow, who commanded Co. K, 148th
Infantry, during the offensive, writes as follows regarding the
operations of the Third Battalion of that regiment:

I commanded Company K, 148th Infantry. The Third
Battalion was Division Reserve when we jumped off. Late the
afternoon of 26th September my company mopped up the Bois
de Chehemin. The battalion reformed on the ridge north of
this woods and we received orders to storm the ridge running
between Montfaucon and Ivoiry. The battalion formed for the
advance with my company on the left front. It was almost
dusk when we advanced against the ridge and we were met
with rifle fire and heavy machine gun fire from the ridge and
the edge of Montfaucon on our right flank.

The enfilade fire from Montfaucon was quite heavy and we could see the flashes of the machine guns and the moving figures of the Germans, although it was almost dusk. The ridge, which was our objective, had an orchard on its south side and when we arrived there the trees protected us from the view of the Germans in Montfaucon. As we advanced against this ridge I saw no American troops on either our right or left and I am certain that there were none in Montfaucon.

We took the ridge, captured several cannons and considerable enemy material. That night our flanks were in the air and we were occupying the so-called Crocodile Trench, which ran along the top of this ridge (an old German trench).

The next morning a counter-attack seemed impending. The fog lifted and we could see a number of American troops south of Montfaucon and about to assault it. I was then in the Crocodile Trench probably one thousand yards from Montfaucon. We were bombed from aeroplanes and severely bombarded all that day and I lost track of these troops on our right above mentioned. However, snipers from Montfaucon bothered us all the day and whenever our men got out from the cover of the orchard on the south side of the ridge they were in danger of snipers' bullets.

Col. Pickering was over to see us some time in the afternoon. He then commanded the Division Reserve from which our battalion had been detached on the 26th, to take the ridge.

The expected counter-attack did not materialize, but we suffered a number of casualties from the heavy bombardment we received when on this ridge. About nigh fall on the 27th we were relieved by other troops and drawn off to another position in front of Ivoiry, which we passed through the next day in the advance. (vol. 2, 257-258)

Capt. F.W. Marcolin, commanding Headquarters Company, 145th Infantry, writes as follows regarding the operations of the 145th and 148th Infantry around Montfaucon:

...

In spite of the fact that the supporting fire from auxiliary weapons was not entirely effective; the troops referred to by Lt. Col. William L. Marlin, 148th Infantry, advanced from the edge of the Bois de Montfaucon, and finally, after several attempts, succeeded in reaching the ridge west of Montfaucon and establishing themselves at that point.

I would judge that this was in the neighborhood of 6:00 P. M., 26th September 1918. The fact that such occupation took place, is borne out by the comparative ease with which our Division outflanked Montfaucon on the morning of 27th September, that is conditions indicated that not only the outskirts of the town had been taken on the evening before by mixed detachments of the 145th, 146th, and 148th Infantry, but that through the diminishing of German resistance due to the outflanking movement on the part of the troops of the 37th Division, the 79th Division had been able to occupy the town in question. (vol. 2, 263-264)

From 37th Division War Diary for September 27th, 1918

```
    The attack was resumed at 5.30 A.M. and advance
continued.  The town of Ivoiry was taken about
9.00 A.M. and about 500 meters north of Ivoiry
the enemy delivered his first counter attack,
the counter attack was easily repulsed and the
advance continued to general line Montfaucon to
just south of Cierges, where counter attack was
again delivered by the enemy.  This counter attack
was repulsed, but due to conditions of roads,
artillery support could not be brought forward
and our troops were unable to advance against
enemy artillery, which covered entire line.  One
enemy battery of four 155's captured during day
in forward position was turned on the enemy and
our own artillery beginning to arrive, our troops
were able to occupy enemy 2nd line position and
```

hold. At about 14 hours Montfaucon was entered by elements of the 73rd Brigade and 32 prisoners (the last of the enemy) were taken. At dark our line halted approximately along Ivoiry-Montfaucon road. The weather greatly hindered operations, rain made the roads practically impassable.

> 980 Officers
> 25644 Men
> Rain - Weather
> Poor - Roads
> Dugouts and Trenches.

> Summer Waite,
> Major, General Staff,
> Acting G-3.

Distinguished Service Cross Citation
Clay Eversole
Private, Medical Detachment, 148th Infantry

For extraordinary heroism in action near Cierges, France September 27, 1918. During the advance of Company K, 148th Infantry, Pvt. Eversole frequently exposed himself to great danger by carrying a number of wounded men through heavy machine-gun fire from an open field to a place of safety.

Distinguished Service Cross Citation
Charles M. Smith
Sergeant, Company F, 146th Infantry

For extraordinary heroism in action near Montfaucon, France, September 27, 1918. While leading a reconnaissance patrol sent out to locate enemy machine-gun nests he was severely wounded. Lying helpless where he fell, he disregarded his own wounds and continued to direct his men. Through his courage and fortitude many enemy machine guns were located and subsequently destroyed.

Distinguished Service Cross Citation
Newton Rex
Corporal, Company F, 146th Infantry

For extraordinary heroism in action near Montfaucon, France, September 27, 1918. Leading a patrol of 12 men from his own and another company, he encountered 35 of the enemy in a ravine. Under a terrific enfilading fire from seven machine guns, he led an attack on the enemy in which five of the latter were killed and 15 captured, together with the seven machine guns.

Distinguished Service Cross Citation
Orum Lee
Sergeant, Company H, 146th Infantry

 For extraordinary heroism in action near Montfaucon, France, September 27, 1918. Sergt. Lee, with an officer and noncommissioned officer, advanced 200 yards beyond the objective of the patrol in the face of heavy machine-gun fire and captured three 77 MM. field-pieces and two light machine guns.

Distinguished Service Cross Citation
Ernest R. Rumbaugh
Corporal, Company H, 146th Infantry

For extraordinary heroism in action near Montfaucon, France, September 27, 1918. Corporal Rumbaugh, with an officer and noncommissioned officer, advanced 200 yards beyond the objective of the patrol in the face of heavy machine-gun fire and captured three 77 MM. fieldpieces and two light machine guns.

Distinguished Service Cross Citation
Fred Kochli
Captain (then, First Lieutenant), Company H, 146th Infantry

For extraordinary heroism in action near Montfaucon, France, on September 27, 1918. Lieut. Kochli, with two non-commissioned officers, advanced 200 yards beyond the objective of the patrol in the face of heavy machine-gun fire and captured three 77 MM. fieldpieces and two light machine guns.

Distinguished Service Cross Citation
Daniel S. McSweeney
Sergeant, Company B, 148th Infantry

For extraordinary heroism in action near Ivoiry, France, September 27, 1918. Leaving a place of shelter, he voluntarily crawled about 400 yards in advance of the front-line elements of his battalion and attempted to rescue a wounded officer. He then crossed an area swept by intense enemy machine-gun fire and attempted to capture an enemy machine gun which was causing heavy casualties in his company. While so engaged he was severely wounded by enemy fire.

Distinguished Service Cross Citation
Luther J. Langston
First Sergeant, Company A, 148th Infantry

For extraordinary heroism in action near Ivoiry, France, September 27, 1918. When his platoon was halted by the fire of concealed enemy machine guns, Sergt. Langston dashed ahead of his organization and, alone, captured the enemy machine-gun, forcing five of the enemy to surrender. This act of heroism enabled his organization to resume the advance.

Gallantry in Action Citation
John R. Hubbard
Regimental Sergeant Major, Headquarters Company, 148th Infantry

For gallantry in action on September 27, 1918, near the village of Ivoiry, Montfaucon, France, while engaged in receiving and dispatching urgent messages and orders under intense shell and machine-gun fire, maintaining liaison with regimental and brigade headquarters and observing and directing the fire of the divisional artillery. Constantly exposed to direct enemy fire, with great courage and coolness, he continued throughout the day to perform his duties until late afternoon, when he was killed by enemy shell fire.

From 148th Infantry Regiment War Diary for September 27, 1918

Regiment advanced from Bois de Montfaucon at 6 am. Two battalions in front line, one as regimental support, advance continued to hill south of Ivoiry.... Colonel Jas. A. Lynch became a slight casualty.

Medal of Honor Citation (Posthumous)
Albert E. Baesel
2nd Lieutenant, 148th Infantry, 37th Division

For conspicuous gallantry and intrepidity above and beyond the call of duty in action with the enemy near Ivoiry, France, 27 September, 1918. Upon learning that a squad leader of his platoon had been severely wounded while attempting to capture an enemy machinegun nest about 200 yards in advance of the assault line and somewhat to the right, 2nd Lt. Baesel requested permission to go to the rescue of the wounded corporal. After thrice repeating his request and permission having been reluctantly given, due to the heavy artillery, rifle, and machinegun fire, and heavy deluge of gas in which the company was at the time, accompanied by a volunteer, he worked his way forward, and in spite of a heavy direct machine-gun fire succeeded in reaching the wounded man, whom he just succeeded in placing upon his shoulders when both were instantly killed by enemy fire.

From 3rd Battalion War Diary for September 27, 1918

    1 day rations with troops. Weather: clear. Health: good.
    At 6:30 am moved out as part of Divisional Reserve (road good as far as 69.30-11.80). Heavy congestion of traffic. Great difficulty in keeping unit intact. Proceeded Avocourt-Bois Montfaucon-Bois Chehemin.
    At 18:10 at northeast edge of Bois Chehemin formed for attack at ridge west of Montfaucon. Mission to outflank Montfaucon-accomplished-consolidated position on ridge between Montfaucon and Ivoiry.

From James M. Cain's Short Story
"The Taking of Montfaucon"

I pulled up and hollered out:
"What way to the hunred and fifty-seventh Brigade PC?" [Of the 79th Division]
"The what?" they says. ...
"Never hear tell of it," they says.
"The hell you say," I says. ...
Because that was one of them gags they had in the army. They would ask a guy what his outfit was, and then when he told them they would say they never hear tell of it.

So I rode a little further and come to another bunch. "Which way... "

But they never said nothing at all. Because they was doughboys going up in the lines, and when you hear talk about doughboys singing when the're going to fight, you can tell him he's a damn liar and say I said so. Doughboys when they're going up to the lines they look straight in front of them and they swaller every third step and they don't say nothing....

"What outfit, buddly?" I say to the next bunch I come to. But all they done was look dumb.... I come to another bunch, and I ask them.

"AEF," a guy sings out.

"What the hell," I says. "You think I'm asking for fun?"

"YMCA," says another, and I went on. And then all of a sudden I knowed why them guys was acting like that, and why it was was this: Ever since they come to France, they had been told if somebody up in the front lines asks you what your outfit is, don't you tell him because maybe he's a German spy....

I thought I might as well pretend to be an officer and scare somebody into telling me where I'm at. So the first ones I come to was a captain and a lieutenant setting by the side of the road, and they was wearing bars. But me not having no bars didn't make no difference because up at the front some officers wore bars but most of them didn't....

"Which way is General Nicholson's PC?" I says, and the captain jumped up and saluted.

"General Nicholson?" he says. "Not around here, I'm pretty sure, sir," he says.

"Hundred and fifty-seventh Brigade?" I says, pretty short....

"Oh, no," he says. "That wouldn't be in this Division. This is all Thirty-seventh."

G-3 Section   V ARMY CORPS, A.E.F.,
Ville-sur-Cousances,   September 27, 1918.

12 Noon to 12 Noon, Sept. 26 to 27

1. HOSTILE SITUATION AT BEGINNING OF THE
DAY: About noon the rate of retirement of the
enemy had materially decreased and in many places,
even earlier, our troops were held up by stubborn
machine-gun fire. Due to the lack of thorough
mopping up, many hostile snipers and isolated
machine-gun crews harassed our engineer troops.
These were engaged in work along the roads, just
in rear of the advance.

2. INFORMATION RECEIVED OF ENEMY DURING
THE DAY: The enemy held Montfaucon entire day,
despite numerous reports to the contrary, and were
successfully defending it up to noon of the 27th,
when it was reported captured. (This capture
is confirmed but time has not been verified.)...
Captives also report that the 151st Prussian
Guard was brought up and placed in line. A Uhlan
captured yesterday in sector on our left states
that the 2nd Division of Uhlans is in back of
third position in the sector of the 77th Division.
No activity of these troops has been yet reported.
During the afternoon interrogation of German
prisoners established the fact that they had
expected an attack on a large scale.

3. HOSTILE MOVEMENTS, CHANGES AND CONDUCT
DURING DAY: Serious resistance was encountered by
the center and right divisions in their endeavor
to reach the corps objective. The advance of the
79th Division was checked at Montfaucon for over
24 hours and the 37th Division encountered similar
opposition across their path just west of this
town. During the early afternoon enemy artillery
became very active on the line Montfaucon to the

east, and also their guns were located to the
north and west of this line. Enemy air patrols
operating over Montfaucon at this time, and other
activity of hostile avions, resulted in two Allied
balloons being brought down in flames.
. . .

   5. OWN SITUATION AT BEGINNING OF DAY:
Center and right divisions had been checked in
their endeavor to reach the corps objective. The
91st Division on the left had occupied the left
portion of their objective but their line sagged
towards the east on the other flank.

   6. OWN CHANGES, MOVEMENTS AND ACTIONS
DURING DAY: The advance of the 79th was hindered
by machine-gun fire during entire afternoon.
Resistance in Montfaucon and vicinity proved so
serious that this division awaited the arrival of
their artillery before they could advance further.
Guns were delayed in coming up by bad conditions
of roads and by congestion on those that could be
utilized. Engineer units are working continuously
to put them in shape for heavy traffic. A special
report from the 79th Division is as follows:

   Our 304th Engineers have been under fire
all day (Sept. 26). Vicinity of 1173 (Bois de
Montfaucon), while they have been repairing this
road. The engineers, themselves have cleaned
up one machine-gun nest and taken some prisoners
in this vicinity. The 91st Division reported at
14:55 o'clock that the corps objective had been
reached and that two battalions of their artillery
had advanced across trenches behind them that
would be supporting infantry later in the day.

   Movement of one group of 105's and one of
155's up to the 79th Division sector commenced
at 15 o'clock. Tanks assisted in the cleaning up
of wood in this sector. P. C. of 32nd Division

moved from Brabant-en-Argonne to Verrieres-en-
Hesse Greme at 18 o'clock. The 91st Division
reports their line at 18 o'clock as running from
a point one kilometer north of Very through the
town of Epinonville. Great congestion occurred on
all roads leading up through corps sectors during
afternoon and night. At 19:10, 79th Division
reports P. C. moved to a point 500 meters N. W.
of Esnes. At nightfall a message was received
from this division expressing the opinion that the
machine-gun nests, on its right and left, had been
mopped up. Our left division at 19:25 o'clock
gave their order of battle from right to left as
follows: 363rd, 364th, 361st and 362nd Regiments
of Infantry, practically occupying the corps
objective on the left and bending around just
below Epinonville on the right. Information from
tank commander states that at 16 o'clock they had
cleaned up Bois de Cuisy after many difficulties.
Other units were progressing very slowly in Bois
de Montfaucon. The 37th Div., in a midnight
report, states that their line runs along the
northern slope of Hill 256 south of the town of
Ivoiry and then along the Trachee de Montfaucon.
P. C. 79th Div. reported moved to Haucourt at 7:15
a.m. After having been repulsed the 79th Division
again attacked Montfaucon and about noon were in
possession of it....

10. RESULTS OF ACTION, OWN AND ENEMY: The
37th Division at 16 o'clock reported 10 officers,
88 noncommissioned officers and 627 privates taken
prisoner by the division.

At 6:55 o'clock the I Corps reports
everything going smoothly.

At 20:40 o'clock the 91st Division reports
that they had captured 10 officers and 1,451 men...

12. ESTIMATE OF SITUATION: Center and
left divisions have not advanced as rapidly
as expected, being held up by strong point
in Montfaucon. This place has not been taken
and with strong artillery support which is now
available opposition in Bois de Beuge should be
quickly overcome.
13. PLANS FOR FUTURE: Vigorous continuance
of the attack.
14. VISIBILITY: From poor to good. ROADS
being repaired. MORALE excellent. SUPPLIES:
difficult in forwarding them due to conditions of
roads....

                         T. H. Emerson,
                         Colonel, Engineers,

Distinguished Service Cross Citation
Leland M. Barnett
First Lieutenant, 148th Infantry

For extraordinary heroism in action near Ivoiry, France,
September 27, 1918. Becoming detached from battalion
headquarters, Lieut. Barnett, battalion adjutant, voluntarily
undertook to locate machine-gun nests under heavy shell
and machine-gun fire, continuing in this hazardous work
until he was killed.

From 148th Infantry Regiment War Diary for September 27, 1918

Regiment advanced from hill south of Ivoiry, two
battalions as Brigade reserve, one as Division
reserve, continued to vicinity south and south
west of Cierges.

Distinguished Service Cross Citation
George E. Ackley
Sergeant, Company L, 148th Infantry

For extraordinary heroism in action near Montfaucon, France, September 27, 1918. While leading his platoon he stormed and destroyed two machine-gun nests. Later he again displayed utter disregard for his personal safety when he extricated his platoon from a perilous position, forcing a passage through the enemy and rejoining the remainder of the company.

From 3rd Battalion War Diary for September 27, 1918

Battalion ordered from Divisional to Brigade Reserve. All copies of messages except those lost on field of battle attached.
Weather: clear (rain at night). Health: good.
At 14:30 Battalion relieved by 146th Infantry and returned to Divisional Reserve. Bivouacked on southern slope of ridge 76:00-between 10:00 and 11:00.

William L Marlin

Major, 148th Infantry
Commanding, 3rd Battalion

Distinguished Service Cross Citation
Mark W. Mails
Private, First Class, Company F, 146th Infantry

For extraordinary heroism in action near Cierges, France, September 28, 1918. After his platoon had withdrawn about 50 yards to an established line, a wounded comrade was seen lying ahead in the position they formerly occupied. The enemy had just launched a strong counterattack, but Pvt. Mails, with another soldier, volunteered to go to the assistance of the wounded man. In the face of terrific fire of enemy artillery and machine guns, and the fire of their own comrades, who were resisting the attack, Pvt. Mails succeeded in bringing his man to a place of safety.

Distinguished Service Cross Citation
Louis Pearl Patten
Captain, Company A, 147th Infantry

For extraordinary heroism in action near the Forest of Argonne, France, September 28, 1918. Capt. Patten was seriously wounded in the shoulder while leading his company, but after being tagged for evacuation at the dressing station, his insistent request for permission to return to his command was granted and he continued to lead his company until the division was relieved.

Distinguished Service Cross Citation
George W. Atkins
Sergeant, Company D, 135th Machine Gun Battalion

For extraordinary heroism in action near Cierges, France, September 27-28, 1918. After being twice wounded, Sergt. Watkins continued to lead his section in action against the enemy under severe machine-gun and direct artillery fire. Though he had been ordered to the rear by his platoon commander, he returned to his section as soon as his wounds had been dressed.

Distinguished Service Cross Citation
Thomas B. Welker
Private, Company B, 146th Infantry

For extraordinary heroism in action near Cierges, France, September 28, 1918. When his company had become disorganized under intense machine-gun fire, Pvt. Welker assumed leadership of a group of men and courageously charged a machine-gun nest in plain view of the enemy, losing his life in this heroic attempt.

Distinguished Service Cross Citation
James Neely
Private, Company F, 146th Infantry

For extraordinary heroism in action near Cierges, France, September 28, 1918. After his platoon had withdrawn about 50 yards to an established line, a wounded comrade was seen lying ahead in the position which they formerly occupied. The enemy had just launched a strong counterattack, but Pvt. Neely, with another soldier, volunteered to go to the assistance of the wounded man. In the face of artillery and machine-guns and the fire of their own comrades, who were resisting the attack, Pvt. Neely succeeded in bringing his man to a place of safety.

Distinguished Service Cross Citation
Ben Mileski
Private, Company I, 147th Infantry

For extraordinary heroism in action near Cierges, France, September 28, 1918. When a platoon of Company I, 147th Infantry, was held up by machine-gun fire from the left flank, Pvt. Mileski, without orders, rushed forward through heavy machine-gun fire, killed the machine gunner, and caused a number of the enemy to surrender.

Gallantry in Action Citation
Frank L. Stratthan
Mess Sergeant, Company K, 148th Infantry

For gallantry in action near Ivoiry, France, September 28, 1918. Under heavy enemy machine-gun and artillery fire he entered the town of Ivoiry with his rolling kitchen, drove it into the remains of a building, and in spite of intense enemy fire continued to serve hot food to the exhausted and wounded men of his regiment, thus materially raising the morale of the men, enabling many of them to return refreshed to the lines and continue fighting.

Distinguished Service Cross Citation
William Seigle
Private, Company A, 146th Infantry

For extraordinary heroism in action near Ivoiry, France, September 28, 1918. He repeatedly volunteered and carried messages under enemy bombardment until he was severely wounded.

Gallantry in Action Citation
C. Upham Gillis
Color Sergeant, Headquarters Company, 145th Infantry

For gallantry in action near Montfaucon, France, September 28, 1918. When his regiment was hard pressed and was temporarily held up under a heavy artillery and machine-gun fire Sergeant Gillis armed a number of men with rifles and automatic rifles of the wounded and killed of the regiment and gallantly led them forward to become a part of the firing line, in order to assist in repulsing an impending counterattack, remaining with them until wounded, and then returned to the detail after having his wounds dressed.

Distinguished Service Cross Citation
Vartan Aghababian
Private, First Class, Medical Detachment, 146th Infantry

For extraordinary heroism in action northwest of Montfaucon, France, September 28, 1918. He voluntarily accompanied the first attack wave of the 146th Infantry, seeking out the wounded under terrific enemy machine-gun and artillery fire, carrying them to places of safety and applying first aid until he himself was seriously wounded. This soldier's heroic conduct and devotion to his comrades greatly inspired the men of his regiment.

Gallantry in Action Citation
William H. Meyers
Colonel, Infantry Officers' Reserve Corps, Lieutenant Colonel, 147th Infantry

For gallantry in action near the town of Cierges, France, September 28, 1918. In command of the 3d Battalion of the regiment in its attack and finding it faltering in the face of terrific machine-gun fire, he advanced through the center of the battalion and led the attack. Encountering an enemy strong point, he led a charge against a concrete machine-gun nest, capturing the gun and its crew. Despite three wounds he remained in command of his advance elements until the fall of darkness.

Distinguished Service Cross Citation
Cecil B. Whitcomb
Sergeant, Headquarters Company, 148th Infantry

For extraordinary heroism in action near Montfaucon, France, September 26-28, 1918. Attached to the Regimental Intelligence section of the 148th Infantry, he, with several men of his section, accompanied the first attacking wave of the regiment on September 26th. Losing contact temporarily with the assaulting wave on account of a smoke barrage, he halted momentarily, and upon resuming the advance encountered enemy machine-gun and sniper fire near a swale in the Bois de Montfaucon. Leaving his men in a place of safety Sergeant Whitcomb discovered an enemy machine-gun nest which covered a bridge across the swale. He captured several unarmed enemy soldiers and an officer; the latter he forced to return to the machine-gun nest and to deliver to him the gun crews, a number of men, as well as several enemy snipers who had been inflicting heavy casualties upon his men; this action permitted the infantry to advance without further heavy losses.

Distinguished Service Cross Citation
Nathanial C. Triplet
Mechanic, Company F, 146th Infantry

For extraordinary heroism in action near Montfaucon, France, September 27-28, 1918. He was a member of a patrol which encountered severe hostile machine-gun fire. He assisted in getting several wounded men to cover and administered first aid until his supply of bandages was exhausted. Returning to company headquarters across a field swept by artillery fire, he secured more bandages, came back with them to his comrades, and resumed his first aid work. On the following day he again displayed exceptional courage under machine-gun and shell fire by carrying a wounded officer to safety.

From 37th Division War Diary for September 28th, 1918

The attack was resumed at 5.30 this morning and at 7.35 the 73rd Brigade reported to be entering the Bois de Beuge, and the 74th Brigade the Bois Emont.

At 10.40 the enemy destroyed our observation balloon at Montfaucon; Balloon destroyed by enemy planes. Enemy planes very active all day in spite of the weather and continually harassed our infantry with machine gun fire and... directed enemy artillery. One enemy plane brought down near Montfaucon.

Enemy artillery fire, and bad weather, resulting in exhaustion to our troops prevented any considerable advance.

Material captured during days operations included, in addition to field pieces and machine guns, thousands of rounds of artillery and small arms ammunition, 5 railway cars and one 3-ton truck.

980 Officers
256483 Men
Rain - Weather
Muddy - Roads
Trenches and Bivouac.

Summer Waite,
Major, General Staff,
Acting G-3.

Distinguished Service Cross Citation
Samuel J. Covert
Private, Sanitary Detachment, 146th Infantry

For extraordinary heroism in action near Montfaucon, France, September 28, 1918. Voluntarily leaving cover, he

went through intense machine-gun and artillery fire to the
assistance of a wounded soldier and was himself killed
while administering first aid to the latter.

G-3 Section   V ARMY CORPS, A.E.F.,
            Ville-sur-Cousances, September 28, 1918.

      12 Noon to 12 Noon, September 27/28

      1.   HOSTILE SITUATION AT BEGINNING OF DAY:
The taking of Montfaucon by our troops caused a
further withdrawal of the enemy before the advance
of the 37th and 79th Divisions. The hostile
delaying action in the vicinity of this town
halted for one full day the progress of our center
and right divisions. Reports indicate that the
enemy had but few troops engaged in the defense of
Montfaucon and that they relied principally upon
machine-gun fire to check our forces.

      2.   INFORMATION RECEIVED OF ENEMY DURING DAY:
Hostile troops opposing the advance of the V Corps
are identified as follows: (From west to east) 1st
Guard Division, 5th Guard Division, 37th Division,
117th Division, and 7th Reserve Division.
      Information is also received that units of
many of the opposing divisions are far below the
average strength in effective, companies averaging
between 50 to 80 rifles. During the day numerous
convoys moving northward had been reported.
The principal resistance by the enemy has been
from machine-gun groups and scattered artillery
fire. No counter-attacks of serious proportions
have been reported. A captured officer gave
the information that we might expect determined
resistance when we reached the vicinity of Dun-

sur-Meuse. Prisoners from the 5th Guard Division captured at 15:30 o'clock, state that they had been in rest camp at St-Juvin for six days. They were brought forward the night of the 26th. They claim the Germans have but few reserves.

3. HOSTILE MOVEMENTS, CONDUCT AND CHANGES DURING DAY: The enemy continued his harassing fire on the entire corps front during the early afternoon of the 27th, making the advance very slow and halting it entirely in many places. Following the capture of Montfaucon the enemy delivered a severe bombardment between this town and Ivoiry, shells of large calibre falling in the region of Ivoiry. This shelling was followed by a counter-attack which was checked.

During the afternoon harassing fire on our first line and outposts in region of Eclisfontaine was fired by hostile batteries causing a slight retirement of the 91st Division.

Boche planes, working with artillery, caused the shelling of troops and train of the 91st Division. Several enemy batteries were observed with horses hitched to them, N.E. of Ivoiry, showing the complete retirement of the enemy.

Fire from enemy's batteries and minenwerfer from Bois de Beuge, and on the road north of it, greatly hindered the advance of the 37th.

Numerous hostile planes were observed during the late afternoon, one was brought down in flames about 18:23....

5. OWN SITUATION AT BEGINNING OF DAY: The V Corps continued its attack with same divisions in line. The 91st Div. on the left, the 37th in the center and the 79th on the right. The 91st Div. was about 1 km. in advance of the left half of

their portion of the corps objective and running
east, their line skirted south of Epinonville and
then bent down in the direction of Ivoiry. The
37th Division held positions, roughly speaking,
about one kilometer south of Ivoiry and running
in an irregular line northeast of this point. The
79th Div. occupied a line about one-half kilometer
beyond Montfaucon which they had captured shortly
before noon.

6. OWN CHANGES, MOVEMENTS AND ACTION DURING
DAY: The advance of our troops was hindered
everywhere by machine-gun fire and intermittent
shelling by the enemy. The movement of the 37th
and 79th Divisions commenced again during the
afternoon. The 37th Division met determined
resistance from the direction of Bois de Beuge,
and artillery fire from the direction of Cierges.
Request was made for artillery concentration
on these points. The 91st Div. states at 14:
35 they were receiving enfilade fire from German
artillery from a position Northwest of Very.
Aviation reports received at 17 o'clock indicate
that friendly troops were advancing about 250
meters north of the Epinonville-Ivoiry Road with
small groups of the enemy occupying shell holes
about 300 meters in advance. The advance of the
artillery continues with the forward movement, but
great difficulty is experienced in hauling it and
supplies forward.
    . . .
10. RESULTS OF ACTION, OWN AND ENEMY: The
action of the day resulted in overcoming obstacles
in the paths of the 37th and 79th Divisions
and permitted the forward movement to be again
commenced.

To noon, the number of prisoners having been sent through the corps cage was approximately 3,000. This of course does not represent total capture, but the number only that have been evacuated to these headquarters. Casualties lists not available, and authentic reports on captured material have not been received.

. . .

14. VISIBILITY: From poor to fair. ROADS: Repair being pushed. SUPPLIES: Road and traffic conditions still prevent prompt delivery. MORALE: Excellent.

> T. H. Emerson,
> Colonel, Engineers,
> A. C. of S., G-3

Found in *The 37th Division in the World War*

At twenty minutes after midnight on 28th September, Fifth Corps Headquarters issued Field Orders No. 45:

"Indications point to withdrawal on the part of the enemy. The Fifth Corps will continue the attack today at 7:00 o'clock....

The 2nd Bn. 145th Inf. Was in the attacking line on the right, with the 3rd Bn. 145th Inf. In support. The 1st Bn. 145th Inf. Was a part of the Division Reserve. In the 2nd Bn. Companies F and G were in the first line, with E and H in support. The 2nd Bn. 146th Inf. was designated as the attacking unit on the left of the brigade sector, followed by the 1st and 3rd Bns., respectively.

On the left of the sector, the 147th Inf. led the attack, with its 1st and 3rd Bns. In line, and its 2nd Bn. In support. The 2nd Bn. 148th Inf. relieving the 3rd Bn. Of that regiment as part of the Division Reserve and moved to hill 266, a little more than a kilometer east (and slightly to the north) of Ivoiry where, the battalion war diary gleefully relates, the "ration train came up and men were fed: at 3:00 P.M., the Division Reserve ordered to Cierges via Bois Emont. Resistance met in this wood, but Companies E and F got through when the enemy gassed the woods and G and H were ordered back and took up a position east of Epinonville." The 3rd Bn. 148th Inf. advanced as part of the Brigade Reserve. The 1st Bn. 148th Inf. advanced as a supporting battalion on the right of the brigade sector, 1000 meters in rear of the first line. The 3rd Bn. 148th Inf. as part of the Brigade Reserve, took position to advance through Ivoiry. (vol. 2, 286-287)

"During that afternoon," Gen. Farnsworth's report stated, "the 73rd Brigade was greatly weakened and the 74th somewhat weakened by gas casualties in the Bois de Beuge, the valley of l'Angon, and in the Bois Emont."

"The men," his report continued, "were now much exhausted from being continually wet and from constant exposure for two days to artillery fire which at times was very intense for periods of half an hour to an hour and a half. During this day (28th September) there had been crowding up of rear elements into front lines due to the slowness of the advance and to the eagerness of those in the rear elements to push the movement along. The result was that more men were actually occupying the line of resistance each night than there should have been; the men were more subjected to fire than they should have been; they got but little rest; and they had no shelter from the weather...." (vol. 2, 289)

From 37th Division War Diary for September 29, 1918

The attack continued today beginning at 7.00 A.M. - the 74th Brigade moved forward to attack from Cote 265. Enemy airplanes appeared over the line... immediately followed by artillery and machine gun fire, which compelled our troops to seek cover in shell holes. The same conditions took place in the 74th Brigade and inflicted heavy losses on both Brigades. One Bn. of the Division Reserve was ordered to proceed through the Bois Emont... up the machine gun nests, it had proceeded by at short distance when Major Houts (commanding) was killed, and the battalion stopped.

Shortage of artillery ammunition, due to road conditions, prevented active retaliative fire and our troops were compelled to dig in and hold where they were, after having penetrated Cierges and having been forced back.

At 15.30 one battery of hostile artillery was put out of action and one hostile observation balloon shot down.

Casualties for operation about 250 killed and missing, 1150 wounded, 450 gassed.

955 Officers
25109 Men
Rain - Weather
Muddy - Roads
Excellent - Health
Trenches and Bivouac.

Summer Waite,
Major, General Staff,
Acting G-3

Distinguished Service Cross Citation
Frederick W. Galbraith, Jr.
Colonel, 147th Infantry

For extraordinary heroism in action near Ivoiry, France, September 29, 1918. When an enemy counter-attack was

imminent he went into the front lines under a violent artillery and machine-gun barrage, and by the coolness and
certainty of his orders and the inspiring example of his
personal courage reorganized his own command and took
command of other units whose officers had been lost or diverted in the confusion of battle. Knocked down by a shell,
he refused to be evacuated and continued to carry on the
work of reorganizing his position and disposing the troops
to a successful conclusion.

From 148th Infantry Regiment War Diary for September 29, 1918

```
Regiment advanced - preceded by light tanks -
... Cierges, two battalions in front line, one
in support.... Colonel Best relieved of command,
Major Marlin... C.O.
```

Distinguished Service Cross Citation
Ernest G. Bozenhart
Private, Medical Detachment, 147th Infantry

For extraordinary heroism in action near Ivoiry, France, September 29,
1918. Making his way through heavy artillery and machine-gun fire,
he rendered valuable medical treatment to the wounded and assisted in
bringing the men to safety and forwarding them to a first aid station. In
the performance of his duties he was shortly afterwards killed.

From 3rd Battalion War Diary for September 29, 1918

```
Bois Emont gassed, moved Battalion Post
Command from 07.10-80.20 to 06.60-79.16.  Line
held 80.20 extending from Bois Emont to Bois de
Cierges.  Flanks 100 yards into either woods.
```

Weather: Cloudy (rain at night). Health: good.

Moved from 76.00-10.50 to 76.80-08.80 and took position for advance on Cierges as part of Brigade Reserve.

Advanced through Ivoiry. Halted on ridge north of Ivoiry and reorganized P.C. at 79.15-08.50.

Moved on to envelope Cierges from the west. Arrived at 79.60-06.80 and formed for attack and advanced north between Bois Emont and Bois de Cierges under hostile machine gun fire. Consolidated position from northwest edge of Bois Emont to east edge of Bois de Cierges. P.C. at 07.10-80.20. Line extended on both flanks.

William L Marlin
Major, 148th Infantry
Commanding, 3rd Battalion

Distinguished Service Cross Citation
Philip R. Colebank
First Lieutenant, 147th Infantry

For extraordinary heroism in action near Ivoiry, France, September 29, 1918. This officer with two soldiers went out in the face of heavy machine-gun and artillery fire to bring in a wounded soldier. As they reached the wounded man a shell burst, killing him instantly.

G-3 Section   V ARMY CORPS, A.E.F.,
No. 31

Verrieres-en-Hesse Ferme, September 29, 1918.

12 Noon to 12 Noon, September 28/29

1.   HOSTILE SITUATION AT BEGINNING OF DAY:
At the beginning of the period covering this
report the enemy was slowly withdrawing before our
advance. He continued his interdiction fire and
constantly harassing our troops with considerable
machine-gun and T. M. activity.
2.   INFORMATION RECEIVED OF ENEMY DURING DAY:
The presence of a new division is reported on our
front in the vicinity of Eclisfontaine.... No new
enemy work has been reported by the Air Service.
A prisoner from the 108th Labor Battalion states
that the whole eastern edge of woods along road
Montigny to Mont-devant-Sassey is mined.   An
ammunition dump and pioneer park reported at
Montigny.
3.   HOSTILE MOVEMENTS, CHANGES AND CONDUCT
DURING DAY: The enemy's tactics are approximately
the same as they have been since the start of the
offensive.

Small machine gun groups, favorably located
have proved a constant hindrance to the attackers.
Artillery activity of the enemy is on the increase
and with the assistance of their observation
planes they are beginning to accurately locate
our forces. Strong hostile opposition was made
by the enemy in the vicinity of Cierges and a
concentration of their forces was reported here at
about 16 o'clock. Enemy gassed the front line and
rear elements of our center division during the
night 28/29 and again in the early morning.
. . .
5.   OWN SITUATION AT BEGINNING OF DAY:
Favorable. Serious opposition on a large scale
has not been encountered.
6.   OWN CHANGES, MOVEMENTS AND ACTION DURING
DAY: In the early afternoon our troops were

observed passing into Bois de Beuge, while bodies
of the enemy were reported on the northern edge.

All our divisions made steady but slow
progress during the afternoon but were constantly
opposed by resistance which gradually became
stronger.

At about 14:55 the 79th Division sent in
report that their advance elements were entering
the Bois des Ogons and the Bois du Fays. Progress
is being steadily made and it appears that the
enemy is slowly falling back. The 37th Division
at 4 p. m., sends the information that they were
pushing ahead, all their light artillery has
caught up and also 3 battalions of heavy.

The line at 19 o'clock may be roughly
described as follows:

The 91st Division holding a line running
along the northern edge of Bois Communal de
Baulny, Bois Communal de Cierges, connecting with
the 37th Division whose front is slightly curved
to the south, about 300 meters below Cierges,
and then to the northeast around the northern
edge of Bois de Beuge. The line then bends up
sharply to the northeast running slightly to
north of the center of Cote 274 and continues in
the same direction to the eastern limit of the
79th Division zone of action. The attack was
continued along the entire front this morning.
Communication with the front line was very
difficult and only a few messages were received.

The 37th Division reported that they opened
their attack at 7 a.m., and that they were
advancing in Cierges. Machine-gun and rifle
fire not very heavy, but there was considerable
artillery activity from direction of Romagne.
The front lines and reserves of this division
were gassed last night and again this morning,

just before the attack.   The town of Cierges was
reported captured and passed at 8:30 a.m.
        Latest information on the line of 91st
Division, from Air Service reports, has its right
flank just west of Gesnes and running along and
just beyond the Gesnes-Exermont Road, with a
front of about 2 kilometers and still advancing.
Complete reports not received up to noon from
center and left division, but understand they are
progressing steadily.   P. C., V Army Corps will
open at 22 o'clock, Sept. 29, at Verrieres-en-
Hesse Ferme....
        12.   ESTIMATE OF SITUATION: Favorable for
continuance of advance....
        14.   VISIBILITY: Generally poor.   ROADS and
traffic conditions improving.   MORALE: Excellent.

                            T. H. Emerson,
                            Colonel, Engineers,
                            A. C. of S., G-3

Distinguished Service Cross Citation
Victor Heintz
Captain, 147th Infantry

For extraordinary heroism in action near Cierges, France,
September 29, 1918. Heeding a call for help from a severely
wounded soldier, Capt. Heintz immediately left his place of
shelter and crawled through heavy artillery and machine-gun
fire to the aid of the man and carried him to a place of safety.

From 148th Infantry Regiment War Diary for September 29, 1918

Regiment holding dug-in position south and east
of Cierges awaiting relief.   Three battalions

less two companies in front line, two companies in support.

Gallantry in Action Citation
William E. Suter
Private, First Class, Company B, 148th Infantry

For gallantry in action at Cierges, France, September 29, 1918. While serving as a runner he repeatedly crossed terrain under intense enemy machine-gun and artillery fire. His courage and soldierly devotion to duty greatly encouraged the men with whom he served.

Distinguished Service Cross Citation
John Lawrence Letzing
First Lieutenant, Company B, 148th Infantry

For extraordinary heroism in action north of Montfaucon, France, September 29, 1918. During the attack Lieut. Letzing exposed himself to heavy artillery, rifle, and machine-gun fire to lead tanks against enemy machine-gun position. After the tanks had been withdrawn he walked up and down the firing line of his platoon and encouraged his men to greater efforts.

Gallantry in Action Citation
Thomas S. Falkner
First Sergeant, Company I, 146th Infantry

For gallantry in action near Montfaucon, France, September 29, 1918. His company having exhausted its ration supply, he voluntarily led a detail under enemy observation and intense enemy fire and secured rations for the company. The courage and devotion to duty greatly inspired the men with whom he served.

Distinguished Service Cross Citation
Nicholas L. Tairmie
Private, Headquarters Company, 147th Infantry

For extraordinary heroism in action south of Cierges, France, September 29, 1918. Volunteering to attempt the recovery of the barrel of a 37 mm. gun abandoned the previous day when the gun crew was gassed and when his battalion had retired to a more advantageous position, Private Tairmie advanced alone in broad daylight and under observation of the enemy 200 yards in advance of his own lines under intense machine-gun fire recovered the missing part and returned in safety to his own lines. His conduct was a splendid example of devotion to duty and proved an inspiration to the men of his battalion.

From 37th Division War Diary for September 30, 1918

Attack suspended for the day.

Colonel Best relieved of command of 148th Infantry, account physical exhaustion. During night 147th Infantry withdrawn to north end of Bois Communal. Enemy continues to shell Montfaucon. Orders issued in compliance with 5th Corps order relief of 37th Division by 32nd Division.

The relief started during afternoon of 30th and continued throughout the nights.

916 Officers
24646 Men
Cloudy & Rain - Weather
Muddy - Roads
Excellent - Health
Trenches & Bivouac.

Summer Waite,
Major, General Staff,
Acting G-3.

Gallantry in Action Citation
Richard J. O'Brien
Second Lieutenant, Company B, 148th Infantry

For gallantry in action in Bois Emont, near Cierges, France, September 30, 1918. He was mortally wounded while seeking places of shelter for the men of his platoon. He declined first aid until all the wounded men of his command had received medical attention. His splendid leadership and devotion to his comrades greatly inspired the men of his battalion.

Gallantry in Action Citation
Abner L. Fraser
Captain (then First Lieutenant), Chaplain, 146th Infantry

For gallantry in action September 30, 1918, near Cierges, France. Voluntarily directing and assisting in the burial of the dead of the regiment, under heavy shell fire and under observation of the enemy in broad daylight. His utter disregard for his own safety and his devotion to duty proved an inspiration to the men of his regiment.

Distinguished Service Cross Citation
Floyd A. Hughes
Mechanic, Company C, 146th Infantry

For extraordinary heroism in action near Montfaucon, France, September 26-30, 1918. This soldier was constantly on duty as a runner during the offensive west of the Meuse River, many times carrying messages through heavy machine-gun and shell fire. On September 30, when the enemy was reported to be forming for a counterattack on the left flank, he volunteered to take the information to the battalion commander. Passing through heavy shell fire, he delivered the message in time to enable the battalion commander to protect the threatened flank, but he was killed by a shell on his return trip to his company.

Distinguished Service Cross Citation
Milo E. Terry
Captain, Company H, 145th Infantry

For extraordinary heroism in action near Montfaucon, France, September 26 to 30, 1918. Although severely wounded while leading his company in the assault, he refused to be evacuated and courageously continued in command of his company for four days in action under heavy fire of all arms and constantly in contact with the enemy. On September 30, he was again severely wounded, but remained with his company until evacuated in a delirious condition after the company's relief had been completed. By his intrepid conduct and disregard of personal danger, he inspired the men of his company and contributed greatly to the success of the operation.

Distinguished Service Cross Citation
Timothy J. Moynahan
Lieutenant Colonel, 146th Infantry

For extraordinary heroism in action near Cierges, France, September 28-30, 1918. Displaying remarkable personal courage and leadership, he personally led his battalion, without support on either flank, through terrific artillery bombardment, in the face of direct machine-gun fire and enfilading fire from 1-pounder guns on the right, capturing his objective on the ridge east of Cierges and repelling four hostile counterattacks.

G-3 Section   V ARMY CORPS, A.E.F.,
     Verrieres-en-Hesse Ferme, September 30, 1918

12 Noon to 12 Noon, September 29/30

1. HOSTILE SITUATION AT BEGINNING OF DAY:
The enemy is strongly resisting the advance of
this corps.

His line has been reinforced and volume of
hostile artillery fire has increased.

2. INFORMATION RECEIVED OF ENEMY DURING
DAY: We received a report about noon that an enemy
radio message had been picked up by an Allied
station ordering a retreat....

3. ENEMY MOVEMENTS, CONDUCT AND CHANGES
DURING DAY: The enemy is making stubborn
resistance along entire front.

Local counterattacks have been made on our
line and also on those of the adjoining corps.
Heavy artillery fire, of high explosives, gas and
shrapnel, is making progress very difficult. A
large concentration of hostile forces was seen
during afternoon of the 29th, just southwest of
Romagne, and roads in that vicinity. Caissons
were observed moving north from Batheville at
this time. About noon the 30th, aerial observer
reported that seven small German tanks and one
large tank, going south through the field, two
kilometers south of Romagne. A long truck train
was seen on the St-Juvin-Romagne Road was going
towards Romagne.

    ...

6. OWN MOVEMENTS, CHANGES AND ACTION DURING
DAY: About noon liaison officer with 37th Division

states that their line had advanced north of
Cierges and still progressing with the assistance
of tanks. Corps observer reports at noon, at
Montfaucon, that our lines are advancing slowly,
being constantly harassed by high explosives,
shrapnel and gas. The 91st Division at this time
had passed the Gesnes-Exermont Road and was slowly
moving forward. The 79th Division reports troops
in Nantillois and beyond it, no indications of a
counterattack.... At noon today the 37th Division
states no change in front line except slight
adjustment to conform to line prescribed by corps.
Enemy artillery activity continues. Montfaucon
being shelled with shrapnel and high explosives.
The 32nd Division arrived during the morning in
the rear of the 37th Division which they will
relieve. Relief by small detachments will be
attempted during day.
    . . .
    13. PLANS FOR FUTURE: Relief of two
front line divisions. The 79th Division by the
3d Division and the 37th Division by the 32nd
Division.
    14. VISIBILITY: Poor. ROADS: Being
repaired. SUPPLIES: Delivery conditions
improved. MORALE: Excellent....

                              T. H. Emerson
                              Colonel, Engineers,
                              A. C. of S., G-3.

Distinguished Service Cross Citation
Albert L. Hechtl
Sergeant, Company C, 146th Infantry

For extraordinary heroism in action near Montfaucon, France, September 26 to October 1, 1918. Throughout the five days' offensive he commanded his platoon with rare coolness and was always in the first wave of his company, facing the greatest danger. He personally took charge of a thin line of outposts on the flank and broke up a German counter-attack that was forming under the protection of a barrage. On the fourth day of the drive this soldier was severely gassed, but he concealed this fact from his officers until he was exhausted.

Found in *The 37th Division in the World War*

That night, 29th-30th September, it was apparent to all that the division had spent at least its initial force and that the constant shelling, hunger, cold and the almost unceasing rains had done their work. Field Order No. 46, Fifth Corps Headquarters stated that "the attack of the corps will not be continued tomorrow. The present lines will be held and every effort made to prepare for a resumption of the offensive on the following day". The order established as a line of defense, a line one kilometer north of Nantillois, through the northern edge of the Bois de Beuge, through the center of the Bois Communal de Cierges, and thence southwest to Hill 231, north of the Bouleaux woods. It directed that a "covering force of at least one regiment for each division would be pushed sufficiently forward to protect this line, supported by at least one regiment of artillery." And at 5:45, Field Orders No. 48, Fifth Corps Headquarters, ordered the relief of the division. (vol. 2, 323).

From 148th Infantry Regiment War Diary for October 1, 1918

Regiment relieved, proceeded to Bois de Montfaucon, later to area 1 kilo. north of Recicourt, arriving... bivouac camp....

Total losses 26 Sept-1 Oct 18: Officers, 5 killed, 25 wounded... Enlisted men, 79 killed, 523 wounded, 107 missing.

Distinguished Service Cross Citation
Vincent C. Porter
Corporal, Company C, 146th Infantry

For extraordinary heroism in action near Montfaucon, France, September 26 to October 1, 1918. Though he was acting as company clerk throughout the drive west of the Meuse River, he volunteered for service as a runner and also took charge of the delivery of rations under constant shell fire in a highly exposed position. He performed valuable service in giving first aid to wounded, and at one time carried a wounded soldier much heavier than himself up a hill through shell and machine-gun fire.

Distinguished Service Cross Citation
Percy S. Blond
First Sergeant, Company C, 146th Infantry

For extraordinary heroism near Montfaucon, France, September 26, to October 1, 1918. Crossing an exposed area under heavy shell and machine-gun fire, he went forward and rescued a wounded comrade carrying him 200 yards up a steep slope. On another occasion during a severe artillery and machine-gun bombardment, he crept alone to an advanced post and carried back another wounded soldier. During the five days' action he gave first-aid treatment to 20 members of his company, inspiring every one by his valiant conduct in ministering to the wounded.

Found in *The 37th Division in the World War*

It should be noted here that there are no reliable reports available as to the number of casualties suffered on the successive days during which the division was engaged in the Meuse-Argonne offensive. Neither are there reports indicating the number of officers and men present for duty with the division. Scores, if not actually hundreds of men lost their way early in the advance and fought with neighboring divisions for days. Similarly, men became separated from platoon, company, battalion, regiment and brigade, and attached themselves to units other than their own, pursuant to orders. During the entire offensive, however, the division lost 16 officers killed 113 wounded and two missing: 352 men killed, 2,287 wounded and left the sector with 690 missing. By 18th October, however, when Maj. Gen. Farnsworth rendered the report from which these figures are taken, the number of missing had been reduced to 128 by known deaths, location of men in hospitals, and by the return of men who had become separated from their organizations. (vol. 2, 219)

From 3rd Battalion War Diary for October 1, 1918

```
        P.C. at 06.60-79.16.  Battalion relieved
by 32nd Division.  Marched to Recicourt where
battalion bivouacked.
        5 days rations and 5 days forage in supply
train.  Weather: fair.  Roads: poor, traffic heavy.
Health: good.

Thomas H. Morrow
Captain, 148th Infantry
Commanding, 3rd Battalion
```

From 3rd Battalion War Diary for October 2, 1918

Day spent equipping troops and reorganizing. Inspection.

5 days rations and 5 days forages in supply train. Weather: fair and good. Roads: soft. Health: fair.

                                    Thomas H. Morrow
                              Captain, 148th Infantry
                              Commanding, 3rd Battalion

FIELD ORDERS   FIRST ARMY, A.E.F.,
No. 34   October 3, 1918--18 h.

    3.   RELIEFS:...

      (b)   The 37th Division now assembling in the rear zone of the V Corps will be relieved from duty in that corps as soon as it is assembled and ready to move by bus and marching. The corps commander will determine the date that the division (less artillery) is ready to move and will give these headquarter timely notice of same. The artillery attacked to the division will remain with the V Corps until its relief can be effected.

Upon relief from V Corps the division will be assembled for rest and refitting in the region of Toul, as a reserve of the IV Corps.

Special orders will be issued directing the movement.

                    By command of General Pershing:

                                    H. A. Drum,
                              Chief of Staff.

From 3rd Battalion War Diary for October 3, 1918

P.C.-Recicourt. Battalion entrained in motor trucks and moved towards back area. Traveling all night.

5 days rations and 5 days forage in supply train. Weather: fair. Roads: soft. Health: fair.

Thomas H. Morrow
Captain, 148th Infantry
Commanding, 3rd Battalion

From 148th Infantry Regiment War Diary for October 4, 1918

Routine duty. Day spent in cleaning up.

Operations Section   FIRST ARMY, A. E. F.,
                      Bar-sur-Aube, January 5, 1919.

THE MEUSE-ARGONNE OPERATION
THE PLANS FOR THE ATTACK

1. Mission: The mission assigned the army on September 3 (Directive, General Headquarters, Allied Armies, G-3, No. 3537; September 3, 1918) was to penetrate the Hindenburg Position on the line Dun-sur-Neuse--Grandpre. This was to be followed by a development toward the line Stenay--Le Chesne which would turn the line of the Aisne River. The Meuse was the eastern limit of the attack. The attack was to be made in conjunction with an attack of the French Fourth Army between the Aisne and the Suippe.

2.   Terrain: The terrain presented unusual
difficulties.   The attack had to be made along the
high ridge or water shed between the Meuse and
the Aisne Rivers, and it was flanked on the east
by the commanding heights of the Cotes de Meuse
and on the west by the wooded hills of the Argonne
Forest.   Along this high ridge, and forming
obstacles to the advance, were: The commanding
hill of Montfaucon, the wooded heights of Romagne
and Cunel, and the heights of Andevanne and the
Bois de Barricourt.   The terrain over which the
attack was made may be likened to a deep defile,
blocked by three successive barriers.

3.   This position, strong by nature, was
heavily fortified and well protected with wire.
The enemy's first position ran generally through
Malancourt--Vauquois--Boureuilles.   There was an
intermediate position through Cuisy and Cheppy,
and a second position through Montfaucon.   Through
Conel-Romagne heights and Gradpre, there was a
third position, the Kriemhild Stellung, a part of
the famous Hindenburg Line.   At the time of the
attack, the enemy held the front with about six
divisions.

4.   The mission assigned required first, a
penetration of about sixteen kilometers to reach
the line Dun-sur-Meuse--Grandpre and second, an
additional penetration of about sixteen kilometers
to reach the Stenay--La Chesne line.   In order
to accomplish this double mission, two operations
were planned, one for each penetration.   The
preliminary plans were prepared September 7, and
forwarded to General Petain September 10.   The
sector from the Moselle to the Meuse was to be
held from right to left by the American IV Corps,
the French II Colonial Corps and a French corps.

September 22 was given as the date when the attack
would be ready.

5. The general plans... were amplified into
a set of battle instructions drawn up in the form
of a proposed field order. The battle instructions
were issued September 16, together with Operations
Map No. 12. Additional instructions were given
the army corps September 17. The French Second
Army was to control the movements of all divisions
in its army area. The normal elements of this
army were to occupy the front line positions
during the concentration in order to conceal the
movement. The American First Army was to take
over command of the sector west of the Meuse on
September 20. The French battalions in the front
lines were to be completely relived by the night
D - 1D. The battle instructions directed corps
and services to submit their plans in the form of
the appropriate field order and annex to the field
order.

6. Field Orders No. 20, with its annexes,
were prepared September 20, and issued September
20 and 21. The attack of September 26 was made
under this field order. The plan of operations was
as follows: To attack west of the Meuse with three
army corps and hold east of the Meuse with three
army corps.

In the attack, the general missions of the
army corps were:

a. Right Corps: To protect the right of the
operation by building up a defensive line along
the Meuse and by assisting in neutralizing with
its artillery the enemy artillery and observation
on the heights east of the Meuse. By advancing
its left division, it was to assist in the capture
of Montfaucon and in the penetration of the
Kriemhild Stellung.

   b.   Left Corps: To reduce the Argonne Forest
by flanking it from the east and to assist in
cutting off hostile artillery fire and observation
from the eastern slopes of the Argonne. With its
right division it was to assist in the capture of
the Bois de Gesnes.

   c.   Center Corps: To make the deep drive to
penetrate the Kriemhild-Stellung.

   d.   General Missions: Corps were to advance
independently to the corps objectives.

   Corps were to advance to the American Army
objective in conjunction with the center corps.

   All corps were to obtain the corps objective
before further advance was to be made.

   Advance beyond the American Army objective
was to be ordered by the army.

   The Kriemhild-Stellung was to be reached by
the afternoon of D day....

                    Prepared by Operation Sector
                         3d Section, General Staff
                             First Army, A. E. F.

                             R. T. WARD,
                         Colonel, General Staff.

The Stars and Stripes, French, October 4, 1918

FIRST ARMY AGAIN IN MAJOR ATTACK, GAINS IN ARGONNE

Americans Strike Between River Meuse and Great Tangle of Forest

-----

NEW DIVISIONS IN BATTLE

Yanks Who Push Ahead Northwest of Verdun Never Knew Rigors of Winter in France

-----

At dawn on September 26, 1918, the First American Army, flushed with its first swift success at St. Mihiel, struck its second blow on a wide front northwest of Verdun--struck and drove the Germans from many a town and village, from many a hill and valley they had held since the first weeks of the world war.

All that region the night before had been blasted by such a concourse of guns as had had no precedent in American history, and by sundown of the second day the Infantry, which swarmed forward through the mist of Thursday morning, had found its way far into the wild forest of Argonne, had carried by storm the forbidding height of Montfaucon, had restored village after village to France, and had sent more than 8,000 prisoners trotting back through the chill September rain to the waiting pens behind.

The attack was made on a 20-mile front. The communiqués of the first two days announced that troops from 12 states--Pennsylvania, Kansas, Missouri, Ohio, New Jersey, Maryland, Virginia, Oregon, Washington, Colorado, Wyoming and Montana--were participating in the action.

In all that battle-line there was not a gunner at his lanyard not a cook straining to push his kitchen forward, not a doughboy crouching ominous in the mud who did not know--and who was not immensely heartened by the knowledge--that at his own Army's left the French were fighting victoriously in Champagne; that to the north the British, Belgians and Yankees were forging ahead.

News Flashed by Wireless

He knew that he and his were taking part in the largest combined military movement the Western front had ever known--that they were taking part in a battle which, with intervals of quiet and taut expectancy, stretched from Lorraine to the North Sea.

The impression of a rain of blows upon the enemy's stupefied head was conveyed through the air from the high wireless station on the Eiffel Tower in Paris, which sped to the uttermost reaches of the tingling front not only the news of progress in other sectors of France, but also the tidings of German disaster in far Macedonia and the Holy Land.

The proof of such concerted fighting could be read on every slope and crest on the American front. It could be noted in the feebleness with which the German artillery made answer to our own during the first two days of the battle. It could be noted in the scramble with which reserves came to the rescue on the third and fourth days and in the nature of those reserves.

Here was part of a division of which the other part was mixed up with the French in Champagne. Here was another division that had been caught and thrown into the gap while on its way from Alsace to some part of the German line in Flanders that had been shrieking for help.

On Memorable Ground

And in all that battle-line from Verdun to the other side of the great forest there was not a Yankee who did not know he was fighting on ground hallowed far beyond our power to add or detract; that he was starting out from Hill 304 and Le Mort Homme of tragic memories; that he was advancing from blighted fields immortalized by those dead soldiers in horizon blue who stood fast there throughout the bitter months of 1916 and said of the invading horde: "They shall not pass."

Ahead of the doughboys, and beckoning to them, loomed Montfaucon, that village on a hilltop which is the highest point between the Ainse and the Meuse, and from whose church steeple, one visible for miles and miles around like a finger pointed to Heaven, the Crown Prince watched in 1916 the vain slaughter of his countrymen.

Now that watch tower is but crumbled stone--crumbled stone of which some has been spread and packed to make a road over which American kitchens are trundling with slum and coffee for American doughboys.

Never Knew a French Winter

But to those Americans whose prayer every morning and every night of their lives is that this young Army should do the home folks proud the factor in this battle of greatest interest is just the fact that the initial attack on the whole 20-mile front was launched by divisions of which not one could tell what a winter in France is like. The attack was launched without taxing a single one of the really veteran divisions of the A.E.F.

What is more, two of the newly arrived divisions had never been in the line before, had never entered even the quietest sector, had never ducked their heads before the banshee wail of a German shell nor heard an American gun fired in anger.

One of these two newcomers--and surely this single fact will thrill a hundred million hearts back home--one of these green divisions, these Freshmen of the A.E.F., was met on the first day by a division of the celebrated Prussian Guard, and on that day chased those famous troops across seven kilometers of devastated France.

Guns Begin to Speak

It was at 2:30 on Thursday morning that from every ridge and hillside from the Meuse to the Argonne, the guns began to speak. From far to the west in Champagne and from over to the east of Verdun there had come the sound of distant firing for three hours past, and now and again one of our own great shells had gone howling overhead.

The day had been one of shifting clouds and occasional autumnal rain-squalls. Now the moon shone clear and the stars were brilliant, but over the land a heavy white mist lay like a wet cloth, a sheltering mist through which the ever thickening traffic crept silently along the roads that led to the battlefield.

Then, quite suddenly, all the guns spoke at once. It was the beginning of a three-hour bombardment which smashed German roads and wires, muted German batteries, sought out and pulverized German P.C.'s. fell like a rain of death on moving German troops, and drove scuttling under ground all living creatures over there.

No Answer Awakened

There was no answer. If there had been, it could not have been heard. For as many miles as once could see by the myriad, ceaseless flashes in the night, our own guns were cursing from every crest and clump. At first you could hear the whine of our own shells, the echo from hill to hill, the harsh swishing of the water in the swamps, the angry rattle against the hogbacks and even, sometimes, the shrill, sharp commands, heard like foot ball signals from some nearby battery. But as the fury reached its crescendo toward dawn, all these overtones were lost in the instant succession of the shots.

The cargo of many a ship, the strain and sweat of many a stevedore, the sale of untold thousands of Liberty bonds, the toil of many millions of devoted hands came into their own in that bombardment.

Its intensity can be estimated from the fact that the count of the rounds fired on one-third of the American front amounted to 10,000 from the larger guns and 70,000 from the 75's.

Its sound can be guessed by the fact that when, after dawn, the firing subsided somewhat and the batteries were content to shoot only one gun a minute, it seemed to the toilers underneath as though a strange restful hush had settled over the world. One of these toilers, a driver on the high seat of an ammunition truck, shivered inside his leather jacket and confided to his steering wheel:

"Oh, Lord, thanks be I'm not on the other end of that noise."

Just Before Zero

That noise reached its most deafening climax in the last few minutes before the zero hour. That is the period of most painful expectancy, when anxious eyes follow the creeping mount hands on thousands upon thousands of synchronized watches. At 5:30 the first faint sign of dawn would be showing in the east, the long waiting would be done, the Infantry would be up and over the top. And every one behind them, from the generals to the cooks, knew in his proud and confident heart that for a time there would be only one problem. For all the rest, there would be only the problem of keeping up with the doughboys.

Then 5:30 came and an observer, crouched in such a vantage point, say, as any one of those look-outs which indent the parapet on the crest of Hill 304, must needs strain his eyes through the mist that blanketed the valley below. The trenches and those within them were completely hidden from view. Then, a few moments later--and it was a sight to carry with him to his grave--out from under the edge of the mist, swarming like a multitude of tawny bees from some giant hive, out and on and up the hill the doughboys went.

In an instant, the wires hummed with the news. Signals flew from the hill tops, pigeons sprang into the air with the tidings and overhead the hovering aircraft paused, wheeled and started back. Soon from each of them would drop to some open field a gleaming cylinder, tracable in its passage through the air by its fluttering stream of white, messages from the air to the waiting commanders in the rear.

"Over on the Minute"

The burden of all these messages was pretty much the same along the whole 20 mile front. Take one flashed back by a corporal, squatting, telephone in hand, at his look-out station. He may have tried to keep his voice level and military. His report, as it was caught on the typewriter in some message center far behind, will some day gather dust in the archives of the War Department at Washington. It read:

"Troops over the top with a yell on the minute."

It meant that the line--which had held at least that much ground for four long years and which had not moved an inch either way for more than a year--the line was moving at last, and toward Germany.

Then, as the Infantry rushed forward, smothering or passing by the rear guard machine gun nests and rounding up the disorganized German troops whose retreat had been cut off by the barrage, every other arm of the service took up the strain of moving forward. At the end of the second day, the counter attack began, came thicker and faster in the days succeeding as the resistance stiffened, brought with them fierce, close hand-grenade fighting as the battle line swayed back and forth. But for the first two days it was a matter of pursuit, and for all the Army, the sleepless task of keeping up with the Infantry.

Moving Up Starts Early

That movement had begun at midnight the night before. At midnight some battalions of 75's had fired a few rounds and then packed up to start forward through the mud and darkness, starting so early that before sundown they were pitched on new hillsides and, without waiting for camouflage or good emplacements, were firing steadily into the receding German lines.

The pace set for them can be gauged by the fact that one regimental aid station, after patching up the first wounded at its old stand until 9 on Thursday morning, jumped forward eight kilometers and was at work in Cuisy by noon of the first day. By sundown of that first day the Infantry lines in some places had gone forward more than five miles, and through the maze of traffic which clogged the crazy roads, the urgent message ran back: "Guns, before all else, and then food for the guns. Rations second, ammunition first."

To get the guns up, meat and coffee must wait. Everything--except ambulances--must wait. If horses dragging the 75's through the mud should be killed or, having done their level best, should drop from exhaustion, then human muscles must push the guns on their way. If a big gun should capsize in some shell hole and despair of moving on to its assigned position, then it must make that shell hole its position and open fire from there. More than once these things happened.

The problem of moving up the guns and the other supplies was made both supremely important and supremely difficult through the first three days by the nature of the terrain over which the Americans were fighting--one of the most difficult battlefields in Europe--and by the condition in which four years of battle had left that terrain.

Here was a stretch of French countryside all little hills and valleys. In the summer of 1914 it was beautifully carpeted with green, field after field of well husbanded farms, with here and there a golden wheat crop embroidered with scarlet poppies and here and there a village of stone homes with red-tiled roofs.

Now it looks as though the hand of some grotesquely gigantic leper had reached out of the East and touched it. It is a dead country. There are no homes, no life, no verdure. Here and there is some crumbled stone where a house once stood, here and there the blackened stump of a blasted tree. For the rest there is only a scorched, bleak countryside, putted with shell holes and mine craters like the face of the moon.

From these shell holes German rear-guards turned their machine guns on the backs of the advancing Yankees. From them, as the mists of the first morning cleared away, Germans emerged in batches large and small, to be taken into custody by the mopping-up parties and sent to the rear to swell to thousands the number of prisoners captured on the first day.

Still the Prisoners Come

Not only that first morning, but off and on through Thursday, Friday and Saturday, little groups of them would trickle out of the underground hiding places wither they had taken refuge when the shelling began and whence they had been afraid to come out, so deep-rooted was their conviction that Americans were accustomed to boil their prisoners in oil. There they would be found by Yanks on a still hunt for souvenirs.

Two famished Boches emerged as late as Saturday from a deep dugout that was not more than a good rifle shot from the dugout of a general commanding an American reserve battalion.

Aside from these shell holes and remnants of abandoned trenches, the waterless, godless land for several kilometers in depth offered not a vestige of shelter, not a hedge or even a clump of green behind which a gun might hide, or in the scant protection of which a line of trucks might move unobserved.

One Wall for a Village

As for the villages which the first few days recaptured, some are so completely obliterated that runners passed through them in broad daylight, never once dreaming that a village had ever stood there.

One messenger, knowing that a general's P.C. had been set up in a certain town which looked imposing enough on the map, found when he came to the place that only a part of one wall of one house remained to identify it. Against this wall, a telephone was placed.

"Where is the divisional P.C.?" the runner asked of the officer at the telephone.

"You're in it now," replied the officer with a grin.

Of other towns, such as Cuisy and Montfaucon or Bethincourt, more is left, but not enough on which to build anew, and sometimes you can recognize the church, where weeds grow rank through the stones of the floor, only by the remnants of painted angels lettering a heap of stones which was once an altar.

But it was neither in terms of battle nor in terms of restoration that this terrain presented its most serious problem during the first few days of the battled. It was in terms of traffic.

Roads over which no vehicle had passed since the summer of 1914, roads recognizable after four years only as serpentine paths weaving disconsolately among the shell holes, roads in which mine craters yawned past all hasty bridging, these had to receive and bear during the first three days a volume of heavy, ceaseless traffic that would have worried a dozen Lincoln Highways.

In Terms of Traffic

That is why the pioneers both Engineer and Infantry went for days and nights without stopping to sleep or eat. That is why the clink of pick and shovel working ahead of the trucks, will ever be music to the ears of the

American Army. Theirs was the task of getting the guns up, and get them up they did, faster in some places than in others, but still the guns moved on through the rain, and the ammunition followed.

Even had the roads been perfect from the start, the traffic problem would have been enormous, and those who went through it will never forget the paralyzing congestion. Every one helped. Everyone had to help. The sight no one could stand was the spectacle of a long train of ambulances stalled in the rain, the drivers raging, the onlookers cursing, only the wounded within silent and uncomplaining save when one of them might reach out and ask for a smoke or a pull on a passing canteen.

Perhaps, when it meant just a short but impassable blockade, an officer would leap down from a truck and call for volunteers. "These men have paid the price," he would call out in the darkness, "and we've got to see them through to the hospitals. Maybe we can cut a road through this wire and mud that will skirt these foundered trucks blocking the way. Pitch in, everybody."

Road Built in Twinkling

Then down from the trucks, out from under tarpaulins, emerging here from a hastily made bed beside the road or there from a roadside kitchen, the volunteers would come. The improvised road would be made in a twinkling, the litters would be carried across its torturing bumpy surface, the ambulances would trundle after and a little later the train of wounded would be creeping on its way to beds and warm food and expert, compassionate hands.

In such traffic jams, when an occasional ill-advised cart full of officers' baggage would be chucked ruthlessly to the side and when stubborn drivers must be coerced to breed in them then and there the right commonly spirit, the strong-armed M.P. was the king of the road and the hero of the hour.

Every cross roads clamored for him over the wires. Things went best where the M.P. at the corner was a square-jawed, hard boiled Yankee who, when a truck seemed disinclined to do his bidding on the instant, would waste no words but draw his gun suggestively and say:

"You do what I tell you or I'll blow what little brains you've got to the other end of Hell."

At the End of the Sixth Day

With roads laid under and in front of the moving traffic, with such M.P.'s to straighten out the tangles, slowly through the mud and rain the guns moved up.

By the end of the sixth day the Yankees in the Argonne had pushed on in some places to a depth of 12 kilometers, and everywhere held fast their new won territory, despite an ever stiffening resistance, which took the form of repeated small-scale counter-attacks and the turning loose on the Americans of all the German tricks in machine guns, shrapnel, hand grenades, minnenwerfers and gas.

On the extreme right the troops working up along that curve in the meandering Meuse, which fairly pocketed the enemy, had pushed through the troublesome woods above Septsarges and reached almost as far as Brieulle. Toward the center the lofty height of Montfaucon was serving American observers as a watchtower, and the battle line had passed Cierges.

Most difficult of all had proved the Forest of Argonne itself, but into this treacherous woods the New York troops had found their way foot by foot for a distance of over five miles. Found their way? Hewed their way, rather, for the Forest of Argonne is such a wild tangle of ancient trees, rank underbrush and barbed wire as no American doughboys have had to face since the first troops went into the trenches.

Chopping a Way Through

The path would baffle a rabbit, and the machine guns are strewn through the woods like snakes in the grass, but somehow the Infantry have pushed and fought and cut and chopped their way through.

Ahead of our line on the sixth day, the Germans had retreated to that third retirement position which they left half constructed in the late autumn of 1917, a position strong in its natural defenses but reinforced to no such extent as the Hindenburg line, with which it cannot be tactically compared. It is rather a continuation of that retirement position to which the Germans were driven when the Americans sliced off the St. Mihiel salient. This retirement line in the Argonne they have named the Kriemhilde line, in honor of a bouncing lady who figured large in the Niebelungen Lied.

Gallipolis Newspaper and year not established

FRIENDS OF 37TH TO FIGHT TO LAST DITCH

Washington, Feb. 5.--Friends of the 37th Div. are preparing to fight to the last ditch the claims of the 79th Div. for congressional recognition as the division that captured Montfaucon. Captain Fred Kochli of Alliance, O., called at Representative John C. Speaks office today and prepared a statement in writing to the effect that he himself led a patrol of the 37th Div. men that put the Montfaucon machine gun nests out of business on the day before the 79th Div. came up.

According to Captain Kochli's statement the 79th Div. walked into Montfaucon without encountering anything but nominal resistance. Lieutenant Colonel Ralph Cole, historian of the 37th Div., is here trying to effect an adjustment of the controversy. Representative James T. Begg, who introduced a resolution authorizing the 37th Div. to erect a monument to the valor of its troops at Montfaucon, said today that the controversy is creating a deadlock which probably will result in no legislation being enacted.

Lieut, Alfred Barlow of this city led two squads beyond Montfaucon and assisted in the capture of the city.

The Stars and Stripes, France, October 4, 1918

ECHOES FROM THE ARGONNE FIGHT

An American private spied a rooster prowling around a farm house in No Man's Land just after the Americans had captured Very. Being angry, and having an appetite for roast chicken, this American private decided to crawl up on the rooster and trap him in the building.

`The American was about to lay his hands on the astonished rooster when a German entered the rear door of the building bent on the same mission. Both were so surprised that they stood for a moment and glared at each other, then the American motioned for the German to do a right flank on the prey they were after and both closed in on him. The rooster was captured by the American, who later returned to the American lines with both rooster and German in tow.

Later, at the regimental P.C., the German roasted the chicken for his captor, who shared it with him.

The following letter was written by an American soldier to his mother in California a few hours before the beginning of the Argonne drive:

"Dear Mother: We are going in to battle the Boche tonight. It is our first time in, as you know, so of course I am thinking of you more or less. But don't forget, Mother, my thoughts are of you.

"I am taking advantage of a few hours' rest and writing to you, as I know you are always wanting to hear from me. But don't worry one bit, Mother Dear. If the Boches get me I will get ten of them while they are about it.

"This will be all until next time.
"Lovingly,
"Bennie."

The "next time" never came for Bennie. When the burial squad found this letter in his shirt pocket he was lying with his face toward Germany, his right front finger pressing the trigger of his rifle. A few yards in front of him was a German machine gun nest. There were nine dead Germans in the pit.

One Artillery unit worked hard during the afternoon of the second day of the attack to get its pieces into position. It had moved up for the second time, and had not fired a shot.

It was four o'clock when the lieutenant in command gave orders for everyone to stand by. The gunners were to fire their first volley into the German lines.

Everyone stood waiting for the final word when the telephone rang and word came that the Infantry had advanced so far that it would be necessary to move up again before going into action.

"Oh, hell!" said a gunner; "those Infantry guys ain't got no respect for us at all!"

A German Artillery unit was in the act of being relieved the first night the Americans swept forward. The advance was so swift that both the old unit and the relieving unit were captured at the gun positions.

A truck train was lined up on a dark road running parallel with the front and only a few kilometers back while a company of Pioneers mended a broken culvert.

A colonel who was unfortunate enough to be at the rear of the jam and who was quite anxious to be on the move, turned on the electric lights of his limousine in hopes that the light would enable the men toiling on the roads to work faster.

A Pioneer private paused, pick above his head, when he saw the sudden flare of light.

"Hey, you rube!" he shouted. "What are you trying to pull off down there? Do you want all the German artillery in the country turned on us? Can that stuff or I'll come down and kick a lung out just to pass the time."

There was no reply. But the light went out.

A Yankee truck driver's right forward wheel had just sunk with an air of finality into a half-filled shell-hole on the road near Avocourt, and he was throwing over a terrific barrage of profanity when he suddenly stopped short and his jaw dropped.

Then it closed in a grin as broad as the Sacramento, from whose distant shore he had gone forth to war. He was contemplating the approach along the roadside of four stalwart and imposing officers of the famous Prussian Guard. On their shoulders, as they marched along in the drizzling rain, was a stretcher, and on the stretcher lay a wounded doughboy smoking a cigarette.

When the mud is knee deep and German shells are falling all around, the officers in the line have been known to reflect audibly and sarcastically on the luxurious life led by the staff officers far behind, and sometimes even to call those more secluded directors of the war by the disrespectful name of "Old Waffle-tails."

But one colonel from an American Army corps emerged from the fight near the Argonne with the glove torn from the back of his hand by a piece of shrapnel and a shattered riding crop as further evidence of a narrow escape.

A lieutenant of Engineers was scouting a few days ago along the road which forks on a hill-crest, one branch mounting toward Montfaucon, on branch dipping into the valley that cradles Cuisy. As to this latter road, he would have to do some prospecting to see how much stone and how many men would be needed to make it bear all the big trucks and ponderous tractors that would have to pass along it in the wake of the Infantry.

Along came a doughboy, rifle on shoulder, a doughboy taking very seriously his new responsibility, which was the escort to the rear of three German prisoners. However, though thus engrossed, he might possibly have noticed the condition of the road.

"Hey, Buddie, are you from Cuisy?"

The doughboy halted and saluted.

"No, sir," he said, "from Philadelphia."

He and his prisoners were both many meters on their way before the lieutenant recovered sufficiently to go on with his inquiry.

One of the hardest jobs any one had in the first drive west of Verdun was the job of a grizzled old mess sergeant in charge of a roadside kitchen set up to nourish, at proper intervals, a company of Engineers at work on the roads. He had just enough rations to feed them for one day, and except for the occasional casuals any kitchen can handle, he knew he must refuse all stragglers.

Yet his kitchen was in full sight of the road, along which all day long there straggled those slightly wounded youngsters from the line who were quite able to foot it to the nearest ambulance camp. Some of them had had nothing to eat for three days. Every one of them, at the smell of the hot coffee, would stop wistfully and ask for a bit of bread or something. Always the old sergeant had to shake his head. By noon he had aged ten years.

"It'll kill me yet," he said at last. "I know they have only to cross the next crest to find food and drink a-plenty, but I remember how my mother never turned any one from her door who asked for something to eat. They might be burglars, but she wouldn't take a chance!"

A young sergeant from Baltimore limped on his way. The mess sergeant could hear him explaining to the other wounded boy with him.

"We can't blame him. If he fed us, he'd have to feed them all, and then where'd he be? I guess he's a good old scout, at that."

From 148th Infantry Regiment War Diary for October 7, 1918

Relieved 353rd Infantry 89th Division in S/S
Benoit, command passed at 23 o'clock: all combat
positions occupied.

From 148th Infantry Regiment War Diary for October 9, 1918

Headquarters Company and 3rd Battalion moved
via truck occupying positions in S/S. 3rd Bn. to
be Brigade Reserve.

From 3rd Battalion War Diary for October 9, 1918

En route to reserve position 74th Brigade at S-
S St. Benoit.

Chapter Nine

The Stars and Stripes, France, October 4, 1918

ONE PACKAGE FOR EVERYONE IN A.E.F., CHRISTMAS PLAN

Soldiers Will Send Special Label to Home Folks, G.O. Explains

-----

RED CROSS TO COOPERATE

Standard Size and Weight Limit of Three Pounds Specified for Holiday Bundles

-----

We are going to get Christmas packages, after all.

Every one of us will get one--exactly one--a small one, to be sure, but the real thing; and nobody will be left out. And here, in a new General Order which will be read to each organization in the A.E.F. as soon as it arrives, is the whole arrangement:

"The following regulations will cover the sending of Christmas packages to members of the American Expeditionary Forces for Christmas, 1918:

"1. The Adjutant-General, A.E.F., will issue through organizations and station commanders an official coupon to each officer and soldier or other member of the American Expeditionary Forces which, when properly filled out by the person to whom it is issued and mailed to a friend or relative in the United States, will permit the person receiving it to send one Christmas package not larger than 9 inches by 4 inches by 3 inches, and not exceeding 3 pounds in weight.

May Use Standard Container

"2. Standard boxes or containers for this purpose may be obtained in the United States from the local or nearest Red Cross chapter, but it is not necessary that these Red Cross boxes be used, provided the package conforms in weight and size to the conditions of Paragraph 1.

"3. Packages not conforming to the standard form adopted by the Red Cross will not be accepted.

"4. Each soldier will write as clearly as possible (printing in block letters preferred) on the line provided therefor, in ink if possible, his name, rank, Army serial number, company, regiment, and arm of service. The following is a specimen copy:

Approved by P.O. Dept.   OFFICIAL COUPON
Approved by War Dept.
                    AMERICAN EXPEDITIONARY FORCES.
                    CHRISTMAS PACKAGE COUPON.

John Doe	Pvt.	123456789
(Name)	(Rank)	(Army Serial Number)
Q	711th	Infantry
(Company)	(Regiment)	(Arm of Service)

PASTE THIS COUPON ON THE PACKAGE

DIRECTIONS: One Christmas package not heavier than three points and not larger than 9 by 4 by 3 inches will be carried free from Hoboken, N.J., to each American soldier in Europe. Standard boxes of these dimensions will be furnished, upon application, by local chapters of the American Red Cross in the United States. Christmas packages must not contain perishable articles, or any articles prohibited by the postal laws from transmission by mail. PACKAGES NOT CONFORMING TO STANDARD FURNISHED BY RED CROSS WILL NOT BE ACCEPTED. This coupon is authority for any post office to accept on or before November 20, 1918, a Christmas package conforming to the above regulations for the soldier named hereon. Postage to Hoboken, N.J. must be prepaid.

THIS COUPON MUST BE PASTED ON THE PACKAGE TO INSURE ITS TRANSMISSION.

"5. After properly addressing the coupon as above described, the soldier will immediately mail the letter to the person in the United States from whom he expects his Christmas packages. He will request the person in the United States receiving the coupon to paste it on the Christmas package which that person may desire to send to him. So affixed, this coupon will form the address of the soldier and the authorization for the shipment of the package overseas. The person in the United States, after affixing the coupon, will then prepay postage to Hoboken, N.J. If the soldier has no parent or relative to sent the coupon to, he may mail it to the Red Cross in Washington, D.C., which has agreed to send one package to every soldier whose parents or relatives are not able to do so.

"6. Commanding officers will personally supervise the issuing of coupons.

"7. It is especially necessary that soldiers... [send] their coupons to the United States at the earliest possible moment.

"8. The bulk of transportation which will be diverted from war purposes in shipping and distributing these packages is of such moment that the co-operation of every officer and soldier is requested to see, first, that every soldier gets one coupon; second, that he understands the necessary method of filling it out and dispatching it promptly; third, that the spirit of Christmas and fair play obtains so that but one coupon will be issued to each soldier."

Distinguished Service Cross Citation
Albert Schlesinger
Second Lieutenant (then, Sergeant), Company G, 147th Infantry

For extraordinary heroism in action. On the night of October 11, 1918, at Bois Dommartin, near Beney, France, he volunteered to recover the body of an American officer who had been killed while leading a raiding party, the body being left about fifty paces in front of the enemy positions. With a patrol of six men he proceeded on his mission, meeting heavy rifle and machine gun fire. Ordering his men to retire, he, with one man of his patrol, covered the retirement, which was successfully accomplished. Although severely wounded he continued his covering fire with automatic rifle and grenades, unassisted, and eventually reached his own lines.

The Stars and Stripes, France, October 11, 1918

WEEKLY NEWS REEL TO BRING HOME OVER

Battle Line, Mary Pickford and Charlie Chaplin Also Booked

State Street, Chicago; Market Street, San Francisco; Canal Street, New Orleans; Broad Street, Philadelphia, and Fifth Avenue, New York, with all their dens and denizens, are now being shown on the screen to as much of the Army as they can possibly be shown to, in France and England and Italy, through the medium of the Overseas Weekly, a news film being gotten out over here by the Community Motion Picture Bureau for distribution through the huts of the Y.M.C.A.

In addition to live news scenes from American cities, the weekly includes views of wheat harvesting in the Middle West, salmon runs in Washington, and lumbering in Maine. It aims to bring home to the A.E.F. through the medium of the movies.

Supplementing the scenes from the States, the bureau's service includes new pictures taken with the French, British and Australian forces, and it also has the pick of the United States Army Signal Corps films, including many scenes of actual combat filmed in the forward areas.

From Monday to Saturday

These war views are gotten out and around in the minimum time required to develop and edit them, and it is therefore quite possible for Lieutenant Snookums, Inf., to lead a charge on Monday and on Saturday evening, in a rest area hut, to see himself leading the charge, thus giving him valuable opportunity to note professional defects in charge leading.

At present the bureau has three separate shows running every evening, multiplied by duplicated films to cover not only the A.E.F., but the movie-loving populace of the British, French and Italian forces. With 300 film projectors here in France now and in working order, there should not a week pass by without every man's having a chance to see what home looks like, what the front looks like, if he hasn't been to the front, or what other people's fronts look like.

The last includes the famous front of Mary Pickford and that of Charlie Chaplin, for, with the single exception of one by film, the Community

Motion Picture Bureau has been given the refusal of every picture made in the States.

Distinguished Service Cross Citation (Posthumous)
Junius I. Boyle
First Lieutenant, 147th Infantry

For extraordinary heroism in action in the Bois Donmartin, northwest of Thiacourt, France, October 11, 1918. He voluntarily and alone made a reconnaissance of the Bois Donmartin, a strongly fortified enemy position, and returned with valuable information. Later, accompanied by another soldier, he again made a reconnaissance, and while returning with valuable information was attacked by a superior force and killed.

```
Adj. #970.              Headquarters 37th Division,
                  American E. F., 12 October, 18.

Memorandum for all Commanding Officers:-

     1.   Inspections show that the sanitary
conditions of troops in this command are
rapidly becoming unsatisfactory due to the non-
construction of latrines and to the non-observance
of sanitary regulations on the part of this
command.  Many organizations have not constructed
latrines as required by regulations and no steps
have been taken to insure the cleanliness of
localities in which troops are living.

     2.   The Commanding General directs that
each and every detachment and organization in this
Division at once proceed to the construction of
latrines of a suitable type which must be used
by each officer and enlisted man in this command.
Infected areas will be cleaned up and guards
```

posted to enforce compliance with this order.
Commanding Officers of organizations will be
responsible that the provisions of this order are
carried out. It shall be the duty of all medical
officers to make a daily inspection of their units
and of their latrine facilities and to report any
failure of non-compliance with this order to the
proper commanding officer, who will at once take
proper corrective action. Organization commanders
will require a daily inspection by their surgeons
and will hold commanding officers as well as their
surgeons strictly responsible for the sanitary
condition of their command.

Official: Dana T. Merrill,
                         Lt. Colonel, General Staff
                              Chief of Staff.

From 148th Infantry Regiment Strength Return for October, 1918

Co. L:
Capt. Estel L. Stewart
1st Lt. Alfred M. Barlow
1st Lt. Nathan S. Clark
2nd Lt. George J. Waterhouse

Co L 148 Inf.
A.P.O. 763
Amer. E F
Oct. 13, 1918

Dear Mamma,

*Since I wrote you I have received your letters of Sept. 2-9 and 16th. I am
enclosing a clipping that will show you more than I am supposed to write of what I
have been doing. The night of the 25 and 6 of September we were in the woods with
the artillery. Using the word in its true sense the sound was "awful."*

The last three days I was in command of my company. In fact I was the only officer left with the company. One was killed, one was gassed, one was shot thru the leg, one who was shot in the legs by shrapnel had to have both amputated six inches below the hips and one was sick. Do you see I've had a warm time of it.

One never knows how one is going to act under fire until one has been thru it. Now I know. I am proud of myself and proud of my men. No one need tell me anything in future about war as butchery. I know it. It is forbidden or I would tell you what proportion of my company are casuals. I was very highly complimented on my work and my whole battalion was [by the] commanding general.

In order to be able to march well and fight well I took only a light rain coat leaving my baggage that I usually carried. When I returned I was unable to obtain any of it. I lost my address book and many papers unable to be replaced.

I am now in a dug out in another sector. I am still the only officer with the company.

For 5 days on the drive we had 2 days food. It rained constantly many are now sick in the hospital.

Gee! but I'm tough.

Lots of love,

Alfred

OK A M Barlow 1st Lt

Distinguished Service Cross Citation
Bryan Hamilton
Sergeant, Company E, 145th Infantry

For extraordinary heroism in action at Olsene, Belgium, October 14, 1918. He was leading a detachment forward which was caught in a heavy enemy counter barrage. Though he was badly wounded by shell fire, he kept his men organized, and, pushing forward, dislodged the enemy from a strong position, where he was again wounded.

Translation from the French, found in
The United States Army in the World War

MESSAGE CENTER, FIRST ARMY,
October 14, 1918.

No. 4779. Very urgent. For General Pershing: The action that has been undertaken today by the Belgian, French and British troops in Belgium has made sufficient progress to enable us to expect important results if it is pushed through, and with that object, followed up with sufficient forces.

Under those conditions and to that effect, I order that two American divisions chosen among those that have taken part in offensive operations, be sent to that region. The first of those divisions will be ready to entrain by October 16 at noon, the second on October 17. One of those divisions could be sent without artillery.

Please let me know by telegram on October 15 before noon the numbers of these divisions, which, it seems, ought to be chosen among the 26th, 89th, 90th or 78th divisions.

It is always understood that this reduction of the American forces will to no extent change the mission assigned to the American Army especially between the Meuse and the Aisne.

Foch.

Field Order No. 13.
1. The following organizations will be relieved tonight:
     Companies N. F. I. K. L. M., 148th Infantry and Machine Gun unit attached to 3rd Battalion 148th Infantry in the Bois de Beney and St. Benoit.
     2. Embussing point will be on Pannes-Nonsard Road. Head of column will be at Pannes, on the Pannes-Beney Road.

3. Commanders 2nd and 3rd Battalions will make arrangements for representative of the relieved organizations to be at Essey as soon as possible tonight to meet representatives from the incoming organizations.

4. Battalion Commanders, 2nd and 3rd Battalions will also provide for representatives at their respective embussing points.

5. All organizations will proceed by bus to Foug. Other instructions will follow.

By order of Lt. Colonel Van Corder

From 3rd Battalion War Diary for October 15, 1918

Movement made from reserve position to Pannes by marching, from Pannes to Cholloy by trucks. Companies received replacements prior to embussing.

5 days rations and 5 days forage in supply train. Weather: cloudy. Roads: muddy. Health: fair.

William L Marlin
Major, 148th Infantry
Commanding, 3rd Battalion

Found in *The 37ᵗʰ Division in the World War*

The entire tour of duty in the sector was a dismal, trying experience; there were no tears when, on 15th October, the "warning order" to prepare for relief and movement to another area came:

"This division will move to a new area. Relief will take place tonight and tomorrow night. Details will follow as soon as secured." (vol. 2, 356)

Translation from the French, found in
The United States Army in the World War

General Staff
No. 4784   HEADQUARTERS, ALLIED ARMIES,
                                                    October 15, 1918.
                                          Received 12:20 p.m.

Headquarters Bacon

To Headquarters at Souilly

For General Pershing. Pursuant to the recommendations which you transmitted to me, the American 91st and
37th Divisions will be moved to Belgium. The 91st Division
will start entraining October 16 in the Revigny region; the
37th Division will start October 16 in the Toul region.
French General Headquarters in agreement with your
headquarters will regulate the conditions of entraining.

                                                    Foch.

Found in *The 37th Division in the World War*

Orders were received, while it was in the salient where
American troops had first operated as an independent command to move to "another sector". The destination was known
to only a few; five or six days rations were issued and there was
more than the usual amount of speculation—many thought
the organization was to be sent to Italy. On 15th October,
however, Colonel Ralph D. Cole, in conversation with the division commander, Major General Charles S. Farnsworth, was
informed that the organization was ordered to Belgium. The
sector to be taken over, as indicated on the map, showed that
the division was soon to find itself moving in the direction of
the battlefield of Waterloo. Colonel Cole remarket that, for
the division to end its operations on such historic ground
would present a striking climax to the part it had played in

the great drama that was drawing to a close. He pointed out that although other divisions had had longer combat service in Europe, few if any had had wide, more varied experiences in the many phases of modern warfare than the Thirty-seventh.... (Vol. I, 5)

Found in *The United States Army in the World War*

FIRST ARMY, A. E. F.
October 15, 1918

MEMORANDUM for Troop Movement Section, G-3.

1. The 91st Division with the 53rd Field Artillery Brigade will be entrained on October 16. Please make arrangement for this movement and notify division.

2. The 37th Division (less artillery), now on the front of the American Second Army will be entrained on October 17 or 18....

G. C. MARSHALL, Jr.
Colonel, General Staff
Asst. G-3

From 3rd Battalion War Diary for October 16, 1918

Battalion debussed at Foug at 7:00 and awaited assignment of billeting area. At 10:00 o'clock... to Cholloy and went into billets.
5 days rations and 5 days forages in supply train. Weather: cold-cloudy. Roads: hard. Health: fair.

William L Marlin
Major, 148th Infantry
Commanding, 3rd Battalion

Found in *The United States Army in the World War*

G-3 ORDERS

No. 9 SECOND ARMY, A. E. F.,

October 16, 1918.

  1. 37th Division is relieved from duty with the IV Corps and will proceed to another area by rail beginning on the 18th instant....

     By command of Major General Bullard:

       Stuart Heintzelman,
       Chief of Staff.

FIELD ORDERS   37th DIVISION, A. E. F.
No. 32

MAPS: Northern France
October 17, 1918---19 h.

  1. Pursuant to G-3 Orders, No. 9, American Second Army, this division, less motorized units, will entrain on October 18, 19, and 20....

  11. Division headquarters will close at Pagney-sur-Meuse at 8 a.m., Oct. 19 and will open at a point to be announced later.

     C. S. FARNSWORTH
      Major General, U. S. A.,
       Commanding

3d Section, General Staff

No. 282/3   GROUP OF ARMIES OF FLANDERS,
October 18, 1918.

GENERAL ORDER NO. 3954

I.   At midnight, October 19, the French Army of Flanders is placed under the orders of General de Boissoudy, who will have at his disposal the staff and the services of the French Sixth Army, less the elements designated in Special Orders No. 3955.

II.   The Commanding General of the French Army of Flanders will have at his disposal all troops now within the zone, said zone determined by Instructions No. 3948 of October 16, 1918, limits are: North: Lichtervelde---Wynghene---Lootenhulle---Nevelle (all to the French army). South: Zonnebeke (to the French army)-Oyghem (to the British army).

III.   The French II Cavalry Corps and the French 11th and 12th Infantry Divisions remain under the direct orders of His Majesty the King of the Belgians.

The American 37th and 91st Divisions, upon detraining, will also be under the orders of His Majesty the King of the Belgians.

IV.   C. P. of the General commanding the French Army of Flanders: Hoondschoote, then Roulers as soon as possible.

In the name of the King:

Degoutte,
General.

From 3rd Battalion War Diary for October 18, 1918

Reorganizing companies and replacements received on night of 15th October, 1918.

P.C. at Cholloy.

5 days rations and 5 days forage in supply train. Weather: fair. Roads: hard. Health: good.

William L Marlin
Major, 148th Infantry
Commanding, 3rd Battalion

Oct. 18, 1918

Dear Mother,

I am sending you a card which by following directions will enable you to send me a Christmas box.

There are certain things I need much I cannot buy and which are easily broken.

Therefore please send me

1 Conklin Fountain Pen

    good, about $3.50

1 Cheap fountain pen about 2.00

    Self filling

2 Ingersol wrist watches -

    Illuminated Dial

1 "Baby Ben" alarm clock.

We are only allowed to receive one package so I am writing Judith to send to you and you can send it to me. I know of nothing I need except those articles

I mentioned. I do not know what Judith will send as it could hardly be anything bulky. She can knit a pair of sox perhaps. I really don't particularly need them as I have several good pairs.

I have been on three fronts now. I am well and am still in command of the company. I shall be glad when the captain gets back as it is a lot of work.

I am sorry Grandma did not get to Camp Lee while I was there.

None of the Ohio boys liked Camp Lee. We did not like Virginia people. I expect I will live in Alabama after the war.

If possible I would like to send you something for Christmas, but if I do not get to a city I cannot.

At least I send you my love and wish you a most joyous Christmas & happy new year.

Alfred

O.K, A M Barlow 1st Lt US Inf

From 148th Infantry Regiment War Diary for October 19, 1918

Division moving to a new area north of Ypres by rail; equipment entrained by battalions, usual intervals between trains.

From 3rd Battalion War Diary for October 19, 1918

Battalion moved from Cholloy to Toul where they entrained. Left entraining point 18:15 o'clock.

5 days rations and 5 days forage in supply train. Weather: fair. Roads: good. Health: good.

William L Marlin
Major, 148th Infantry
Commanding, 3rd Battalion

Distinguished Service Cross Citation
James G. Haverfield
Sergeant, Company G, 145th Infantry

For extraordinary heroism in action near Olsene, Belgium, October 21, 1918. He advanced alone under heavy machine-gun fire and killed two of the enemy who were delivering effective machine-gun fire on the attacking wave of his companyand delaying its progress.

From 3rd Battalion War Diary for October 21, 1918

```
    Battalion arrived Valmertinge 14:30 o'clock
detraining at this point.
    5 days rations and 5 days forage in supply
train.  Weather: cold and wet.  Roads: soft.
Health: fair.

                          William L Marlin
                      Major, 148th Infantry
                   Commanding, 3rd Battalion
```

From 3rd Battalion War Diary for October 22, 1918

```
    Routine duties, cleaning equipment and
organizing.
    5 days rations and 5 days forage in supply
train.  Weather: cold and wet.  Roads: soft.
Health: fair.
```

From 148th Infantry Regiment War Diary for October 23, 1918

```
    Entire regiment billeted in Gits area;
cleaning equipment, resting, animals... checking
up property shortage.
    Colonel George W. Stuart Inf U.S.A. reported
```

for duty and assumed command of regiment at 11:00
AM.

October 25th 1918

Dear Friend,

Many thanks for your very nice letter of the 13th which I have received yesterday morning. I was glad to hear that you are in good health, but your friends are not well. Chas, the American officer who plays the piano so well, is very sick. Poor fellow! I am pitied of his unfortunate. I cannot believe the doctor is dead! He was so respectable! So devoted! Tell me, if you can, how he was killed. I thought so often to him! I shall keep his souvenir during my life! I shall always remember of him. I know you are in a pretty active sector and now you are very busy. Since you left our Lorraine sector, you did fine work, but how many men are dead! Poor soldiers! Poor officers!

When do you think go to Paris in "permission"? You will all make a great pleasure, where you will come back at home! You can be with us as in the old days! You will always remain our good friend!

Soon, we shall be in winter, and already it is very cold. You need, of course, your overcoat. Yesterday, I have been in station for send it to you. My mother and my sister give you their kind regards. I wish you a good luck. Good bye, dear friend, and I am awaiting a long letter from you.

> *I am always*
>> *yours very sincerely*
>>> *Adelina Jacques*

Please excuse me for my English mistakes. I cannot write very well. Since you are away, I shall have no more the opportunity to talk that language. Soon write me again, and don't forget us! My better thanks.

From 3rd Battalion War Diary for October 26, 1918

Prescribed drill schedule carried out and work done burying dead in assigned area.

19 officers and 562 men available for
all duty. Weather: fair-warmer. Roads: Fair
conditions. Health: good.

William L Marlin
Major, 148th Infantry
Commanding, 3rd Battalion

Translation from the French, found in
The United States Army in the World War

3d Section, General Staff

GROUP OF ARMIES OF FLANDERS,

No. 74/3   October 26, 1918.

INSTRUCTIONS No. 9

I. The resistance offered by the Germans on the front
of the French Group of Armies of Flanders, the reinforcement
of the enemy who has put new divisions in line, and the present political situation in Germany permit consideration of a
combined operation assigned to throw the forces opposite us
behind the Escault and enables us to seize a footing beyond
that river.

The offensive preparations on the front for this operation must be completed by October 29. The date of the attack
will be designated later.

II. The Belgian army will cross the secondary canal
north of the Ghent-Brussels Canal, to establish bridgeheads
and subsequently, be ready to exploit any weakening which
might develop on the hostile front.

It will make its main effort south of the Ghent-Brussels
Canal in liaison with the left of the French army, its mission

being to drive the enemy beyond the Lys and to establish itself beyond that river, south of Ghent.

The French army will clean up the region between the secondary canal and the Lys, with its left, and will debouch beyond that river.

It will make its main effort with its right, in close liaison with the British army, while its center advances in the direction of the Escault.

Concentrating the major portion of its means on its left wing, the British army will decisively break enemy resistance between the Lys and the Escault by outflanking, with the French right, the enemy forces along the Lys.

With its center and right, it will seek to cross the Escault and establish bridgeheads on the right bank of the river.

III. From these directives, it develops that, the main effort of the Group of Armies of Flanders being directed between Deynze and the Escault, it will become necessary to concentrate the greatest possible amount of artillery in that region.

Consequently, the Belgian army will have to provide a certain number of heavy batteries from its own means, for the purpose of the artillery action on the French front.

Likewise, the British Second Army will, in so far as is compatible with its own mission, support the attack by the right of the French army.

The commanders of the Belgian, French and British armies will reach an agreement on this point.

IV. For the proposed operation, the French army will have at its disposal: the two American divisions, now in the reserve of the King (the American 37th and 91st Divisions), and all of the French infantry divisions. [Two] are to be designated by the army commander and will be placed in reserve, at the disposal of the King, presumably, in the region east of Roulers.

The French II Cavalry Corps, whose employment cannot be foreseen at this time, will also be placed in the reserve of the King in the region west of Roulers, actually occupied by the American divisions. All of its artillery is left at the disposal of the commander of the French army.

V. The attack units will not be moved into position until the last moment. Movements will be carried out by night.

VI. In so far as the French army is concerned, it should improve its base of departure, between now and the moment for the attack by minor operations designed to advance its front to Deynze-Courtrai Railroad and to the Waereghem-Anseghem Road.

In the Name of the King,

Degoutte,
General.

Sunday October 26, 1918

Dear Mamma,

We have been traveling around so much lately that I have received no mail from you for a long time.

In my last letter I sent a card which will enable you to send a Christmas box. If there is room please put in a flash light and as many extra batteries as possible.

As I did not get to write to Judy yet, I do not suppose she will send anything.

I am on my fourth front now. I am kept rather busy as I am still in command of the company. I have only one lieutenant to help me while a captain usually has five lieutenants.

I find Flemish much more difficult to understand than French. I was becoming quite proficient in French. I passed thru some of the devastated portions of Belgium. It is no exaggeration to say that if a crow wished to pass over this region he would have to carry rations with him. We could tell only where villages had been by observing a few bricks among the piles of mud around the shell craters. We walked an hour thru a once rich and populous city of which you have read much that had not a sing habitable room left in one of the houses.

It is very damp here, thou it has not rained for two days and only sprinkled for a little while.

Belgium is certainly the richest country I ever saw. The soil is a dark loam, like woods dirt down as deep as the deepest shell crater I've seen.

I hope you are still well and that you will be able to send the things. Do you still get your money? What of Ruben Gerd?

Write often. With love,

Alfred

OK A M Barlow 1st Lt US Inf

Translation from the French, found in
The United States Army in the World War

3d Section, General Staff

GROUP OF ARMIES OF FLANDERS,
No 84/3   October 27, 1918.

SPECIAL ORDERS No. 10

The American 37th and 91st Divisions are placed at the disposal of the General commanding the French Army of Belgium, effective at midnight October 27/28.

Translation from the French, found in
The United States Army in the World War

3d Section, General Staff

GROUP OF ARMIES OF FLANDERS,

No. 65/3   October 27, 1918.

General Degoutte

To Marshal Foch, Commander-in-Chief of the Allied Forces

The American 37th and 91st Divisions have joined the French Group of Armies of Flanders lacking equipment; in particular, the 37th Division did not have its artillery. This artillery, the 62nd Field Artillery Brigade, was recently resting at Toul, according to information furnished by the division commander.

It is requested that, in view of forthcoming events, these divisions be completed as soon as possible: (1) The American 37th division, by sending its artillery, ammunition trucks, and the 100 ordinary trucks it lacks. (2) the American 91st Division by sending its motor ambulances, 80 ordinary trucks, and 120 ammunition trucks which it likewise lacks.

```
FIELD ORDERS                    37th Division, A. E. F.,
No. 34                          October 27, 1918---17 h.

MAPS:          ROULERS  ) Scale 1/40,000
          THIELT        )
```

1. Pursuant to Special Orders No. 8 Op. French Army of Belgium, October 26, 1918, this division will proceed by marching to a new area.

2. The 73rd Brigade will be billeted in the Thielt Zone, the 74th Brigade in the Pitthem Zone.

. . .

10. Division headquarters at Lichtervelde will close at 14 h., October 28, 1918, and open at Meulebeke at same date and hour.

By command of Major General Farnsworth:

Dana T. Merrill,
Colonel, General Staff
Chief of Staff.

From 148th Infantry Regiment War Diary for October 27, 1918

Orders received at 10 AM to be prepared to move to a new area by marching at a moments notice.

Headquarters
148th Infantry
AMERICAN E. F.

27 October 1918.

Field Order
No. 14

Par.1. This regiment proceeds to a new area 28 Oct. 1918.

Par.2. Route: Gits - Gitsberg - Winnendaale - Beveren - Ardeve - Rysseleinds - Pitthem.

Par.3.   (a) Order of March of troops:
            Headquarters Company
            Machine Gun Company (less wheel transportation except kitchen)
            1st Battalion
            3rd Battalion
            2nd Battalion

Each company will be followed by its own rolling
kitchen.
      (b) A distance of 200 meters will be
maintained between companies and battalions.
      (c) A strict observance of the rules of
march discipline is enjoined.
      (d) If any aeroplane is observed
all movement on road will cease and troops take
shelter from view if available. Otherwise remain
immovable until plane has passed.
      (e) Distance of march is about Nine
miles - suitable rate of march and rests will be
maintained to obviate struggling or necessity for
men to fall out.

    Par.4. Initial Point: South-east exit e.g.
Gits, head of column passes initial point at 8:30
A.M. 28 Oct. 1918.

    Par.5. The Regimental Trains (less Company
kitchens) will be assembled at Gits and reported
to the Regimental Supply Officer at 9:30 A.,. ready
to march via northeast exit of Gits to Roulers -
Theureut Road - Lichtervelde - Oelscamp - Pitthem.

    Par.6. Immediately upon arrival in new area
location of units will be reported to Regimental
Hq. at Litthem.

    Par.7. Regimental Headquarters closes at Gits
at 8:30 A.M. 28 Oct. 1918.

        By order of Colonel Stuart:

                R.F. Ohmer,
            Capt. 148th Inf.,
             Adjutant.

Translation from the French, found in
The United States Army in the World War

FRENCH ARMY OF BELGIUM

No. 96/3   October 28, 1918.

Special Orders No. 10 Op.

Pursuant to Instructions No. 2 Op. dated October 28 (sent only to generals commanding army corps):
...
II. The American 37th Division is placed at the disposal of the French XXXIV Army Corps (Headquarters at Ondank), effective October 29....

Found in *The 37th Division in the World War*

At 8:00 A. M. on 29th October, Field Order No. 35 was issued from Division Headquarters, directing that the unit relieve the 132nd (French) Division on the nights of 29th and 30th, 31st October, pursuant to Special Orders No. 29, from the 30th (French) Army Corps....

The left or northern boundary of the division sector passed just to the north of Pitthem, then through Thielt and curved gently south passing Petegem about one kilometer to the south. The sector had a front of about seven kilometers, extending northeast and southwest; Denterghem was in the center and about five kilometers to the rear of the line of departure; and Olsene was about one and one-half kilometers from the right boundary and slightly less than one kilometer behind the line of departure. The order of battle from right to left was:

Seventh Corps, 91st (American) Division, 128th (French) Division; Thirtieth Corps, 37 Division, 12 (French) Division; and the 34th (French) Corps. For the coming attack, the 73rd Brigade was on the right, and the 74th on the left, each with two battalions in the first line, echeloned in depth. Thus, on the extreme left of the sector was the 2nd Bn. 148th Inf., on the right the 3rd Battalion of that regiment. Following these units was the 1st Bn. 148th Inf., with one platoon of engineers as regimental reserve....

The mission of the corps was to cross the Escault. The chief task of the 37th Division, in the early stages of the battle, was to surround Cruyshautem from the north and south "by using the regiment on the north (the 148th Infantry) in order that the regiment on the south (the 145th Inf.) may reach the heights of Lindenhock as soon as possible. (vol. 2, 369-372)

Translation from the French, from
The United States Army in the World War

FRENCH 132nd ARTILLERY DIVISION.

No. 3,098/3   October 29, 1918---3 p.m.

I. Attached:

...

The American 37th Division will have: on the right, the French 128th Infantry Division; on the left, the French 12th Infantry Division.

II. Disposition of Attack:

The division will be disposed by brigades abreast, the 73rd Brigade to the right, the 74th Brigade to the left.

Each brigade will attack with one regiment having two battalions in first line.

The limit between the two brigades will be fixed later.

From now on the 73rd Brigade will have a front of attack narrower than the front of the 74th Brigade in view of realizing the echeloning in depth adequate to the projected maneuver....

From 3rd Battalion War Diary for October 29, 1918

Company L from Pitthem at 14:30 to Olsene at 23:45. 18 kilometers.

Battalion moved from Pitthem to Olsene and relieved French units.

2 days rations with troops. 5 days rations and 5 days forage in supply train. Weather: fair part of day. Roads: good. Health: good.

William L Marlin
Major, 148th Infantry
Commanding, 3rd Battalion

Translation from the French, found in
The United States Army in the World War

3d Section, G.S.   FRENCH XXX CORPS

No. 169/3   October 29, 1918

OPERATION ORDER No. 33

1. The American 37th Division will relieve the French 132nd Division in the night of October 30/31, 1918.

The details of this relief will be regulated by the commanding general of the French 132nd Division after agreement with the commanding general of the American 37th Division.

H Penet,
The General,
Commanding the XXX C.A.

From 37th Division War Diary for October 29, 1918

702 Officers/18758 Men
Relief of units of 132nd Division (French)
completed. Field Order No. 36... covering Plan
of Attack by 37th Division under 30th Army Corps
(French) Objective - To drive the enemy back of
the Escault River.

From 148th Infantry Regiment War Diary for October 30, 1918

2 & 3 Battalions Support positions in
reserve.
Division orders covering operations for "D" day
received at PC at OLSENE at 9.15 PM via courier
from 74 Brigade. Notice of "zero" hour and "D"
day received 10.25 PM by officers from Division
Headquarters.
Losses during the day in 2nd & 3rd Battalions from
"surprise fire" (shrapnel) from the enemy.

U.S. ARMY FIELD MESSAGE

From: C.O. 3d Bn - 148th Inf.
At: PC Marlin at OLSENE
Date: 30 Oct 18 Hour: 22hr50 No.   How sent: Runner
To: C.O. 148th Inf.
Have you any information as to the disposition of Capt. Stewart.

The above seems to indicate that Lieutenant Barlow was still in command
of Company L. Family lore has it that he was in charge of the company when he was
wounded just days later, but no proof of that has been found.

From 3rd Battalion War Diary for October 30, 1918

Moved Battalion P.C. from Olsene to 200.80-
469.05. Companies formed up for attack.

Companies K and M for up as first line. Companies
on line of departure thereby relieving French
units. Companies I and L form as second line
companies along railroad east of Olsene.

   2 days rations with troops. Weather: cloudy.
Roads: good. Health: good.

   T. H. Hume
   1st Lieutenant, 148th Infantry
   Battalion Adjutant

Found in *The 37th Division in the World War*

At 5:30 A.M., 31st October, the attack started according
to schedule and progressed steadily. Little resistance was offered by enemy fire, excepting occasional machine gun nests
which were promptly knocked down by accompanying artillery, and at the close of the day the Division was on the crest
of Cruyshautem, almost to the second objective; casualties
reported were "very light." The enemy artillery tried coun-
ter-battery work, using large quantities of phosgene which
the wind wafted back to Division Headquarters, but, General
Farnsworth reported "the advance was steady right from
the start and all enemy resistance was methodically broken
down." ...

Enemy artillery continued active, shelling the roads leading forward but casualties continued light and the advance
moved steadily; the German infantry had apparently fallen
back to the ridge southwest of Cruyshautem, although machine guns offered considerable resistance. Shells from heavy
enemy field pieces continually broke telephone wires strung
by signal troops, and Division Headquarters experienced considerable difficulty in maintaining communication with the
advancing units. The roads, however, were generally hard
surface highways, and were in good condition; the use of
motor ambulances insured prompt attention to and evacua-

tion of the wounded—an experience differing from that in the
Meuse-Argonne offensive. (vol. 2, 374-375)

The 1st Bn. 148th Inf. reported:

"Started on drive in support of 2nd and 3rd Bns. On the
line. Co. D had platoon on left of 2nd Bn. to connect with the
French. Co. A acted as moppers-up. Company's B and D
caught in Boche barrage, Lt. H. Hess instantly killed. At 5:30
started over the top. Confusion on account of darkness. 8:00
A. M. relayed message that left flank of 2nd Bn. exposed to machine gun fire. French not keeping up. 12:00, have relayed
several messages about French not keeping up. 2:30, French
now advancing. 2:45, relayed message to Co. 2nd Bn. to push
forward. 3:15, relayed (same message). 6:00 P. M., received
word that 2nd Bn. had reached top of hill—objective.

The war diarist of the 2nd Bn. 148th Inf., reported that his
unit "attacked southeast of Olsene, Co. E and F in front line,
G and H in second line. The French on our left did not advance and at 10:00 A. M., Co. H was sent into the line to cover
the left flank. Battalion advanced under very strong opposition to hill 1,000 meters east of Huttengen. Approximately
100 prisoners taken. Two officers wounded, 36 men killed, 70
(men) wounded, 40 missing." The 3rd Bn. 148th Inf. "formed
for attack, Co. K and M in first line, I and L in second along
railroad." ...

At 8:36, the 148th Infantry reported that "attack began
per schedule. Battalions advancing satisfactorily. Numerous
prisoners of the 6th Guard and 6th Landwehr regiment. Front
line almost to its 1st objective. Losses apparently slight.
Enemy line not heavily held except for machine gun nests."
(vol. 2, 376-378)

At 3:22 Gen. Jackson reported that "our right flank is
advancing satisfactorily. Our left flank has been held up by
machine gun fire from our left front. Have no definite information as to the location of advancing lines of French troops
on our left. After verifying position of Marlin's troops, reported

to have reached crest of hills in his immediate front, will authorize artillery to put heavy barrage on crest north of Marlin's troops...."   (vol. 2, 381)

Distinguished Service Cross Citation
Robert L. Tavener
Captain, 148th Infantry

For extraordinary heroism in action near Cierges, France, September 29, 1918, and near Olsene, Belgium, October 31, 1918. Without regard for his own safety Capt. Tavener personally conducted a tank in an attack on a machine-gun nest. After several of the tanks had been put out of action and the others had withdrawn, he walked up and down the firing line under heavy machine-gun fire, cheering his men, who despite severe losses, fought till all of their ammunition was exhausted. On October 31 he was severely wounded while making a personal reconnaissance of the enemy's position.

Distinguished Service Cross Citation
John A. Doll
Private, First Class, Company E. 145th Infantry

For extraordinary heroism in action near Olsene, Belgium, October 31, 1918. While leading a squad forward, Pvt. Doll suddenly found himself in the midst of an enemy barrage, but he exposed himself to the severe fire in trying to keep his men organized and continued with the advance. He was killed while thus engaged.

Gallantry in Action Citation
George Daniel Kingrey
First Lieutenant, 148th Infantry

For gallantry in action at Olsene, Belgium, October 31, 1918, while directing his company after having been wounded.

Distinguished Service Medal Citation
William R. Hughes
Major, Chaplain Officers' Reserve Corps, Captain, Chaplain, 148th Infantry

For gallantry in action near Ivoiry, France, September 27-28, 1918. With complete disregard for his own safety he voluntarily and repeatedly made his way under intense enemy fire to the position held by the advance elements of his regiment carrying medical supplies thereto and assisted in carrying wounded men to the dressing stations. His devotion to his comrades had a marked effect upon the morale of his regiment. For gallantry in action near Olsene, Belgium, October 30-31, 1918. On October 30 he volunteered to direct troops to their positions in the line, and in accomplishing this mission remained throughout the night exposed to concentrated and continuous enemy artillery fire. On October 31 he again exposed himself to intense enemy machine-gun and artillery fire while assisting wounded men of his regiment to the dressing stations. Later, he directed under heavy enemy fire the burial of more than 60 men of his regiment whose bodies were lying in exposed positions.

Chapter Ten

From 37th Division War Diary for October 31st, 1918

Troops of the 37th Division began offensive,
at 5 hours 30 (H hour) under supervision of
30th A.C. in accordance with Field Order #36,
these Headquarters, 30th October. Very little
resistance offered by enemy forces, except
for machine gun nests, which were overcome by
artillery fire. At close of day, troops of this
Division occupied rest of Cruyshautem Heights;
almost to 2nd Objective.
Casualties reported very light.
Considerable gas shells dropped by enemy.

From 148th Infantry Regiment War Diary for October 31st, 1918

 D Day Today - Zero hour 5.30 AM. Regiment
advanced with 2nd & 3rd Battalions in first lines,
1st Battalion in support, all organized 500 meters
in depth. 1st Objective reached at 6.30....
Losses not definitely known, reported from
slight to heavy by different organizations. 3rd
Battalion on right reached crest of hill command
by Cruyshautem... at 3.30 PM and dug in awaiting
advance of 2nd Battalion and 145 Infantry on its
right.

U.S. ARMY FIELD MESSAGE

From: Commanding General 74th Brigade
At: OLSENE - Chateau
Date: 31 October/18 Hour: 14.45 No. 20 How sent: Runner
To: Commanding Officer 148th Infantry

Division orders a prepared attack on heights at Cruyshautem at 3:
00 PM. An artillery barrage will be laid down extending from the
crossroads north of Cruyshautem to He Bunter and territory
immediately to the west of this line & use this as a cover for your
advance.

Jackson

U.S. ARMY FIELD MESSAGE

From: Commanding Officer 3rd Battalion - 148th Infantry
At: N of Tulle S. E.
Date: 31-Oct-18 Hour: 6:45 No.   How sent: Runner
To: Commanding Officer 148th Infantry

1st Objective gained 6:30 a m. Am re-organizing and correcting with
flanking units. Very few casualties. Have no signal section. 37 mm are
Stokes. Will advance at 8:30.

Marlin

U.S. ARMY FIELD MESSAGE

From: Commanding Officer 3rd Battalion - 148th Infantry
At: PC Marlin
Date: 31-Oct-18 Hour: 12hr55 No.   How sent: Runner
To: Commanding Officer 148th Infantry

Relief of French companies has been completed (at 12hr.40). So far
no special arms have reported.

U.S. ARMY FIELD MESSAGE

From Stuart, CO 148
To Battalion Commanders

Intelligence Reports indicate that almost all cross roads, bridges and RR crossings from here to Escault River have been mined....
If you will, take all necessary precautions to avoid possible loss at such points.

U.S. ARMY FIELD MESSAGE

8:30
Am advancing again....

Marlin

U.S. ARMY FIELD MESSAGE

3 hr 45
Where are the Stokes - one pounder and Signal Sections Headquarters Company assigned to this Battalion?

Marlin

U.S. ARMY FIELD MESSAGE

12 hr 55
Need V.B. and hand grenades. Am trying to secure same from my Battalion supply officer.

Marlin

U.S. ARMY FIELD MESSAGE

from Commanding General 74th
to Commanding Officer 148th
4:45

Lieutenant McSweeny of the Divisional Staff reports that he has
command of Company G - 148 nearly all day as he found company
without an officer. Request an officer be sent to this company as
Lieutenant McSweeny has left to report back to the Commanding
General.

Jackson

U.S. ARMY FIELD MESSAGE

3:00
2 mopping-up platoons B Company and A Company just in rear of
my position. As I have my entire battalion on a circular line to protect
flanks - I have ordered A & B to dig in as a support.

Marlin

U.S. ARMY FIELD MESSAGE

3:00
Am digging in and will hold.... Don't overlook our shortage of
ammunition. Many wounded who should be evacuated - cannot have
men from line for this task. 145th holding on right. - have sent word to
Hance to swing his left forward if possible and Sergeant who brings
this is looking for stragglers who can carry ammunition.

Marlin

SECRET

Headquarters 74th Inf. Brig.
American E. F.,
31 October 1918

23 Hrs. 50 Min.
MAPS: THIELT - 1/40,000
1/20,000

FIELD ORDERS NO. 22

    1.   The Division occupies the crest of the Cruyshautem heights. The 128th Division, on the right, has its left at approximately 23 -25, and the 12th Division on the left has its right at approximately 45.73 - 40.72.

    2.   The Division resumes the attack.

    3.   (a)   The attack will start at 6 hours, 30 minutes (H hour), tomorrow, 1st November 1918. This Brigade will attack on the left of the Division Sector and the 73rd Brigade will attack on the right. The objectives and limits of the Brigades are shown on the map furnished by Division Headquarters. The attack will be made at H hour after an artillery preparation of 5 minutes, commencing at 6:25, and will be preceded for a distance of 600 meters by a rolling barrage which will move at the rate of 100 meters in 5 minutes. There will be a pause on the 2nd objective until H plus 5 hours (11:30), at which time the attack will move forward to the final objective.

    (b)   The attack will be made in the zone of this Brigade by the same units and using the same formation as used in the attack of this morning.

(c)   The plan of artillery support will be made by the commanding officer of the artillery attached to the Division and the artillery attached to the several battalions and regiments will support their advance.

(d)   Liaison will be established as prescribed in Field Order No. 36, Headquarters 37th Division, 30 October 1918; liaison combat groups as prescribed in Field Order No 21, these Headquarters, 30 October 1918.

(e)   One-half (1/2) of Co. E, 112th Engineers, will report to the Commanding Officer, 148th Infantry, to be used for repairing bridges and roads.

4.   Combat trains, rolling kitchens and water cars will follow their units as closely as possible.   Field Trains under command of Commander of Trains.

5.   (a)   No change in axial road or traffic rules and supply route.
(b)   Rail head - THIELT.

(c)   Distribution point, Quarter Master supplies, vicinity of Man on the first cross-road east of the river bridge, 1/2 kilometer northeast of axial road.

(d) Ammunition.   Ammunition for the units of this Brigade may be obtained from the present Post Command of the Brigade at Olsene and also at point prescribed as distributing point of Quarter Master supplies.

Found in *The 37ᵗʰ Division in the World War*

The advance started at the hour fixed, and at 7:20, the 3ʳᵈ Bn. 148ᵗʰ Inf. had passed through Cruyshautem, from which, apparently, the enemy had withdrawn. At 7:40, the second (now the first objective) was reached and Wanneghem-Lede was occupied.   Civilians, joyously waving handkerchiefs, confused aeroplane observers and it was impossible for the infantry to mark its front line positions for them. Division Headquarters cancelled the order for a halt at the second position, and at 10:40 the attack "was ordered pushed forward with all possible speed to the final objective." Because of the rapid advance, liaison between headquarters and the front line units was difficult.   Refugees returning from the front, however, said that by 11:00 A. M., units of the division were within one kilometer of the Escault River.   Reports at 6:00 P. M. established our lines on the west bank of the Escault River and in compliance with orders received from the Commanding General, of the 30ᵗʰ Corps, all units were ordered to prepare for crossing the Escault during the night, the artillery had moved forward to bring its 75's in position, 3,000 meters west of the Escault, and its heavy guns, 6 kilometers west of the river. An officer and five enlisted men were captured during the second day of the drive. By early afternoon, the 2ⁿᵈ Bn. 148ᵗʰ Inf. had reached the west bank of the Escault and established its line from Heuvel southeast to Heurne. The 3ʳᵈ Bn. 148ᵗʰ Inf. arrived on the right of this unit fifteen minutes later (1:45 P. M.) and the 2ⁿᵈ Bn., 145ᵗʰ Inf. advanced steadily, uninterruptedly, until held up at Eyne by enemy artillery and machine gun fire. They consolidated for the night in that village, and along the road to Ghent. The 3ʳᵈ Bn. 145ᵗʰ Inf. consolidated for the night along a road about 100 meters west of the railroad, its left resting in Heurne with outposts on the railroad. (vol. 2, 382)

From 37th Division War Diary for November 1st, 1918

Headquarters at Denterghem, Belgium
650 Officers/18734 Men
Resumption of advance by this Division at 6 hours
30 with 128th Division (French) on right and 12th
Division (French) on the left. Advanced elements
reached 2nd objective by 8 hours and paused there
for reorganization of troops, after which advance
was continued. Resistance light, except for
enemy machine gun nests. Village of Cruyshautem
occupied by our troops during the morning.
Enemy airplanes very active during afternoon. One
German plane was brought down near Denterghem,
Belgium.
Crossing of Escault River (final objective),
conditions warranting, by elements of this
Division, ordered in Operations Message #13...

1 November 1918.
Time received 10:35 hours.

MESSAGE:

From: Post Command Stuart, 9:30 o'clock
      (thru Headquarters 74th Brigade).

      3rd Battalion passed through Cruyshautem at 7:20 o'clock.
2nd Battalion on left slightly behind. 2nd Objective taken at 7:40
o'clock. 3rd Battalion at 7:50 o'clock occupied Wannegem Lede
with outpost line. No casualties, little resistance, no prisoners. 3rd
Battalion, will advance at H plus 5 hours.

                                              Stuart

U.S. ARMY FIELD MESSAGE

From Commanding General 37 Division
Date: 1 Nov 18   Hour: 10:30 AM   How sent: Phone
To; Commanding General 74 Brigade

The Corps Commander directs that provided there is very little resistance being offered, our advance be stopped at second objective only such length of time as to enable you to reorganize units & formations. You will therefore move forward to final objective as soon as you can move your Brigade in unison. Consult your accompanying artillery to insure no artillery fire by them into our own troops.

                                        Farnsworth

Division Headquarters

11:33 - For Major Waite,

Aeroplane reports no Germans seen west of Escault and inhabitants everywhere wave handkerchiefs. A few enemy seen east of the Escault. If your observation shows enemy to be in confusion east of the Escault River you will cross the Escault with platoons & entrench there on east bank to secure bridge head. Assure their protection and additional strength of bridge head by machine guns, 37mm, Stokes, properly placed, at the halt this evening, final objective, depth of command will be insisted upon. 112 Engineers are now moving forward with light bridges for crossing the Escault.

                                    signed Farnsworth

C.O. 148
    Comply
         Jackson

Distinguished Service Cross Citation
George Reed
Cook, Company G, 145th Infantry

For extraordinary heroism in action at Eyne, Belgium, November 1, 1918. After the remainder of his company had withdrawn, he crossed the Scheldt River alone, under terrific machine-gun and artillery fire, and rescued a wounded comrade.

Distinguished Service Cross Citation
Rudolph S. Ursprung
First Lieutenant, 145th Infantry

For extraordinary heroism in action near Eyne, Belgium, November 1, 1918. Seeing a wounded soldier lying 150 yards in front of the line, after his company had withdrawn to a more secure position, Lieut. Ursprung crawled through heavy fire and administered first aid to him. He then picked up the wounded man, carried him across the open, wading a canal through water waist deep, and succeeded in taking him to a place of safety.

1 November 1918.
Hour 12:25
From: Major Light, 74th Brigade.
To: G-3

Stewart intends to move forward to new Post Command along axis of liaison probably to vicinity of Wanneghem-Lede, time and place dependent upon progress of troops. Have directed troops to dig in and consolidate upon making final objective. Request dumps be advanced at least as far as vicinity of Cruyshautem as soon as possible. Ammunition and pyrotechnics left at Olsene. Troops moving faster than it can be brought forward. Post Command 74th Brigade 202.9 - 465.9. Request dumps and ammunition be moved forward before dark.

U.S. ARMY FIELD MESSAGE

From: Commanding General 74th Infantry Brigade
At CRUYSHAUTEM
Date 1 Nov/18   Hour: 14:40 No. 37   How sent: Runner
To: Commanding Officer, 148th Infantry

The officer in charge of aviation just now interviewed at 2:40 (PM) gives me the impression that you will find some resistance on the east bank of the Escault. I send this to you merely for your information and suggest that it might be wise to get it to the Battalion Commanders for their information.

Jackson

Send us your dispositions whenever you can.

From 148th Infantry Regiment War Diary for November 1st, 1918

Remarks: Regiment continued advance at 6:30 PM, preceded by 5 minutes artillery preparation and barrage; same formation -- 2nd Battalion on the left 3rd Battalion on the right; 1st Battalion in support; advance made thru Cruyshautem at 7:20 AM; outpost line at Wanneghem-Lede; 3rd objective reached by leading Battalions at 14:43,... occupied Heurne on the best bank of the Escault River. Impossible to make crossing in face of Machine Gun and artillery fire due to lack of Engineers... to construct bridges. Night PC's -- 1st Battalion in support... 2nd Battalion left of line... 3rd Battalion right of line.

R.F. Ohmer
Captain, Adjutant

Regiment continued advance at 6.30 preceded by 5 minutes artillery preparation and a barrage; same formation 3rd Battalion on the left, 3rd

Battalion on the right, 1st Battalion in support.
Advance made through Cruyshautem at 7.20 AM
outpost line at Wanneghem-Lede at 7.50 AM. 3rd
Objective reached by leading Battalions at 14.45
which occupied Heurne on west bank of the Escault
River.

      Impossible to make crossing in face of
machine gun and artillery fire owing to lack of
engineering materials to construct bridges.

U.S. ARMY FIELD MESSAGE

From Commanding Officer 14th to Commanding Officer 3rd
Battalion 4:50 PM

1. Brigade directs that this regiment push across the Escault River
tonight without fail to establish a position strong enough to hold and to
send forward patrols to get contact with the enemy if possible.
2. You are charged with the execution of this order within your sector
limits.
3. Show your position on sketch so that artillery can furnish barrage
on your signal.

U.S. ARMY FIELD MESSAGE

148th to 3rd
9:05 P
1. Here with copy of Brigade order.
2. Take note of the words "without fail tonight," an aide states that this
order emanates from the Army and the Corps Commander considers it
urgent.
3. If the Engineers fail to construct the light bridges which they
were bringing forward this afternoon, construct many small rafts or
devise some similar scheme. If you effect a crossing make it a strong
detachment at least a halt   [marked "not sent"]

U.S. ARMY FIELD MESSAGE

Marlin at Thielt to Commanding Officer 148
Battalion well in hand, morale good. Wounded evacuated.
Ammunition received.

U.S. ARMY FIELD MESSAGE

Marlin to Commanding Officer 148

Arrived at final objective at 14:45 o'clock. 2nd Battalion here at same time. Germans have evacuated all territory west of River Escault. Advance made today without resistance from enemy. Am having passages of the River Escault reconnoitered and will start later. P. C. at present in Priest's house in Heurne.... No shelling of town as yet by enemy but expect it soon. Will need rations and ammunition tonight. Kitchens should have come forward and ammunition wagons can reach us at Heurne. In fact entire train can advance practically here.

Marlin

1st Aid Station should be advanced to this town.

Marlin

U.S. ARMY FIELD MESSAGE

from 148 to Marlin
16:30

Push across the Escault without fail tonight. Establish yourself strong enough to hold the East bank. Send patrols forward and get contact with enemy if possible. Report Action.

Jackson

U.S. ARMY FIELD MESSAGE

From C.O. 3rd Battalion-148th Infantry
At P.C.-HEURNE
Date: 1-Nov-18   Hour: 17:50   How sent: Runner
To Commanding Officer - 148th Infantry

Germans are placing a few shells in Heurne - evidently in retaliation
for harassing rifle and machine gun fire today. Have report our own
artillery fired short. Machine guns brought down a German aeroplane
this afternoon but unfortunately it fell across the river. Have two
Stokes now - but certainly would enjoy the use of a one-pounder.

Marlin

U.S. ARMY FIELD MESSAGE

From Commanding General 74th Brigade at Cruyshautem
to Commanding Officer, 148th Infantry
Date: 1 Nov/18   Hour: 22:30   How sent: Runner

In order to expedite matters the following message was sent to Major
Marlin, he being the senior officer present which the advanced
Battalions:—
     "To C.O., 3rd Battalion, 148th Infantry. The 112th
Engineers have been directed by the Divisional Commander to
put a bridge across the Escault River tonight. You are directed to
give Colonel Sage all assistance possible. Upon completion of the
bridge you will push at least one (1) Battalion and one (1) machine gun
company across the river and protect the bridge from being destroyed."

JACKSON

U.S. ARMY FIELD MESSAGE

from Commanding General 74th Brigade at Cruyshautem
to Commanding Officer, 148th Infantry
Date: 1 Nov/18   Hour: 22:45   How sent: Runner

Send report by runner size of force sent across the Escault as
directed in orders, both verbal and written today. Orders are most
insistent that troops be pushed across the river tonight and the 74th
Brigade wishes the honour of having part of the 148th Infantry as first
troops on the east bank.

JACKSON

Found in *The 37ᵗʰ Division in the World War*

Field Orders No. 38, issued for 2nd November, announced
that "the division will cross the Escault today with strong
advance guards. In order preserve depth, not to exceed
one regiment of each brigade will proceed beyond the line
Beltenshoek-Huysee-Klien-Gavere."

During the night, Companies K and M 148th Inf., with a
detail under Lt. Schumaker, made a temporary bridge from
fallen trees and material from destroyed houses in Heurne,
over which a few men from these companies had crossed at
7:00 A. M. under heavy artillery and machine gun fire. During
the afternoon a detachment of 20 men from the 3rd Bn. 145th
Inf. under Lt. S. S. Beard, crossed another bridge they had
improvised to act as a "bridge-head guard for the protection of
the troops who were to build a bridge during the night." One
pontoon foot bridge was laid by the infantry and engineers at
Heurne early in the night and the entire 3rd Bn. 145th Inf. and
attached companies crossed without incident and dug in near
and behind the opposite bank. At the same time a portion of
the 2nd Bn. extended its flank on the west bank of the river for
the purpose of supporting the troops on the other side." (From
War Diary 145th Inf.) The 146th Inf. removed in reserve.

Gen. Farnsworth's report stated that "small detachments of our troops began to cross the river by 8:25 A. M. The 148th Inf. made temporary bridges of fallen trees and material from destroyed houses in Heurne. The enemy had taken position on the east bank and disputed the crossing with both artillery and machine gun fire. Artillery was particularly heavy along the roads and on the town of Heurne, making the bringing forward of bridge material extremely slow.

At 10:30 the 2nd and 3rd Bns. Of the 148th Inf. began a definite movement across the river by the protection of artillery and machine gun barrage and by noon, approximately 300 men had succeeded in crossing and establishing a position on the east bank. (vol. 2, 389)

Late in the afternoon the 145th Inf. succeeded in getting 52 men across on the temporary bridge constructed by the 148th Inf. One pontoon bridge was completed by 7:00 P. M. and at 8:00 P. M. the entire 2nd and 3rd Battalions of the 148th Inf., less one company, Company L, were across the river and a second pontoon bridge was completed. Ammunition, pyrotechnics and rations were carried across by carrying parties. Because of the heavy shelling directed against Heurne, all troop movements through the town were stopped at 11:00 P.M. At this same hour, the engineers completed their bridge in the 73rd Brigade sector and one battalion of the 145th Inf., the 3rd, crossed the river and established liaison with the 2nd and 3rd Bns. Of the 148th. All other units of the 37th Division remained on the west bank, that night of 2nd-3rd November. (vol. 2, 291)

At 4:35 P. M. division headquarters received the message from the commanding officer of Co. M, 145th Inf., written at 2:30, which stated:

"Company L reports no men across the river. The 148th has some men across. I have five or six men across with them. Co. K will try to go across as soon as they can use bridge. Companies L, I and M will follow them in turn."

At 2:35 Regimental Headquarters of the 145th Inf. reported that the Commanding Officer of Co. L had reported at noon that "the 148th is held up in crossing on account of machine guns, artillery and one pounders. Major of 148th would not allow Lt. Meyers of 145th to continue crossing. Companies will cross in following order if advance can be resumed; K, L, I and M. (Artillery fire) and plenty of Boche planes directing it." (vol. 2, 392-392)

It's quite likely that Lieutenant Barlow wrote that Company L report. As indicated earlier, he had recently been in command and may have remained so.

Distinguished Service Cross Citation
Paul A. Smithisler
Sergeant, First Class, Headquarters Detachment, 112th Engineers

For extraordinary heroism in action near Heuvel, Belgium, November 2, 1918. Under cover of darkness he swam the Scheldt River at a point where it was covered by hostile machine guns and reconnoitered a road for a distance of 500 meters, returning with valuable information.

Distinguished Service Cross Citation
Walter C. Mack
Private, Company B, 135th Machine Gun Battalion

For extraordinary heroism in action near Eyne, Belgium, November 2, 1918. In the face of intense machine-gun fire, he voluntarily swam the Scheldt River to obtain information regarding the enemy. His successful return with the desired information enabled his company commander to so place his guns that they could be fired with great advantage.

Distinguished Service Cross Citation
John Warman
Private, Company B, 135th Machine Gun Battalion.

For extraordinary heroism in action near Eyne, Belgium, November 2, 1918. In the face of intense machine-gun fire he voluntarily swam the Scheldt River to obtain information regarding the enemy. His successful return with the desired information enabled his company commander to so place his guns that they would be fired with great advantage.

Distinguished Service Cross Citation
Clifford C. Loucks
Private, Company B, 112th Engineers

For extraordinary heroism in action near Heuvel, Belgium, November 2, 1918. Pvt. Loucks, with two other soldiers, crossed the Scheldt River after two attempts and succeeded in stretching a line for a bridge across the stream. They were discovered and fired upon by the enemy, but they continued at work driving stakes and made a second trip across the river to obtain wire, despite the fact that a violent artillery barrage had been laid down on their position.

Distinguished Service Cross Citation
John Friel
Corporal, Company K, 145th Infantry

For extraordinary heroism in action near Eyne, Belgium, on November 2, 1918. In full view of the enemy and under heavy artillery and machine-gun fire, Corpl. Friel, with two other men, swam the Escault River and assisted in the construction of a footbridge. The construction of this bridge aided materially in the later successful operations of American troops in this vicinity.

Distinguished Service Cross Citation
William L. Marlin
Lieutenant Colonel, Infantry Officers' Reserve Corps
(then Major), 148th Infantry

For extraordinary heroism in action at Heurne, Belgium, November 1-2, 1918. While commanding the 3rd Battalion, 148th Infantry, Major Marlin displayed exceptional qualities of personal courage and leadership in forcing the crossing of the Escault River, establishing a bridgehead on the right bank of the river, and maintaining his position against repeated and vigorous counterattacks, all under heavy artillery and aeroplane fire. Major Marlin exposed himself fearlessly and audaciously and without regard for danger, thereby greatly enhancing the morale of the troops and contributing materially to the success of this operation. His personal bravery in this act was markedly conspicuous and outstanding.

Distinguished Service Cross Citation (Posthumous)
Charles Mzik
Corporal, Company K, 145th Infantry

For extraordinary heroism in action near Eyne, Belgium, on November 2, 1918. In full view of the enemy and under heavy artillery and machine gun fire Corporal Mzik, with two other men, swam the Escault River and assisted in the construction of a footbridge. The construction of this bridge aided materially in the later successful operations of American troops in this vicinity. Corporal Mzik was killed in the performance of this act.

Distinguished Service Cross Citation
Joseph T. Atkinson
Private, Company B, 112ᵗʰ Engineers

For extraordinary heroism in action near Heuvel, Belgium, November 2, 1918. Pvt. Atkinson, with two other soldiers, crossed the Scheldt River, after two attempts, and succeeded in stretching a line for a bridge across the stream. They were discovered and fired upon by the enemy, but they continued at work driving stakes, and made a second trip across the river to obtain wire, despite the fact that a violent artillery barrage had been laid down on their position.

Distinguished Service Cross Citation
Herbert W. Flesher
Sergeant, First Class, Company B, 112ᵗʰ Engineers

For extraordinary heroism in action near Heuvel, Belgium, November 2, 1918. Sergt. Flesher, with two other soldiers, crossed the Scheldt River after two attempts and succeeded in stretching a line for the bridge across the stream. They were discovered and fired upon by the enemy, but they continued at work driving stakes and made a second trip across the river to obtain wire, despite the fact that violent artillery barrage had been laid down on their positions.

From 148th Infantry Regiment War Diary for November 2nd, 1918

```
March Table:
Supply, etc.:

                                   3 days rations
                                     supply train
2nd and 3rd
Battalions -           ) Banks of Escault R to enemy
                          Cloudy weather
```

```
1st Bn in support    ) side of river slight
                       Fair roads
of 2nd and 3rd       ) advance of Heurne
                       Fair Health
Supply Company
                Camp: Under Fire in rear
                     Olsene
```

Remarks: Advance continued across the Escault River; 3rd Battalion on the right 2nd Battalion on the left in assault; 1st Battalion in support; 3rd Battalion gained east bank of the Escault in face of heavy artillery and Machine Gun fire, using trees thrown across river as bridges. Passage assured at 12:30 PM. Location of farthest advance of line beyond which advance was not to be made from 213.2-461.9 SW to 211.9-460.8. Flank regiments did not entirely accomplish crossing during day.

R F Ohmer

Capt Adj

148th Inf

2 November 1918
Hour: 11:45
MESSAGE:
FROM: Liaison Officer, 74th Brigade.

At 10:30 o'clock temporary bridges of fallen trees were thrown across the Escault in front of the 148th Infantry. The 2nd and 3rd Battalions of the 148th Infantry are crossing the Escault, supported by the Machine Gun Company. 148th Infantry at 10:30 o'clock. Major Marlin has arranged with artillery for a 5 minute concentrated barrage and a 30 minute specific barrage on certain targets, both to be called for my signals if needed. 1st Battalion will support the 2nd Battalion.

Cavanaugh.

2 November 1918
Hour: 17:50
MESSAGE:

FROM: Headquarters 74th Brigade

At 17:50 o'clock, received telephonic communication from Captain Baehr, Operations Officer, 148th Infantry, that Major Marlin's battalion had crossed River Escault and was holding the line from point 213.20 at east bank of river, to 211.90 - 460.85, with small outposts extending from the latter point west to east bank of the Escault River.

Moore.

37TH DIVISION, A. E. F.,
November 2, 1918.

From: Commanding General, 37th Division
To: Commanding General, 91st Division

SUBJECT: Passage of the Escault

1. With reference to your request to cross regiment of infantry within the zone of action of 37th Division, I have to inform you that the construction of two small foot bridges across the Escault, one at 300 and the other at 600 meters north of the Eyne--Neder-Eename Road, was begun at six o'clock this evening. I believe that these bridges have been finished by this time and can be used by troops. The pontoon bridge being constructed at the crossing of the last named road will probably not be completed until very late tonight or tomorrow forenoon. It is possible, however, that this pontoon bridge will be finished earlier than I anticipate. I will be very glad

to have you pass a regiment of infantry over any one of these three bridges. I will also be glad to assist the passage in any way that I can with my troops or arms. Machine guns now in position might be able to assist and I would suggest that the commander of the regiment to cross might consult the commander of my battalion in Eyne with a view to use his machine guns. My divisional artillery will also be placed in part at your disposal to fire on targets at times and with kind of ammunition as you may designate to me. If there is anything further that I can do to assist your passage, please advise me.

   2. I now have seven companies across the river in the left of my sector and at least two and possibly five, have crossed the river and are in position from 300 to 600 meters northeast of Eyne--Neder-Eename river coursing. Nearly all of the above crossed on bridges made of fallen trees and material secured in Heron and by wading.

C. S. Farnsworth,
Major General, U.S.A.

From 37th Division War Diary for November 3rd, 1918

During the night of 2/3 November, the 148th Infantry succeeded, by use of foot bridges and one pontoon bridge, in placing a total of six companies on the east bank of the Escault.

Gallantry in Action Citation
William Perry
Sergeant, Headquarters Company, 145th Infantry

For gallantry in action near Eyne, Belgium, November 3, 1918, in securing valuable information under heavy fire.

Gallantry in Action Citation
Floyd Kimball
Private, First Class, Headquarters Company, 145th Infantry

For gallantry in action near Eyne, Belgium, November 3, 1918, in securing valuable information under heavy fire.

Distinguished Service Cross Citation
Francis X. Schumacker
First Lieutenant, Company K, 148th Infantry

For extraordinary heroism in action near Heurne, Belgium, November 3, 1918. In the face of terrific machine-gun and artillery fire, he gave valuable assistance in the construction of a log bridge over the Scheldt River, which enabled his battalion to cross and establish itself in its objective. He remained with his company after being wounded until he was forced to be evacuated.

Distinguished Service Cross Citation
Morris Aamodt
Sergeant, Company K, 148th Infantry

For extraordinary heroism in action near Heurne, Belgium, November 3, 1918. He advanced alone through violent artillery fire to reconnoiter the new position to be occupied by his company beyond the Escault River. He made the reconnaissance and returned with valuable information for his company commander, but was wounded while advancing to the new position with his company.

From 148th Infantry Regiment War Diary for November 3rd, 1918

Positions help being consolidated; balance of
2nd Battalion being pushed across Escault River
at Heurne to left of 3rd Battalion. Heurne and
vicinity severely shelled.   Construction of
pontoon bridge impossible on account of same....
Tonight, 2nd and 3rd Battalions holding positions
won.

Supply, etc.:
Cloudy weather
Fair Roads
Fair health
Under Fire - Camp

148 Infantry
March Table
HQ PC From Chateau at 207.463, 2nd and 3rd
Battalions, east of Escault River at Heurne, 1st
Battalion and Machine Gun Company west of same
- support; Supply Company at Olsene -- all to
Appelhoek area.

Remarks:
Positions held being consolidated and balance of
2nd Battalion being pushed across Escault River
at Heurne to left of 3rd Battalion. Heurne and
vicinity severely shelled; construction of pontoon
bridge impossible on acct. of same. Line of
furthest advance from 213.1-461.9 southwesterly
to 211.9-460.8. 1st Battalion and attached
Machine Gun Company (148th Infantry) ordered to

withdraw to rear area in vicinity of Appelhoek
near Cruyshautem tonight.   2nd and 3rd Battalions
holding positions won.

                                    R.F. Ohmer
                              Capt 148th Infantry
                                    Adjutant

Distinguished Service Cross Citation
Wilk Gunckle
Private, Company M, 148th Infantry

For extraordinary heroism in action near Heurne, Belgium,
November 3, 1918. He volunteered and guided ammunition
carriers to advanced positions, despite the fact that he was
seriously wounded in the face, which made it necessary to
hold a bandage in place during the journey to and from the
front. After receiving treatment at the first-aid station he
returned to his duties.

Distinguished Service Cross Citation
Alfred M. Barlow
First Lieutenant, Company L, 148th Infantry

For extraordinary heroism in action near Heurne, Belgium,
November 3, 1918. Although suffering from a painful
shrapnel wound in the leg, he led his company, with excellent leadership and command, over the river, and not until
he had received wounds in both legs would he give his consent to be taken to a dressing station.

Found in *The United States Army in the World War*

Operations Report   37th DIVISION, A. E. F.

REPORT OF OPERATIONS OF THE 37TH DIVISION IN
FLANDERS OFFENSIVE, FORCING THE CROSSING OF
THE LYS AND ESCAULT RIVERS, OCTOBER 31,
NOVEMBER 4, 1918 INCLUSIVE

October 18:   Pursuant to Field Order 32,
headquarters 37th Division, October 17, 1918
issued in compliance with G-3 Order No. 9 of
Second Army, entrainment of division for new
area was commenced at 18 hour. Detraining point
unknown. Before commencing this movement, 75%
of truck transportation of ammunition and supply
trains was taken from the division and ordered
turned over to American Second Army.
October 20:   Troop trains began to arrive and
detrain at points Wieltje--Boesinghe--St. Jean-
-Vlanertinghe in the neighborhood of Ypres. The
P.C. of the division was established at Hooglede,
Belgium, and troop movements by march to billeting
areas in Staden-Hooglede and Gits area started on
the 21st.
October 21:   Difficulties immediately began to
arise in equipping and rationing of troops, due to
extreme shortage of transportation and devastation
of country, which was "No Man's Land" from Ypres
to Hooglede, difficult and slow for transportation.
Efforts to obtain from French, English and
American sources, additional transportation, were
unsuccessful.
October 22:   Pursuant to Special Order 5 A.F.B.
October 22, the 37th Division was put at the
disposal of the King of Belgium and attached to
the French Army of Belgium for operations.

October 23/24: Detraining and march to billeting areas completed by all troops.

October 25: The billeting area of the division was enlarged to include the area of Lichtervelde.

October 26: Division headquarters and 73rd Brigade moved to Lichtervelde.

October 27: Pursuant to Special Order 8, A.F.B., October 26, the division advanced one stage nearer the front lines and P. C. was established at Meulebeke October 28, at 14 hour.

October 28: Pursuant to note from XXX Corps, the 37th Division, on order of A.F.B., was attached to that corps for pending operations. Another step forward was taken by the division and the P. C. (advanced) was opened at Denterghem at 8 hour October 29.

October 29: Special Order No. 29, from the XXX C. A., dated October 28, was received this day, ordering relief of French 132nd Division in the Cruyshautem sector and Field Order 35, headquarters 37th Division, dated October 29, was issued from these headquarters. Relief to take place in night of October 29/30 and 30/31.

October 30: Operations Order No. 32, Headquarters XXX French Corps, of October 29, 20:35 hour, was received this date. The order directed the attack by the corps at a day and H hour to be fixed later. The French 132nd Divisional Artillery Balloon Company 87, Aero Squadron 287, and the Cavalry Squadron on the 132nd D.I. were attached to this division for the projected operation. Based upon Operations Order No. 32, XXX Corps, Field Order 36, Headquarters 37th Division, October 30, was issued.

    At 17:30 hour memo was received from French XXX C. A. fixing D day as October 31 and H hour as 5:30 a.m.

Order of Battle from Right to Left
VII A.C. American 91st Division
French 128th Division
XXX A.C. American 37th Division
French 12th Division
XXXIV A.C. French

Mission to drive the enemy across the Escault.

Disposition of troops of this division for the attack was a follows:

The Infantry Brigades abreast, 73rd on the right, 74th on the left, each with two battalions in 1st line....

To each infantry battalion was attached a machine gun company.

One company, 112th Engineers, was employed in keeping in repair the bridges over the Lys River and approaches thereto.

After an artillery preparation of 5 minutes the infantry went over the top at 5:30 a.m., following a rolling barrage of high explosives and shrapnel, moving at a speed of 10 meters in 3 minutes. Enemy counterbattery work commenced immediately and contained a great many arsine gas shells. The wind being from the east, the effects were felt as far back as division headquarters then located at Denterghem.

The advance was steady right from the start and all enemy resistance was methodically broken down.

Prisoners began to arrive at 7:35 and reported the first enemy line thinly held, and that the main resistance would be met on the ridge west of Cruyshautem.

At 8:15, the division had reached its first
objective--Ruisseau de Katterbeek--Boqueteau est
de Karreweg--Lisiere est de Huttegem--junction of
Tichelbeek with the route Olsene to Cruyshautem
Point 1450.

A pause until 8:30 was made at the first
objective, when movement was begun toward the line
Merhaaghoek--Ferme de Recte--Waterhoek--Neder-
Rechem, on which line the attack was to be resumed
at 13:30 hour. The enemy artillery was very
active, especially upon roads leading forward.
Casualties, however, were not heavy and the
advance continued steady. The resistance of the
enemy was mostly by machine guns, the greater part
of the hostile infantry having fallen back to the
ridge southwest of Cruyshautem. The heavy enemy
artillery fire continuously broke the telephone
lines of communication of this division and
difficulty was had in keeping accurately in touch
with the advanced elements. The roads were good,
being generally paved and this permitting the use
of motor ambulances and assuring prompt attention
to and evacuation of all wounded.

During the enemy retirement the enemy
heavily shelled the town of Olsene, wounding
many civilians and blowing down two houses
which temporarily blocked forward movement. A
detachment of engineers immediately cleared away
the debris and permitted traffic to proceed with
little delay. Between the hours of 10 and 11, our
artillery held the ridge worthiest of Cruyshautem
under very heavy shell fire and at 10:15, the
advance was ordered continued regardless of the
progress of the adjoining units.

At 13:05, the division reserve was ordered
to advance to a point within 2000 meters of the
reserve of the 73rd Brigade and to be prepared for

action at a moment's notice. At this time, the 74th Brigade was held up on the crest of the ridge west of Cruyshautem and a pause was ordered until 15 hour, when a strong attack was ordered by all units to take the ridge.

At 15 hour the Commanding General of the French XXX A.C. was requested to move that part of the 147th Infantry in the corps reserve to the area between the railway and Houtstraat. This request was made because of the delay of the 12th Division, on our left, and the consequent exposure of our left flank.

The advance was ordered to cease shortly after 17 hour and all units were directed to deeply intrench. The line rested for the night on the crest of the Cruyshautem Heights....

Total prisoners taken for the day, 11 officers, 306 enlisted men.

November 1: Field Order No. 37, Headquarters 37th Division, dated October 31, was issued at 22 hour and ordered the attack for November 1 to commence at 6:30 hour, artillery preparation to commence at 6:25, the infantry to make the attack at 6:30, preceded by a rolling barrage at a distance of 600 meters and which was to move at the rate of 100 meters in 3 minutes. The first objective of the day was the 2d objective of the original plan, upon reaching which a pause was to be made until 10 o'clock.

The advance on the morning of the 1st proceeded as per schedule and at 7:20 o'clock the 3rd Battalion, 148th Infantry had passed through the town of Cruyshautem. All indications were that the enemy had withdrawn. At 7:40 the second objective had been reached and the town of Wannegem-Lede was occupied.

Attempts to make out the front line by aeroplanes were unsuccessful due to civilians everywhere waving handkerchiefs.

The pause at the second objective was ordered cancelled and at 10:40 the attack was ordered pushed to the final objective with all possible speed.

Liaison with the advanced units was very slow in reaching headquarters due to the rapid advance. However, reports of refugees indicated that at 11 o'clock our troops were within one kilometer of the Escault River.

Advance dumps were established by the division and all available transportation used in hauling up ammunition and supplies from the division dumps at Hooge.

Reports at 18 hour established our line on the west bank of the Escault River and in compliance with Memo Orders received from the Commanding General in the XXX Corps, all units were ordered to attempt to prepare for crossing the Escault during the night and establish outposts on the east bank.

Advanced P.C. of Headquarters 37th Division, closed at Denterghem and opened at Cruyshautem at 18 hour this date.

During the night the artillery of the 132nd Artillery Division supporting this division, was ordered to move forward and to have 75 mm guns in position at 3,000 meters west of the Escault and heavy artillery in position 6 kilometers west of the river.

Prisoners taken, one officer, five enlisted men.

November 2: Small detachments of our troops began to cross the river by 8:25 in the morning. The 148th Infantry made temporary bridges of fallen trees and material from destroyed houses in the town of Heurne. The enemy had taken position on the east bank and disputed the crossing with both artillery and machine guns. Artillery fire was particularly heavy along the roads and on the town of Heurne, making the bringing forward of bridge material extremely slow.

At 10:30 o'clock the 2nd and 3rd Battalions of the 148th Infantry, began a definite movement across the river under the protection of artillery and machine-gun barrage and by noon, approximately 300 men had succeeded in crossing the river and establishing a position on the east bank. Request was made of the French 128th D.I. and the American 91st Division to cover the right flank of this small party with artillery. The enemy artillery reaction increased during the afternoon, both high explosives and gas shells being used.

The town of Heurne was practically demolished and movement on the banks of the river was almost impossible.

Due to the impossibility of getting material through the town of Heurne, the pontoon bridge to be erected at that place was shifted to Eyne where a bridge was to be constructed at 6 p.m. under cover of darkness.

Late in the afternoon the 145th Infantry had succeeded in getting 52 men across on the temporary bridge constructed by the 148th Infantry. One pontoon bridge was completed by 19 h. and at 20:50 h. the entire 2nd and 3rd Battalions of the 148th Infantry, less one company, were across the river and a second pontoon bridge completed. Ammunition, pyrotechnics and rations were carried across the river by carrying parties during the night.

All troop movements through the town of
Heurne were stopped at 23 h., due to the terrific
enemy bombardment of high explosives and gas
shells.

At 23 hour the engineer bridge in the
sector of the 73rd Brigade was completed and one
battalion of the 145th Infantry crossed the river,
and established liaison with the battalions of the
148th Infantry already across.

One regiment of the American 91st Division
on our right, was authorized to cross the river
during the night on the footbridge constructed by
the 37th Division near Eyne.

Prisoners taken; 5 enlisted men.
November 3: The crossing of the river was resumed
early on the morning of this day in the face of
continued heavy enemy artillery and machine-gun
fire.

The French 12th Division began to cross the
river on the footbridge of the 148th Infantry
early during the morning and at 6:30, two
companies of infantry and one machine gun company
were securely established on the east bank. The
regiment of the 91st Division, on our right, did
not succeed in crossing and organized a position
near the village of Marolle.

All during this entire day, small parties
filtered across the river. The enemy concentrated
all means at his disposal to prevent this
crossing. Aeroplanes numbering as high as ten at
one time harassed the position with machine-gun
fire and aerial bombs.

As fast as enemy battery positions were
located our artillery would concentrate their
efforts upon the known target and at times during
the day the heavy concentration of enemy artillery
would be greatly decreased.

At 18 hour, three and one-half companies of the 148th Infantry, four machine gun companies, and six companies of the 145th Infantry, as well as four companies of infantry and two machine gun companies of the French 12th Division were established on the east bank of the river, securely holding the line.

One deserter from the 5th Prison Company surrendered.

Operations Order No. 43, XXX C.A. directed the relief of the 37th Division by the French 12th Division for the day of November 3 and night of November 4/5....

Distinguished Service Cross Citation
Ralph T. Trew
Sergeant, Company K, 145th Infantry

For extraordinary heroism in action near Heurne, Belgium, October [November] 4, 1918. Volunteering to construct a footbridge across the Scheldt River, Sergt. Trew crossed the stream in plain view of the enemy under violent machine-gun fire and, after the bridge had been completed, returned and led the first detachment of his regiment across.

Distinguished Service Cross Citation
Joe W. McGraw
Private, Company D, 145th Infantry

For extraordinary heroism in action near Heurne, Belgium, November 4, 1918. He displayed exceptional personal bravery when, with one other soldier, he went to the aid of a comrade who had been attacked and wounded by a patrol of eight Germans, putting the patrol to flight and rescuing the wounded man.

Distinguished Service Cross Citation
William E. Moore
Private, Company D, 145ᵗʰ Infantry

For extraordinary heroism in action near Heurne, Belgium, November 4, 1918. He displayed exceptional personal bravery when, with one other soldier, he went to the assistance of a comrade who had been attacked and wounded by a patrol of eight Germans, rescuing the wounded man and putting the enemy patrol to flight.

Distinguished Service Cross Citation
Mat A. Kohx
Corporal, Company K, 145ᵗʰ Infantry

For extraordinary heroism in action near Heurne, Belgium, November 4, 1918. He went through heavy shell and machine-gun fire for a distance of 100 yards, and carried a wounded comrade to safety.

Distinguished Service Cross Citation
Herbert C. Fooks
Major, 3ʳᵈ Battalion, 145ᵗʰ Infantry

For extraordinary heroism in action near Eyne, Belgium, November 4, 1918. Although severely wounded and his jaw shattered by a machine-gun bullet, he refused to be evacuated, administered first aid himself, and continued to fearlessly direct his battalion during a strong counter-attack. The personal example of this officer was a vital factor in the success of the operation.

Distinguished Service Cross Citation
Harold J. Gordon
Captain, 148th Ambulance Company, 112th Sanitary Train

For extraordinary heroism in action near Heurne, Belgium on November 4, 1918, at the crossing of the Escault River. Although in command of an ambulance company and not required to work so far forward, he voluntarily crossed the river and sought out wounded among the troops in the advance line. Finding two severely wounded men. he gave them first aid under withering machine-gun, rifle, and shell fire, arranged such shelter for them as he could, then sought assistance to carry them on to safety. Returning with three men of his company, the bearers placed one of the wounded on an improvised litter, while the other was carried on the shoulders of the officer until the latter was exhausted. The fire becoming more intense, the wounded man was placed on the ground and encouraged by the officer to crawl to safety, the latter crawling beside him and protecting him from the enemy's fire with his own body.

Gallantry in Action Citation
Robert M. Johnson
Sergeant, Company, Company K, 148th Infantry

For gallantry in action near Heurne, Belgium, November 3 and 4, 1918, while in command of a company which repulsed an enemy counterattack.

Gallantry in Action Citation
George Toliver
Private, First Class, Company I, 148th Infantry

For gallantry in action near Olsene, Belgium, October 31 to November 4, 1918. He repeatedly carried messages under intense enemy fire despite painful wound in foot.

Distinguished Service Cross Citation
Robert L. Baldridge
Private, 148th Ambulance Company, 112th Sanitation Train, 37th Division

For extraordinary heroism in action near Heurne, Belgium, November 4, 1918. With two other soldiers he volunteered to rescue two wounded men who had been lying in an exposed position on the opposite bank of the Scheldt River for two days. Making two trips across the stream in the face of heavy machine-gun fire, he and his companion succeeded in carrying both the wounded men to shelter.

Distinguished Service Cross Citation
Stuart S. Donaldson
Private, 148th Ambulance Company, 112th Sanitary Train, 37th Division

For extraordinary heroism in action near Heurne, Belgium, November 4, 1918. With two other soldiers, Pvt. Donaldson volunteered to rescue two wounded men who had been lying in an exposed position on the opposite bank of the Scheldt River for two days. Making two trips across the stream, in the face of heavy machine-gun and shell fire, he and his companions succeeded in carrying both the wounded men to shelter.

Distinguished Service Cross Citation
Edward N. Gillen
Private, 148th Ambulance Company, 112th Sanitary Train

For extraordinary heroism in action near Heurne, Belgium, November 4, 1918. With two soldiers he volunteered to rescue two wounded men who had been lying in an exposed position on the opposite bank of the Scheldt River for two days. Making two trips across the stream in the face of heavy machine-gun and shell fire he and his companions succeeded in carrying both the wounded men to shelter.

Periodical and Date Not Identified

ALFRED BARLOW SHOT IN LEGS
Nephew of B.S., M.C. and J.C. Barlow, War Victim

M.C. Barlow, who recently left this city and is now back in his old home at Gallipolis, Ohio, has sent to this office a newspaper clipping telling of the serious injury in battle of his nephew. The young man is also a nephew of B.S. Barlow of the Ind. Times, and of J.C. Barlow, late of this city, and now of California. The father of the young man was Marion Barlow, who, at one lime lived in this city. The article from the Gallipolis Tribune regarding the soldier follows:

"Lieut. Alfred Barlow, while doing the work of his captain and several lieutenants, lost in battle, was shot through both legs and one foot, and lay on the field of battle from four o'clock in the afternoon, all night, before he received medical attention.

"His mother's word is that the surgeons hope to save both legs. The story that he lost both legs is wrong. It is possible that he may lose neither, and his friends will hope and pray that complete recovery may come.

"Gallipolis is being hard hit by the after-the-war casualty reports."

"Gallipolis is being hard hit by the after-the-war casualty reports." This has to be one of the saddest lines of all the sad lines written about the United States involvement in WWI. Given communications of the day, it was not surprising that the big news—the Armistice—got to Gallipolis before the little news—the heavy casualties suffered by the 37th Division in the last week of the war. Many people celebrated, believing their loved ones in the service were now safe, only to find, over the next week or two, that they had died or been wounded during that last week of fighting.

Publication and Date Not Determined

SOLDIERS MEET AGAIN
After Undergoing Hardships Together on Belgian Front in November 1918

Tom Hughes makes Gallipolis for The Chatfield & Woods Paper Company of Cincinnati. He gets around every month or so and calls on The Times, The Tribune and The Booton Press as well as other establishments which use paper in large quantities. Several weeks ago while waiting on Mr. Booton, he picked up a Rio Grande Year Book and noticed a familiar face in one of the pictures. He called Mr. Booton and said "I know that guy, he gave me some Melachrino cigarettes in Belgium."

The picture happened to be one of Lieut. Alfred Barlow of who was then out of the city. Friday morning Hughes returned and hunted up Barlow. They spent most of the morning talking over the experiences of November 1, 2, and 3, 1918.

Barlow was in charge of an infantry unit near the village of Heurne, Belgium, near Olsene. He was with the 148th Infantry, Company L. Hughes, a Sergeant, was in command of a machine gun company, his officers having all been killed. Barlow and his infantry outfit had advanced to a canal and the Germans had their machine guns and artillery trained along the canal nicely. As they were working their way across, Hughes came up with his machine guns and covered Barlow and his men as they advanced.

When Hughes met Barlow, Barlow gave him some cigarettes, gaining his everlasting gratitude. A short time later in the same action both received wounds that sent them to the same field hospital, where Hughes listened to Barlow in delirium. Later in another hospital they occupied beds ten feet apart.

Hughes was a member of Company D, 136th Machine Gun Company. His wound was in the shoulder. Barlow was struck in both legs, making necessary the amputation of one.

They spent a comfortable morning talking over the three days activity on the Belgian front. Strange as it may seem to many readers, their reminiscences were along the lines of food and amusing experiences rather than of the horrors they went through.

Friday, June 20, 1941

Bravery Recalled

A feature story in the Cleveland Press concerning the World War activity of Capt. Alfred Barlow will revive among his friends here the memory of his bravery for which he was later awarded the Croix de Guerre, with palm, and the American D.S.C. He now lives in Cleveland.

The young officer, a native Gallipolitan, headed a company assigned to cross a river and deep canal in Belgium and establish a bridgehead on the other side facing the German forces. A tree was felled across the canal and Lieut. Barlow, head of his company, crossed first, a wire serving as a hand rail. A shell fragment scored his right shin. A few of his men followed when the enemy put down a box barrage at the crossing. Barlow stopped action until dark. While waiting a shell landed far away but ricocheted by chance in such a way that it crushed his right foot. He got his company across after dark and the bridgehead was established.

Meanwhile one of his messages got back to headquarters. His high superiors couldn't understand why his advance had been held up. If his disregard for orders had been unsuccessful he would have been reprimanded, perhaps court marshaled. Since it turned out all right he received the honors mentioned above.

Now he is chief attorney for the United States Veterans Hospital at Brecksville, near Cleveland. He is the son and only child of Mrs. Eva Barlow, Island Side.

WESTERN UNION

TELEGRAM

16D WX 45 GOVT

Washington DC346P DEC 2

MRS EVA BARLOW

1066 1ST AVE GALLIPOLIS O

DEEPLY REGRET TO INFORM YOU THAT IT IS OFFICIALLY REPORTED THAT FIRST LIEUT ALFRED M BARLOW INFANTRY WAS SEVERELY WOUNDED IN ACTION ABOUT NOVEMBER FOURTH FURTHER INFORMATION WHEN RECEIVED

HARRIS THE ADJ GENL

334PM,

Chapter Eleven

Anglo-American Hospital
A.P.O. 538
B.E.F.
France

November 10, 1918
Sunday 9:30 a.m.

Dear Mother,

I suppose long before you will receive this you will have heard that I was wounded. I hope you have not been worried. I was hit in the left shin about one o'clock November 2nd. We were crossing a river. I had to stay where I was, and was again hit, this time in the right foot about 5 p.m. I was lying on my back and the piece of shell hit me in the bottom of the foot and traveled up towards my instep.

I did not get back across the river until just before day light.

The wound in the left leg is all right now but the other will take some time to heal. There was dirt in it and they thought at one time they might have to amputate but now they say it's coming fine.

It's only by special intervention of Divine Providence that I'm alive. I'm certainly lucky to get off so easy.

I am in a fine hospital which is for British and American Officers only. It is kept up by Lady Hadfield whose husband is a big Shefield manufacturer and who before her marriage was a Wichersham of Philadelphia. I met her yesterday. She is very pleasant.

I will be in hospital about two months the doctor says. As soon as I start mending fast they will probably send me to London.

Write soon. Letters will reach here soon.

Lots of love,

Alfred

OK A M Barlow 1st Lt, U.S. Inf.

The Anglo-American Hospital,
Wimereux,
PRES BOULOGNE.

Nov. 14th

Dear Mrs. Barlow.

I regret to inform you that your son Lieut A. M. Barlow, U.S.I. has been admitted to this hospital with severe wound in the foot. I'm sorry to say it was found necessary to amputate at the ankle joint. Rest assured that anything possible will be done for your son & if his condition does not progress satisfactorily I will write again.

Yours truly,

Brasie,

Matron

THE HALL WALKER HOSPITAL FOR OFFICERS
(MRS. HALL WALKER)

Telephone
SUSSEX LODGE,
  Paddington 1878.
Regent's Park, N.W.

16 . 11 . 18

Dear Mr. Barlow,

How is the poor foot going on and is there any hope of your coming to London?

Are you still in the same room and have you got any fellow suffers since Waunth left? We often speak about you.

Enclosed is the ten francs note you so kindly lent W. the day he was coming away and which should have been returned to you long ago. Remember us to everyone. Every best wish for Xmas & New Year.

> *Yours sincerely*
>
> *Golden*   *(per SMC)*

No 5 B.R.C.S. Hospital
B.E.F.

18/11/18

Dear Mrs Barlow

    I am writing this for your son who is in hospital here. He has been wounded in the foot, and has been suffering a good deal of pain, so that he has been unable to write himself. The wound is going on as well as could be expected, however, but he will probably have to stay in hospital some time. Your son asks you to write to the above address, instead of to his former one. If by any chance he has been moved to England, or to any other hospital in France your letters will be forwarded to him at his new address. This is one of the very best hospitals, and your son asks me to say he is receiving the utmost kindness and the very best of attention.

    If your son is not well enough to write in a few days I will write again to let you know how he is progressing.

    He sends his best love.
        Yours very sincerely

        W P Jones, Chaplain

Publication and Date Not Determined

LIEUT. BARLOW WAS DECORATED FOR BRAVERY IN BATTLE.

Writing from Brussels, Belgium, under date of Nov. 22, Captain Tom Jones states that his Division is on a long march across Belgium to the Rhine, following the retreating Germans, and that the boys are being royally entertained. "Yesterday," he writes, "we paraded here, and helped King Albert again ascend his throne, which he had to leave so suddenly more than four years ago. Tomorrow we march across the historic old Waterloo battlefield.

"Our division is to be decorated for bravery, as we have had three French citations, which gives us the Red and Blue shoulder cord. We have also been cited twice by Gen. Pershing, which entitles us to a medal for each man.

"I do not think it is generally known back in the States that the 37th Division has done a lot of hard fighting. We went over the top five times and fought on nine different fronts, and advanced every time and always gained our objective. The German artillery we captured will all be sent to Columbus for the statehouse yard.

"I have just received the sad news from the hospital at Bologne that the surgeons had to amputate Lieut. Alfred M. Barlow's foot at the ankle, and the other foot is badly crippled. One of his brother officers just told me of it. To bad he had to lose it in our last fight.

"I want the people of Gallia County to honor this brave officer when he returns, and I want to help do it, as no braver man ever led his men in battle. He was in command of Company L, 148th Infantry, when he was wounded. He was leading his men in one of the worst artillery barrages we ever saw. On the banks of a river hundreds of machine guns on the German side were working on us and it was a veritable hell. The Germans had blown up all the bridges and it looked like the old 37th Division had been stopped for the first time. The order came to cross the river, and Lieut. Barlow and his company sprang from their hasty "dug-ins" and began to construct rafts and fell trees. For hours they worked, and one after another was picked off. Lieut. Barlow was wounded in the leg by a piece of high explosive shell, but he being the only officer left with his company, refused to go to the rear. The little band got across the river in many ways and they dug in and held their position until reinforcements got to them. Then after his brave feat Lieut. Barlow was wounded in both feet by shrapnel and carried to the rear. Many of my old boys from Company C were with him and one, John Bennett from Middleport, was killed. I am glad to say that Lieut. Barlow has been awarded a medal for distinguished service. He is a real hero, and Gallia County may well be proud of him. In fact, she can feel proud of all her old Company F boys, as they are all fighters."

The Stars and Stripes, France, November 22, 1918

WOUNDED AND SICK GET FIRST CHANCE AT HOMEWARD TRIP

Serious Cases Should Be Back in American Within Three Months

BED TO EVERY 14 MEN

Many Hospital Construction Plans Suspended--Medical Units Will Continue to Arrive

-----

All seriously wounded men of the A.E.F. now in hospitals in France probably will have been transported to the United States before three months have passed, according to the office of the Chief Surgeon. Seriously ill patients also will be taken back as transportation will permit.

With approximately 250,000 beds in A.E.F. hospitals now, the Medical Department plans to have a hospital bed to every 14 men in the A.E.F. Plans for the fighting period called for one bed for approximately every seven men, statistics so far having shown that sickness and battle casualties made about equal demands on hospital facilities.

There are 21 complete hospital trains now in service, and contracts for 29 more have been held up. Contracts for 20 trains designed to carry sitting cases only have also been held up.

Many Plans Suspended

Fifteen thousand additional beds in new hospitals, mostly converted hotels, in the district about Nice and Mentone will be taken over according to plan.

New medical units will continue to arrive from the States for some time, because with the rapid transportation of fighting troops to France the Medical Department had not been able to maintain its authorized proportional strength.

A number of A.E.F. hospital units which have been attached to the British forces since the United States entered the war will probably learn soon whether they will be returned for duty with the American forces.

November 24, 1918.

Anglo American Hospital
A.P.O. 538
British E. F.
France

Dear Mother,

It is now one o'clock Sunday afternoon. My leg is dressed at 11 a.m. Today I had gas so that I did not know it was being done.

I received Half Communion this morning - the first time since I have been in France.

Received a fine letter from Cousin Morley, how sad about his son.

Don't let on I want to know but find out from Bob Switzer if possible if I will get any government compensation (pension) for my foot being off. Also please find out if I get any government insurance for the same reason. I've heard I would get a pension and $2,500 insurance but I don't know. I will be home not earlier than February 1st. I will I think stay permanently in G. or at least make it my headquarters.

Who is principle of the Mill Creek School? (Grant School) May-be I can get it next year. Don't say anything about this. At odd times I can finish college and then be a superintendent of schools. Don't you worry about my foot being off. I shall be able to get around pretty well.

I'd like to get a Ford if I can afford it when I come home. DO write soon & often. It's been at least 6 weeks since I've heard from you. Tell everyone to write. I get so lonesome no one I know here.

Loads of love,

Alfred.

Hill House Farm

Nov 24 . 18

- Wadhurst -

Dear Cousin Eva

Since writing you I heard from Alfred yesterday and I enclose you his letter so that you will see, the Hospital that he is in is at Boulogne. I know the place so well and I have written him and told him if I can get a permit to travel I will go over and see him and as well. I have asked him in the meantime to write me if he can to let me know how he is progressing I do hope that he will soon be out of pain but they cure and look after them better than you or me could do especially in a case like his it is so hard to see these Brave Boys suffer. We have about 45 in the hospital opposite us - but they get every care and everything they want and every thing they have to help and prevent them suffering. All the shipping is very busy bringing over the wounded & prisoner that it is most difficult to travel across the Channel unless I could get a permit from the American Embassy in London. Dear Eva you have the consolation to know that Alfred is alive and we hope he will soon be restored to you. I have told him anything that he wants or would like I will send him with our united love to you.

From your affectionate Cousin,
Morley Browne

November 27, 1918

Anglo American Hospital
A.P.O. 538
British E. F.
France

Dear Uncle Tell,

    I've been wanting to write you ever since I received your letter way back in the States but - as father would say - I've been too busy dying for my country.

    We certainly had about as much war as any soldiers ever had in so short a time. We were on four fronts - two to hold and two to drive.

    I had many narrow escapes, so miraculous in fact that I thought I had a charmed life until while crossing a little river in Belgium November 2nd (about the size of Chickimaugua) - than deep. I was hit by a piece of shell in the left leg. That was early in the afternoon, then about dark I was hit in the right foot. I got to 1st aid station next morning and then on back.

    They thought at first they could save my foot but it was torn up pretty bad and became so poisoned they had to amputate leaving only my heel.

    The pain is intense but I am getting along all right & my right leg is about well.

    I am in a good hospital & I got good treatment but I'm very lonesome.

    Please write me as soon and as often as you can.

    The doctor says I will probably be up by Christmas & able to go home by Feb. 1st.

                With lots of love

                   Your nephew,

                     Alfred Barlow

The Stars and Stripes, France, November 29, 1918

BASE PORTS MADE READY FOR YANKS HEADED WESTWARD

S.O.S. Dolling Up Brest, St. Nazaire, Bordeau for Exodus

NEW OUTFITS TO EVERYONE

Class B, C and D Men to Depart in Casual Companies Bound for Home Districts

-----

Preparations for the reception of members of the A.E.F. returning homeward are being pushed by the various departments of the Service of Supply at the three base ports of Brest, St. Nazaire and Bordeaux, and in a few weeks everything will be organized to care for troops as fast as they are ordered home.

Commanding officers of the different services involved have visited these ports during the past week and gone over the plans for the returning soldiers of the A.E.F. in detail. Great stocks of clothing and equipment are being massed there, so that every last doughboy will be completely outfitted and equipped when he starts off on the voyage for the old home town. The forgotten individual clothing and equipment slips will be resurrected there and one complete outfit charged to each soldier. The old stuff about "lost in action" won't go if he is shy anything when he gets back to the States. The price of the missing articles will be deducted on his final statement.

Those Best Camps Again

Existing rest camps at these base ports are being renovated and refurbished to receive the homegoing business this winter and spring, and other camps in the process of construction are being rapidly pushed forward to construction. Every effort will be made to avoid overcrowding and discomfort. One camp that was originally designed to hold about 80,000 men will be used by 55,000 men instead.

At present the embarkation ports are caring for wounded officers and men who can be safely transported as well as those of B, C and D classes. All C class officers and soldiers now on duty in the S.O.S. and B class officers and soldiers who will require at least two months for restoration to class A will be returned to the United States as rapidly as they can be relieved without serious detriment or handicap to the service, and be replaced, where needed, by men of class A.

Casual companies are being organized at the First Dept Division at St. Aigman, at the base depot at Blois and at the rest camps at the base ports, consisting of two officers and 150 men, with necessary medical attendants and supplies. Embarkation instructions direct that every casual company be deloused at the point of organization and each soldier provided with a neat and well fitting uniform and serviceable equipment.

No Rifles for Casuals

Rifles, bayonets and pistols will not be carried, but every soldier will carry the rest of his ordnance property, three blankets, shelter tent half, change of underclothing and a complete toilet kit among other things. Casuals will be assigned as far as practicable to companies according to the geographical area or district from which they were recruited according to the following grouping of States:

District No. 1--New England, New York.

District No. 2--Pennsylvania, New Jersey, Delaware, Maryland, District of Columbia, West Virginia, Virginia, North Carolina.

District No. 3--Ohio, Indiana, Illinois, Wisconsin, Michigan, Kentucky.

District No. 4--Tennessee, Mississippi, Alabama, South Carolina, Georgia, Florida.

District No. 5--Minnesota, Kansas, Iowa, Nebraska, Missouri.

District No. 6--Oklahoma, Arkansas, Louisiana, Texas.

District No. 7--North Dakota, South Dakota, Montana, Wyoming, Idaho, Washington, Oregon.

District No. 8--California, Nevada, Utah, Arizona, Colorado, New Mexico.

Marines Going, Too

Each casual company will be designated as going to the depot or camp where organized and also according to grouping by district, as "Blois Casual Company No. 301 (District No. 1)." Officers and soldiers returning to the United States as casuals will be sent to depots or rest camps and thence to ports of embarkation as follows:

Advance and Intermediate Sections to 1st Depot Division at St. Aignan-Noyers, thence to St. Nazaire; Paris District to Blois, thence to Brest; Base Sections Nos. 4 and 5 to Brest; Base Section No. 1 to St. Nazaire for organization, equipment and shipment; Base sections Nos. 2, 6 and 7 to Bordeaux. Special arrangements will be made to care for Base Section No. 8. Men in Base Section No. 3 will be sent home through English ports.

Marines in B and C classes will be organized into provisional companies composed entirely of officers and soldiers of the Marine Corps, and no attempt will be made to segregate them according to the district where they were recruited.

Pay for Every Soldier

While the return home will be a happy one, it will still be the same old Army game aboard the transports, as the opening paragraph of embarkation instructions No. 2 issued by Major-Gen. Harboard, Commanding General of the S.O.S. will convey:

"In the case of units and casuals that do not appear to be properly disciplined, all available time preceding embarkation will be devoted to intensive disciplinary training. It must be borne in mind that the reputation of the A.E.F. will to a large extent depend upon the physical and mental condition in which the troops reach home."

The commanding general at each jumping off place for the A.E.F. has been directed to see that every enlisted man is paid before he embarks. Organizations will receive the pay due them on the rolls. Casuals will be paid on detachment rolls or partially paid on their paybooks, service records or supplementary service records. Arrangements have been had to change French and English money into American money or checks.

Officers of the Regular Army will be retained in France in preference to others to the fullest extent to which their services can be utilized. Until the facilities at the base ports have been organized to handle large movements of troops, the following policy will be in force:

Each ship will be filled as completely as possible with the sick, wounded and convalescent, as much troop space as possible being utilized with men requiring no special treatment for who those accommodations are suitable. The remainder of the troop space will be utilized by such casual and other units as may be gotten to the ports and made ready for embarkation, reserving sufficient officer accommodations for the necessary number of officers to accompany those units.

Staterooms for Wounded

As the Medical Department has at all base ports more than enough sick and wounded to occupy all stateroom accommodations, the minimum number of casual officers should be returned to the United States, at least with the first shipments. Certain cargo ships have limited passenger accommodations will be utilized for the return of casual officers, civilian personnel and small organizations, for which the accommodations are suitable. A reservoir of casual officers will be maintained at ports for duty with causal organizations.

Commanding officers of organizations returning home will be held responsible that records of both officers and soldiers under his command are complete. In the case of officers, the records will consist of the qualification record card, securely wrapped and sealed, and if a captain or lower grade, the officer's record book. Each soldier will be accompanied by his qualification card, service record, pay card, pay record book and individual equipment record.

Commissioned and enlisted personnel of the Air Service and of the staff departments and technical services directly under the Service of Supply may be returned to the United States if in the opinion of the chief of the service concerned such personnel can be spared from their present duties in the A.E.F. The order making such action possible does not include commissioned and enlisted personnel temporarily assigned to the S.O.S. for labor, guard or other duty.

December 2, 1918

Anglo-American Hospital

Use this address

A.P.O.
538British E. F.
France

Dear Mamma,

My pain is not now so intense. The dressing do not hurt so much. The doctor says I am getting along fine. My temperature remains constant. Soon after

Christmas I expect to be transferred to London. I will probably remain there until I am able to go home. While I am confined to my bed I might as well be here as anywhere else as this is one of the best hospitals anywhere. The food is excellent. We have breakfast, luncheon, tea and dinner. I should like to see London & Paris while I am here.

Just received a fine letter from Cousin Morley. He is coming to see me if possible. He said he had just written to you and to Aunt Mattie.

I do not need anything but I would like to hear from you. My mail will be forwarded from the company but it takes a long time. Is Grandma with you. Give her my love.

Lots of love to you

Alfred.

OK A M Barlow 1st Lt U.S. Inf.

Publication Undetermined, Sunday, March 4, 1928

FINDER OF BILLETS ALSO SAVED HEADS

Holder of Cross for River Work Still Counsels Wounded Vets.

EDITOR'S NOTE--What has become of the men who served with unusual gallantry in the World War? Ten years have passed since they laid down their arms and entered into that trying period of readjustment. This is the fifteenth of a series of stories of the deeds of men of Great Cleveland and northern Ohio who dragged muddy boots along the road that led to the great red dawn.

BY ROELIF LOVELAND.

"Bon jour," said First Lieut. Alfred M. Barlow, casually enough, when his outfit landed in France to attend the big show. "Combien des kilometers au Pontenazen? Sept? Merci."

"Seven kilometers to the Pontenazen barracks," Barlow announced.

"Excelsior," said the major in command of the Third Battalion, 148th Infantry, 37th Division--"he can talk it"--and he made Barlow billeting officer.

The price was standardized. The citizens of France got 10 centimes a day for every horse billeted on their property, providing said horse was provided with a manger. The price, without a manger, was five centimes. For every enlisted man enjoying the comfort of the lofts of their barns they got 10 centimes. Rooms for officers brought a franc--and the officer was supposed to pay another franc for having his bed made and the room swept.

And after the deal was closed Lieut. Barlow attacked the general topography to the main street with shovels and civic ferocity--but this did not detract one sou from the amount due, and was, in fact, looked upon as a decided waste of time and energy by the natives. They never had found it necessary, or even advisable to do what the Americans were doing.

The outfit moved up to the Baccarat Sector. Lieut. Barlow went out to look for billets. Yes, the French people of the town would be happy to provide rooms for officers--but they just didn't have room for enlisted men. They were sorry.

Memories of Marines.

"Hell," said Lieut. Barlow after he had inspected the town. "There's plenty of room. Wonder what's wrong." And he went out sleuthing for information. Finally someone told him that some of the marines had been billeted in the town--and that they had become very, very drunk.

Lieut. Barlow went to the center of the town, hopped up on the watering trough and made a speech. He waved his arms, intoned the Marseilles, and assured the wondering citizens that the men who were coming in were not Marines, but a regiment of the Guards, who never got drunk. If they did, the were socked into the calaboose pronto--but they never did. "Regiment des guardes" sounded good to the citizens, and they discovered it would be possible to make room.

The 148th started action in the Argonne. Lieut. Barlow, a young farmer from Gallipolis, O, never had heard of the Argonne, or yet Verdun. Yet, here he was with orders to lead his platoon up a certain dark road at 11 p. m. to face the north in line of combat groups and wait further orders. * * * "No one told us where we were, but I imagined up ahead I could see the first line trenches, thinly lined by French. Suddenly shells seemed to crash all around us--and we waited to get blown to bits. When day broke we saw that we were up around our own naval guns which had been hurling shells into German territory."

Jack Rabbit Starts Rumpus.

Later, in the first day of its advance at the Argonne, Company L was moving along to the left of Montfaucon in two waves. Suddenly a big jack rabbit hopped out of the underbrush, and the outfit started banging. Those in the second wave had jumpy nerves, and fired too, forgetting that they might hit their own men in front of them. Barlow blew his whistle and firing ceased before anyone, including the jack rabbit, got hurt.

But the war became more grim when they started up a hill. Machine guns spat down at them. They flopped and waited. That night German raiders came over and stumbled into an American with a chauchet. He let 'em have it. Next morning they found a German lieutenant with a dozen holes in his body. The only way they could explain the fact that the chauchet hit anything was that it was shooting at very close range. When they advanced in the morning under cover of fog, the found the pill box deserted. When they went into the Argonne, Company L had 170 men. When they came out there were 70, and Lieut. Barlow was the only officer left.

They proceeded to St. Mihiel and lay in the mud. Lieut. Barlow was very miserable for a time because the company pay roll had been sent to him and there were few men left to pay. He wore a money belt stuffed with 1,000 franc notes and spent most of his time mentally subtracting $3,000 (the approximate amount on him) from $10,000, his insurance policy.

Thence to Belgium. They rested first at "Dirty Bucket Camp," a British institution famous for the size of its rats. * * * "Speaking conservatively, they were twice as large as any rat I ever saw in the Unites States--and when I'm an old man I suppose I will imagine they were the size of sheep.

On Nov. 2, 1918, the Third Battalion of the 148th was hot on the trail of the Germans who had taken up position on the opposite side of the Scheldt Canal, which ran swift and deep with water which had been diverted from the Escaut River. Battalion scouts felled a tree, wired it across the stream, stretched a wire hand rail and the battalion started over the next morning. A German plane spotted the bridge and German artillery opened up.

Barlow had just crossed with twelve men about 1:30 p. m., four hours after K company, the first to cross, had established a line on the other side. A shell fragment snapped the wire hand rail. Barlow went to fix it. The shells were coming over steadily now. One dropped near him and a jagged piece of steel buried itself in his left leg. He sat there by the wire rail, unable to walk, and urged another man to fix the wire. By this time the shelling was terrible. Barlow ordered the crossing stopped until dusk to prevent further slaughter and sent back word of his action to battalion headquarters.

At 5 p. m. another piece of shrapnel tore into his right foot. He kept his post and organized the crossing. The dead were buried in the river to prevent needless strain on the morale of troops coming up. The river was swift--and deep.

He stationed a man on the bluff whence troops were arriving to caution them to crawl, as they were easy marks for the German gunners. He stationed a corporal and three men at his end of the bridge to pull out of the canal such as fell from the slippery makeshift bridge. Night came and still they came over. Barlow saw them coming over the bluff silhouetted against a burning town.

"Down," he shouted, sitting there by the end of the bridge with two useless legs, faint with pain and loss of blood. By 3 a. m. the headquarters was established. The men were over and at 5 the next morning a runner from headquarters brought word that the engineers had put over a pontoon bridge farther down. Lieut. Barlow sat on his cane and two men carried him back.

He was awarded the Distinguished Service Cross and the Croix de Guerre for that day's work. Although suffering from a painful shrapnel wound in the leg, he led his company, with excellent leadership and command, ever the river, and not until he had received wounds in both legs would he give his consent to be taken to a dressing station.

His left leg healed. His right leg turned green. Infection had started while he sat there warning his men coming over the hill. They took off his foot, first. Then they whittled eight inches off his leg at intervals. Thirteen operations. He left his last hospital March, 1925.

Alfred M. Barlow, regional attorney for the United States Veterans' Bureau, Hanna Building Annex, twice prosecuting attorney of Gallia County, O, explained that his sires had always answered the call to arms.

"And you figured you had to maintain the tradition?"

The man who swapped his leg for a D.S.C. nodded.

FLINT BROWNE, F.S.I., F.C.I.S.,
LICENTIATE, R.I.B.A.
30 Watling Street,
ARCHITECT & SURVEYOR.
TELEPHONE
CITY 2952.
London, E.C.4.

4th Dec. 1918

Dear Eva,

I was very sorry to hear your son is wounded and hope it may not be so serious as it was thought at first to be; If he comes to England I shall be pleased to see him and hope he will let me have his address as soon as he arrives.

I was pleased to receive your letter. What a good thing that horrid war is over; No doubt you know that Morley has lost a son in it.

With kind regards,

> *I remain,*
> *yours truly,*
> *Flint Browne*

                    Headquarters 37th Division,
                    A.P.O. 763, American E. E.,
                         18 December, 1918.

Special Orders,   )
)
)

        The following General Order of General
Degoutte, Commanding the French Army in Belgium,
is published for the information of this command:-

"11th December, 1918.

                VI ARMY FRENCH
GENERAL ORDER NO. 31.

In addressing myself to the Divisions of the United States of America, who had covered themselves with glory in the Chateau-Thierry Offensive, I said that orders given by the Chief were always carried out, in spite of the difficulties and the sacrifices necessary to win.

In the 37th and 91st Divisions U.S., I found the same spirit of duty and the willing submission to discipline which makes gallant soldiers and victorious armies.

The enemy was to hold the heights between the Lys and the Escaut "to the death". American Troops of these Divisions, acting in concert with the French Division of the Group of Armies of Flanders, broke through the enemy on the 31st of October, 1918, and after severe fighting, threw him across the Escault.

Then attempting an operation of war of unheard of audacity, the American units crossed the overflooded Escaut, under fire of the enemy and maintained themselves on the opposite bank of the river in spite of his counter attacks.

Glory to such troops and their chiefs. They have valiantly contributed to the liberation of a part of Belgium territory and to final victory.

Their great nation may be proud of them.

The General Commanding the Army,

Degoutte".

By command of Major General Farnsworth:

Official: Dana T. Merrill,
                                        Colonel, General Staff
                                             Chief of Staff.

R. E. Fraile,
Adjutant General,
Division Adjutant.

ON ACTIVE SERVICE
WITH
American EXPEDITIONARY FORCES.

December 22 1918
American Base Hospital No. 29
St. Ann's Rd.
Tottenham N15
London

Dear Cousin Morley.
    I arrived here last night. My foot is coming fine although I felt a bit seedy after the trip will be delighted to see you whenever you can come to London.
    With the best of wishes for a merry Christmas and a most happy and prosperous new year. With love to all.
                    Your cousin,
                    Alfred M. Barlow

Hill House Farm
Wadhurst

Dec 28 18

Dear Eva

I received your letter this afternoon and I received one from Alfred this morning and I have replied to his and have made an arrangement to see him in London at the Hospital on Monday. I have enclosed his letter for you with his address as well for you to know that he is progressing & getting on so nicely -- his case being a surgical case he will get every kindness and attention and if it is possible for him to come to us - when able we will look after him - and he will not want for anything. As I mentioned I asked Nurse Ramsden to call and see him at Boulogne but the Hospital where he was is at Wimereux about 4 miles from Boulogne & being in route for Rouen she had not time to go. But now he is in London I can see him. I told you I wrote the American Embassy but they could not give me a permit. So I wrote the British Passport & I had their reply that I should have to get a Permit from the Medical Office in France but that does not matter now he is in England. After I have seen him I will write you at once & tell you all & what arrangements I make. I will close so that his letter gets off by next mail with our love to you also from your affectionate Cousin

Morley Browne

POST OFFICE TELEGRAPHS

[stamped: 30 Dec 18]

Morley Browne
Hill House Farm Woodlawn

At American Hospital ninetyeight Lancaster Gate expect to go to America January fourth

Barlow

Hill House Farms

Wadhurst

Dec 31st 1918

Dear Eva

    My daughter Dorothy Eva and myself went up to the American Hospital at Tottenham yesterday to see Alfred but found when we arrived that they had removed him from the North of London to the West so we journeyed on to the West and found him at the present address

> *American Hospital*
> *98 Lancaster Gate*
> *London   W*

He was delighted to see us although it was 5 o'clock in the afternoon before we could get there and after the time for visiting. But when the matron found we had been travelling all day, they permitted us to see him. Eva he is looking very bright but unable of course to get about yet & looked very delicate after having passed through so much suffering. But my opinion is that he is gradually getting better. The place where he is is a beautiful home and every care and attention is given to him and his foot is healing up. But as he said they have a small tube inserted in the wound & that has to be kept perfectly clean & clear of puss. But when they see to it or the wound gathers his temperature goes up but yesterday his temperature was normal. He expects to leave England for America on Jan. 4th. I enclose for the telegram he sent me after I had started to see him. You certainly have no cause to feel uneasy about him as every thing that is possible to be done is being done for him but it will take some months before he will be quite well. Uncle Flint has been to see him & I can telephone to him from my home so I shall find out at once if he is alright. Alfred mentioned that your letters had not come to hand so I am sending the ones you sent me for him to see. I hope he may be able to come & stay with us if he remains in England which I am very doubtful about but we will do all we can. Now I must close so that you can get this as quickly as possible. With our love to you also

    from your affectionate Cousin

    Morley Brown

We were so please to see him & hope we shall have him with us before he returns. Alfred says he has not seen any thing of England or France but only the Battle Fields.

Gallipolis Daily Tribune, January 8, 1919.

LIEUT. BARLOW WAS DECORATED FOR BRAVERY IN BATTLE.

Word has been received from the hospital at Bologne that the surgeons had to amputate Lieut. Alfred M. Barlow's foot at the ankle, and the other foot is badly crippled.

A soldier in France says no braver man ever led his men in battle. He was in command of Company L, 148th Infantry, when he was wounded. He was leading his men in one of the worst artillery barrages of the war.

Hill House Farms

Wadhurst

Jan. 9th 1919

Dear Cousin Eva -

Your welcome letter I received today with enclosures for Dear Alfred, but, as I wrote you and I suppose our letters have crossed, Alfred returned to US on Jan. 1st. It was very fortunate for me that I was able to get away or I should have missed seeing him. I hope by now that you have news of him. I suppose they would all go to New York, we all of us shall be very anxious to know how he is progressing. I am very sorry he could not come and stay with us at my home, but under all circumstances it is the wisest plan to get him well first and then pay visits afterwards. Well Cousin Eva I must say I feel very proud of your Son although we could not have him now possible later on we may again have the pleasure. I enclose your letter you sent and I hope your Mamma's cold is better. We all of us have colds. So much pain. The Farm is always well.

With our love
Your affectionate Cousin

Morley Browne

Chapter Twelve

738 Ten Eyck St.
Brooklyn, NY
Jan 19, 1919

Dear Mrs. Barlow,
    The enclosed paper was thrown to me, from the boat on which this "War Hero" arrived. He is well and happy and will write to you as soon as he reaches camp.
    I am a member of the Mayor's Receiving Committee of New York and we meet all the incoming transports, ask Alfred about them.
    Wishing him the best of luck.

                              Anna Graife

[enclosed:]

Mrs. Eva Barlow

    1066 First Ave.

       Gallipolis O.

Arrived in New York today. Wire Grace to look me up.

           Alfred.

Gallipolis Daily Tribune, January 20, 1919
GALLIPOLIS OFFICER

Arrives With Wounded at New York Sunday.

New York, Jan. 19--Four steamships their decks crowded with American fighting me, hundreds of whom gazed upon the home shores from cots and convalescent chairs, passed the Statue of Liberty today amid a din from harbor craft bringing home 4,992 heroes.

The climax of the demonstration came when the hospital ship Comfort, with 271 sick and wounded entered the upper bay and was hailed by cheers from the throngs on shore and the strains of "Home Sweet Home" from a band on board a vessel carrying Mayor Hylan's committee of welcome. As the Comfort came abreast the Statue of Liberty a great shout arose from her decks, crowded to the rails with soldiers in bandages, supported by crutches and canes or seated in easy chairs. Through the portholes of the hospital ship glimpses were caught of the more seriously wounded.

Germany was in dire straits when the war ended, according to Captain Robert W. Hudgens of Laurens, S.C., who arrived on the Comfort. He was attached to the 118th infantry, 30th division, and when the town Bellecourt was captured, the Captain said the Americans found the bodies of German soldiers being prepared to be rendered into fats. A complete rendering plant was found in a tunnel beside the Bellecourt canal, Captain Hudgens said.

Gallipolis, O. Jan 19, 1919.

Dear Friend Barlow: --

Your splendid letter of Dec 18 received a few days since, and you have doubtless received my other letter ere this. I wrote it before I heard of your misfortune; so of course, you can not learn the things we inquired about; but we have learned where he was buried and about all the essential things. I am enclosing Luther Broyles's letter taken from the Bulletin, which will tell you about our boys from here more than I can. Leo Carter has returned to Camp Sherman, waiting for discharge, and if he and Ben were sent to same hospital he <u>may</u> give us more particulars. I congratulate you on your admirable spirit of resignation to your misfortune, for of such are true soldiers made. Your fine tribute to Ben would read like flattery if we did not know his noble spirit so well; and while we are bowed with grief we are filled with pride over his pure unselfish character. He never in his life tried to deceive us, much less tell us an untruth.

Gallia County will never blush for the record of old original Co F, no matter to what units you were attached, and woe to the future of any country that can forget the sacrifices you boys have made. God bless you one and all.

Memorial services will be held tonight at the Presbyterian church for Minturush Hall who died of fever soon after landing over there. There will likely be some kind of public services for all the boys some time probably when most of the boys return. Some talk of the 37th Div. being home by March.

Six of our letters to Ben have been returned; one sent Aug 25, balance up to Sept 16 and all rest of September, October, November and possibly some August letters unaccounted for; but we hope he received the August letters and his pay for July, August and September so the poor boy could have the use of them while he lived.

Your mail service and pay system looks to us here like a huge failure. As I have no news which you are not already familiar with I will close.

The family joins us in best wishes for your health and early return. As ever

Your friend

A J Starmont

Ben Starmont was one of the old Company F soldiers to die in the final days of the war. This letter was probably returned to A.J. Starmont, who then gave it to Eva Barlow.

Saturday Jan. 1919
Disembarkation Hospital #,
Hoboken N.J.

Dear Mamma and Grandma,

I've just been down stairs on my wheel chair and on coming back found letters from you, Aunt Mattie & Alice, Cousin Nellie Henking & Grace also awaiting me.

Grace enclosed the clipping from the Times. It was of course greatly exaggerated. It was mightily fine of Capt. Jones to write of me.

Grace and the Machelhenies bring me more magazines than I can read and more candy than I can eat.

My foot gives me very little pain now. I am still too weak to walk much on crutches but my strength is growing daily. I am sitting up writing now. Caroline M said she was going to write to you. She told me about her Aunt Frankie.

I am enclosing a clipping from today's N.Y. Tribune which is the first sure news I have had of the D.S.C.

I read a good deal and go to a show down stairs in my wheel chair in the evening.

I was feeling seedy in London. They opened my foot on the boat and got out about a half a cup of puss and since I've been feeling much better ever since.

What is this I hear about Charley Summers? I hope he gets 10 years in the Ohio Penitentiary. Keep still about it. Have you any money in his Banking & Loan? If so get it out.

Put whatever I send in the Ohio Valley Bank savings dept.

Lots of love,

Alfred.

Gallipolis Daily Tribune, January 24, 1919

LIEUT. BARLOW IN HOBOKEN

Mrs. Eva Barlow received a wire from her son Lieut. Alfred Barlow who is now in embarkation hospital No. 1 at Hoboken expecting to remain there ten days and will then be sent to camp Sherman. He says he has seen several persons residing in New York that are well known here.

Office of the Commanding Officer
Detachment of Patients

WALTER REED GENERAL HOSPITAL
Takoma Park, D.C.

February 1, 1919.

Mrs. Eva Barlow
1066- 1st. St. Ave.,
Gallipolis, Ohio.

Dear Madam:-

I beg to report that your son, 1st. Lieut. Alfred M. Barlow was recently admitted as a patient to this hospital having returned from service overseas.

Your son is not seriously ill and his general condition is good but further hospital treatment is necessary to determine the proper disposition in his case.

Yours truly,
A. Ragan
Lieut. Colonel, USA, Retired
Commanding Det. of Patients.

W/pw

Publication and Date Unknown
LIEUT. BARLOW LOSES ONE LEG

The Gallipolis Daily Tribune of Saturday contains an announcement of an operation for the removal of a leg, upon Lieut. Alfred Barlow, who has been previously mentioned in this paper as having been awarded the medal for distinguished service, he having won it by extraordinary heroism in Belgium while heading his company after he was wounded. The Ohio paper shows a picture of Col. Glennan pinning the service cross on the soldier at Washington, D.C.

The distinguished soldier is a nephew of B.S., J.C. and Tel Barlow, who are all so well known in this city.

Gallipolis Daily Tribune, February 10, 1919
Lieut. Alfred Barlow to Undergo Second Operation

Lieut. Alfred Barlow expects to have to undergo another operation soon for the removal of his leg to about nine inches below the knew, the former operation where the greater part of his foot was taken off, not being successful and he has not been getting along as was hoped for.

He will come home though before the operation.

Feb. 15 1919

Dear Mamma & Grandma,

I just received your letter of February 12. I will try to answer it in order.

If my foot were reamputated now it would take six months more to get well. If they let this heal up and I get so I can walk around for a month or two and get my system in good condition it won't take more than a month. I've been in bed a long time you see and my recovery would be much more rapid if I get out and get some exercise first. Then too my wound is still infected and they want my blood to be in good condition so my next wound will not be infected. I will be home for a month or two first.

I can go out and they encourage us to as much as possible. The only trouble is that I soon get tired walking on crutches.

I was down town to church last Sunday then in the afternoon to the House & Senate memorial service for President Roosevelt. Then to dinner with Congressman Switzer. Tomorrow I shall go to church then to dinner with some Parkersburg girls who are doing war work here next Tuesday Miss Maysus Congressman Mason's daughter who Grace wrote to about me invited me to the Congress Hotel for dinner and to watch the dance afterwards so you can see I am not dead by a long shot. My foot still hurts some - pretty badly also at times - but they say it always will. Some peoples toes cramp twenty years after their limbs have been amputated.

I am sorry to hear of Uncle Alfred's wife's illness if you want to go, go by all means if you want a hundred dollars let me know and I will send you a check.

Thanks for the clippings. I am enclosing them in the letter.

No I do not get the Tribune. I received yesterday several letters from France from you, Aunt Mattie, Mrs. Morgan and Judith.

I have just been looking over my unanswered letters (which are many) and I found one from you dated Feb. 7th which I had not seen before. I don't know how I over looked it.

I have still my glasses. I cannot read without them. Before I leave I shall have my eyes tested again as now I can get it done for nothing.

Is Tell going to remain in town long? I wrote him from France. Did he get it? I am glad you rented the farm. I want to have it put in my self next year.

Tuesday Morning

While I was away Sunday Mr & Mrs Poulchet & Miss Meadham & Miss Mills were here. Sorry I missed them. I received a note from your friend Miss Allen I will write her today. This p.m. there is a special theater down town and people are coming after us in autos. Then to this Mason's. Tomorrow night Ernie Stower's husband is coming in an auto to take me to dinner.

Don't worry about me I expect to be hone about April 1st for my leave.

Lots & lots of love,

Alfred

P.S. Just received one letter from you from Hoboken

Knights of Columbus
WAR ACTIVITIES
Camp...Walter Reed Hospital'Washington.D.C.

March,5th   19~~18~~,9,

Dear Mamma and Grandma,
        This is the first letter I have ever written
on my tipewriter,This is the first day I have had
it , I received your letter enclosing the one from
Montgomery. The other day I received thirty-five
from France:about eight of them were from you,
I owe letters to every one for I as ever find it
verry hard to write letters.
            This machine cost me forty dollars and
fifty cents($40.50) If I had not bought it at an
army commissary it would have cost fifty dollars
$(50.) , I expect to use it in school next year.
        I am still in bed but my foot does not hurt
much now, I will be able to be out in a few days.
        I understand what you mean about Mrs. A.
Don't worry your darling boy is no infant.
The Masons have certainly been fine to me. Miss
Mason has been out several times to see me and
brought me candy. Congress is over now so they
are going to New York and then to Chicago. I hope
to see them when they come back next term.

Wednesday.

Yesterday was rainy and miserable,but today is clear and beautiful . I have just had my first lesson. Iknow I shall enjoy it especially after I become a little more accustomed to it and am able to write more rapidly.

Go ahead and sell the farm. I imagine it will always be a bother to us anyway. We can make more on our money Ihave no doubt.

I expect to receive my D.S.C. this week.

> Lots of love,

> *Alfred.*

Gallipolis Daily Tribune, March 20, 1919

LIEUT. BARLOW RECEIVED DECORATION

Gallipolis Soldier Awarded the Distinguished Service Cross

A letter received from Miss Carrie Needham of Washington by Mrs. J. E. Halliday, contains the welcome news that Lieut. Alfred Barlow, now in a Washington hospital with wounds received in battle in France last summer, has received the Distinguished Service Cross for heroism in the face of the enemy.

Lieut. Barlow was a gallant soldier of whom Gallipolis is justly proud, the first and only one to be decorated, so far as we know. He is a lineal descendant of Joel Barlow, the early American poet and ambassador to France who assisted in the organization of the colony that started the existence of Gallipolis as a community.

WAR DEPARTMENT,
Washington, March 11, 1919.
GENERAL ORDERS,)
    NO. 37.   )

E X T R A C T

     vi--AWARDS OF DISTINGUISHED-SERVICE CROSS.-
- By direction of the President, under the
provisions of the act of Congress approved July 9,
1918 (Bul. No. 43, W.D., 1918), the distinguished-
service cross was awarded by the Commanding
General, American Expeditionary Forces, for
extraordinary heroism in action in Europe, to the
following-named officers and enlisted men of the
American Expeditionary forces and of the allied
armies:
                 ***   ***   ***   ***
     ALFRED M. BARLOW, first lieutenant, Company
L, 148th Infantry. For extraordinary heroism in
action near Heurne, Belgium, November 3, 1918.
Although suffering from a painful shrapnel wound
in the leg, he led his company, with excellent
leadership and command, over the river, and not
until he had received wounds in both legs would he
give is consent to be taken to a dressing station.
                 ***   ***   ***   ***
     BY ORDER OF THE SECRETARY OF WAR:

                         FRANK McINTYRE,
              Major General, Acting Chief of
Staff.
     OFFICIAL:
     P. C. HARRIS,
     The Adjutant General.

Gallipolis Daily Tribune, April 5, 1919

Lieut. Barlow Operated On.

Lieut. Alfred Barlow underwent the operation for the removal of his leg at Walter Reed hospital last Saturday and it is good news to friends here to learn he stood the operation well and will soon be able to come home.

I, Alfred M. Barlow, C-364689, give the following as summary of medical record:

I was in command of Company L, 148th Infantry and was ordered to establish a bridge head across the Scheldt Canal at Heurne, Belgium November 2, 1918; got across with about a dozen men by 1: 30 P.M. At that time I was hit by small piece of high explosive in left leg; artillery fire was so intense I held up advance until 6:00 P.M. when crossing could be made under cover of darkness. In the meantime at 5:00 P.M. was hit by high explosive fragment in right foot. About five companies crossed Canal by 3:30 A.M. November 3rd. Reached battalion dressing station back on American side of Canal at six o'clock. Had clean bandage put on wounds and left in ambulance; reached Ambulance Dressing Station at 12:00 noon November 3rd. They were too busy to operate; they had too many bad cases. Left early the next morning and reached Evacuation Hospital #5 about 10:00 o'clock P.M.; was operated on immediately for removal of shell fragments. Left at six o'clock A.M. next morning, November 5th; arrived at British Red Cross #5, A.O.O. S.38, Wiemereaux, Bologne Base, France November 6th at 3:00 A.M. Bone fragments and pus removed November 9th. Sims operation November 16th. Was in this hospital until the Saturday before Christmas (I do not

remember the date). During this time had four
operations for removal of pus and to establish
drainage. Then went to Tottenham Hospital, Queen
Anne's Road, London; there until after Christmas;
December 26th transferred to American Women's Club
Hospital at Lancaster Gate, Hyde Park

        Was there a week or ten days and then
transferred to Danforth Hospital near London. Was
there a few days and then was sent to Plymouth,
where I embarked for New York on Hospital Ship
"Mercy". Was operated on to establish drainage
and for removal of pus when two days out. Put
in at Madiera Island to coal because of storm.
Arrived in New York about January 20, 1919; was
taken to Embarkation Hospital #1, St. Marys,
Hoboken, N.J. Was operated on shortly after
arrival for removal of pus and to establish
drainage.

        Left for Walter Reed Hospital, Washington,
D.C. January 29, 1919; had reamputation two weeks
before Easter; had neuroma removed in November
1919; was discharged February 28, 1920. Had
operation at Mount Carmel Hospital, Columbus, Ohio
June 1921. Had another operation for removal of
neuroma at same hospital in November 1921. Had
small pus pocket and nerve removed February 1922.
(I am not sure about the last two dates.)

Gallipolis Daily Tribune, Date As Yet Unknown
CO. F BOYS COMING HOME.

J. C. Butz received a telephone message Sunday from Lieut. Alfred
Barlow at Camp Sherman stating he and 21 others of old Co. F would be
discharged at noon today and wanted to come home.

Early this morning the following men left in cars to bring them in:
Paul Switzer, J.W. Miller, J.C. Butz, George Tabit and two cars sent by the Swanson-Swigert hardware firm.

Gallipolis Daily Tribune, April 21, 1919

GALLIPOLIS SOLDIER IS KILLED IN AN ACCIDENT SIX MILES FROM HOME

Dr. J. R. Rathburn of Russel received a telephone message last night from his brother at Gallipolis O., giving news of a serious accident which marred the homecoming of Company F boys from Gallipolis who were discharged yesterday at Camp Sherman at the same time the Co. I boys were released from service.

It seems that a number of patriotic citizens of Gallipolis took a number of automobiles to Camp Sherman and brought the boys home in a body.

In one of the machines, an Oldsmobile Eight, owned and driven by Warren Miller, well known produce dealer was Miller, Sergeant Albert Mays, several other privates and Lieut. Alfred Barlow, who is the real hero of Gallipolis in the present war having distinguished himself for gallantry in action, and sustaining wounds which resulted in the loss of one leg and serious injury to the other, for which he was awarded the distinguished service cross.

About six miles out of Gallipolis Miller's machine jumped the road and turned over, killing Sergeant Mays and breaking another soldier's jaw. The machine took fire and was completely destroyed. Miller, Lieut. Barlow and the other soldiers escaped with only slight injuries.

Strangely coincident with this fatal accident is the fact that about two years ago Mr. Miller's produce building collapsed and in the wreck Sergeant May's father was killed.

The accident will do doubt interest Company I boys as the victims probably were known to them. It was particularly pathetic for the reason that the dead soldier had survived all the arduous campaigns of the 37th division on the Flanders front, only to meet death six miles from the home he had not seen for nearly two years.

Gallipolis Daily Tribune, April 22, 1919.

ARRIVAL HOME MARRED BY TRAGEDY
Returning Gallipolis Soldiers in Fatal Motor Car Accident.
Sergt. Mayes Instantly Killed and Others Badly Hurt.

Dead:
Sergeant Alfred Mayes.
Injured:
First Lieut. Alfred Barlow.
Pvt. Earl Comley.
J. Warren Miller.

Returning in motor cars from Camp Sherman after gallant service in France, about twenty members of old Company F reached Gallipolis a little after six Monday evening--one dead and two injured, as the result of an automobile wreck, in which the driver and owner of the car, Mr. J. M. Miller, was also badly hurt.

In the many conflicting reports of the tragic accident there seems to be this much truth: The wrecked car, a fine 8-cylinder Oldsmobile, was approaching Gallipolis at a high rate of speed, preceding and followed by a number of other cars, all filled with soldiers and driven by men who had felt their business and driven to Chillicothe to get them home early.

At the railroad crossing beyond the Fox dairy the Miller car left the road, and turned over, head on, once or twice. At any rate it landed upside down. Its occupants suffered severely as follows:

Sergeant Alfred Mayes, a splendid specimen of physical manhood, was instantly killed, the whole top of his head being crushed in and both legs broken above the knees. He was one of the squad who personally accompanied the King of Belgium on his triumphal entry into Brussels after the Armistice.

Lieut. Barlow got two bad scalp wounds. He was the Distinguished Service Cross for gallantry, was severely wounded in battle, and lost a leg in the service. He was given first aid at the Holzer Hospital.

Pvt. Earl Comley had his jaw broken at the chin, hip bruised, and nose and hand cut. His jaw was wired together and other injuries dressed by Dr. Holzer.

Mr. J. W. Miller received a bad cut on the head, and the ligaments of his back were all torn loose. He was taken to BR. Bean's office and given immediate attention. Dr. Bean is as yet uncertain as to whether he received internal injuries.

The body of Sergeant Mayes was taken to the Hayward undertaking establishment on the fire wagon and prepared for burial.

News of the tragedy spread like wildfire over the city, and filled the public with deepest regret. That soldiers should have such a sad homecoming depressed the entire community. All sorts of wild stories as to the cause of the accident, and its results, gained currency. Those in the accident were so hurt and shocked that their ideas of it was hazy, while those coming behind the Miller car knew only what they saw. After the plunge they saw the car burst into flames, and arriving on the spot they pulled the body of Sergt. Mayes away from it. The car itself burned up, a total loss.

The burnt men were carefully and tenderly brought to the city as related above, and this (Tuesday) morning were all in much better condition. It is hoped by everybody that all the survivors will recover little the worse for their frightful experience.

Gallipolis Daily Tribune, April 24, 1919

Lieut. Barlow Addresses High School Students.

Lieut. Alfred Barlow, of whom Gallia county has every reason to be proud, told the students of the High School this afternoon his experience in the great war. It was highly entertaining from start to finish and given in an eloquent and forceful manner.

The lieutenant has endeared himself to all our loyal citizens.

A.D.
GRAND QUARTIER GENERAL
DES
ARMEES FRANCAISES DE L'EST
ETAT-MAJOR
BUREAU DU PERSONNEL
(DECORATIONS)
ORDRE No 13.092 "D." (EXTRAIT)

APRES APPROBATION DU GENERAL COMMANDANT EN CHEF LES FORCES EXPEDITIONNAIRES AMERICAINS EN FRANCE, LE MARECHAL DE FRANCE, COMMANDANT EN CHEF LES ARMEES FRANCAISES DE L'EST CITE A L'ORDRE DE L'ARMEE.

....

LIEUTENANT ALFRED M. BARLOW, COMMANDANT LA COMPAGNIE "L" DU 148 REGIMENT D'INFANTERIE :
"LE 2 NOVEMBRE 1918, A FAIT TRAVERSER L'ESCAULT A SA COMPAGNIE, A HEURNE (BELGIQUE). BLESSE A LA JAMBE PAR UP SCHRAPNELL, EST RESTE A LA TETE DE SA COMPAGNIE, JUSQU'A CE QUE BLESSE UNE DEUXIME FOIS AUX DEUX JAMBES, A ETE INCAPABLE DE SE MOUVIOR ET D'EXERCER SON COMMANDEMENT."

....

AU GRAND QUARTIER GENERAL, LE 25 JANVIER 1919

LE MARECHAL,
COMMANDANT EN CHEF LES ARMEES FRANCAISES DE L'EST
PETAIN
POUR EXTRAIT CONFORME:
LE LIEUTENANT-COLONEL,
CHEF DU BUREAU DU PERSONNEL,

Gallipolis Daily Tribune, May 12, 1919.
Get Croix de Guerre.

First Lieut. Alfred Barlow, recently decorated with the Distinguished Service Cross, has another honor, the French Croix de Guerre--a greatly coveted decoration.

Knights of Columbus
WAR ACTIVITIES
Walter Reid Hospital

May 20 1919

Dear Mamma & Grandma,

I had a fine time in Chicago and got here Saturday night with the Masons. I attended Uncle John's funeral. Was to Morley's for dinner.

I was measured for a leg yesterday & go again Wednesday.

When I get my leg I may get another leave.

The weather is fine.

I may be home in two weeks.

Lots of love,

Alfred

P.S. More next time.

Publication and Date Undetermined
TWO HEROES AT W.R. HOSPITAL AWARDED D.C.S.
New Commander Presents Honor Medals with Impressive Ceremony.
BOTH ARE LIEUTENANTS
"For extraordinary Bravery in Action," Says Pershing in Citation.

The presentation of the distinguished service cross comes to two officer-patients at the Walter Reed Hospital, Monday afternoon was attended by full military honors. This is the third occasion that the parade grounds of the institution have assembled therein the entire Medical Detachment, and swarms of interested spectators to witness the reward of bravery.

The post band played and the four medical companies were drawn up in company front as the new commanding officer of the hospital, Co. Glennan, with the Adjutant Capt. Master, as his assistant, stepped forward to pin the distinguished service cross on the broad chest of First Lieut. Alfred M. Barlow of Company L, 148th U.S. Infantry.

To state that the ceremony was an impressive one would be a very conservative remark, for with the bright sun, which had burst forth from its three days' hiding as if for the occasion, shining down in all his glory; the folds of "Old Glory" fluttering defiantly above, and the long rows of khaki, ever ready to protect it and the brave men who had risked their all for God and country awaiting their reward: the spectacle presented was one that will live forever in the minds of all who witnessed it.

The official government reported stating that the Commanding Officer of the American Expeditionary Forces had awarded the medal to Lieut. Barlow cited that he had earned it by "extraordinary heroism in action near Heurne, Belgium, on November 3, 1918, and although suffering from a painful shrapnel wound in the leg, Lieut. Barlow led his company, with excellent leadership and command over the river, and not until he had received wounds in both legs would he give his consent to be taken to a dressing station."

Chapter Thirteen

During the earlier part of convalescence, Skip involved himself with a campaign to grant National Guard officers the rights and benefits as Regular Army officers. The effort failed, getting inadequate support from Congress and none from the President. Skip would later say that he was "an officer and a gentleman nevertheless, Congress and the President notwithstanding."

Publication and Date Unknown

On Behalf of Soldier Boys.

In reading the Congressional Record we find a splendid sensible address in it made by Hon. William E. Mason of Illinois, and were surprised to find that he made allusion in applying his remarks. We reproduce the address in full:

Mr. Speaker, I have been deeply stirred by most eloquent remarks made by my colleagues on this Memorial Day. I know you will pardon me if to my mind there comes this thought--that the best way to honor the dead soldier is to protect the living, to take care of those who have been left to us, and those who are dependent upon the soldier who died. The pay envelope of soldiers will be much more useful to his family if it has in it some of the coin of the realm and it is not filled entirely with glory. It is a beautiful thing and a due and proper thing to place flowers upon the graves of our dead, but it is up to the Congress of the United States in the next few weeks to provide flour and bacon and bread for the living. I trust it will not be improper to suggest on this sacred day the high duty that lies at the door of this Chamber to equalize and make just laws for those soldiers who have come back, to bring those back home who ought to be home, to hurry the confirmation of the treaty of peace, that American soldiers may be brought back to American shores. In my city there are 600 women who have sons or husbands in Siberia. You can do no greater honor to the men who died for this country than to bring back those boys from the country to which they were not sent by order of the Congress of the United States.

One of my friends, Lieut. Alfred M. Barlow, who has just left the gallery, decorated by medals of honor for bravery, who lost a leg; under our present laws, although he was a farmer and can never work at it again--under the law of compensation fixed by Congress he will enjoy the magnificent income of $7.50 per month. He was a volunteer soldier. If a man in the Regular Army of the same rank, met with he same misfortune he would draw fifteen times that amount for life. Let us correct some of these things; let us pledge ourselves on this Decoration Day to satisfy the mothers of the boys who are buried over there. I know I realize the heroic desire of those who wish to educate the mothers that it is heroic to leave their sons' remains over there; but, Mr. Speaker, human nature is the same the world over. The mother's love wants her son's remains brought back. It lies at the door of this Chamber to see to it that it is done, and that the son of the poorest mother shall have the same chance, and the same opportunity, and the same honor, of being brought back by his government as the son of those more prosperous in life.

There are 10,000 questions pressing upon us now; and may I not ask in this one minute that is given to me that we pledge ourselves within the splendid thought of my colleague who has just taken his seat and forget partisanship, forget everything but the actual debt that we owe to the loved and to the dead, and that the highest honor we can pay to the soldiers who made the sacrifice is to deal justly and fairly with the old Grand Army of the Republic, the Spanish War veterans, and the soldiers of this war who are left living with us? [Applause]

RED CROSS CONVALESCENT HOUSE
WALTER REED HOSPITAL
WASHINGTON, D. C.

June 2, 1919

Dear Mamma & Grandma,

I was mighty glad to get the Tribune. Keep it up. It is terrifically hot here. Go to Columbus or anywhere else for I expect to be home in about two weeks. Yesterday and the day before I wore my new leg with two canes.

I asked you to send my right shoe for my new leg, but I found I had it here in my baggage. I am working hard down at Congress. We want to be retired on the same basis as that of the regular army.

If it goes thru I'll get $1500 a year. In any case I'll get a lot more than 7.50 per month. Use your money don't try to save. I'll have enough whatever happens so enjoy yourself now and fix up the house. Have it painted. All white would be fine. We could have it washed when it gets dusty.

The croix de guerre is for you to wear. Wear it.
I expect to get 2 or 3 months leave soon.

Lots of love,
Alfred.

State of Ohio
Executive Department
Columbus

July 15, 1919.

Lieutenant Alfred M. Barlow,
Gallipolis, Ohio.

My dear Lieutenant Barlow:

Your activity in behalf of the recognition of national army and national guard officers on the same basis as regular army officers has been brought to my attention. I will take this matter up as opportunity offers with those who are best in position to aid you. It seems to me there should be no trouble in getting the proper action.

With every good wish, I am,

Very truly yours,

[signature illegible]

The campaign for National Guard benefits led Skip to his decision to go to law school, so that he could better work for veterans' rights. Most of his law career would be spend with the Veteran's Administration, from its founding in 1926. In the meantime, however, his political activities occasionally bore strange fruit.

REPUBLICAN NATIONAL COMMITTEE
SUITE A-16-18 CONGRESS HOTEL
CHICAGO

July 26th, 1919.

Lieut. Alfred M. Barlow,
Gallipolis,
Ohio.

Dear Lieutenant:

Recalling your having told me that you were a socialist before the war, and had now become a firm believer in Republican principles, I thought that I might be able to obtain an agreeable appointment for you to disseminate your convictions among those who are still of your former belief.

I am writing now to ask your plans, and to ask how much salary you would require in addition to your expense to work as a field man in Ohio localities where socialism has taken the firmest root, for example, Toledo and Hamilton. I am doing this entirely at my suggestion and will be glad to communicate to the Ohio authorities your ideas on the matter.

Kindly write me immediately at the above address as I am hoping to be in Columbus for a conference Saturday, August 2nd.

      With best wishes, I am,
              Yours very truly,
                    Victor Heintz
VH-J

REPUBLICAN NATIONAL COMMITTEE
SUITE A-16-18 CONGRESS HOTEL
CHICAGO

                       July 29th, 1919.

Lieutenant Alfred M. Barlow,
Gallipolis,
Ohio.

Dear Lieutenant:
    I neglected to mark my last letter to you confidential, and it being the first letter I have written you on a political subject, I should have done so. Please understand that everything I write you hereafter regarding politics is strictly confidential, which means not only that they are not for publication, but are not to be shown even to your intimates. I know that you will well understand that this is essential and it probably was not necessary to call it to your attention.

      With best wishes, I remain,
              Very truly yours,
                    Victor Heintz
VH-J

For the present, I think it just as well for you to keep your Republican conversion under cover.

Skip's response to the letters isn't known. He did not, however, become an underground Republican operative.

Knights of Columbus
WAR ACTIVITIES

Sept 9 1919

Dear Mamma & All,

It is now 11:30 p.m. I just returned from down town. I was to have met Tish. Mills and Mable Thomas at the Union Station & to have taken them to Keith's. I arrived there just on time 8 p.m. but got quite a fall. I was all in for a while and when I was able to move I could not find them.

I had bought tickets so went with Congressman Juell of Chicago & his son.

My left thumb is much swollen and I am waiting for the surgeon & nurse on duty to come over & fix me up. It is not broken but is so swollen I can scarce move it.

My claim has been allowed so if you need any money <u>let me know</u>. I am intending to start a bank account here.

I expect to go to the commissary for your sugar tomorrow.

As soon as my thumb is well I expect to take type writing & stenography. I will start to law school Oct. 1st.

It is now twelve o'clock and the medical officer of the day has not been here yet-- He has been here and fixed me up. My left thumb was out of place and now in. It hurts a good deal but will be all right in a few days. My stump bled a little and he fixed it up too. It will be all right in a few days.

Loads & loads of love

Alfred.

THE OHIO NATIONAL GUARD

To all whom it may concern:

Know ye, that Alfred M. Barlow a Sergeant of Co. D of the Seventh Regiment of Infantry who was enlisted on the 15 day of June one thousand nine hundred and sixteen to serve 3 years is hereby Honorably Discharged from the Ohio National Guard by reason of muster out of company Par. 1. S.O. 256 p. b. A. G. O.

The said ALfred M. Barlow was born in Gallipolis in the State of Ohio and when enlisted was 25 years of age 6 feet - inches high, Fair complexion, Blue eyes, Brown hair, and by occupation a Farmer.

Given under my hand a Hdq. 7th Inf. vvv+ Lexington, Ohio this 25 day of December, in the year of our Lord one thousand nine hundred and nineteen

Tom O. Crossan

Colonel 7th Inf. Commanding.

Character

No objection to his reenlistment is known to exist

```
-----Excellent-----
```

Bennett

Russell

1st Lieut. Commanding Co. d 7th Inf.

ARMY OF THE UNITED STATES OF AMERICA
TO ALL WHO SHALL SEE THESE PRESENTS, GREETINGS:
THIS IS TO CERTIFY THAT

by direction of the President and under the provisions of section nine of the act of Congress, approved May eighteen, nineteen hundred and seventeen,

```
Alfred M. Barlow.
First Lieutenant, Infantry.
```

was honorably discharged from the military service in The United States

Army at Walter Reed General Hospital, Takoma Pk., D.C. on the Twenty-Eighth day of February, 1920.

> W K Bennett
> Major, Inf., U.S.A.
> Personnel Adj.

Lieutenant Barlow, though honorably discharged, took the phrase "no objection to his reenlistment is known to exist" literally and applied to the Officers' Reserve Corps. Obviously, he did not want to leave the service. If not for his wound, he would likely have become a career officer, so strong was his devotion.

WAR DEPARTMENT,

OFFICE OF THE CHIEF OF STAFF,

WASHINGTON.
WTM-CBS--395

May 7, 1920.

Lieut. Alfred M. Barlow,
1066 1st Ave.,
Gallipolis, Ohio.

Sir:

Your application for appointment in the Officers' Reserve Corps, has been referred to this office for consideration. It appears from the record of physical examination at the time of your discharge from the service that because of injuries sustained during your service in France, you would be physically unable to perform full duty were you called for active service. Only those persons who are physically qualified for active service are being appointed in the Officers'

Reserve Corps, and for that reason it is not considered advisable to appoint you at this time. Should you later feel that you have sufficiently recovered from the injury to pass the necessary physical examination, you may make application to the Adjutant General for a reconsideration of your case with a view to appointment in the Reserve Corps.

It is regretted that you are ineligible at this time for the appointment you desire, and the Department wishes to express its full appreciation of the service rendered by you during the emergency. Your willingness to serve, would future emergency arise, will be made a matter of record in the War Department.

Yours very truly,

P. Bishop
Colonel, General Staff,
Chief, Personnel Branch,
Operations Division.

By

T. MacMillan,
Captain, General Staff.

Unable to stay in the military, Skip devoted himself even more passionately to Veterans' affairs. In law school and later, he helped found a number of American Legion posts, becoming involved in the Legion's state-wide matters.

Publication and Date Not Determined
LIEUT. BARLOW WINS APPLAUSE
By Bold Stand Against the Ku Klux Klan at Legion Meeting at Toledo

Special to The Times,

When a resolution condemning the Ku Klux Klan as unAmerican was presented to the convention of the Ohio Department of the American Legion last Tuesday in Toledo, a debate lasting an hour ensued in which the Lafayette Post No. 27 came into the lime light through its delegate, Alfred M. Barlow, one of Gallia County's war heroes. Barlow's speech, which was a feature of the meeting, was spoken of by the Toledo News-Bee in a front page story as follows:

Alfred M. Barlow of Lafayette Post 27 of Gallipolis, formerly a first lieutenant, made a speech opposing the klan because of discrimination against creeds. He said there is no place in this country for such things and referred to the company which he commanded in which there were many Jewish soldiers.

Barlow argued that private vengeance and outrages can be committed under the guise of the klan, even tho its members do not commit the outrages, and referred to the Texas instances where robed riders beat people and the klan denied responsibility.

"You can't get around the fact that the klan does discriminate," declared Barlow.

"How do you know? How do you know?" came the calls from the floor.

"I know," continued Barlow calmly, "because I can read and write the English language, and their very application blanks that state that their members must be white gentiles is discrimination."

Cheers followed Barlow's reply.

"If the courts can't enforce the laws then it's time to repeal the constitution. We, the American Legion, carry on Americanism, but we do it in the open American way--not thru fear. We do it thru education."

When Barlow finished there was a clamor to be heard. E. H. Huber of the Cleveland Post gained the floor. He said his ancestors had been members of the klan up until 1871, when lawless people secured control of the organization. He said that he is opposed to the klan.

Publication and Date Unknown

BARLOW FIELD SECRETARY LEGLESS ENDOWMENT

(From American Legion News Service.)

"The man most operated on" has become the unwanted title of Alfred M. Barlow, one of Ohio's thrice decorated World War heroes and field secretary of The American Legion Endowment Fund campaign for disabled veterans and war orphans in the Buckeye state.

Every time the stump of his right leg begins to behave too painfully, they take off just a little bit more. Fifteen times under an anesthetic, that is Barlow's record.

It began with Barlow's foot--then the foot of First Lieutenant Barlow of the A.E.F.

Twenty-four hours on a river bank just within the arc of German artillery fire, he lay. Wounded in both legs, he cajoled, cursed, entreated and demanded a company of Belgium soldiers, whose command he assumed when his captain had been killed, to follow him across a treacherous stream.

Unable to speak the "lingo" of his men and with little knowledge of French which might have aided him, Barlow's position was difficult. A narrow but deep and swift stream near Heurne, Belgium, had impeded carrying out an order to advance. By means of slippery, rolling logs, an effort was made to cross in the face of punishing fire from the enemy. Lieutenant Barlow hesitated only a second and plunged into the stream. He made the opposite bank but was wounded in both legs.

There he lay, inside the range of German guns, dangerously wounded. The men behind were recalcitrant. They either would not heed or failed to understand the command to follow. Whipping out his automatic, he trained it on them and got the message home.

Over they came, all the long afternoon and into the night. Numbers were drowned and many were killed as a result of direct hits by the Germans. But they reached their objective.

It was twenty-four hours before medical attention could be obtained for Barlow. Gangrene had set in. His right foot was taken off but the left one saved.

Lieut Barlow, a native son of Ohio and of American stock that ante-dates the revolution, was decorated by Belgium, France, and the United States for his deeds. His Croix de Guerre bore the double palm.

His citation from the United States government reads:

"For extraordinary heroism in action near Heurne, Belgium, November 3, 1918. Although suffering from a painful shrapnel wound in the leg, he led his company with excellent leadership and command over the river, and not until he had received wounds in both legs would he give his consent to be taken to a dressing station." Lieutenant Barlow was definitely out of the war as a result of that engagement which took place just eight days before the armistice. While the war was over for many, it had just fairly begun for him.

After long days and nights in hospitals on his return to the states Barlow became a trainee of the United States Veterans Bureau at Columbus. He had studied law at George Washington University, so he went to Ohio State University and finished. While studying law, he taught in the Columbus Boys School.

Returning to Gallipolis, Barlow began the practice of law. They had offered to make him prosecuting attorney to get him to come back home to practice. They did. Later he was elected for a second term but he did not serve it.

When The American Legion, of which Barlow was an active member of Lafayette Post No. 27, Gallipolis, began its national $5,000,000 Endowment Fund campaign for disabled veterans and orphans of the World War, Barlow resigned as prosecuting attorney.

"I've got to do something in this," he said. Going to Indianapolis, national headquarters of the Legion, he asked to be made field secretary of the campaign in Ohio for "those who gave the most," the disabled men and the 35,000 orphans whom the Legion wants to help.

Because of his background, his training, and his indomitable courage, and because Ohio knew him and he knew Ohio, the Legion wanted him. Then came the fifteenth operation. Unlike fourteen others, it was not on the stump of that right leg but was for appendicitis. He's over that now and is actively on the job in Ohio getting ready to put his own state 'over the top' in what he says is the "biggest and most patriotic undertaking since the war."

"Aux Grand Chefs - Aux Officiers - Aux Soldats - A Tous, Heros connus et anomymes, vivants et morts, qui ont triomphe de l'avalances des barbares et immortalise son nom a travers le monde et pour les siecles futurs, la Ville de Verdun inviolee et debout sur ses ruines, dedie cette medaille en temoignage de sa reconnaissance."
(Deliberation de Conseil Municipal De Verdun du 20 Novembre 1916)

Tous ceux qui ont dresse ici le mur de leurs poitrines meritent d'etre a l'honneur, vont pouvoir se retrouver dans l'intimite glorieuse de votre "Livre d'Or".
Andre Maginot
Depute de lat Meuse, Ministre de la Guerre, Citain de Verdun
27 Aout 1922

Les Soldats de Verdun, fiers de l'insigne qui leur a ete donne et leur est reserve, montreront a leurs enfants sur le "Livre d'Or" conserve dans ce monument l'attestation de leur valeur et lad preuve de lat victoire glorieuse qu'ils emporterent ici de haute lutie.

Victor Schleiter,
Depute-Maire de Verdun
29 Juin 1929
Le nom de   Alfred M. Barlow
Private, 148th Infantry,
U. S. Army,

est inscrit sur le "Livre d'Or des Soldats de Verdun" 1918

When the Purple Heart was initiated as an award, veterans were allowed to request citations for wounds received in earlier wars. Barlow did so, probably as soon as he was able to.

AG 201 Barlow, Alfred M.
(4-11-32)EX   Purple Heart
                                                     May 13, 1932.

(COPY)
WAR DEPARTMENT
THE ADJUTANT GENERAL'S OFFICE
WASHINGTON

The Quartermaster General.

   1.   The Secretary of War directs that a Purple Heart,
engraved with the name of the recipient, be issued to

Copy for
Alfred M. Barlow
327 Hanna Building Annex,
Prospect at 14th
Cleveland, Ohio.

on account of wound received in action November 2, 1918, while
serving as a 1st Lt., Co. L, 148th Infantry.

                                        Adjutant General.

   Barlow probably wrote this about 1950, probably in hopes of receiving another posting to Mexico, where the VA had previously arranged for him
to be for his health:

   Alfred M. Barlow was born July 18, 1890, at
Gallipolis, Ohio. The family settled in Ohio in
1803, coming there from New England where they
settled in 1630. He is of the same family as Joel

Barlow, the poet who was Minister to France under President Madison.

Barlow was graduated from the local public schools and later attended Rio Grande College and Ohio State University. He took a two year Normal Course at Rio Grande and later taught in the public schools of Gallipolis, Ohio. After attending Ohio State University for two years and a half he was graduated afterwards from Rio Grande College with the degree of A.B. After the war he attended the Law School of George Washington University for one year and later received his L.L.B. degree from Ohio State University. At one time he taught History and English at the Columbus Academy, a Preparatory School for Boys at Columbus, Ohio. Several years after being admitted to practice, he took a post-graduate course at Baldwin Wallace College and received the degree of Doctor of Juridical Science.

At the beginning of World War I, he joined the Ohio National Guard and served throughout the war with the 37th "Buckeye" Division and was discharged as a First Lieutenant. During the war he was wounded and suffered the loss of his right leg below the knee. He was given the Croix de Guerre with palm and the Distinguished Service Cross.

On being admitted to practice, he returned to Gallipolis, Ohio, and engaged in the general practice of law. He was twice elected Prosecuting Attorney, and as it was a small County, attended personally to all the legal business of the County, both civil and criminal. In 1925 he resigned to become the Secretary for National Headquarters of the American Legion and had charge of raising an endowment fund for the Legion in Indiana and Ohio. In Ohio he superintended all

of the organization work which resulted in a
successful campaign which raised over $400,000.00.

On October 1st, 1925 he accepted a position
as legal adviser and guardianship officer with
the Cleveland Regional Office of the Veterans
Administration. He held that position with
varying titles until July 1, 1949, when he was
retired.

During the time from November 1946 to April,
1949, he was on load to the Department of State
as attache for Veterans Affairs at the American
Embassy, Mexico City.

Barlow started with the V.A. at $3,000 a
year and at the time of his retirement his Civil
Service grade was that of P-6 at a salary of
$7,912 a year.

On returning to Cleveland from Mexico, Mr.
Barlow contracted pneumonia and was for some
time in a hospital. On his discharge doctors
recommended that he seek a warmer climate. His
health is now greatly improved and he feels that
he can pass such physical examinations as may be
required.

Barlow did return to Mexico, but was never really able to work again.
He died in 1959 in a Veteran's hospital in Houston and was buried at Arlington
National Cemetery in Washington, DC.

Made in the USA
Monee, IL
29 October 2024

68880958R00298